Cause Lawyers and Social Movements

Cause Lawyers and Social Movements

Edited by

AUSTIN SARAT

STUART A. SCHEINGOLD

STANFORD LAW AND POLITICS

An imprint of Stanford University Press • Stanford, California 2006

Stanford University Press
Stanford, California
© 2006 by the Board of Trustees of the
Leland Stanford Junior University.

Printed in the United States of America on acid-free, archival-
quality paper

Library of Congress Cataloging-in-Publication Data
Cause lawyears and social movements / edited by Austin Sarat and Stuart A. Scheingold.
    p. cm.
  Includes bibliographical references and index.
  ISBN 0-8047-5360-1 (cloth : alk. paper) – ISBN 0-8047-5361-X (pbk. : alk. paper)
  1. Cause lawyers–United States.   2. Social movements–United States.   I. Sarat, Austin.
II. Scheingold, Stuart A.
  KF299.P8C38 2006
  344. 73—dc22   2005036242

Original Printing 2006

Last figure below indicates year of this printing:
15   14   13   12   11   10   09   08   07   06

Typeset by TechBooks, New Delhi, in 10/13 Minion

Special discounts for bulk quantities of Stanford Law and Politics
are available to corporations, professional associations, and other
organizations. For details and discount information, contact the
special sales department of Stanford University Press.
Tel: (650) 736-1783, Fax: (650) 736-1784

To My Sweet Prince (A.S.)
And
To Joel Handler and in memory of Gary Bellow—they paved the way
(AS and SS)

Acknowledgments

This is the fourth edited volume in an ongoing collaboration that began about a decade ago. It has been a real pleasure for us to work together, the kind of pleasure that is all too rare in the academy. We are grateful to many wonderful scholars who have joined us in giving meaning to the phrase "cause lawyer." We are particularly grateful to the School of Law at UCLA

Thanks to UCLA'sDeanMichael Schill for making possible the conference at which the essays collected in this book papers were first presented. Thanks also to David Delaney for his insightful comments on our introductory essay. For generous financial support we acknowledge the Office of the Dean of the Faculty at Amherst College and the H. Axel Schupf '57 Fund for Intellectual Life. For invaluable research assistance we thank Conor Clarke. Finally, a special word of thanks to Rick Abel for his energetic commitment to, and support of, this project.

Contents

Contributors

SCOTT BARCLAY, Political Science, SUNY, Albany

SUSAN BIBLER COUTIN, Anthropology, University of California, Irvine

SCOTT L. CUMMINGS, School of Law, UCLA

KEVIN H. DEN DULK, Political Science, Grand Valley State University

JEFFREY DUDAS, Political Science, University of Connecticut

KATHLEEN M. ERSKINE, Geffner-Bush, Los Angeles, California

SHAUNA FISHER, Political Science, SUNY, Albany

JENNIFER GORDON, School of Law, Fordham University

THOMAS HILBINK, Legal Studies, University of Massachusetts

LYNN JONES, Criminal Justice, Northern Arizona University

SANDRA R. LEVITSKY, Political Science, University of Wisconsin

JUDY MARBLESTONE, Gladstein, Reif, and Meginniss, New York

ANNA-MARIA MARSHALL, Political Science, University of Illinois

MICHAEL MCCANN, Political Science, University of Washington

STEPHEN MEILI, Law, University of Wisconsin

AUSTIN SARAT, Law, Jurisprudence and Social Thought and Political Science, Amherst College

STUART SCHEINGOLD, Emeritus, Political Science, University of Washington

COREY S. SHDAIMAH, Social Work, Bryn Mahr College

Cause Lawyers and Social Movements

What Cause Lawyers Do *For*, and *To*, Social Movements

An Introduction

AUSTIN SARAT AND STUART SCHEINGOLD

The last half of the twentieth century in the United States was, in part, a story of law's role in movements for social change—from the struggle for African-American civil rights to efforts to secure equal rights for women, from the struggle to expand the reach of human rights to efforts to secure gay rights (Sarat, Garth, and Kagan 2002). In this story cause lawyers played an important, though controversial, part (Lobel 2003). They pressed the claims of oppressed people and disadvantaged groups and reminded Americans of our shared aspirations and ideals. They used legal institutions to energize a political process that all-too-frequently failed to live up to those aspirations and ideals (see Kinoy 1983; Hilbink 2003).

In the most idealized version of this period of American history, litigation mobilized movements, informed the public about particular injustices, and re-framed political struggles (for a discussion of this point see Epp 1998). This version is replete with the vindication of lawyers who fought skillfully on be-half of what, at the time, seemed to be the most hopeless of causes (Lobel 2003). It is also a reminder to lawyers of the importance of resisting the temp-tation to choose strategies that have the highest likelihood of prevailing in court in favor of those that push the envelope of conventional understand-ings and, in so doing, speak both to a broader political context and to history itself.

In our previous work we have attended to the ways lawyers construct causes and causes supply lawyers with something to believe in (Scheingold and Sarat 2005) as well as to ways commitment to a cause challenges conventional ideas of lawyer professionalism (Sarat and Scheingold 1998). In *Cause Lawyers and Social Movements* we shift the focus in two ways. First, we move from an analysis of causes to a concern with social movements. Second, we turn our attention from the way cause lawyering articulates with the project of the organized legal profession to the explicitly political work of cause lawyers.

From Causes to Social Movements

For our purposes, a cause becomes a movement when it provides the basis for "a sustained series of interactions between power holders and persons successfully claiming to speak on behalf of a constituency lacking formal representation, in the course of which those persons make publicly visible demands for changes in the distribution or exercise of power, and back those demands with public demonstrations of support" (Tilly 1992: 306).[1] If causes are abstract and disembodied, movements tend to be more concrete and embodied in the people who work in and for them, the organizations that represent them, and in the actions taken to advance the movement's goals (see McCarthy and Zald 1977; Jenkins 1983; Buechler and Cylke 1997). If lawyers have great freedom in constructing causes, movements constrain lawyers in various ways, for example by setting their agendas, dictating strategic considerations, and/or offering distinctive sets of incentive and rewards (Handler 1978; Burstein 1991).

As this book demonstrates, although all cause lawyering cuts against the grain of conventional understandings of legal practice and professionalism, social movement lawyering poses distinctively thorny problems—taking most lawyers out of their comfort zones (Scheingold 1998). As we will show, causes and movements both invigorate and constrain lawyers. In associating themselves with a movement, lawyers are likely to find that they are called upon to sign over elements of their independence—asked, in effect, to surrender some of the autonomy they earned by becoming members of the bar and the sense of agency they sought in cause lawyering. On the one hand, they may be asked not to deploy the tools of their trade and, on the other, they may find themselves relegated to "second-chair" status within the movement.

In addition, because lawyers are by training and temperament comfortable in a courtroom, litigation is for them the line of least resistance. Of course, lawyers are not strangers to bargaining in the shadow of law, to trying their cases in the court of public opinion, nor to the rough and tumble of "inside the beltway" style politicizing—at every level of government. All of these activities were long ago incorporated into full-service lawyering in the profession as a whole (see, e.g., Kritzer 1991; Heinz, Laumann, and Nelson 1993). On the other hand, grass roots organizing and conducting political campaigns to broaden support for a movement's agenda are not activities that lawyers qua lawyers are likely to welcome or to feel well equipped to carry out.

One obvious solution to this problem is a division of labor between movement activists and cause lawyers. And, indeed, as McCann and Silverstein (1998) have argued, if lawyers are to resist the allure of litigation, they are best able to do so from within a social movement where legality will, perforce, be viewed within the broader context of movement strategies and the prioritizing of long- and short-term goals. However, to divide labor in this fashion tends to reinforce the second class, indeed the dependent, status of lawyers within the movement hierarchy.

Movements, in any case, tend to be resistant and intractable, thus forcing the burden of adaptation mostly on their lawyers (e.g., Silverstein 1996). However cause lawyers may wish to construe the cause, their influence is filtered through the perceived needs of leaders of the movement who must in turn take account, to a greater or lesser degree (depending on the structure of the movement), of the needs and desires of rank and file members (see Olson 1984; Burstein 1991). The problem thus posed is whether lawyers, with their penchant for taking charge, can serve, rather than seek to control, political organizations.

Independence is, of course, most likely to be compromised when cause lawyers work, not only for, but also, within the movement as, in effect, salaried employees. Alternatively, being a movement lawyer may entail remaining in private practice—perhaps on retainer for the movement or perhaps serving episodically as the movement's counsel. Well-organized and well-established movements are likely to expect cause lawyers to enlist for the long term, while ad hoc movements will feel constrained to accept cause lawyers on their own terms. In *Cause Lawyers and Social Movements* we ask what the uncertainty of autonomy and dependence tells us about the dependability of cause lawyering as a social movement resource, about what cause lawyers can do *for*, and *to*, a social movement.

From the Professional to the Political

Although our previous volumes were attentive to social movement issues—reporting the findings of numerous studies of cause lawyers working with social movements (see, e g., Kilwein 1998; Morag-Levine 2001; Israel 2005), in making social movements the centerpiece of this book we enter a political terrain that, although readily recognizable, introduces a notably new perspective. Instead of thinking of cause lawyers as professionals making independent choices among political and legal strategies in their very personal quests for something to believe in, the essays collected in this book start with social movements and examine what cause lawyers do *for*, and *to*, them. In so doing, the essays foreground issues about the political nature and efficacy of cause lawyering.

Put another way, the paradoxical consequence of treating cause lawyers as role players in social movement dramas is to enhance the relevance of cause lawyering as political and social practice. Viewing cause lawyering through the prism of social movements, rather than vice versa, this book underscores the primacy of the political. It describes the distinctive resources and skills that cause lawyers can and do bring to social movements as well as the limits of those resources and skills and the dangers that law, legal action, and lawyers pose to movements.

Although scholars sometimes warn of lawyer domination of movements (Handler 1978), patterns of interaction generally are more complex and multi-dimensional than such scholars recognize (Silverstein 1996). During the earliest phases of organizational and agenda formation, lawyers help define the realm of the possible, offering advice about the relative efficacy of legal versus political strategies (Milner 1986). With their help, marginalized groups can "capitalize on the perceptions of entitlement associated with (legal) rights to initiate and to nurture political mobilization" (Scheingold 1974: 131). They contribute to what McCann (2004: 511) calls "'rights consciousness raising'" by providing a vocabulary drawing on, "legal discourses to 'name' and to challenge existing social wrongs or injustices."

Yet there is no guarantee that lawyers working for a cause or with a movement will offer distinct advantages (Milner 1986). Rights are, in some cases, tremendously significant, but lawyers are themselves often the most skeptical about the capacity of rights-based legal action to effect change. As McCann (2004: 519) observes, "Legal mobilization does not inherently disempower or empower citizens. How law (and therefore lawyers) matters depends on the complex, often changing dynamics of context in which struggles occur. Legal relations, institutions, and norms tend to be double-edged, at once upholding the larger infrastructure of the status quo while providing many opportunities for episodic challenges and transformations in that ruling order."

The Civil Rights Example

Close to the heart of any version of the history of the United States in the last half of the twentieth century, and of contemporary images of cause lawyers and social movements, is the story of civil rights and of the elimination of de jure discrimination from the lexicon of American law (Kluger 1975). And, at the heart of the story of civil rights is the Supreme Court's landmark 1954 decision in *Brown v. Board of Education* (1954). Yet it did not end the indignities that the law itself had heaped on African-Americans. Its legacy, like the legacy of all great historical events, is, even today, contested and uncertain. *Brown* was at once a turning point and a source of resistance, a point of pride and an object of vilification.

As is now widely recognized, until 1954 the project of establishing the American Constitution was radically incomplete. It was incomplete because, in both chattel slavery and then Jim Crow, the law systematically excluded people from participating fully, freely, and with dignity in America's major social and political institutions on the basis of their race. But *Brown* changed everything. "*Brown*," J. Harvie Wilkinson (1979: 6) contends, "may be the most important political, social, and legal event in America's twentieth-century history. Its greatness lay in the enormity of the injustice it condemned, in the entrenched sentiment it challenged, in the immensity of law it both created and overthrew." It stood for the proposition that "race is an impermissible basis for governmental decisions" (Tushnet 1994b: 176). As the then-editors of the *Yale Law Journal* (1984: 981) put it in their celebration of the thirtieth anniversary of *Brown*, "No modern case has had a greater impact either on our day-to-day lives or on the structure of our government."

Ours is, however, a time of revision and mixed views about *Brown* and its legacy. Although some commentators have noted that it has not resulted in the elimination of racism in American society (Lawrence 1980), or even of segregation in public education (Orfield 1969), others suggest that *Brown* has been given too much credit for sparking racial progress (Rosenberg 1991). "[F]rom a long-range perspective," Michael Klarman (1994: 10) argues, "racial change in America was inevitable owing to a variety of deep-seated social, political and economic forces. These impulses for racial change ... would have undermined Jim Crow regardless of Supreme Court intervention."

For scholars like Klarman, *Brown* stands not as a monument to law's ability to bring about social change, but instead as a monument to its failure to do so. In their view, whatever racial progress America has achieved cannot be traced back to *Brown*. "[C]ourts," Gerald Rosenberg (1991: 70–71) contends,

> had virtually no effect on ending discrimination in the key fields of education, voting, transportation, accommodation and public places, and housing. Courageous and praiseworthy decisions were rendered, and nothing changed ... In terms of judicial effects, then, *Brown* and its progeny stand for the proposition that courts are impotent to produce significant social reform.

Still others remain unsatisfied with the doctrinal basis of the *Brown* opinion (see Washburn 1994). And some now say that the integrationist vision that is most closely associated with *Brown* is inadequate to deal with the continuing subordination of African-Americans in contemporary American society (Flagg 1994).

A clear understanding of the record of civil rights lawyers is essential to working through the claims and counterclaims in which *Brown* continues to be embroiled (for an example see Mack 2005). This record also serves as an instructive point of departure for much of the research reported in *Cause Lawyers and Social Movements.* Specifically, the civil rights era in the United States supplies the most notable and the best documented example of cause lawyers working in ways that complicated, and perhaps frustrated, the work of building a social movement (see Greenberg 1994).

In that instance, attorneys for the National Association for the Advancement of Colored People (NAACP) who took the initiative in attacking racial segregation and achieved its milestone victory in *Brown*, fought tooth and nail against direct action politics of more radical organizations like the Student Nonviolent Coordinating Committee (SNCC) and the Reverend Martin Luther King, Jr.'s Southern Christian Leadership Council. Thus, although a civil rights *social movement* did eventually take shape and is generally credited with success in ending de jure segregation and in advancing integration, it did so in spite of, and in conflict with, the cause lawyers of the NAACP (see Morris 1984; also Mack 2005).

It would be easy, particularly in retrospect, to portray NAACP attorneys as shortsighted and misguided individuals who were simply blind to what others could readily see and understand. NAACP lawyers were, however, inspired by a faith in the efficacy of courts and law—by "the myth of rights." According to the myth of rights, "politics *is and should be* conducted in accordance with patterns of rights and obligations established under law" (Scheingold 2004: 13). In other words, once the courts speak, respect for the law is supposed to take over and compliance to follow—perhaps sooner, perhaps later. The underlying point is that the lawyers for the NAACP subscribed to a widely shared belief system, one embedded in the popular conscience as well as in the education and professional socialization of lawyers (Greenberg 1994).

Accordingly, the NAACP's campaign on behalf of civil rights should be seen less as an aberration than as a cautionary tale concerning the inertial tendencies of legal process, the validation of these processes by the prevailing political and legal cultures, and of the shortcomings of cause lawyers as movement leaders (see Tushnet 1987). It was their faith in the courts and in the law that initially led NAACP lawyers to pursue a litigation strategy and that sustained them even as a campaign of "massive resistance" was mounted against the *Brown* decision (Tushnet 1994a; for a contrary view see Mack 2005). After all, the surest way to poison the ultimate fruits of litigation, according to this way of thinking, is to undermine respect for the law by giving up on the courts and resorting to direct action politics like sit-ins, freedom marches, and the like.

With all that said, cause lawyers were instrumental, in spite of themselves, in constituting the civil rights movement. The myth of rights not only fueled the original NAACP campaign but also generated hopes and fears once the *Brown* decision had decisively invalidated legally segregated schools. Belief in the myth of rights and thus in the *Brown* decision generated fears in the south that led to the counter-campaign of "massive resistance." Conversely, the televised spectacle of angry crowds at schoolhouse doors, the use of cattle prods, and the unleashing of dogs during desegregation demonstrations, as well as the murder of civil rights workers, were indirectly instrumental in sparking the civil rights movement and its achievements (Scheingold 1988).

Cause Lawyering for Right Wing Social Movements

If the history of the last half of the twentieth century was a history of civil rights activism, its successes, and its failures, the history of the early part of the new century may be a story a counter-mobilization and its apparent triumph (Crawford 1980; Diamond 1995; Hodgson 1996). Today it has become clear that the right has taken its cues from the left—constructing its own cultures of victimization and resistance as well as its own social movements—on behalf of property rights, against abortion rights, and so on—and deploying them legally and politically (Himmelstein 1990). They have recruited their own cadres of cause lawyers, who have crafted conservative versions of the politics of rights (Teles 2003).

Conservatives have both challenged egalitarian inflections of rights and pro-posed culturally resonant alternatives (Southworth 2005). In claiming that the fetus has rights, abortion foes are, of course, attempting to expand the meaning of rights beyond its traditional boundaries—altogether analogous to the efforts of their egalitarian counterparts on the left. Similarly, opponents of affirmative action argue for a color-blind interpretation of rights—a return in effect to a for-mal, decontextualized conception of equal rights and equal opportunity (Glazer 1975). Gay rights and American Indian treaty rights are then reinterpreted as special rights and thus at odds with equal rights (Goldberg-Hiller 2002; Dudas 2004).

Right wing cause lawyers have been particularly successful at establishing and funding foundations dedicated in part or in whole to legal advocacy (Hatcher

2002). At least three distinct camps of cause lawyering have emerged on the right. Two of them—*neo-liberal* advocates of property rights and *libertarians* who embrace a much wider range of the private rights—are well within the legal mainstream. Accordingly, they are inclined to privilege litigation because they can expect, at the very least, a sympathetic hearing from the courts. In contrast, *evangelical cause lawyering* repudiates rights as a cornerstone of politics and society. For evangelicals, the problem with rights is that they are secular, individualistic, and privilege personal entitlement. Evangelicals are, therefore, more inclined toward political mobilization and regularly engage in a politics of rights (den Dulk 2001).

Either way political mobilization proceeds from contested meanings with the objective of enlisting support not only from a core of true believers but also from the political mainstream. Not the least of the objectives of evangelical movements is, of course, to alter the composition of the courts to make them more receptive to evangelical aspirations. In sum, conservative counter-mobilization, although politically at odds with egalitarian evocations of the politics of rights, seems analytically indistinguishable from them (Heinz, Paik, and Southworth 2003).

Social Movement Politics

In order to fully appreciate the complex relations of cause lawyers and social movements of the kind exemplified in twentieth century civil rights movements or twenty-first century right wing movements, it is necessary to understand what is distinctive about movement politics whether of the left or the right—and in particular how they differ from conventional interest group politics. At first glance, there does not seem to be much to distinguish a social movement from an interest group (McCarthy and Zald 1973, 1977). And, indeed from an organizational perspective there often is considerable overlap. Labor unions and a host of advocacy organizations working on behalf of environmental protection, property rights, racial justice, right-to-life issues, and so on are primarily interest groups, but they may also serve as sites of social movement politics.

An organizational perspective is, however, inadequate for understanding social movements that are not so much organizations as collective voices of political protest or moral visions (see Tilly 1992). Social movements may or may not be represented by an umbrella organization, though they may well be sustained by component organizations—each representing a divergent strand within the movement. But thinking in these organizational terms obscures what is most distinctive about movements and what cause lawyers contribute to building, maintaining, and realizing the aspirations of social movements.

It is the breadth of their aspirations and a distinctive mode of politics that are the defining traits of movements (Tilly 1992). As McCann (2004: 509) puts it, "social movements aim for a broader scope of social and political transformation than do most more conventional political activities . . . they are animated by more radical aspirational visions of a different, better society." Given these objectives, it follows that social movements draw sustenance from, and give voice to, aggrieved—indeed deeply aggrieved—elements of the population. Because the normal channels of politics tend to be impervious to their needs, and/or are so perceived, movements may turn to unconventional political action. As McCann (2004: 509) observes, "they are far more prone to rely on communicative strategies of information disclosure and media campaigns as well as disruptive 'symbolic' tactics such as protests, marches, strikes, and the like to upset ongoing social practices."

As a result, cause lawyers may find themselves in court, defending movement activists who have participated in direct action campaigns that disrupt public order. As defense counsel, they can offer preventive assistance by clarifying the boundary between lawful and unlawful disruptions. And when movement activists cross that boundary, or are deemed to have done so by the authorities, cause lawyers can either mount a conventional defense in hopes of securing an acquittal or they can, ordinarily at the behest of and under instructions from the activists, politicize the trial so as to generate public support for the movement (Kinoy 1983). These strategies need not be mutually exclusive. Thus, a defense directed at jury nullification creates an intermediate stage that is part conventional, and part political, trial. Whatever the tactics, defense of movement activism puts cause lawyers, by definition, in the position of responding reactively to initiatives undertaken by movement leaders. Still, when cause lawyers take an active role in the politicization of criminal trials, they are in effect seeking resonant social meaning beyond the realm of positive law.

Insofar as cause lawyers think of law as more than a set of authoritative institutions, written rules and established doctrines, and instead view it as part of a cultural process in which rules resonate within the broader culture, law can serve as a useful site for articulating and advancing alternative visions of the good. As Judith Butler (1990: 1716) reminds us, ". . . [T]he law posits an ideality . . . that it can never realize, and . . . this failure is constitutive of existing law." Law exists both in the "as yet" failure to realize the Good and in the commitment to its realization. Confronting this tension in law is the distinctive work of "cause lawyers" wherever they practice, and whatever movements they serve. Cause lawyers use their professional skills to move law away from the daily reality of injustice and toward a particular vision of the Good. For them, the

Good is known in the causes for which they work even as its realization may be deferred.

These more expansive aspirations are more likely to emerge when cause lawyers switch from defense to offense and deploy law and litigation as a sword rather than a shield. The courtroom becomes an arena of movement activism, and cause lawyers, almost by definition, are elevated from support staff to positions of leadership. In this sense cause lawyers' service to social movements begins with legal expertise and access to the courtroom, but that access can be leveraged so as to contribute to the construction of causes and the mobilization of movements. This leveraging relies less on legal expertise than on a willingness to participate with activists in the politicization of the law.

Politicization, in turn, is dependent on the recognition and exploitation by both cause lawyers and movement leaders of the cultural resonance of rights and legality. Simply put, cause lawyers contribute most compellingly to movements not as a result of the direct consequences of litigation but indirectly through deploying courtroom encounters strategically—irrespective of whether judicial decisions go in their favor (McCann 1994). There are, thus, ample opportunities for cause lawyers to make meaningful, indeed seminal, contributions to the building, maintenance, and success of social movements.

To the extent that they are prepared to deploy legality as a political and cultural resource, cause lawyers are uniquely positioned to politicize grievances, mobilize activists, and leverage law and rights within public and private institutional arenas. To do so, however, means lawyering outside the lines of mainstream practice and of established patterns of cause lawyering as well. Today's cause lawyers are less likely to be constrained, as were the NAACP lawyers of the mid-twentieth century, by an internalized belief in law as a necessary and sufficient condition of social change.[2] Nonetheless, the politicization of legal practice is neither free of costs nor, as the chapters in this volume make abundantly clear, is it unproblematic.

Constituting Social Movements: Rights as a Political Resource

Cause lawyers who are willing to confront the costs and problems of politicization can, however, make seminal contributions to the building of social movements. McCann (2004: 511) describes a four-stage process of movement building that draws its sustenance from legality and more specifically from the cultural resonance of legality, four ways in which cause lawyers do things *for* social movements. The process begins with building a collective sense of grievance and entitlement that generates, "processes of cognitive transformation in the movement constituents." Rights claiming, thus, becomes intrinsic to the construction of a cause rooted in grievance and validated by discursive association with constitutional and legal rights. The base is activated not so much by grievances, as such, which in all likelihood have been long experienced—or even by giving voice to those grievances. Instead, activation is a product of identifying grievances with the sense of legitimacy, entitlement, and the collective identity attaching to legality.

The second stage entails the use of litigation, or the threat of litigation, to negotiate concessions directly and/or to generate exogenous pressure to soften up the opposition. In the former instance, movement leaders use the costs and the uncertainties of litigation to avoid litigation. "For one thing, organizations targeted by reformers often are well aware that litigation can impose substantial costs in terms of both direct expenditures and long-term financial burdens . . . More important, powerful public and private interests typically fear losing control of decision-making autonomy . . . to outside parties such as judges" (McCann 2004: 514). In the latter instance, legal and extra legal tactics are combined to generate political support for movement goals. As McCann notes (2004: 515), "Political scientist Helena Silverstein (1996) has demonstrated how . . . [i]n a variety of instances . . . litigation has been used to dramatize abuses of animals to embarrass particular institutional actors, and to win favorable media attention." Thus the second stage combines the institutional and the cultural resources of legality to shift the focus of movement activity from raising the consciousness of its members to generating pressure against its opponents.

In the third stage the institutional levers of legality are deployed to gain compliance with court decisions and to pursue their policy implications. This ordinarily takes shape as institutional reform litigation in which courts, in effect, become executive agencies—by, for example, providing injunctive relief and deploying special masters (Chayes 1976). "Social movement groups often use litigation specifically to create such formal institutional access to state power as well as to apply pressure to make that access consequential. In this way, legal resources often provide a series of more refined tools—basic procedures, standards, and practices—along with blunt leveraging tactics for shaping the 'structure' of ongoing administration at the 'remedial' stage of struggles over policy" (McCann 2004: 517). As McCann acknowledges this may be the most problematic stage of movement building either because courts are short on coercive resources or because "judges and other legal officials shrink from cases requiring great technical knowledge and experience" (McCann 2004: 517).

Finally, McCann calls attention to what he terms the "legacy" that legal struggle can leave to social movements. He draws upon his own research on the pay equity movement to discuss the potentially transformative secondary consequences of litigation. "[W]orkers," he says (2004: 518), "repeatedly talked to me about matters of...workplace empowerment. They told me how their sense of efficacy as citizens was greatly enhanced, and even how their identification with other women workers had been increased markedly. This was related to a growth in the organizational power of women within their unions, and of their unions relative to their employers." Here, the focus turns from tangible results back to consciousness raising and from outside agencies to the internal energy generated within the movement itself. But perhaps even more noteworthy is McCann's finding of the broad sense of empowerment that flowed from the struggle itself.

Yet it is clear that as much as law and lawyers may do *for* social movements they may do things *to* them as well (see generally Morris and Staggenborg 2004). Deploying law within the context of movement mobilization and political action has undeniable advantages over simply allowing legality, as such, to follow its own doctrinal and institutional logics. However, the mobilizing capacity of litigation may not survive a string of judicial defeats that make the law less and less resonant to movement activists. In addition, the record tells us that, as was the case with abortion rights, mobilization can lead to counter-mobilization— resulting in a standoff or something worse (Meyer and Staggenborg 1996). The point is not so much that politicization is a high-risk strategy, although it is, but rather that just as the status of cause lawyers within the movement may be unstable and unpredictable, so too may be the strategy itself.

In addition, cause lawyers may continue to think more like lawyers than like activists, and indeed if they are to have any distinctive value to movements it is precisely by being and thinking like lawyers. However, because they are comfortable with, and professionally attuned to, litigation they may push movements to legalize their agenda with a resultant narrowing of focus and loss of momentum (see Zald and Ash 1966; McCarhy and Zald 1987). Similarly, cause lawyers may, whether wittingly or unwittingly, parlay their expertise and their social capital to redirect the trajectory of the movement. In so doing, they may undermine the leadership and stifle the grassroots energies necessary for success of the movement (Handler 1978; Burstein 1991). If so, law becomes not the ally of politics but its enemy, and legal expertise works at cross-purposes to democratic participation.

Overview of the Book

The first section of the book—*The Life Cycle of Movements and Movement Lawyering*—highlights the importance of history in shaping what cause lawyers do *for* and *to* movements. Here history has two referents. In the first, the chapters in this section attend to the broader historical contexts and time periods that offer particular opportunities and challenges for cause lawyers and the movements with which they work. What happens to the work of cause lawyers and the activities of social movements in periods of "rights activism" or when rights activism recedes? In addition to addressing this question, these chapters also examine the significance of the history of a movement itself. They show how lawyers fashion and respond to periods of mobilization, maintenance, and decline in movements.

In the opening chapter, "Retrenchment and Resurgence?: Mapping the Changing Context of Movement Lawyering in the United States," Michael McCann and Jeffrey Dudas examine cause lawyering in social context, arguing that the analysis of the latter is essential for that of the former. They contend that explorations of context are important for studying the relationship between cause lawyering and movements for two related reasons. First, they maintain that "scholarship about social movements . . . is overwhelmingly focused on analyzing context, on the specific institutional and organizational factors that shape political struggle." Second, they argue that "the potential contributions of cause lawyers to movement activity everywhere are variously enhanced or constrained by key features of the historical context."

McCann and Dudas explain "how the relatively favorable context for rights-based, legally oriented social movement activity in the United States in the middle part of the twentieth century gave way to an increasingly unsupportive, hostile context by the century's end." And in so doing, they both provide a specific historical backdrop for many of the other chapters in this book and highlight the need for "greater scholarly attention to the social context of cause lawyering activity in general."

Specifically, they suggest that these changes have made the modern presidency "an obstacle to progressives." Matters are more muddled in the federal courts where, the authors contend, there is a "curious mix of judicial restraint, on the one hand, and judicial activism, on the other hand," that "represents an occasionally incoherent compromise" between entrenched constitutional norms and the "hybrid New Right political vision." In Congress, however, there is little compromise, and the "ideological character" of the institution, McCann and Dudas contend, makes it "unsurprising that the progressive legislation and appropriations bills . . . have largely disappeared from the legislative agenda."

With social organizations and foundations, the authors see a similar trend. They suggest that nowhere "is the conservative appropriation of progressive tactics over recent decades more apparent than in tapping . . . social foundations for support." The same is true, they argue, of the legal profession as a whole: "Organizing themselves into such groups as the Manhattan Institute, the Pacific Legal Foundation, and the Federalist Society, right-wing advocates have emulated the tactics used by left cause lawyers." Finally, McCann and Dudas's analysis of popular culture is similarly bleak, because for them the "outstanding fact of contemporary America," the "right turn" toward conservative ideals, is as much a product of popular cultural resentment as of shrewd political elites.

McCann and Dudas, thus, "map" the changing macro context of cause lawyering in the United States. They find, in sum, that many of the "changes in the larger American political map can be traced through the rise and fall of the Democratic Party's New Deal coalition," but temper this claim by noting that even these broad transformations were themselves situated within a larger, domestic and international context. The result is that "American lawyers (who) would take rights claims to court in the hopes of sparking a movement, generating public sympathy, and winning elite support typically face a far more hostile cultural environment in 2004 than they did in 1954."

Thomas Hilbink, in "The Profession, The Grassroots and the Elite: Cause Lawyering for Civil Rights and Freedom in the Direct Action Era," examines the life cycle of movement lawyering through the experiences of cause lawyers involved in the "direct action phase of the civil rights movement" and considers how their understanding of cause lawyering "reflected and reacted to social and professional experiences, circumstances, and beliefs." Hilbink contends that over time this resulted in "a new concept of lawyering that challenged contemporary conceptions of practice and professionalism both within and outside the movement."

Specifically, Hilbink documents the emergence of "Grassroots" cause lawyering and the displacement of "Proceduralist," "Elite/Vanguard," styles of cause lawyering. At the start of the direct action phase, Hilbink argues, the approach of lawyers working for the NAACP Legal Defense Fund was most prominent—an approach that was dominated by "a belief that society's ills can be cured through legal action." In its "focus on law as the primary means for bringing about change," Hilbink argues that those lawyers embraced an "elite/vanguard" method of lawyering.

The next group Hilbink examines, the Lawyers' Committee for Civil Rights Under Law, was, on the other hand, less concerned with helping activists than it was in evincing a "strong dedication to the legal system itself." In this sense, Hilbink contends, the Lawyers' Committee represented a prime example of "proceduralist" cause lawyering: the group was "dedicated to defending the legal system and upholding the duties of the profession."

Finally, he looks to a different set of legal organizations—the Congress for Racial Equality (CORE), the Student Nonviolent Coordinating Committee (SNCC), and the Lawyers' Constitutional Defense Committee (LCDC)—that fall under the "grassroots" umbrella. These lawyers viewed the civil rights struggle "in much the same terms as the activists themselves." Indeed, for these particular organizations, lawyers "acted as collaborators rather than directors, even in the realm of litigation"; they were "not the leaders of the movement, and not the heart of the movement," but they were, nonetheless, "a part of the movement."

Despite these distinctively different frames of reference, organizational affiliations, and initial agendas, Hilbink finds that "the experience of lawyering in the South had a significant impact on many (if not most) of the attorneys, forcing them to reenvision the legal system, the cause, and the role of lawyers within the cause." For example, many volunteers for the Lawyers' Committee experienced violence first hand and, more generally, concluded "that progress could not be made through the existing power structure." Others "went to the South with the belief that they were representing individuals," but returned knowing "that they were defenders of a movement."

Hilbink concludes that "experience in the field . . . forced attorneys to reconsider understandings of the profession and the profession's role in American society, and, perhaps more importantly, their role as lawyers working in the context of (if not directly with) the movement." The assumption that "lawyers must be neutral, disinterested, and dispassionate representatives of individuals" was challenged, and, for many civil rights lawyers, it would remain so forever.

The next chapter in this section explores the shifting role of cause lawyering in more than thirty years of same sex marriage litigation. Barclay and Fisher take as their starting point two cases decided by the Washington Court of Appeals: the first of which, *Singer v Hara*, held that "the state's denial of a marriage license" to same sex appellants is "required by our state statutes and permitted by both state and federal constitutions"; the second, *Anderson v King County*, found that Washington's prohibition of same sex marriage violated the state's constitution. For the authors, the switch in outcomes "demonstrates the dynamic nature of legal interpretation in relation to an unchanged set of laws." Despite the fact that "the legal claims presented on each occasion are remarkably similar," and that "each claim was initiated and litigated by a cause lawyer" the outcomes were markedly different. Barclay and Fisher suggest that these snapshots of legal history "offer insight into the role of litigation at divergent moments in the development and promotion of new social definitions with obvious legal overtones."

The two cases appear so different from each other that it would seem easy to assume there is no relationship between the two, or that the earlier serves only as a "substantial and negative precedent" for the subsequent same sex marriage litigation. And yet, Barclay and Fisher argue, not only did *Singer* present no obstacle to later same sex marriage litigation, but also "the 1974 case represents a different aspect of cause lawyering," and, as such, "was a necessary predecessor" of the latter case. Indeed, given the social and legal context of the time, it is, the authors note, "hard to imagine the 1974 case in Washington leading to a legal success." What it did do, they argue, is create publicity: the 1974 case (and others like it) "can be identified as the first shot across the bow of the socially accepted."

Because, law "plays a role in the production of naturalized patterns of behavior," the filing of the claim and associated publicity begins the process of "denaturalizing the current notions of sexuality, marriage, love, and commitment." Early litigation was also important because it let the gay and lesbian rights movement "publicly proclaim [its] presence and signal that [it] was active." Litigation "reappropriates the idea of same sex marriage and returns its 'ownership' to lesbian and gay individuals." In short, Barclay and Fisher maintain, in "the act of litigating, same sex marriage is transformed from the ridiculous to the possible."

The 2004 case occurred at a very different historical moment. Barclay and Fisher maintain that "the robust and serious national discussion" about gay marriage, and the "myriad of lesbian and gay rights organizations" that were active in it changed the atmosphere in which litigation occurred. It was in this context, they argue, that "litigation played a substantially different role than it did for the 1974 case." Indeed, in the case of Washington, they contend, "the litigation appeared designed to place the state legislature on notice to accept the idea that same sex marriage was about to become reality." Barclay and Fisher argue that in "the 1974 and the 2004 Washington cases we can observe cause lawyers adjusting effectively to the social context of the era and the related social recognition of the relevant cause at each stage."

From the social movement perspective, "litigation acted as a means," according to Barclay and Fisher, "to allow membership involvement in defining the direction of a movement in light of its geographically dispersed and organizationally divided structure." Put simply, litigation operated as "an informal referendum of the future direction of the movement," with strong support for the direction indicated by "repeated emulation on the same litigation in new locations by different local organizations." Relative lack of emulation in the early 1970s indicated a lack of organization and enthusiasm; repeated emulation thirty years later, by contrast, indicated a robust interest and organizational effort, including "relative unity among organizations and cause lawyers." Early litigation efforts may have started out as a means to "effectively reclaim ownership and legitimacy over the idea of same sex marriage," but they became a way of developing "input into the direction and goals of the larger movement." Arguably, then, Barclay and Fisher provide another example of the shift in direction, called to our attention by Hilbink, from "elite/vanguard" cause lawyering toward "grass roots" cause lawyering.

Susan Coutin examines the life cycle of movement lawyering by focusing on efforts of lawyers working on behalf of Central American refugees and suggests that the recent history of this movement has been fueled and reshaped by cause lawyering. Legal developments in this area, she contends, have "redefined causes, constituencies, and agendas, even as changed circumstances gave legal developments new meanings." Drawing on three decades of research, Coutlin first analyzes the efforts of "cause lawyers and solidarity workers to obtain political asylum for Central American refugees during the 1980s." Next she describes "how Central American peace accords and US immigration reforms forced both advocates and cause lawyers to change strategies." Third, she delineates recent realignments that have produced unprecedented legal regulations. Throughout, Coutin attends "to the shifting relationships between causes, lawyers, and law."

She begins her chapter by noting that, during the 1980s, efforts to secure asylum were undertaken by religious groups, political activists, and legal advocates who "sought to establish that the US government was discriminating against Salvadoran and Guatemalan asylum seekers due to foreign policy considerations." To prevent Salvadorans and Guatemalans from being deported, Coutin continues, "solidarity workers sought to mobilize the law": "Volunteers connected Salvadorans and Guatemalans who were in deportation proceedings with attorneys who were willing to represent asylum seekers on a pro bono basis." Other legal advocates "filed class action suits designed to force the INS to change its treatment" of these asylum seekers—actions that, Coutin says, were part of a broad attempt to challenge immigration officials' treatment of Central Americans.

Some advocates, in addition to filing class action lawsuits, (unsuccessfully) sought legislative change that would have granted "Extended Voluntary Departure" status to Salvadorans. Although the bill "languished in Congress," other lawyers brought suits to bar future prosecutions of sanctuary workers. Ultimately, they had some success: a settlement was reached establishing that "every Salvadoran and Guatemalan who was in the United States prior to certain dates "had the right to apply or reapply for political asylum." But the settlement was not without its drawbacks, because the agreement put the asylum seekers "in an ambiguous position," leaving them legally vulnerable and granting them only precarious residency.

In the early 1990s, Coutin notes, "the Central American solidarity movement declined significantly," as a result of several factors, including the fact that "sanctuary, which had been a key component of the solidarity movement, was no longer perceived as the most appropriate form of advocacy." But still, she notes, "cause lawyers and Central American activists continued to seek a permanent immigration remedy for" the precarious immigration settlements of the 1980s. But matters were complicated by "the fact that peace accords were signed with El Salvador in 1992"—putting the question of asylum and deportation in a new light. And when "efforts to obtain a blanket grant of permanent residency foundered," and "antiimmigration sentiment in the United States grew"—resulting in legislation like the Illegal Immigration Reform and Immigrant Responsibility Act—that dramatically altered the terrain.

This new legislation led, in Coutin's words, to "unlikely alliances and unprecedented regulations." Indeed, through a multiparty process "that one participant described as 'torturous' . . . regulations that created unprecedented solutions to a series of debates were crafted." This process resolved debates over who should adjudicate asylum claims; debates over "the enumeration of hardship factors" that would be of importance in determining the appropriateness of deportation; and debates over "whether or not the INS could grant a blanket finding of hardship" to the asylum-seeking groups in question. The new regulations were "a victory for Salvadoran and Guatemalan refugees."

In the end, Coutin maintains that the work of cause lawyers in this instance "not only reshaped refugee law and procedures but also empowered immigrants and inspired renewed activism." It demanded that lawyers serve the movement with both their legal skill and their political commitments.

Stephen Meili's "Consumer Cause Lawyers in the US: Lawyers for the Movement or a Movement unto Themselves?" examines cause lawyering and US consumer protection over the past fifty years and assesses the efficacy and legacy of legal mobilization strategies in the consumer protection movement. Drawing on a "political process model," he claims that "social movements are rational attempts by excluded groups to mobilize sufficient political leverage to advance collective interests through noninstitutional means." In the consumer movement cause lawyers have not focused obsessively on a single tactic, like litigation, but have rather "altered their strategy depending on a host of factors, including the existing political climate." Context is important, and what cause lawyering does *for* and *to* movements responds to it. Thus it is only within the past decade "that litigation has become the primary legal mobilization strategy in the consumer movement." Prior to that time, Meili says, "consumer lawyers were far less prominent in the overall movement, and those who were involved focused their efforts more on community-organizing" and "legislative advocacy" than they did on litigation.

This began to change in the 1980s, when, with the rise in Ronald Reagan and free market conservativism, "legislative advocacy on behalf of consumers became much more difficult." Because the federal government drastically reduced funding for "legal services programs around the country"; because "it became virtually impossible to enact new laws that would in any way regulate the private sector"; and because "the Reagan Administration appointed leaders to consumer protection agencies who were either hostile or indifferent to those agencies' underlying mission," pursuing legislative change became far more difficult. The changing political realities of the 1980s created a kind of "pragmatic shift" in how cause lawyers operated: they "altered their strategy so as to maximize their own political leverage as well as that of individual consumers." This shift led to a number of strategic and organizational changes beginning with an increased emphasis on litigation.

Not surprisingly, the increased prominence of litigation led to a tremendous expansion of consumer cause lawyering within the movement and the growth of a significant distance between consumer cause lawyers and the consumer movement. This finding offers the volume's first, and perhaps, its most dramatic example of the concern of scholars, mentioned at the outset of this introductory chapter, who "warn of lawyer domination of movements." In this instance, Meili argues that the distance between consumer lawyers and consumer activists doesn't just change the relationship between lawyers and the social movement. It has, in addition, transformed the lawyering organization into something akin to its own social movement.

Surprisingly, the increased prominence of litigation has led not toward but away from consumer *rights*. "One of the most striking aspects of the rise in prominence of consumer cause lawyers within the US consumer protection movement," he submits, "has been the concomitant deemphasis on consumer rights within the movement as a whole." Although the consumer movement had great success creating rights in the middle of the twentieth century, many of the lawyers and advocates Meili interviewed "downplay the importance of rights in movement work"; some even see rights as "harming the overall movement." For others, the lack of emphasis on rights stems from "the sheer breadth of issues and concerns that fit within the umbrella of 'consumer protection.'"

The next section—*Lawyers and Activists/Lawyers as Activists: Professional Identities and Movement Politics*—explores the role of legal expertise in social movements, the professional identities of cause lawyers, and the ways in which movement activism shapes the practice of law. It describes the various roles that cause lawyers play in social movements and asks whether lawyers can be activists and still remain faithful to their professional role. It describes the way nonlawyer activists understand what cause lawyers do *for* and *to* social movements. The chapters in this section highlight the suspicions that seem endemic to the activist–lawyer divide while also taking up the complex negotiations that go on between activists and lawyers.

We begin by considering the question of how influential cause lawyers are in social movements. In "To Lead With Law: Reassessing the Influence of Legal Advocacy Organizations in Social Movements," Sandra Levitsky claims that "legal advocacy organizations stand in a formidable position to both dictate the terms of interorganizational relations and influence the direction of movement activity." Taking as her example interorganizational relations in the Chicago gay, lesbian, bisexual, and transgender (GLBT) movement, she argues that "while legal advocacy organizations do assist other organizations in the movement, interorganizational relations are defined by unilateral, rather than interdependent, cooperation." Specifically, "there was little evidence that law organizations . . . relied on the expertise or experience of nonlegal GLBT organizations." Indeed, they "rarely solicited assistance or advice from other organizations in their own legal efforts," and none of the lawyers in her study "could point to a single case in which street protest organizations assisted their efforts."

This often leads to a sense among the social movement organizations that "the agendas of legal advocacy organizations were formulated in an insular, exclusionary way." The feeling that legal organizations were "imposing their agenda on the rest of the movement" leads to resentment. Even when the legal work has been positive and effective, the activists Levitsky interviewed "returned again and again to the point that" legal organizations "have 'forced' their issues onto the rest of the movement." One of the reasons they are able to do so, she argues, is that with budgets that "dwarf those of the rest of the GLBT community," these organizations are able to cultivate media attention and hire full-time professional staffs.

Her findings, Levitsky argues, "stand in stark contrast to the depiction of legal advocacy organizations as just one group among many equivalently positioned actors in a pluralistic movement." In fact, she concludes, actors within movements are "very differently situated"; and, as a result, social movements activists who work with cause lawyering groups risk being (or feeling) overshadowed and marginalized.

Levitsky's picture of lawyer dominance is, however, not replicated in other contexts. Indeed in the next chapter, Anna-Maria Marshall, focusing her analysis on the movement for environmental justice, describes its efforts to challenge environmental hazards, promote democratic participation in important public decisions, and connect environmental quality to broader issues of social injustice. In each of these areas lawyers "get involved by educating activists about the obscure regulatory and administrative procedures that characterize environmental decision making and by litigating disputes among activists, corporations, and the government." Nonetheless, lawyers are considered outsiders to the movement. Thus, although "environmental justice organizations turn again and again to litigation to pursue their goals," they "often find the legal system inhospitable to their claims, and without the political support of a dynamic movement organization, these legal campaigns usually fail."

At the heart of the matter, according to Marshall, are the conflicting demands faced by social movements when choosing their strategies and tactics: they need to be "convincing with respect to political authorities, legitimate with respect to potential supporters, rewarding with respect to those already active within the movement, and novel in the eyes of the mass media." The demands are not entirely compatible; more "confrontational strategies," for example, "appeal to loyal activists," but "risk alienating the public and policymakers whose support is often necessary to make the changes the movement seeks."

Legal strategies "fit uncomfortably" between institutional and confrontational approaches. Although courts are "state institutions that rely on public norms," legal strategies, Marshall maintains, are also "inherently confrontational." They operate on a number of levels: litigation "clearly attributes responsibility for those grievances to identifiable corporate and state elites," and can "be an effective means of framing . . . conflict" by providing "powerful motivation for participation in movement activity." It is the diverse, multifaceted character of legal and social action—the fact that it does "not fall neatly within the dichotomous institutional and extra-institutional categories but rather lies along a spectrum"—that Marshall suggests sets up potential tension between activists and lawyers.

Still, Marshall maintains that, "lawyers and grassroots activists can cooperate in the use of direct action techniques to advance environmental justice goals," especially when they are "enhanced by mass participation." Although there is "at best (a) tenuous relationship" between cause lawyers and environmental movements, such lawyers often are ideologically committed to the cause and contribute "to the overall movement." Indeed, cause lawyers may be in a unique position to "tailor legal strategies" to fulfill the "participatory potential" of social movements, and can frequently, despite the resistance of activists, "shape the direction of the movement itself."

Following Marshall, Lynn C. Jones continues the exploration of the ways in which lawyers impact movement processes—of what they do *to* as well as *for* the movements with which they work. To do so, she introduces the concept of framing and goes on to explore how activists and cause lawyers interact within the framing process. She contrasts her approach to traditional sociolegal analysis, with its focus on lawyers acting as 'hired guns' who help movements accomplish particular goals that are set by movement activists. In so doing, they ignore both the interactive character of framing and its ideological work.

Social movement activists, Jones argues, "single out some existing social condition and redefine as unjust what was previously viewed as unfortunate, yet tolerable." Then they "frame the conditions by assigning blame . . . and then suggest a line of action and who should be responsible for such action." Since "all lawyers are granted the task of defining problems, of fitting a clients' grievance into a nameable offense," it stands to reason that cause lawyers will act in a similar capacity in movements, helping to "frame grievances and construct a remedial plan of action." They do so by articulating frames in "legally relevant ways."

Although their use of legalese and their reliance on professional knowledge often confuses and alienates the movement participants, cause lawyers, particularly those who work closely with movements, are, she argues, very much aware of the broader impact of legalization on a movement over time. Accordingly, "activist lawyers do not always automatically turn to litigation, but work to recognize a point where a lawsuit might work best or is the only solution."

There are, moreover, multiple points of convergence. Perhaps none of these is more central than "the criticism of the system of inequality that is perpetuated in this society"—what Jones calls the "haves come out ahead" frame. Because, in addition, the "rights frame" remains the "master frame used by most movements," it would seem "logical that movements will seek corrective action in the courts." Lawyers also participate in "counterframing," namely "attempts to rebut or neutralize an opposing collective action frame or an articulation made by an opposing movement organization." Finally, Jones analyzes what she calls "prognostic or motivational framing," which occurs when lawyers "describe the chance of success in courts and whether using the courts is even appropriate action for the movement to take." In sum, Jones sees the study of framing as important "for explaining the link between movement ideologies, tactical choice, and cause lawyers, regardless of context."

Kevin den Dulk's "In Legal Culture, but Not of It: The Role of Cause Lawyers in Evangelical Legal Mobilization" describes what cause lawyers do *for* and *to* one of today's most contentious social movements, the evangelical movement that entered public life "during the late 1970s and 1980s" and, unlike Levitsky, den Dulk finds that lawyers and activists exist in a cooperative, if not totally harmonious, relationship.

Focusing primarily on abortion rights and church-state law pertaining to education, den Dulk offers some "theoretical preliminaries" for studying evangelical rights mobilization. First, while many sociolegal scholars view conservative rights mobilization as "simply a status quo reaction to . . . egalitarian rights claims," the "story of evangelical rights mobilization is," den Dulk argues, "more complex than a straightforward account of reactionary conservativism." Indeed, evangelical rights mobilization "did not so much reflect an opposition between egalitarianism and antiegalitarianism as it revealed a conflict over different understandings of equality itself." In other words, evangelical cause lawyers reconstrued and redeployed progressive rights talk.

Den Dulk acknowledges that it is "somewhat surprising . . . that evangelicals have paid so much attention to legal ideas and activism." Indeed, evangelicals "avoided courts as a place for cultural contestation well into the 1970s." On the other hand, although their moral campaigns preceded evangelicalism's overt foray into the legal arena, den Dulk claims that "the movement itself was always intimately linked to the politics of rights," to such an extent that "the distinction between moral/religious grievances and legal rights was thoroughly blurred." It was, however, not until "intellectuals and other elites within the broader world of evangelicalism became convinced that 'secular forces' must be confronted in terms of a theology of activist politics that evangelical cause lawyers emerged." They came to realize that it was necessary "to do more than merely publicize grievances and opportunities for redress"; they had to "provide a religious justification for why progressive rights-mobilization was a threat at all and why their fellow evangelicals ought to mobilize to combat it." It was this realization, den Dulk claims, that led to an "innovative use of rights." Specifically, it was a "confluence of legal and extra-legal ideas" that "shaped the way cause lawyers in the evangelical tradition viewed the efficacy of the politics of rights."

Among the earliest steps in this direction was Jerry Falwell's Moral Majority Legal Defense Foundation, which sought to "defend believers from abridgments of their freedoms and help reclaim a Judeo–Christian heritage that had been lost in thirty years of 'secularist' interpretations of the Constitution." In the area of educational rights, evangelical groups like the Center for Law and Religious Freedom (CLRF) argued for "equal access"—the principle that "religious and nonreligious individuals and groups alike ought to have the same opportunities to [access] public goods." In addition, evangelical leaders made explicit calls for Christian cultural (and particularly legal) engagement, drawing analogies "between civil disobedience in the civil rights movement and civil disobedience against abortion rights."

The agenda of lawyers for the evangelical movement was, however, broader and more ambitious than can be captured by comparisons to the NAACP Legal Defense Fund and the battle against the legal discrimination suffered by African-Americans. "It is one thing," den Dulk points out, "to defend one's slice of culture, as equal access efforts attempted to do for evangelicals; it is another to attempt to transform the culture as a whole." Evangelicals want to use law to secure a particular kind of freedom, "the freedom to be a certain kind of person, not simply freedom from constraints." For this reason, den Dulk contends, "many evangelical firms expanded their agendas to include matters that are not directly related to the autonomy of religious practices and institutions"—and nothing was (or is) higher on those agendas than abortion. In the evangelical movement, then, we have an instance of cause lawyering motivated by "both legal and extralegal ways of evaluating the social and political world."

"Intersecting Identities: Cause Lawyers as Legal Professionals and Social Movement Actors" concludes this section by exploring "the meaning of lawyers' intersecting professional identities" and focusing on "lawyers' own perceptions and understandings of their roles" in social movements. Drawing on two sets of interview data, Corey Shdaimah argues that cause lawyers see themselves "as part of broader movements for social change and measure themselves against such movements." This is true, Shdaimah contends, "even if the movements with which they identify are incipient [or] otherwise latent."

Among the lawyers she studied, commitment to their respective movements runs deep: "Without exception the lawyers interviewed explicitly chose the legal profession as a means to promote social change"; for most, "it is the cause rather than the law that is the centrifugal [sic] force," and so "the profession as such holds less sway than does the social change goals they wish to pursue." Indeed, for many, "a career in law was not . . . their first choice": more than one of the lawyers had been "involved in social movement activities prior to choosing law," and many chose law only after "weighing the instrumental value of a law degree and the leverage that comes with it."

Despite the "initial optimism expressed by left-activist cause lawyers who started their practice in a political and social climate that augured hope, much of that initial hope was not realized." Given the kind of political and legal climate McCann and Dudas describe, these deeply committed cause lawyers were forced to adapt to new realities—coming to terms, that is, with their "inability to bring about more systematic changes." Accordingly, Shdaimah notes that, "the benefits that they are able to secure through the legal processes can seem meager and inconsequential." Yet they recognize that "working within existing systems in order to be relevant is dangerous but necessary." To do otherwise would be, she argues, "to ignore people who experience need in pursuit of some imagined future theoretical integrity."

From a more affirmative perspective, Shdaimah argues that cause lawyers working for progressive social movements still can "give voice to individuals who would otherwise not be heard." Voice can, in turn, "foster a greater sense of citizen participation in the forums in which marginalized citizens are rarely heard." Additionally, lawyers act as "hubs on a metaphoric wheel, with clients as the spokes." In other words, lawyers can create networks of similarly situated individuals and in so doing help build movements. Incremental legal actions, moreover, "expose the system's unfairness by helping clients to express their dissatisfaction in legal forums," and the language of rights "can serve to rally and energize movements." Finally, Shdaimah notes that lawyers can work with clients to create "shared narratives of responsibility and injustice that legitimate clients' grievances and indict oppressive and unfair systems." This legitimation is particularly important "when social movement constituents' experiences are not otherwise validated by the public."

Shdaimah also looks beyond the way left-activist cause lawyers serve social movements and discovers that they, like Meili's consumer lawyers, "see themselves as a social movement sector made up of different social movement organizations that have a common agenda." Such a view allows lawyers working for progressive causes to view resource constraints through social movement lenses and to collaborate in ongoing projects, which "draw on each organization's and individual's expertise in an attempt to garner more funds and to leverage resources." She also notes that, "social movement theories are helpful in explaining the motivation and material support they draw from the collective identity. In particular, she claims that, "most cause lawyers need to see themselves as part of a larger collective with a shared agenda in order to keep social movement fires burning or to nurture incipient social movements."

The next section—*Beyond Litigation: Other Roles, Other Styles for Cause Lawyers in Social Movements*—describes cause lawyers participating in campaigns for legislative change and working in the shadow of new legislation. It highlights the ways in which cause lawyers shape legal change by inventing new legal devices and attending to their implementation. Moreover, the last chapter in this section describes new strategies of cooperation and negotiation, of joint problem solving, between movement lawyers and their counterparts in government that reflect the emergence of new types of legal ordering.

In their chapter, Kathleen Erskine and Judy Marblestone analyze a "localized movement"—the Santa Monica living wage campaign—while "paying particular attention to how lawyers participated in this dynamic fight." They trace the development of a movement that had its roots in "a small group of community activists," and later grew to encompass scores of community volunteers, Santa Monica resident activists, clergy, union members and leaders, city council members, lawyers, law students, and more. Given the wide breadth of involvement, it comes as no surprise that the tactics employed—from legal, to legislative, to direct action—were Erskine and Marblestone note, diverse, and that the movement faced multiple obstacles in its efforts.

But, can one say that such varied actions constituted a social movement? Erskine and Marblestone define a social movement as a "sustained attempt by people on the margins of power, or those working on behalf of the marginalized people, to effect change and thereby reallocate resources or power," and argue that by this definition the Santa Monica struggle counts as a social movement. Nonetheless, the authors acknowledge that the Santa Monica living wage movement's leaders and activists themselves "have different views on whether the living wage struggle was a "social movement." Although there is "consensus that the fight for a LWO (Living Wage Ordinance) in Santa Monica" was "part of a nationwide effort to advance rights of low-wage workers," it also occurred under a "largely sympathetic city council," in a city "historically known for its radicalism and political activism, and when the differences between the 'haves' and the 'have nots' were starker than they had perhaps ever been." For this reason and others, Erskine and Marblestone choose to characterize the Santa Monica LWO campaign as simultaneously separate from, but connected to, a larger national living wage movement.

As for the place of cause lawyering in this movement, Erskine and Marblestone stress that "the attempt to pass a living wage in Santa Monica involved a large and diverse coalition," and, within that coalition, "lawyers played at most a supporting role." By and large, these lawyers "did not develop strategy," and even those "lawyers acting in a traditional lawyer's role were not the leaders of the coalition." They were "not closely involved with the framing of the issue"; by and large "they took direction from the movement's leaders and provided specific assistance, or acted simply as volunteers and activists in the various mobilizing efforts of the coalition." Their services included "shaping strategy, drafting an ordinance, and waging campaigns to get the ordinance passed and defend against multiple anticipated challenges."

That lawyers could play such diverse, multifunctional roles is a testament to the range and complexity of cause lawyering today, but it also is a consequence of the structural constraints of California's political process. Erskine and Marblestone point out that "individual groups can use the electoral process to challenge legislative mandates via the referendum and ballot initiative process." This means that litigation may be "much less likely [to succeed] than in states where citizens do not have the power to challenge laws directly."

Not surprisingly, then, Erskine and Marblestone find that the Santa Monica LWO lawyers "do not fall easily" into any recognizable cause lawyering categories. They are a kind of unique hybrid, resembling "with some overlap, staff activists, independent cause lawyers, and nonpracticing lawyers." Indeed, "several attorneys who were very active in the Santa Monica LWO campaign rarely viewed themselves as 'lawyers' in their participation." Many of them "were drawn to the cause as interested citizens or volunteers and only acted as lawyers when specifically asked to do something requiring their particular legal knowledge and skills." What emerges is an image of lawyering consistent with what Scheingold (2004) calls "the new politics of rights," which focuses on "the indeterminacy of rights and their negation through competing myths." In this view, litigation is only "one arrow in a quiver that includes" many other options that can be brought out under the right circumstances.

In "A Movement in the Wake of a New Law: The United Farm Workers and the California Agricultural Labor Relations Act," Jennifer Gordon examines a facet of the relationship between cause lawyering and social movements that has received little attention in traditional sociolegal studies: the question of how new legislation affects social movements and cause lawyering. The passage of a law establishing new rights is, Gordon argues, "a moment of great importance in a social movement's history"; it is "a triumph, a measure of the movement's power." But, "it is also a pivotal time, when the movement must negotiate a shift in its relationship to the state as it moves from an outside force to at least something of an inside player."

Because labor law and its impact on the labor movement have received a wealth of attention from historians and legal scholars outside the law and social movements field, Gordon examines the National Labor Relations Act's "relationship to the social movements that beget it." She describes a sharp upward surge in the wake of the new law, followed by a long, slow process of co-optation, restriction, and decline and argues that this trajectory contrasts with much law and social movement scholarship says a movement should expect in the wake of the establishment of new rights. In this scholarship, the legacy of new rights is seen as growing "richer over time," and the period immediately following new legislation is supposed to be "particularly challenging for movements."

To complicate this picture Gordon describes the impact of the passage of the California Agriculture Labor Relations Act in 1975 on the United Farm Workers (UFW). This case is particularly apt, she says, because "the UFW was as much or more a social movement as it was a union." UFW organizer Cesar Chavez acted creatively: using collective action tactics like fasts and providing community services. This creativity also involved the use of law, which "played an important role in the union's success." The controlling question UFW lawyers asked was never "what are our rights here?" but rather "how can we best turn this legal situation to the union's organizing advantage?"

This led, most prominently, to legislative victories for the UFW—legislative victories that, Gordon contends, produced mixed results. She describes the "implementation phase"—the phase that follows a major legislative victory—which she defines as "the period when the precise contours of the new right that the movement has won are delineated and the mechanisms for its enforcement are established and put into play." She observes that "legislative proclamations of rights are at least as vulnerable to subversion as their judge-made cousins," given their often "high public" visibility and "potentially more far-reaching character." Although legislative action can provide "a window of opportunity in which the advantaged side can press its advantage if it is ready to do so," such an opportunity is "tempered by a variety of challenges that the law itself introduces," creating "an inherently unstable situation."

Beyond backlash and delayed implementation, and "in addition to the obvious route of repeal or amendment," Gordon notes that there are "many other ways for powerful opponents to invalidate a law." And yet, she ends by pointing out that "these tactics do not rob a movement of its agency, its capacity to continue to work in innovative and strategic ways in the face of new challenges," or its ability to "maintain an independent stance vis-a-vis the state."

Cause Lawyers and Social Movements concludes by examining the stance of movements and their lawyers toward the state in an emerging "postregulatory" era. In "Mobilization Lawyering: Community Economic Development Movement in the Figueroa Corridor" Scott Cummings argues that we are witnessing a transformation in the American political system from "hard regulation to soft governance," and he suggests that the role of cause lawyers is fundamentally different today than it was fifty years ago.

This has its roots, according to Cummings, in the "conservative backlash" against big government politics. The backlash was "framed in terms of moral and efficiency-based critiques"—leading to a reduction in "the role of the federal government in service provision." The result has been "a new set of more localized and market-oriented governance structures that depart from federal command-and-control regulation in favor of public–private partnerships, greater stakeholder participation in rule-making, and greater flexibility in rule structures." These "public–private partnerships [are] designed to leverage outside investment while maintaining a degree of low-income community control"—thus constituting a "pragmatic response" to larger political shifts.

Cummings notes that "litigation strategies of the type pioneered by the NAACP, ACLU, and federal legal services lawyers are suspect in an environment where courts are no longer receptive to expansive rights claims, administrative agencies have lost their centralized authority, and basic welfare entitlements have been eliminated." Accordingly, "legal strategies that emphasize collaboration with political decision makers or cooperation between public and private partners appear more in line with political realities." Cummings maintains, this new "governance lawyering style" is also "a potentially superior method of social change, capable of mobilizing grassroots resources in a way that traditional rights strategies cannot."

He offers Community Economic Development (CED) lawyering as an example of this new method and this new lawyering style. The CED, itself, is neighborhood-based and dedicated to the building of affordable housing and is typically served by "transactional lawyers." Their goal is to "mediate between community-based nonprofit organizations, public funders, and private investors in order to design institutions that foster economic revitalization." Whereas traditional movement lawyers might deploy litigation in an effort to "mobilize claims of legal rights to advance large-scale political reform, CED lawyers attempt to mobilize community participation to change local economic circumstances through the creation of innovative institutional structures." But unlike other social movements' tactics, "CED is not connected to protest politics and broad-based movements"; indeed, it is "parochial" and "seeks to preserve community boundaries while increasing their control of resources."

Because of its "orientation toward the market, its rejection of rights strategies against the state, and its involvement in grassroots organizations," CED lawyering "occupies an ambiguous position along the spectrum of cause lawyering." Resisting Hilbink's typology, which distinguishes among categories of cause lawyers by "comparing their views about the fairness and legitimacy of the legal system," Cummings contends that CED lawyering is in fact defined in large part by "its relative disinterest in the legal system as such." CED, he continues, "does not map nicely onto a 'law versus politics' divide, largely because CED operates within the domain of private law, where negotiated economic relationships are privileged and political considerations are submerged." In sum, the CED movement itself "appears to diverge from conventional understandings of social movements." And, not surprisingly, CED lawyering "does not break down neatly along the political axis of left and right."

Cummings analyzes in detail the tactics of CED organizing, but the unconventional nature of the movement and its lawyers remains the prominent theme throughout—a reminder that, in the postregulatory state, lawyers and social movements are often difficult, if not impossible to classify by old norms or rigid standards.

The research assembled in *Cause Lawyers and Social Movements* provides a comprehensive overview of what cause lawyers do *for* and *to* the movements they serve. The chapters in this book highlight the benefits activists derive when they enlist legal expertise as well as the costs they incur and the ways in which cause lawyering itself is transformed by movements. They assess the circumstances under which legalizing social and political conflict spurs on, as well as siphons off, the kind of grassroots energy that gives social movements their distinctive character and power. Furthermore, they examine ways in which cause lawyers can help to politicize legality and thus serve social movements in their own idiom. Throughout, they remind us that contingencies shape what cause lawyers do *for* and *to* movements, that movements have their own histories, and that both movements and their lawyers are responsive to the constraints our legal, political, and social history imposes and the opportunities that they make available.

Notes

1. McCann (2004: 508) suggests the need for a broader perspective on social movements. In his view, "Social movements aim for a broader scope of social and political transformation than do most more conventional political activities. Although social movements may press for tangible short-term goals within the existing structure of relations, they are animated by more radical aspirational visions of a different, better society. *Second*, social movements often employ a wide range of tactics, as do parties and interest groups, but they are far more prone to rely on communicative strategies of information disclosure and media campaigns as well as disruptive "symbolic" tactics such as protests, marches, strikes, and the like that halt or upset ongoing social practices.... *Third*, social movements tend to develop from core constituencies of nonelites whose social position reflects relatively low degrees of wealth, prestige, or political clout. Although movements may find leadership or alliance among elites and powerful organizations, the core "indigenous population" of social movements tends to be "the nonpowerful, the nonwealthy and the nonfamous.""

2. Our view that civil rights lawyers were caught up in the myth of rights is challenged by Mack (2005).

References

Brown v. Board of Education (1954), 347 US 483.

Buechler, Steven and F. Kurt Cylke, eds. (1997), *Social Movements: Perspectives and Issues.* Mountain View, CA: Mayfield Publishing.

Burstein, Paul (1991), "Legal Mobilization as a Social Movement Tactic: The Struggle for Equal Employment Opportunity," *American Journal of Sociology,* 96: 1201–15.

Butler, Judith (1990), "Deconstruction and the Possibility of Justice: Comments on Bernasconi, Cornell, Miller, Weber," *Cardozo Law Review,* 11: 1716.

Chayes, Abram (1976), "The Role of the Judge in Public Law Litigation," *Harvard Law Review,* 89: 1281.

Crawford, Alan (1980), *Thunder on the Right: The "New Right" and The Politics of Resentment.* New York: Pantheon Books.

den Dulk, Kevin (2001), *Prophets in Cesar's Courts: The Role of Ideas in Catholic and Evangelical Rights Advocacy.* Doctoral Dissertation, Madison, WI: University of Wisconsin.

Diamond, Stephen (1995), *Roads to Dominion: Right Wing Movements and Political Power in the United States.* New York: Guilford Press.

Dudas, Jeffrey (2004), "In the Name of Equal Rights: 'Special' Rights and the Politics of Resentment in Post-Civil Rights America," Presented at the Annual Meeting of the Law and Society Association, Chicago, IL, May 27.

Epp, Charles R. (1998), *The Rights Revolution: Lawyers, Activists, and Supreme Courts in Comparative Perspective.* Chicago: University of Chicago Press.

Flagg, Barbara (1994), "Enduring Principle: On Race, Process and Constitutional Law," *California Law Review,* 82: 935.

Glazer, Nathan (1975), *Affirmative Discrimination: Ethnic Inequality and Public Policy.* New York: Basic Books.

Goldberg-Hiller, Jonathan (2002), *The Limits of Union: Same Sex Marriage and the Politics of Civil Rights.* Ann Arbor, MI: University of Michigan Press.

Greenberg, Jack (1994), *Crusaders in the Courts.* New York: Basic Books.

Handler, Joel (1978), *Social Movements and the Legal System: A Theory of Law Reform and Social Change.* New York: Academic Press.

Hatcher, Laura (2002), "Conservative Cause Advocacy: Mapping the Sites of Conservative Legal Activism," unpublished manuscript.

Heinz, John, Edward Lauman, and Robert Nelson (1993), *The Hollow Core: Private Interests in National Policy Making.* Cambridge, MA: Harvard University Press.

Heinz, John, Anthony Paik, and Ann Southworth (2003), "Lawyers for Conservative Causes: Clients, Ideology, and Social Distance," *Law and Society Review,* 37: 5.

Hilbink, Thomas (2004), "You Know the Type. . . . : Categories of Cause Lawyering," *Law and Social Inquiry* 29:657.

Himmelstein, Jerome (1990), *To the Right: The Transformation of American Conservatism.* Berkeley, CA: University of California Press.

Hodgson, Godfrey (1996), *The World Turned Right Side Up: A History of the Conservative Ascendancy in America.* New York: Houghton Mifflin.

Israel, Liora (2005), "From Cause Lawyering to Resistance: French Communist Lawyers in the Shadow of History (1929–1945)," in Austin Sarat and Stuart Scheingold, eds.,

The Worlds Cause Lawyers Make: Structure and Agency in Legal Practice. Palo Alto, CA: Stanford University Press, pp. 147–70.

Jenkins, J. Craig (1983), "Resource Mobilization Theory and the Study of Social Movements," *Annual Review of Sociology*, 9: 527.

Kilwein, John (1998), "Still Trying: Cause Lawyering for the Poor and Disadvantaged in Pittsburgh, Pennsylvania," in Austin Sarat and Stuart Scheingold, eds., *Cause Lawyering: Political Commitments and Professional Responsibilities.* New York: Oxford University Press, pp. 181–200.

Kinoy, Arthur (1983), *Rights on Trial: The Odyssey of a People's Lawyer.* Cambridge, MA: Harvard University Press.

Klarman, Michael (1994), "Brown, Racial Change and the Civil Rights Movement," *Virginia Law Review*, 80: 10.

Kluger, Richard (1975), *Simple Justice.* New York: Knopf.

Kritzer, Herbert (1991), *Let's Make a Deal: Understanding the Negotiation Process in Ordinary Litigation.* Madison, WI: University of Wisconsin Press.

Lawrence, Charles (1980), "'One More River to Cross'—Recognizing the Real Injury in Brown: A Prerequisite to Shaping New Remedies," in Derrick Bell, ed., *Shades of Brown: New Perspectives on School Desegregation.* Jackson, MS: University of Mississippi Press, pp. 17–40.

Lobel, Jules (2003), *Success Without Victory: Lost Legal Battles and the Long Road to Justice in America.* New York: New York University Press.

Mack, Kenneth (2005), "Rethinking Civil Rights Lawyering and Politics in the Era Before Brown," *Yale Law Journal*, 115: 256–354.

McCann, Michael W. (1994), *Rights at Work: Pay Equity Reform and the Politics of Legal Mobilization.* Chicago: University of Chicago Press.

——— (2004), "Law and Social Movements," in Austin Sarat, ed., *The Blackwell Companion to Law and Society.* London: Blackwell Publishing, pp. 506–22.

McCann, Michael W. and Helena Silverstein (1998), "Rethinking Law's Allurements: A Relational Analysis of Social Movement Lawyers in the United States," in Austin Sarat and Stuart Scheingold, eds., *Cause Lawyering: Political Commitments and Professional Responsibilities.* New York: Oxford University Press, pp. 261–92.

McCarthy, John and Mayer Zald (1973), *The Trend of Social Movements.* Morristown, NJ: General Learning.

——— (1977), "Resource Mobilization and Social Movements," *American Journal of Sociology*, 82: 1212.

——— (1987), "The Trend of Social Movements in America: Professionalization and Resource Mobilization," in Mayer N. Zald and John D. McCarthy, eds., *Social Movements in and Organizational Society.* New Brunswick, NJ: Transaction, pp. 337–91.

Meyer, David S. and Suzanne Staggenborg (1996), "Movements, Countermovements, and the Structure of Political Opportunity," *American Journal of Sociology*, 101: 1628.

Milner, Neal (1986), "The Dilemmas of Legal Mobilization: Ideologies and Strategies of Mental Patient Liberation," *Law and Policy*, 8: 105.

Morag-Levine, Noga (2001), "The Politics of Imported Rights: Transplantation and Transformation in an Israeli Environmental Cause-Lawyering Organization," in

Austin Sarat and Stuart Scheingold, eds., *Cause Lawyering and the State in a Global Era*. New York: Oxford University Press, pp. 334–53.

Morris, Aldon D. (1984), *The Origins of the Civil Rights Movement*. New York: Free Press.

Morris, Aldon D. and Suzanne Staggenborg (2004), "Leadership in Social Movements," in David A. Snow, Sarah A. Soule, and Hanspeter Kriesi, eds., *The Blackwell Companion to Social Movements*. Oxford: Blackwell Publishing, pp. 141–63.

Olson, Susan (1984), *Clients and Lawyers: Securing the Rights of Disabled Persons*. Westport, CT: Greenwood Press.

Orfield, Gary (1969), *The Reconstruction of Southern Education*. New York: Wiley.

Rosenberg, Gerald (1991), *The Hollow Hope: Can Courts Bring About Social Change?* Chicago: University of Chicago Press.

Sarat, Austin, Bryant Garth, and Robert Kagan, eds. (2002), *Looking Back at Law's Century*. Ithaca, NY: Cornell University Press.

Sarat, Austin and Stuart Scheingold, eds. (1998), *Cause Lawyering: Political Commitments and Professional Responsibilities*. New York: Oxford University Press.

Scheingold, Stuart (1974), *The Politics of Rights: Lawyers, Public Policy, and Political Change*. New Haven, CT: Yale University Press.

—— (1988), "Constitutional Rights and Social Change: Civil Rights in Perspective," in Michael McCann and Gerald Houseman, eds., *Critical Perspectives on the Constitution*. Boston: Little, Brown, pp. 15–32.

—— (1998), "The Struggle to Politicize Legal Practice: A Case Study of Legal Activist Lawyering," in Austin Sarat and Stuart Scheingold, eds., *Cause Lawyering: Political Commitments and Professional Responsibilities*. New York: Oxford University Press, pp. 118–50.

—— (2004), *The Politics of Rights: Lawyers, Public Policy, and Political Change*, 2nd edn. Ann Arbor, MI: University of Michigan Press.

Scheingold, Stuart and Austin Sarat (2005), *Something to Believe in: Politics, Professionalism, and Cause Lawyering*. Palo Alto, CA: Stanford University Press.

Silverstein, Helena (1996), *Unleashing Rights: Law, Meaning, and the Animal Rights Movement*. Ann Arbor, MI: University of Michigan Press.

Southworth, Ann (2005), "Professional Commitment and Political Identity Among Lawyers for Conservative Causes," in Austin Sarat and Stuart Scheingold, eds., *The Worlds Cause Lawyers Make: Structure and Agency in Legal Practice*. Palo Alto, CA: Stanford University Press.

Teles, Stephen (2003), "The Federalist Society and the Evolution of the Conservative Legal Movement," unpublished manuscript.

Tilly, Charles (1992), "Social Movements and National Politics," in Charles Bright and Susan Harding, eds., *Statemaking and Social Movements*. Ann Arbor, MI: University of Michigan Press, pp. 15–38.

Tushnet, Mark (1987), *The NAACP'S Legal Strategy Against Segregated Education, 1925–1950*. Chapel Hill, NC: University of North Carolina Press.

—— (1994a), *Making Civil Rights Law: Thurgood Marshall and the Supreme Court, 1936–1961*. New York: Oxford University Press.

—— (1994b), "The Significance of Brown v. Board," *Virginia Law Review*, 80: 176.

Washburn, James (1994), "Beyond Brown: Evaluating Equality in Higher Education," *Duke Law Journal*, 43: 1115.

Wilkinson, J. Harvie (1979), *From Brown to Bakke: The Supreme Court and School Integration: 1954–1978*. New York: Oxford University Press.

Yale Law Journal (1984), 93: 981.

Zald, Mayer N. and Roberta Ash (1966), "Social Movement Organizations: Growth, Decay, and Change," *Social Forces*, 44: 327.

The Life Cycle of Movements and Movement Lawyering

Retrenchment . . . and Resurgence?

Mapping the Changing Context of Movement Lawyering in the United States

MICHAEL MCCANN AND JEFFREY DUDAS

Introduction

Part one of the first edited collection of essays about cause lawyering (Sarat and Scheingold 1998) is entitled "Contexts and Conditions of Cause Lawyering." In fact, many of the initial cause lawyering studies devoted significant attention to matters of context. In the first volume, the focus was primarily on the "microcontexts" that motivate individual lawyers to act for causes and the broader constraints of the legal profession on lawyers' advocacy. The second volume made a welcome contribution by, among other things, expanding attention to the varied and changing character of nation-states in the global era. The inquiries contained therein explored a variety of "macro" national and transnational contexts in which cause lawyering ventures are situated, with particular emphasis on those contexts that shape human rights advocacy.

And, indeed, context is also relevant to this new volume on cause lawyering and social movements for two related reasons. The *first* reason is theoretical. Simply put, scholarship about social movements also is overwhelmingly focused on analyzing context, on the specific situational and organizational factors that shape political struggle. Social movement scholarship argues that these factors vary widely in time and place, and that such variation in context matters a great deal for the forms, character, and very possibility of struggle. We posit that this rich legacy of applied theorizing about context can contribute not only to studies of cause lawyering and social movements (such as those that follow in subsequent chapters), but also to studies of cause lawyering generally.

The *second* reason derives from the empirical study of cause lawyering in practice. For, as social movement theorists would insist, the potential contributions of cause lawyers to movement activity everywhere are variously enhanced or constrained by key features of the historical context. In this essay, we map one such context. Specifically, we explore how the relatively favorable context for rights-based, legally oriented social movement activity in the United States in the middle part of the twentieth century gave way to an increasingly unsupportive, hostile context by century's end. Indeed, many of the classic examples of lawyers working with social movements draw from movements—the civil rights movement, other subsequent minority rights movements, the women's rights and feminist movements, the environmental movement, the welfare rights movement, and the disabilities rights movement—that developed in the 1950s and 1960s. But, with a few exceptions, these movements had declined or shifted to mostly defensive action by the 1980s. And, indeed, few would dispute that contemporary America is both more hostile to most familiar types of progressive democratic rights movements and more supportive of neoconservative or reactionary movements.

These reflections on context lead us to a two-part conclusion. *Empirically*, we note how the shifts in the contemporary American landscape, in spite of their generally reactionary direction, may nevertheless be opening up new sites of struggle for progressive movements. We speculate that two strategies in particular—the application of international human rights standards to American domestic politics and the invigoration of class-based struggle—are potentially noteworthy. Wedding these observations to our general *conceptual* focus, we also conclude more concretely, by encouraging scholars to assess cause lawyering as it occurs within these changing contemporary contexts—which are, as in the United States, less amenable to the "classic" liberal social movements that have so far informed analysis.

Accordingly, we here apply theoretical insights derived largely from social movement theory to make sense of this transformation in the context for progressive cause lawyering in the United States. Our goal is twofold. We aim, first, to provide historical backdrop for many of the other essays in this volume. But in so doing, we shall also argue, second, for greater scholarly attention to the social context of cause lawyering activity in general. Although our empirical focus is on the United States, we nevertheless intend our contribution to be relevant also for studies of cause lawyering and social movements in other nations. It is appropriate in this regard that most social movement scholarship is self-consciously *comparative* in character; it aims to develop general conceptual and analytical categories that are useful for comparing different contexts. Moreover, given the reality of globalization, the example of the United States may offer lessons for egalitarian movements elsewhere. Activists around the world—in Central Europe, South Africa, Latin America, and Asia, for example—who have placed great faith in law, rights, and lawyers would thus do well to heed the lessons about changing contexts that are so vividly on display in the United States. We shall argue that these lessons point, on one hand, to the centrality of political and cultural retrenchment against democratic mobilizations of law and, on the other hand, to the possible emergence of new sites, opportunities, and resources for legal mobilization. We turn first, though, to another set of lessons: those derived from social movement scholarship.

Social Movement Theorizing About Context: A Primer

Social movement literature is diverse, but scholars typically focus on three types of factors that matter for struggles against injustice (McAdam 1982; McCann 1994):

1. *Political opportunities*—emerging systemic vulnerabilities, realignments of group power, spaces for creative challenge, or developing tensions between dominant interests or norms that render prevailing relations potentially responsive to struggles waged from below.
2. *Political resources*—organizational, associational, financial, material, ideological, and logistical assets that can be mobilized to exploit opportunities for change.
3. *Frames of collective meaning*—discursive constructions of identity, interest, and aspiration that animate and facilitate movement constituents' common sense about existing wrongs, possible rights, and visions of alternative relations.

Although rarely emphasized, it is important to note that these three concepts do not typically refer to discrete social phenomena so much as they provide three angles to scrutinize the same interrelated, relational features of social life. For example, an appellate court could simultaneously be viewed as opening up (or closing) opportunities, as extending (or withholding) a resource, and as a source of frame construction and validation (or denial and delegitimation). In the discussion of contemporary America that we present here, we see just how intertwined are each of these concepts. It is beyond the scope of our project to systematically trace the intersections of each of these three aspects of social practice. But we do seek to highlight how shifting frames of collective meaning have shaped, and been shaped by, large-scale institutional transformations in American life—transformations that themselves go a long way toward making sense of the varying political opportunities and resources available to social movements over time.[1]

It is also worth noting just how these categories are typically imagined and used in analytical projects. Some social movement scholars tend toward a positivist epistemology. These three conceptual categories are, accordingly, used to identify variables that can be tested for causal influence and the generation of predictive principles. More commonly, however, social movement theorists tend toward interpretive theory, utilizing its key concepts to make sense of social struggle, to analyze and understand politics in more structured ways, and to distinguish what is common and different in varying historical legacies. In this sense, interpretive concepts can be mobilized to "map" the context of struggle in which cause lawyers toil rather than predict the trajectories of their efforts in any precise way.

Our own approach here leans heavily to the interpretive pole of analysis. Not only do we tend to avoid strong causal claims; we also join social movement theory to a constructivist epistemology. Our analysis of social conditions, accordingly, focuses less on identifying objective facts about situations and more on exploring the understandings, aspirations, and worldviews of the actors— cause lawyers, their allies, and their rivals—under study. This requires attention to how subjects are at once constructed by their social context *and* active transformers of that context.[2] We thus deploy the conceptual and research tools of academic scholarship in order to clarify, expand, and analyze in comparative terms the opportunities, resources, and animating frames that construct the worlds of subjects. Our interpretive approach, accordingly, probes the meaning-making activity of subjects and situates their efforts in more general, analytical, historically grounded terms. To do so, we here build on a rich foundation of interpretive sociolegal analysis that explores the ways that law at once constructs social meaning and identity *and,* accordingly, defines the terrain on which instrumental action takes place.

Finally, we should emphasize that most social movement theory highlights the dynamic, volatile character of struggle. Political interaction is viewed as a process whereby interrelated events are inherently unstable and in a constant state of change, often in clashing, inconsistent ways. In particular, scholars in this tradition are attuned to the contextual factors that facilitate the emergence of social movement activity as well as its eventual decline or deterioration. Decline, in fact, often signals a change in context, not only in the reversal of initially favorable social conditions but also in the movement's organization, leadership structure, and animating frames. Such a process-based account is thus a useful way to analyze the development, decline, and shifting of favorable contexts for cause lawyering projects affiliated with social movements.

Mapping the Changing Context of Movement Lawyering
in the United States

We shift now from analytical considerations to the identification of various factors that scholars find important for social movement development and decline. Hence, we here focus upon the contextual features that facilitate and dampen the possibilities for egalitarian, inclusionary movements, and especially for cause lawyering on behalf of such movements. Most factors are manifest at the broad macrolevels, but many of these broad changes have proximate, direct implications for movement lawyers in specific settings. Our goal is to develop a broad, though necessarily truncated, theoretical overview of the terrain of struggle and to make the case that attention to context can enhance the study of cause lawyering and facilitate comparative analysis.

In many ways, the changes within the American context can be traced through the rise and fall of the Democratic Party's New Deal coalition. Aligning working-class ethnic whites with racial minorities and other long-marginalized populations (including women), this coalition dominated American electoral politics from the late 1930s until the late 1960s. It produced a bevy of congressional enactments meant to promote the interests of coalition members, as well as an often-unwieldy bureaucratic apparatus overseen by the executive who administered the new legislative programs. The Democratic Party during this time also presided over a significant expansion of the federal judiciary. Underlying and propelling these institutional transformations was a political vision of welfare-state liberalism. Although never as robust or uncontroversial as advocates sometimes claim, the understanding that government had a responsibility to enforce the rights of citizens to a relatively free but also materially secure social existence was, for a time, widely shared. These transformations in the political context opened up opportunities for left cause lawyers and, then, as political terrain shifted, gave way to roadblocks for progressive politics. Even so, the narrowing of opportunities for egalitarian social movements, and for cause lawyers with whom they are affiliated, has not been complete. As we shall suggest in conclusion, there is reason to believe that new sites of struggle may be opening that are conducive to new types of movement activism.

But we are getting ahead of ourselves. We begin with the broad international context out of which the classic American social movements emerged. This is appropriate, as the transformations in this context prefaced the contextual shifts that define contemporary American experience.

Macrocontext: International Factors

Social movement scholarship on the United States has generally focused on national and subnational contextual factors. However, as a result of re-assessments of the post-World War II era and engagements with contemporary movement activity at transnational levels, international contextual factors have recently assumed prominence as well. Historians have identified the importance of various interrelated international factors: the contributions of Black and other minority soldiers as well as women at home to the American effort in WWII; the optimistic prospects for unparalleled economic growth and full employment at home, which at least momentarily eased class, race, ethnic, and geographic tensions; the promulgation of the International Declaration of Human Rights and formation of the United Nations as a body committed to rights enforcement; the increasing sensitivity of national policymakers to how race hierarchy and other inequalities at home undermined America's claims for freedom, equality, and democracy abroad (Dudziak 2000; Anderson 2003). These international factors provided opportunities and resources specifically for Black leaders to challenge American apartheid and racism on a world stage. They encouraged, in fact, several presidents to nominate civil-rights friendly federal judges, to offer symbolic support for ideals of "civil rights" and integration, and, eventually, to pursue legislative mandates to back up these commitments. Such interrelated international and domestic developments were thus critically important for the emergence of the initial African-American civil rights movement, which in turn inspired other rights-based movements in subsequent decades.

But the Cold War context also placed significant constraints on progressive politics. Demands for loyalty and conformity were complemented by overt repression of dissidents, protestors, and even mainstream liberals, all of whom were condemned as subversives and "fellow travelers." Federal law enforcement agencies routinely violated the law and undermined civil liberties in efforts to undermine Left movements. The forces of reaction in the American South developed strategies and substantive agendas that were slowly nationalized in the 1960s, took root in the administration of Richard Nixon, and contributed to what is often referred to as the "Dixiefication of America" that has attended the rise of the New Right governing coalition. The heating up of the Cold War during the era of the Vietnam War further fueled divisions in the nation, accelerating the reaction that was increasingly evident across the American institutional and cultural landscape. Justified or not, the fall of the Iron Curtain in the 1980s further empowered the Republican Party and social conservatives. Both parties, in fact, became far more conservative in domestic policy following the Cold War than they were at its inception. Finally, the terrorist attacks of September 11, 2001, and the ensuing War on Terror, have arguably intensified the most reactionary trends of the Cold War while supporting few of that earlier era's emancipatory possibilities.

These are only the most obvious of the international factors that shaped US social movements and the roles of cause lawyers in those movements. But the point should be clear: the local and the global became increasingly connected over the course of the twentieth century. And, indeed, the prospects of movement-based cause lawyering in the future will surely continue to be affected by the interplay of domestic and international factors.

We now sketch in greater (though still abbreviated) detail the domestic context for American left cause lawyers. In the sections that follow we shall highlight in particular how broad cultural transformations—shifts in the popular American imagination—have at once shaped, and been shaped by, equally broad transformations in the institutions of the national government. As we shall see, such an interpretive approach has great potential for revealing the sorts of shifting political opportunities, resources, and frames of meaning that social movement theory identifies as the keys to mapping the contexts within which activists struggle. We begin with the Executive branch, where the fates of left-oriented social movements and the opportunities for action by affiliated cause lawyers have shifted with changing patterns of leadership.

Executive Branch

The expansion of the Executive branch into a full-fledged bureaucracy was one of the most obvious long-term products of New Deal America. But perhaps because so many of its critical positions are staffed by political appointees who are directly responsive to the then current presidential administration, the bureaucracy's relationship to left activists has tended to be less complicated than those relationships in other venues. When overseen by an administration sympathetic to more progressive policies, bureaucratic agencies have tended to be both more open to left activists (including lawyers) and more aggressive in implementing egalitarian legislation and policies. Conversely, when overseen by administrations indifferent or hostile to progressive politics, these executive agencies have been unresponsive at best and obstructionist at worst. Like no other institution of government, the fates of progressive activists in the federal bureaucracy are thus linked to immediate, often short-term shifts in electoral fortunes.

Accordingly, under the New Deal coalition that dominated American electoral politics from the early 1930s until the late 1960s / early 1970s, the Executive branch was frequently an indispensable resource for left cause lawyers. Most important, the departments of Justice and Labor during the Kennedy and, especially, Johnson terms provided critical incubators for progressive legal visions, training ground for cause-oriented lawyers, and allies on a variety of egalitarian projects. But as electoral trends shifted, this resource dried up.[3]

Driving and complementing this expansion of the Executive branch was a shift in the character of the presidency itself. Indeed, the normal state of American politics up until the 1930s—domestic decentralization and foreign isolationism—limited the president mostly to the position of administer of congressional will. Not a leader on matters of domestic policy, the president was widely understood only to oversee and enforce the legislation passed by Congress. But with the advent of the New Deal and the increasingly aggressive participation of the United States in foreign relations, the role and influence of the "modern presidency" became far more pronounced.

The first wave of the modern presidents, from Franklin Roosevelt through Lyndon Johnson, governed according to a vision of welfare-state liberalism that was relatively hospitable to activism from progressive social movements. The modern presidency was thus, for a time, an important resource for American progressives. But the modern presidency has more recently been an obstacle for progressives. Indeed, the presidents of the last twenty-five years have been opposed, or indifferent, to progressive causes in general and left legal activism in particular.

Richard Nixon's domestic agenda, propelled by a punitive and exclusionary "politics of law and order," is illustrative of this shift. More so are the presidencies of Ronald Reagan and George W. Bush. Distancing himself from the unrest and progressive activism of the 1960s and 1970s, Ronald Reagan looked to symbolically rewind history to the 1950s when, he suggested, America was strong abroad and united at home in order to recover the impetus for the nation's coming glory (Wills 1987). American renewal thus relied in the first place upon muting the discordant voices that propelled the rights-based movements of the previous generation.[4]

So too is current President George W. Bush committed to salving the open wounds of American community, which in his neoconservative visions is regularly beset by frivolous litigation, activist judges, and weepy juries that favor citizen plaintiffs over corporations. Bush's attacks on the American tort system, and those who rely upon it, are linked to Reagan's both in form and in content. For imagining American community as under assault from a lawsuit crisis implicitly identifies those who have historically had to rely upon courts as subversives whose lack of personal responsibility corrodes the body politic (Haltom and McCann 2004).

Federal Courts

The New Deal programs increased the workload of lower federal judges, who were asked to interpret (often purposively) ambiguous Congressional legislation and administrative guidelines (Lovell 2003). Congress accommodated this litigation by creating new judgeships, with the size of the lower federal bench increasing by over 25 percent to 252 lifetime positions during Franklin Roosevelt's presidency alone (Goldman 1997: 64). That bench further expanded to 481 lifetime positions by 1968 and steadily increased from there to 831 positions in 2003 (Goldman et al. 2003: 294).

And presidents have increasingly envisioned vacant judgeships as opportunities to entrench their policy agendas. Franklin Roosevelt was the first of the modern presidents to fully grasp these possibilities, consciously using his 183 nominations to fill up the federal bench with judges thought to be sympathetic to his New Deal programs (Goldman 1997: 17–64). A pioneer in form and content, Roosevelt's establishment of welfare-state liberalism as the dominant governing paradigm influenced the presidents who followed him. Accordingly, the vast majority of successful judges nominated during the Truman, Eisenhower, Kennedy, and Johnson administrations (even those formally affiliated with the Republican Party) accepted, specifically, New Deal prerogatives and policy initiatives and acknowledged, more generally, the responsibility of government to provide a minimum level of security for its citizens (Keck 2004). The federal bench was by the mid-1960s thus guided by a vision of "rights-based constitutionalism" (Goldman 1997: 104–95; Keck 2004: 67–97). This constitutional vision led judges to be at once deferential to legislatures when dealing with matters of economic regulation and planning and highly skeptical of those same legislatures when they acted on the rights and liberties of minorities.

The unique mix of judicial restraint and activism associated with the federal bench's rights-based constitutionalism—a so-called "double standard"—created unprecedented opportunities for left cause lawyers and their clients. Indeed, the Supreme Court's opinions in the areas of equal protection, religious liberty, and criminal procedure set off a judicially initiated "rights revolution."[5] But this original double standard has been now complemented (perhaps eclipsed) by an alternative, inverted one. As Keck argues, the twin (though often incommensurate) New Right commitments to limited government and traditional social arrangements translate in the judicial arena into deference to legislatures when they deal with matters of criminal policy and civil rights (often on federalism grounds) and extreme suspicion when they deal with matters of economic regulation and planning (often on property rights grounds).[6] At the same time, though, the more right-leaning federal bench (and especially the Supreme Court) has ruled surprisingly in some controversial areas (consider, for example, the high Court's refusal to overturn *Miranda v. Arizona* and *Roe v. Wade* and its overruling of *Bowers v. Hardwick*). But in spite of its occasionally moderate flourishes, the justices of the Supreme Court, as well as many lower federal court judges, have clearly "turned right," a transformation that has made the federal courts a far less promising venue for left cause lawyers than they once were. Indeed, contemporary federal courts exemplify the long-standing insight that the judiciary follows dominant political trends far more often that it challenges them (Rosenberg 1991). The opportunities and resources that expanded to welcome progressive cause lawyering in midcentury not only have contracted, but also have created a favorable context for reaction to earlier shifts in power.

Congress

The widespread commitment to welfare state-liberalism, which had by the 1950s become entrenched in American political practice, arguably helped members of Congress to envision an important role for the national government in protecting individual rights. For, although Congress was initially reluctant to aggressively support attempts to upset the status quo (passing only the watered down *Civil Rights Acts* of 1957 and 1960), by the mid-1960s the legislative branch was passing increasingly expansive civil rights and liberties bills into law. Two sweeping pieces of legislation—the 1964 *Civil Rights Act* and the *Voting Rights Act* of 1965—exemplified Congress' determination to combat entrenched forms of inequality.[7] Moreover, it was during this time that Congress finally began to allocate funds to the Executive branch (to the Department of Education especially) for the implementation of the Supreme Court's decision in *Brown v. Board of Education* and its school desegregation progeny. This spate of legislation at once allocated significant funds to executive branch agencies to oversee its implementation and encouraged left cause lawyers to bring suits in federal court in order to ensure compliance. New statutory forms of "social regulation" for consumers, workers, and the environment in subsequent years continued this trend of leaving future legal construction and implementation to cause-oriented litigators in judicial forums.

During the 1960s and early 1970s, however, the regional cleavage within the Democratic Party also intensified. And the resulting defection of the formerly "Solid South" to Ronald Reagan's 1980 presidential campaign solidified the conservative social and racial character of the once moderate Republican Party. This realignment quickly altered the tenor of American politics, recovering the punitive and reactionary themes associated with our individualist tradition and

reelevating them to prominence.[8] And though it was not as quickly or dramatically felt as it was in the judiciary, the Executive branch, and state legislatures,
this rightward shift did also register in Congress. By the time of 1994's "Republican Revolution," in which the GOP took decisive control of both houses of
Congress, the reactionary tone that infuses the New Right political vision was
entrenched in American political practice, leading to the contemporary "common sense" through which events are interpreted and aspirations are articulated
(Haltom and McCann 2004). Given this environment, it is unsurprising that
the progressive legislation and appropriations bills that characterized Congressional action over the previous three decades have largely disappeared from the
legislative agenda, while Congress' still strong commitment to influencing the
everyday lives of American citizens has been increasingly channeled into law
enforcement and surveillance (Simon 1997; Gilliom 2001).[9] All in all, the legislative texts that social movement lawyers could for a time invoke now provide
many fewer resources and many obstacles for expanding egalitarian change.

Transformations in the character and trajectory of the national government
since the New Deal have thus presented progressive activists (and left cause
lawyers in particular) with steadily dimming opportunities. Government has in
the same time become more open to conservative activism. And much of this
activism, as the next sections highlight, emulates left legal mobilization in form,
if not in content. Pursuing a distinct vision of social justice, many right-wing
advocates have found the tactics of their liberal colleagues to be useful political
tools for challenging and reversing substantive political agendas.

Social Organizations and Foundations

In addition to the institutions of government, social movement scholars also
emphasize the critical role that social organizations play in the development (and
decline) of movement resources. These social organizations are often divided
further into subcategories of indigenous movement organizations, financial
patrons, and third party allies. Even more than elsewhere, our coverage here is
truncated.

Indigenous associational resources refer largely to the formal organizational
structures and informal associational networks and bonds that connect the core
movement constituency and its leaders. The key insight is that durable movements rarely are constructed from scratch, but rather build out of preexisting,
if often not yet politicized, connections among potential activists. The classic
example comes from the American Civil Rights Movement, in which southern churches at once connected African Americans to one another and to the

more well-established advocacy organizations (such as the NAACP [National Association for the Advancement of Colored People] and CORE [Congress of Racial Equality]) and professional networks (such as the National Lawyers' Guild) that facilitated coordination among movement leaders. Such connections were, in fact, crucial for the eventual emergence of organized protest.[10] The women's movement, by contrast, grew initially out of experiences in New Left cadres supporting civil rights and later grew through campus and then professional workplace associations. One of the major ironies of desegregation, however, was to erode many of the bonds among African Americans, especially across class lines, while success for the minority of professional women posed a pervasive individualizing pressure that eroded grassroots solidarity for many potential activists. Environmental and consumer groups, in further contrast, developed a new form of advocacy that was appropriate for its disaggregated middle class, white constituent base: the "checkbook" organizational affiliation, whereby hundreds of thousands of members could contribute money for advocacy staffs to advance campaigns with little alteration in the lives of members themselves.

Nowhere is the conservative appropriation of progressive tactics over recent decades more apparent than in tapping such social foundations of support. Churches throughout the nation, especially in heavily white rural and suburban areas, became highly effective sites for the organization of the New Right beginning in the 1970s. Churches provided a regular place for constituents to hear the message, develop a coherent identity and vision, and develop plans for action. In recent years, churches organized to physically take people to the polls during elections. Moreover, evangelical groups and secular conservative groups employed their abundant resources to tap constituents for support of various moral, social, and economic causes. In so doing, they provided both additional financial support and populist credibility for elite-run advocacy campaigns that supported property rights, welfare reform, and tort reform and which sought to reverse liberal gains in the areas of abortion rights, affirmative action, and environmental protection.

The same reversal can be seen with regard to *financial patrons* and *group allies.* It is a well-told story how such prominent foundations as Ford provided support not just for a variety of race and class-based causes in the 1960s, but specifically provided the financing for many new ventures by liberal public interest lawyers. Other patrons funded the rise of liberal think tanks, policy organizations, and advocacy groups that provided well-respected, "insider" allies for social movement activists and their attorneys. But in the 1970s many of the initial patrons of left causes at home—especially Ford—began to redirect their efforts toward human rights and other campaigns in the international arena. At the same time, labor unions, the core of the old organized Left, continued to decline in member density, financial resources, and political clout. Moreover, conservatives developed scores of well-financed foundations that directed resources toward the formation of their own think tanks, policy organizations, advocacy groups, and legions of "public intellectuals." As Delgado and Stefancic demonstrate, a radical mismatch soon developed in favor of the Right. During the 1980s, a palpable tension between neoliberal business groups and neoconservative groups driven by moral agendas limited the synergies among these developing forces. But by the 1990s common ground was found on a range of individual "responsibilizing" issues such as tort reform, welfare reform, tax reform, and education reform (Stefancic and Delgado 1996).

All told, our account suggests that the "counter-mobilization" efforts of neoconservative and neoliberal forces within and beyond the legal system have produced a stunning reversal of power dynamics in the contemporary United States that dramatically shapes the possibilities for progressive movement lawyering activity. And during this same time, complementary trends were at work in the legal profession itself.

Legal Profession

Social movement scholars typically devote little attention to courts, litigation, and legal rights mobilization, much less to the legal profession and its activist wings. This is, of course, one of the primary contributions that law and society scholarship can make to the study of social movements. As such, we devote a separate section to the topic. And here too, we see a reversal of fortunes for left cause lawyers.

Cause lawyers, defined by Scheingold and Sarat as attorneys who dedicate their careers to the pursuit of specific political and/or moral commitments, first emerged in substantial numbers and public identity during the New Deal period (Scheingold and Sarat 2004: 3–4). Taking advantage of litigation opportunities presented by the expanding federal government, a bevy of young attorneys (many of whom were ethnic minorities historically excluded from the bar by the American Bar Association) who were trained in the legal realist tradition at once put the New Deal's regulatory apparatus into practice and defended it against constitutional challenges in federal court (Scheingold and Sarat 2004: 36; see also Auerbach 1976: 102–129, 158–230). These New Deal lawyers were joined in the 1950s and 1960s by a new generation of cause lawyers who, working both for governmental agencies and for public interest firms, practiced on behalf of the disadvantaged.

Sociolegal scholars have established the importance of these lawyers for the character and trajectory of the social movements of the previous generation. The mobilization of law is, after all, often a useful way for groups that are disadvantaged by the majoritarian political process to access and leverage the power of the state on behalf of their interests. At the same time, legal mobilizations on behalf of the disadvantaged involved the prior and continuous invocation of widely valued legal symbols, conventions, and discourses to legitimize movement goals. The use of rights discourse, in particular, proved to be an important, if conditional, resource for progressive causes (see the following section; Scheingold 1974; McCann 1994; Dudas 2005). Each of these aspects of legal mobilization—litigation and legitimization—were at the fore of progressive activism, providing, directly, a strategy for change and, indirectly, a cultural terrain on which to imagine interests and articulate demands. Left cause lawyers, who deal in each of these components, were thus important actors in the progressive politics of the times.

And they were, for a time, relatively without conservative counterparts. Although the organized bar in America has historically been a force for preserving the status quo, there were few cause lawyers explicitly dedicated to right-wing commitments until the late 1970s.[11] But by the early 1980s cause lawyers had become an integral part of New Right politics. Organizing themselves into such groups as the *Manhattan Institute*, the *Pacific Legal Foundation*, and the *Federalist Society*, conservative advocates have emulated the tactics used by left cause lawyers (Hatcher 2005). Particularly important in this regard has been the use of legal symbols and language to legitimize conservative interests. Proclaiming themselves defenders of federalism and the property rights of ordinary Americans, right-wing cause lawyers appropriate legal discourse in order to reassert traditional hierarchies. Their uses of legal language—of rights especially, see below—thus deflect attention from the specific interests that they promote and instead portray their efforts as defenses of long-standing American values and ideals. Right-wing cause lawyering thus sanctifies an essentially reactionary politics, cleansing it in the symbols of Americana. This appropriation of legalism is a resource of substantial utility for right-wing causes, one that was first exploited with regularity by the progressive activists of the previous generation.

Mass/Popular Culture and Ideology

Rights and resentment. The outstanding fact of contemporary America— its "right turn" toward conservative ideals—is not simply the handiwork of political elites. For that politicking has itself emerged out of, even as it has contributed to, a broad and deep culture of resentment. Constituting American life from the bottom-up, widespread resentment over the "unfair," "irresponsible," and "special" activism of the underprivileged and their allies consumes contemporary culture and politics; it underlies, for example, many of the institutional transformations of American government that we explored above. Resentment is, moreover, tied clearly to egalitarian rights-mobilizations; it provides a substantial resource for those who oppose the successes of the previous generation's rights revolution. Palpable in its intensity and expression but subtle in its impacts, this resentment is, in fact, perhaps the most daunting obstacle for American progressives who seek to use law and rights to realize a more egalitarian society.

The contemporary culture of resentment is, in the first place, motivated by a sense of injustice over the breakdown of the status quo. Understanding themselves, often with good reason, as victims of a world that has displaced them from formerly secure locations (the so-called "Reagan Democrats" who grew increasingly uneasy with the direction of the Democratic Party beginning in the 1960s are particularly noteworthy here), many Americans have associated their insecurity with the activism of the marginalized. In so doing, blame is both displaced away from the impersonal economic and political processes of late capitalism *and* fixed onto the activism of the marginalized, which only partially (at best) explains the circumstances of contemporary America (Dudas 2005). Thus, even as Americans express resentment over the increasing uncertainty of life, they exonerate, and deflect attention from, the major culprits of this uncertainty. And this is a process encouraged by the New Right commitments that we have encountered here, many of which are grounded in mobilizing resentment toward the political participation and social influence of the underprivileged.

The targets of resentment—racial minorities, women, gays and lesbians, welfare mothers, prisoners, greedy litigants, multiculturalists and, especially, their liberal co-conspirators—are thus accosted for irresponsible behavior, which assaults once harmonious communities and maligns once universally accepted American values. There are many examples of such resentful political discourse, including attacks on multiculturalism, academia, Hollywood, and the high-end tastes of the "blue" states. The expressions of resentment that concern us here, though, are those that target the law use of historically disadvantaged Americans.[12] And many of these expressions, as we argue presently, occur in the realm of popular culture.

Legal mobilization and lawyers: the tarnished image. This resentment against social groups and inclusionary causes has been entangled with a manufactured resentment against particular categories of individual plaintiffs, their attorneys, and the judges and juries who respond favorably to them. American popular culture has long been infused with ambivalence about attorneys and their assumed contributions to social life (Haltom and McCann 2004). However, by the 1940s, the production of American cultural texts and sources of meaning production became thoroughly nationalized and corporatized. Leading national magazines and news production sources, popular movies, and television together provided the core media through which a "national culture" was routinely produced and reproduced. Not surprisingly, these new corporatized and technically sophisticated forms of knowledge production reproduced the ingrained ambivalence toward attorneys. Middle class professionals were generally celebrated in these media, reflecting sociological transformations during the previous fifty years and new challenges demanding well-educated, rational, disciplined social leaders during the Cold War.

Indeed, in many ways the 1950s are associated with a momentary elevation of attorneys as key contributors not just to rational order but also to social justice and democracy. Lawyers were a prominent force in constructing the New Deal regime that refashioned state/society relations in the United States and institutionalized progressive social welfare programs, mostly for the middle classes (see above). These heroes were joined by new heroes during the civil rights era (such as Charles Houston and Thurgood Marshall), then by legions of public interest lawyers following the lead of Ralph Nader, and eventually by lawyers for the poor, for women's rights, for environmental causes, for peace, and the like.

By virtually all accounts, however, the currents of popular culture began to shift in the 1970s toward the darker images of law and lawyers. Lawyers became even more prominent in fictional TV dramas, but the new heroes were prosecutors who joined with tough-minded police to apprehend and convict those who betrayed law's order. Images of racial minorities, the poor, and the downtrodden—all represented by civil liberties' attorneys—increasingly became the problem that law must confront and defeat. "Law and Order" and its many spin-offs is just the most prominent indicator of these trends. Scholars have likewise identified marked trends toward portrayals of civil attorneys in an increasingly negative light. In both serious and comic veins, civil attorneys routinely have been portrayed as "satans in suits" (*Devil's Advocate*), duplicitous con artists (*Liar, Liar*), self-centered career climbers (*Kramer v. Kramer*), greedy corporate lackeys (*The Rainmaker*), and feckless and myopic paper pushers (*Jurassic Park*). Even films that celebrated heroes who pursued social justice and citizens' rights—*Erin Brockovich, Class Action, The Insider*—presented a decidedly negative image of lawyers' capacities and motives, while portraying the legal system as unresponsive to the concerns of ordinary people. The heroes of these stories are mostly outsiders to law, the victims who suffer law's failures and the populist, nonlawyer social heroes who compel law to live up to its promises. This is also the era when, as Marc Galanter and others have documented, "lawyer jokes" have recycled old stigmatizing ethnic narratives to make attorneys the social caste we all love to scorn Galanter 1998.

These twin resentments—against plaintiffs who rely on law and on their attorneys—have become carefully intertwined through a convergence of influences. The tort reform movement has since the 1970s fortified and amplified longstanding moral sentiments against rights claiming by civil plaintiffs and their attorneys, orchestrating them into frenzied warnings of a "litigation crisis." The strategic campaign of business-supported groups to tarnish various legal challengers and bolster the prerogatives of corporate power has been supported—mostly unwittingly, it seems—by the routine knowledge production of news reporters, cartoonists, and television talk show hosts (see Haltom and McCann 2004). McCann and Haltom (2005), for example, have generated research demonstrating how the use of legal mobilization tactics by public interest reformers battling with manufacturers and vendors of tobacco products, fat-producing fast food, handguns, silicone breast implants, and other toxic products has been portrayed in decidedly negative terms by the mass infotainment production process. Cause lawyers utilizing litigation to raise public consciousness and bolster calls for responsible government action now find that concerns about "litigiousness," lawyer rapacity, and a legal system out of control overwhelm the substantive policy messages they aim to project. Evidence suggests that these same dynamics have transformed the politics concerning privacy rights (especially those involving abortion), affirmative action, and disabilities rights—all areas of robust cause lawyering activity over the last thirty-five years.

Accordingly, American lawyers who take rights claims to court in the hopes of sparking a movement, generating public sympathy, and winning elite support typically faced a far more hostile cultural environment in 2004 than they did in 1964. The trajectory of Ralph Nader's career is illustrative. No longer the widely revered "people's champion" of a generation ago, Nader is now associated in the public mind with misguided political strategies and anachronistic whining. Nader does, though, remain iconic; he personifies the fall from grace narrative through which ascendant neoliberal values construct progressive cause lawyers.

Continuing and Emerging Struggles

In spite of the general contours of the contextual shift that we have herein sketched, which point to the narrowing of formerly promising sites of struggle for left cause lawyers, it is important to note that many existing struggles remain vital while others appear to be emerging. Indeed, contemporary America is not one-dimensionally hostile to egalitarian politics. For example, many of the death penalty lawyers whom Sarat (2001) describes as "lost" have greater reason for optimism about the pursuit of their abolitionist goals than they did a decade ago. Similarly, the gay and lesbian rights movement is steadily engaged in legal and political battles for same-sex marriage, while the disabilities rights movement remains vibrant. The treaty-rights activism of Native American tribal nations over the last forty years has resulted in many significant victories, including the securing of historic fishing and hunting rights and the sovereignty necessary to operate lucrative commercial enterprises (including casinos). Consider, additionally, how the terrorist attacks of September 11, 2001 have, somewhat lamentably, catalyzed various immigrants' rights movements. Or, finally, note how campaigns for environmental justice, living wages, and AIDS prevention provide venues for activist attorneys.

We invite scholars to use the categories of social movement theory to analyze why some movements have emerged or continued while others have withered, and to consider what is common or unique about contemporary movements and legal engagements relative to past movements. One characteristic of many contemporary movements is striking, for example. These movements are typically based at the local or state level, a reversal of the logic of "expanding the scope" to the federal level, electorally and legally, that characterized the classic mass-based movements of earlier decades. And with that shift "downward" to more specific venues of struggle, the opportunities, resources, and roles for engagement by cause lawyers have changed as well in ways documented throughout this book.

At the same time, we can envision new strategic approaches that might increase the resources and opportunities for progressive lawyers to contribute to social change at the national level. Democratic activists in recent years have looked with increasing frequency to international standards, including especially human rights standards, in order to anchor their efforts. One of the great historical ironies of the Cold War is that the United States played a crucial role in the adoption of the Universal Declaration of Human Rights (UDHC) in 1948, but leaders in both political parties worked to ensure that these rights provisions could not be mobilized as resources for social change at home.

However, progressive lawyers and a host of legal advocacy organizations—Amnesty International, the US Human Rights Network, WILD (Women's Institute for Leadership Development) for Human Rights, the Indian Law Resource Center, the Center for Constitutional Rights—in recent years have invoked human rights standards to challenge existing policies on US treatment of detainees, the death penalty, and discrimination against gays and lesbians. Several US Supreme Court justices, most notably Ruth Bader Ginsburg, and other leading jurists have responded by urging US courts to pay more attention to international norms. Accordingly, activists see great potential for invoking the economic and social rights logics of the UDHC to advance the case for basic guarantees of adequate jobs, education, food, housing, and healthcare for all citizens in our nation. Advances on such fronts could create openings for cause lawyers working with progressive movements (see Jenkins and Cox 2005).

Finally, in a related vein, there is growing reason to believe that the relentless, populist-inflected New Right critique of how identity politics assails the legitimate interests of "ordinary" and "forgotten" Americans has opened to left activists a potential entrée to those latter constituencies. Indeed, such a critique suggests a class-based analysis—one that would emphasize how poorly the New Right coalition has served the economic interests of those many lower income citizens whom it proclaims to champion (Frank 2004). In other words, progressives might reinflect the resentment that the New Right has so successfully parlayed into electoral gain, highlighting the common ties between those whom the New Right vilifies and those whom it celebrates. In fact, Democratic National Committee Chair Howard Dean appears to be pursuing exactly this sort of strategy, tying it specifically to a reinvigoration of Democratic local and state organizations. In so doing, Dean appears to be borrowing a foundational strategy from the New Right itself, mobilizing the resentment of the disaffected at the grass roots in order to rebuild a robust party structure from the bottom-up. The implication of this political maneuver for cause lawyering is unclear, but it might create a more favorable context for renewal of various campaigns for economic and social rights, whether grounded in older US traditions or in appeals to international human rights. Indeed, a number of prominent activists and scholars (Sunstein 2004) in recent years have drawn attention to how much the international human rights system drew from the US experience with the Great Depression and the New Deal, thus laying a foundation for reinvigorating agendas committed to social and economic rights at home and abroad.

Conclusion

We have in this essay briefly described the changing landscape within which American progressives, and especially cause lawyers affiliated with progressive movements, have struggled in the last fifty years. An admittedly hasty sketch, we have nevertheless sought to emphasize that movement lawyering activities do not take place in a social vacuum; the possibility, and character, of struggle is shaped by the various institutional opportunities, resources, and discursive frames that construct the relational terrains in which actors find themselves. By providing a cursory mapping of the institutional and cultural terrain of contemporary America, we have called attention to changes in context that have constrained as well as supported movements for social justice. This seems especially important because studies of cause lawyering often tend to focus on microcontextual factors—on the motivations, aspirations, and strategies for cause lawyers as well as relations among lawyers and with clients, constituents, or adversaries. By attending to matters of broad social context, these individualized features can be understood in more complex, contingent, and dynamic—relational—terms.

More systematic attention to context also facilitates comparative analysis. It provides a common set of markers or variables to distinguish among struggles by different types of groups, in different places, and in different times. We have seen how attending to the specific dynamics of international politics and its effect on domestic affairs, for example, sheds light on how a vital civil rights movement flourished in the 1950s Cold War context, while civil rights activists today face far greater constraints and yet also new and different opportunities amidst the War on Terror. Such analyses of context can also help us to understand similarities and differences in the struggles of lawyers on behalf of indigenous peoples in Chiapas, Mexico, and in South Africa, on behalf of environmental causes in Israel and in the United States, on behalf of disabilities rights in Scandinavia and in Japan, and on behalf of same-sex marriage among different states and countries. We may debate the capacities for prediction that such analyses can produce, but the increased depth of understanding is undeniable. The legacy of social movement analysis underlines this point and can inform our efforts in this regard.

We conclude, finally, by suggesting that our brief outline of changes in the general landscape of American politics provides important lessons for progressive activists beyond our borders. In an age of massive popular struggles for democracy and justice—frequently punctuated by visions of legal rights, a commitment to the rule of law, and left cause lawyering—around the globe, the American legacy provides a cautionary tale. E. P. Thompson's bold claim that law is an "unqualified human good" (Thompson 1975: 266) is simply difficult to accept in light of contemporary history. Law, rights, and legal mobilization by activist lawyers inherently cut both ways, for and against justice, equality, and democracy. What democratic activists can secure in one time or place is often withdrawn in another. The ideal of a rule of law carries with it promises to tame arbitrary power and to increase fairness for all, but it is dishearteningly easy to identify the contributions that law makes to hierarchy. We are thus left with only one certainty in the irrepressibly relational and contextual world that we have in part sketched here: law will continue to be a central terrain on which movements and cause lawyers act as they struggle to realize a more just and humane social order.

Notes

1. Moreover, social organization and activity is often viewed on different scales of proximity to individual actors: *micro*contextual factors are those most proximate and specific to individuals or small groups; *mezzo*-contextual factors refer to broader subnational institutional factors; and *macro*context generally refers to more distant, national, or transnational level organizational influences. Once again, although our account of the American context implicitly casts attention at each of these levels, we are constrained by considerations of space from an in-depth tracing of their interplay.

2. An interpretive study of cause lawyering would thus understand political and legal opportunities in terms of the sensible constructions of the cause lawyers engaged in struggles rather than as demonstrable facts.

3. The *Equal Employment Opportunity Commission*, an independent regulatory agency established in 1964 to administer the newly passed *Civil Rights Act*, is illustrative. Initially committed to dismantling structural inequality in the American job market, the *Commission* has become less committed to its original egalitarian mission under Republican administrations, with its investigative and enforcement activities steadily waning.

4. Reagan's assaults on "welfare queens," "sue happy" plaintiffs, and "ambulance-chasing" attorneys should thus be understood as rebukes of legal rights claiming by marginalized individuals and groups.

5. One should not, though, overstate the progressive tendencies of the federal bench, particularly when evaluating the Supreme Court's jurisprudence. For example, the Warren Court's interpretation of the fourteenth Amendment's equal protection clause was almost completely denuded of any commitment to economic justice. The Court instead followed a meritocratic vision of equal opportunity that led it to tacitly accept the sorts of ingrained, structural inequalities that pervade late capitalism and that intersect with race and gender-based inequalities (but see Keck 2004).

6. The Rehnquist Court has thus become, in Horwitz's formulation, a "master at flipping the rights argument . . . finding rights that no progressive could sanction with ease" (Horwitz 1999: 95).

7. To be sure, much of this legislation emerged primarily because of the sustained pressure and attention of the Civil Rights Movement. Yet Congress was also during this time becoming an increasingly liberal institution, in spite of spirited denunciations by southern Democrats and Republicans. Although this "conservative coalition" had by the late 1950s made common cause (especially on matters of race and federalism), the continued dominance of nonsouthern Democrats in both houses of Congress ensured that the institution remained an important venue for progressive activism until as late as the early 1990s, as evidenced by passage of the

Americans with Disabilities Act of 1990 and the *Civil Rights Act* of 1991 (Ornstein, Mann, and Malbin 2002: 181–82).

8. Richard Nixon's linking of racial and social unrest to criminal and sexual delinquency, for example, was not so much an unprecedented cultural intervention as it was the revival of a longstanding American cultural tradition.

9. The recent passage of federal legislation prohibiting class action lawsuits that challenge court power in state courts, moreover, represents a direct assault on an important tactic used by cause lawyers.

10. Indeed, scholars often note that one of the major resource disadvantages of poor people, in both rural and urban contexts, is the lack of such organized social capital from which to build a movement.

11. Scheingold suggests that the lateness with which conservative cause lawyers arrived on the American political scene is due to the Right's "longtime hostility . . . to the kind of judicial activism that has been intrinsic to cause lawyering" (Scheingold 2001: 401). We also posit that the extensive commitment of the organized bar to protecting existing hierarchies lessened the felt need for right-wing cause lawyering, and once the bar embraced some forms of left cause lawyering in the 1960s conservative attorneys saw the need to reassert their profession's historical commitments.

12. A particularly noteworthy expression of resentment in this regard is the accusation that underprivileged Americans are seeking to promote their interests through the use of "special" rights (Goldberg-Hiller and Milner 2003; Dudas 2005).

References

Anderson, C. 2003. *Eyes off the Prize: The United Nations and the African-American Struggle for Human Rights, 1944–1955.* New York: Cambridge University Press.

Auerbach, J. S. 1976. *Unequal Justice: Lawyers and Social Change in Modern America.* New York: Oxford University Press.

Dudas, J. R. 2005. "In the Name of Equal Rights: Special Rights and the Politics of Resentment in Post Civil-Rights America." *Law and Society Review* 39 (4): 723.

Dudziak, M. L. 2000. *Cold War, Civil Rights: Race and the Image of American Democracy.* Princeton, NJ: Princeton University Press.

Frank, T. 2004. *What's the Matter with Kansas? How Conservatives Won the Heart of America.* New York: Metropolitan Books.

Galanter M. 1998 "The faces of mistrust: The image lawyers in public opinion, Jokes, and political Discourse" University of Cincinnati Law Review 66:80?

Gilliom, J. 2001. *Overseers of the Poor: Surveillance, Resistance, and the Limits of Privacy.* Chicago: University of Chicago Press.

Goldberg-Hiller, J. and N. Milner. 2003. "Rights as Excess: Understanding the Politics of Special Rights." *Law and Social Inquiry* 29: 1075.

Goldman, S. 1997. *Picking Federal Judges: Lower Court Selection from Roosevelt Through Reagan.* New Haven, CT: Yale University Press.

Goldman, S., E. Slotnick, G. Gryski, G. Zuk, and S. Schiavoni. 2003. "W. Bush Remaking the Judiciary: Like Father Like Son?" *Judicature* 86(6): 282.

Haltom, W. and M. W. McCann. 2004. *Distorting the Law: Politics, Media, and the Litigation Crisis.* Chicago: University of Chicago Press.

Hatcher, L. J. 2005. "Economic Libertarians, Property and Institutions: Linking Activism, Ideas, and Identities among Property Rights Advocates." In *From Fate to Responsibility: Cause Lawyers and the Worlds They Make,* edited by A. Sarat and S.A. Scheingold. Stanford, CA: Stanford University Press, pp. 112–46.

Horwitz, M. 1999. "In What Sense Was the Warren Court Progressive?" *Widener Law Symposium Journal* 4: 95–99.

Jenkins, A. and L. Cox. 2005. "Bringing Human Rights Home." *The Nation* June 27, 2005. Available at http://www.thenation.com/docprem.mhtml?i=20050627&s=cox.

Keck, T. M. 2004. *The Most Activist Supreme Court in History: The Road to Modern Judicial Conservatism.* Chicago: University of Chicago Press.

Lovell, G. I. 2003. *Legislative Deferrals: Statutory Ambiguity, Judicial Power, and American Democracy.* New York: Cambridge University Press.

McAdam, D. 1982. *Political Process and the Development of Black Insurgency, 1930–1970.* Chicago: University of Chicago Press.

McCann, M. W. 1994. *Rights at Work: Pay Equity Reform and the Politics of Legal Mobilization.* Chicago: University of Chicago Press.

McCann, M. W. and W. Haltom. 2005. "Framing the Food Fights: How Mass Media Construct and Constrict Public Interest Litigation." Unpublished essay.

Ornstein, N. J., T. E. Mann, and M. J. Malbin. 2002. *Vital Statistics on Congress 2001–2002.* Washington, DC: American Enterprise Institute Press.

Rosenberg, G. 1991. *The Hollow Hope: Can Courts Bring About Social Change?* Chicago: University of Chicago Press.

Sarat, A. 2001. *When the State Kills: Capital Punishment and the American Condition.* Princeton, NJ: Princeton University Press.

Sarat, A. and S. A. Scheingold, eds. 1998. *Cause Lawyering: Political Commitments and Professional Responsibilities.* New York: Oxford University Press.

Scheingold, S. A. 1974. *The Politics of Rights: Lawyers, Public Policy, and Political Change.* New Haven, CT: Yale University Press.

———. 2001. "Cause Lawyering and Democracy in Transnational Perspective: A Postscript." In *Cause Lawyering and the State in a Global Era,* edited by A. Sarat and S. A. Scheingold. New York: Oxford University Press, pp. 382–406.

Scheingold, S. A. and A. Sarat. 2004. *Something to Believe in: Politics, Professionalism, and Cause Lawyering.* Stanford, CA: Stanford University Press.

Simon, J. 1997. "Governing Through Crime." In *The Crime Conundrum: Essays on Criminal Justice,* edited by G. Fisher and L. Friedman. Boulder, CO: Westview Press, pp. 171–90.

Stefancic, J. and R. Delgado. 1996. *No Mercy: How Conservative Think Tanks and Foundations Changed America's Social Agenda.* Philadelphia, PA: Temple University Press.

Sunstein, C. 2004. *The Second Bill of Rights: FDR's Unfinished Revolution and Why We Need It More than Ever.* New York: Basic Books.

Thompson, E. P. 1975. *Whigs and Hunters: The Origin of the Black Act.* New York: Pantheon.

Wills, G. 1987. *Reagan's America: Innocents at Home.* New York: Penguin Books.

The Profession, the Grassroots and the Elite

Cause Lawyering for Civil Rights and Freedom in the Direct Action Era

THOMAS HILBINK

As the civil rights movement moved from the courts to the streets in the early 1960s, three types of cause lawyering came into conflict. In the Fall of 1961, attorney Jack Greenberg replaced Thurgood Marshall as director-counsel of the National Association for the Advancement of Colored People (NAACP) Legal Defense and Education Fund, Inc. (known then as the "Inc. Fund"). A veteran of the litigation campaign that culminated in the *Brown* decision, Greenberg's ascension made the front page of the *New York Times* (N.A.A.C.P Names a White Counsel 1961). In its profile of this lawyer on the "civil rights frontier," the *Times* described Greenberg as a man for whom law "is a religion." Wrote the *Times* (On Civil Rights Frontier: Jack Greenberg 1961), "[H]e once confided that the only place where he really felt he was in a house of religion was when he entered the Supreme Court of the United States." Greenberg's reverent vision of the law was not without its limits—he recognized that law was not the exclusive answer to the problem of racial inequality in America—but he nonetheless believed it possessed God-like powers to change society (Greenberg 1960; Lewis 1960). It was no surprise, then, that Greenberg was personally and institutionally committed to a lawyer-led, court-based campaign for racial equality.

While the Inc. Fund continued its litigation campaign, the direct action phase of the civil rights movement began to spread around the country, meeting with increasingly violent resistance from these bent on maintaining white supremacy. Despite having campaigned in the midst of the lunch counter sit-ins and entered office months before the start of the Freedom Rides, President Kennedy sought primarily to quiet the flames, seeking assistance from lawyers like Burke Marshall, whom the administration had chosen to head the Civil Rights Division of the Department of Justice. Marshall was chosen, according to Deputy Attorney General Byron White, because, "We thought it would be more interesting to get first-class lawyers who would do the job in a technically proficient way that would be defensible in court – that Southerners would not think of as a vendetta, but as an even-handed application of law" (Navasky 1971: 38). Those they recruited saw their primary duty as keeping the peace and defending the rule of law from attacks on both sides.

The attitude of both types of lawyers was an increasing source of frustration for civil rights activists. By the time of the 1963 March on Washington, Student Nonviolent Coordinating Committee (SNCC) leader John Lewis represented the vanguard of the direct action movement. Nearly a decade after *Brown* and after three years of sit-ins, freedom rides, and voter registration campaigns that were making slow progress and suffering serious casualties, Lewis' faith in the law was evidently shaken. Lewis' draft speech expressed his frustration with those who counseled calm and patience from those seeking immediate change in the South.

> This nation is still a place of cheap political leaders who build their careers on immoral compromise and ally themselves with open forms of political, economic, and social exploitation... Mr. Kennedy is trying to take the revolution out of the streets and put it in the courts. Listen, Mr. Kennedy, listen, Mr. Congressman, listen, fellow citizens, the black masses are on the march for jobs and freedom and we must say to the politicians that there won't be a "cooling-off" period (Lewis 1991: 164–65).

Others talked Lewis out of making that speech, but the sentiment was present nonetheless, particularly among the young activists who had ventured into the Deep South in the early 1960s, working with local people who risked their lives defying "southern justice" and demanding equality, dignity, and freedom in the face of lawless, massive resistance to court orders and legislation. Thus, the lawyer on the civil rights frontier, the "first-class," technically proficient lawyer, and the activists skeptical of court-based reform struggled with the place of law and lawyering in the social changes progressing in the United States of the early 1960s.

In his groundbreaking history of the civil rights movement, Aldon Morris (as noted by Michael McCann) contends that in the direct action years, "[t]he two approaches – legal action and mass protest – entered into a turbulent but workable marriage" (Morris 1983: 39 *quoted in* McCann 2004: 512). Although generally true—both approaches to social change were prominently used throughout the 1960s—research demonstrates that those engaged in mass protest at the very least had a long-term affair with a different group of lawyers than those typically seen as *the* lawyers for the movement. These other lawyers' vision of the system, vision of the cause, and approach to lawyering reflected a cognizance of and sensitivity to the worldview of the direct action wing of the movement. What I argue is that new approaches to cause lawyering emerged as a result of "experiences, circumstances, memories and aspirations of lawyers" involved in the movement (Shamir and Chinski 1998). In the context of the civil rights movement, the experiences gained working with movement activists and the impact of exposure to "southern justice" resulted in the reconstruction of cause lawyering to fit the movement context.

Social Movement Theory has gone a long ways toward better understanding the factors that shape and influence movements for social change. As McCann and Dudas discuss in their contribution to this volume, theorists' focus on political opportunities, political resource mobilization, and frames of collective meaning all help us better to understand the commonalities among diverse movements (McCann and Dudas 2006). One of the key debates in the literature focuses on the role of elites and professionals in steering movements. Responding to McCarthy and Zald's contention that the ascendance of social movements in the 1960s was the result of the spread of professional social movement organizations (SMOs), others have vociferously countered that professionalization of movements moderated movement goals and thus blunted the radical social change aspects of those movements, resulting in less change than might have otherwise occurred (McCarthy and Zald 1973; McCarthy and Zald 1977; Piven and Cloward 1977; Perrow 1979; Helfgot 1981; McAdam 1982; Jenkins 1983; Haines 1984; Jenkins and Eckert 1986; Staggenborg 1988). Anna Maria Marshall, in her chapter from this volume, is correct in asserting, "Professional SMOs, by virtue of both their repeated engagement with political elites and their training as professionals, are much less likely than indigenous protest groups to make broad demands for sweeping change" (Marshall 2006). Yet *much less likely* does not mean that professional SMOs always had a moderating effect, or sought to. Thus, the critics are partially correct. In the context of the civil rights movement, some professional SMOs acted as moderating forces that attempted to direct the movement away from radical goals while others adopted themselves the radical goals of the "classical SMOs".

What social movement scholars have generally failed to understand is that professionals—at least in the case of lawyering—are not fungible. Not all lawyers approach lawyering the same way, relate to clients alike, have the same attitudes toward law and the legal system, or share the same beliefs about the cause for which they fight. At its most basic level, the study of cause lawyering contained in this volume and its three predecessors demonstrates the extent to which such a view is misguided (Marshall, 6; Jones, 4). This chapter adds further depth to that observation.

More importantly, however, the chapter also demonstrates the extent to which the understanding of professional action in the social movement context has failed to understand the ways in which professionals and concepts of professionalism can be and are influenced by social movements. "Where one practices influences how one practices," Marshall succinctly states (Marshall 2006). In other words, theorists who have treated professionals *as* professionals have assumed, to paraphrase Lynn Jones, that lawyers act according to their professional role as lawyers, rather than as activists (Jones 2006). This is decidedly not always the case.

In their earlier contribution to the *Cause Lawyering* enterprise, Ronen Shamir and Sara Chinski rightly recognize that a cause is a "socially constructed concept that evolves, if at all, through a process in the course of which experiences, circumstances, memories, and aspirations are framed in a particular way" (Shamir and Chinski 1998: 231). However, Shamir and Chinski's observation of the nature of a cause can be applied to the concept of cause lawyering as well. Cause lawyering is a socially constructed set of practices and concepts that evolve through a process in which experiences, circumstances, and beliefs shape and reshape how lawyers engage in professional practice. Forms of practice are not static. Lawyers' actions change over time in reaction to forces both internal and external, incorporating personal experience and contextual influence, what Sarat and Scheingold describe as "The mutually constitutive relationship among the social, political, and legal worlds in which cause lawyers operate and which they help construct" (Sarat and Scheingold 2005: 2).

This essay looks specifically at cause lawyering in the context of the direct action phase of the civil rights movement (roughly 1960–65) and the ways that concepts of lawyering reflected and reacted to social and professional experiences, circumstances, and beliefs. Activists and lawyers brought to the movement a set of what I call "visions" and practices that reflected understandings of law, the legal system, and professionalism. Within the crucible of the Deep South, those involved reconsidered their visions of the system in which they worked, their visions of the cause, and visions of the lawyer's role in the movement. For many, the result was a new approach to cause lawyering that challenged contemporary conceptions of practice and professionalism both within and outside the movement. In short, the movement changed the professionals more than the professionals changed the movement.

Over the course of the 1960s, four prominent legal organizations provided assistance to the civil rights movement: the Inc. Fund, the Lawyers Constitutional Defense Committee (LCDC), the National Lawyers Guild's Committee to Assist Southern Lawyers (the Guild), and the Lawyers Committee for Civil Rights

Under Law (LCCRUL or the "President's Committee," as it was known).[1] In an earlier essay, I proffered three "types" of cause lawyering that fit under the general rubric of cause lawyering. "Proceduralist," "Elite/Vanguard," and "Grassroots" lawyering can be distinguished, I argue, in looking at the ways in which lawyers conceive of their "visions of the system," "visions of the cause," and "visions of the lawyer's role" (Hilbink 2004). In the case of lawyering within the civil rights movement, each of these types is detectable in the groups mentioned.

At the start of the direct action phase of the movement, the Inc. Fund's approach to lawyering was the most prominent thanks to the fact that it was the most significant national legal organization working in the field. It possessed many of the qualities associated with "elite/vanguard" lawyering. In regards to the "vision of the system," Jack Greenberg's statements in the *New York Times* (discussed above) expressed a reverent attitude toward law and the Supreme Court as an institution—law's majesty inspired faith in the law whereby judges (though, particularly, justices) implicitly gods or oracles. Greenberg believed in (and the Inc. Fund's litigation strategy demonstrated a belief in) law's capacity to "effect larger processes of social change" (Greenberg 1960). The Inc. Fund's approach evinced a set of beliefs common at the time, what Laura Kalman dubs "legal liberalism": a belief that society's ills can be cured through legal action (Kalman 1996: 2).

The Inc. Fund's "vision of the cause" further reflected an "elite/vanguard" approach in its focus on law as the primary means of bringing change. The Inc. Fund believed in the cause of equality and believed law was the *best* way to achieve that goal. In its 1963 annual report, the Inc. Fund, in the wake of the Birmingham protests, warned of a crisis involving the rule of law caused by both opponents of the movement and the movement itself. The Inc. Fund's solution? "There is only one way. *Those who believe that rights must be found in law and ultimately rest upon law must make a massive effort to use law to solve America's race problem*" (NAACP-LDF, 1963 (italics in original)). The Inc. Fund focused on obtaining victories on issues of legal principle as the way to advance equality. It had a "grand plan" and fought "over-all issues" but left people saying, "The Inc. Fund may win a great principle but what about us?" as NAACP head Roy Wilkins put it in a letter to the Field Foundation (Wilkins and Jones 1965). From the organization's perspective, the goal was to establish legal principles first and foremost—putting them at odds with activists who saw protest as not merely a way of establishing a principle, but involving people in their own liberation and thus challenging a culture of oppression.

The movement's growing strategic focus on direct action did Civil disobedience had frustrated Thurgood Marshall when he was head of the organization.

Dismantling Jim Crow, he said in reaction to the Montgomery Bus Boycott, was "men's work and should not be entrusted to children" (Branch 1988: 189–90; Tushnet 1994: 305). The lunch counter sit-ins were similarly galling to Marshall, as Derrick Bell recalls him yelling about, "crazy colored students" violating the "sacred property rights of white folks" (Williams 1998: 287). The law was clear and best left to the lawyers. The attitude remained the same as the movement grew. The Inc. Fund felt that direct action tactics went too far when, according to attorney Len Holt, a "'point had been proven' and there was no need for new cases before the number of old arrests had tapered down considerably" (Holt 1992: 89). This is not to say that the organization refused legal assistance to those in need, but it did so reluctantly while putting pressure on the movement to change its approach.

The Inc. Fund's willingness to pressure activists to change their approach revealed the groups' ideas about the respective roles of lawyers and activists in advancing the cause. The Inc. Fund lawyers had, according to one historian, a "well-established set of practices, a well-defined set of goals" (Bourne n/a). These goals were defined by lawyers, the practices established by them as well, from the offices in New York. According to Ella Baker, a former NAACP field organizer who later became a guiding force behind SNCC, "The legal strategy 'had to be' directed by lawyers and other professionals, leaving most of the huge mass base... little meaningful role in the development of policy and program except raising funds and cheering the victories as they came" (Payne 1995: 87). Marshall made clear to NAACP head Roy Wilkins that the membership could not set the agenda for the lawyers. He resisted suggestions that he and his staff be more "aggressive" and attack a broader array of racist laws (Williams 1998: 258). Lawyers were to be in control. Jack Greenberg's actions reflected a similar attitude, evidenced by the fact that he felt he could set the terms for its representation of activists going South for Freedom Summer in 1964. Greenberg wrote Freedom Summer director Bob Moses informing him that the Inc. Fund would provide legal assistance on condition that SNCC refused offers of assistance from the National Lawyers' Guild.[2] SNCC refused this condition, as Moses informed Greenberg:

> The SNCC Executive [Committee's] feeling was that the only principled position is to accept the offer of legal assistance from the National Lawyers Guild and urge the different associations of lawyers to lay down, if possible, jurisdictional lines, to insure optimum coverage. In particular, they were concerned about the expressed unwillingness of the Legal Defense Fund to file offensive suits, and a feeling on our part of their lack of commitment to handling "criminal" cases involving our civil rights workers (Moses 1964).

Moses' letter suggests that SNCC was bristling not only at the Inc. Fund's attempt to determine from whom SNCC would accept legal assistance, but also that the Fund had been resistant to SNCC's desire to file offensive (as opposed to defensive) suits and was less than enthusiastic about defending activists arrested in the course of protest actions. The Inc. Fund lawyers whom Jenkins and Eckert describe as providing "technical support to the indigenous challenge" were in fact doing much more than that. The Inc. Fund behaved as social movement theorists generally assume professional SMOs do: attempting to moderate the movement and pursuing elite-determined agendas rather than those of the indigenous movement.

In the midst of increasing tension between the Inc. Fund and activists, another group of attorneys threw its hat into the ring that was dedicated not to serving activists, but rather the President and the legal system. In reaction to the violence in Birmingham, Alabama, President Kennedy called together an "elite corps" of the legal profession to enlist them to provide leadership in quelling racial unrest in the American South (Hunter 1963; Connell 2003: 97). In attendance at the White House meeting were three former Attorneys General, law school deans, former American Bar Association (ABA) presidents, and prominent lawyers from cities around the country. The result of the meeting was the creation of a "lawyers' racial communications committee"—the LCCRUL (known as the President's Committee due to its close ties to the Kennedy administration)— headed by Philadelphia attorney Bernard Segal, chair of the ABA's federal judicial vetting committee, and Harrison Tweed, chair of the American Law Institute and name partner in upper-crust New York law firm Milbank & Tweed (Hunter 1963). The last two words of the group's name were added at Tweed's insistence to make clear that the group worked within the legal process and would not condone violence (Connell 2003: 85). From its origins, the group represented an example of "proceduralist" cause lawyering (Hilbink 2004: 665–73).

Emerging as it did from the Kennedy Administration and the "elite corps" of the profession, the Committee evinced proceduralist cause lawyering's strong, primary dedication to (and belief in) the legal system itself (Connell 2003: 97). Journalist Victor Navasky described the Kennedy Justice Department as hewing to the "Code of the Ivy League Gentlemen" reflecting a vision of the world that assumed the system "which had floated them to the top was basically sound, that the main problem was to gain for the Negro admission to that system and that the way to achieve this goal was to think and behave like a lawyer, and a corporation lawyer at that" (Navasky 1971: 164). The code understood the system as formed by discreet, individual matters—case-by-case, person-by-person—unconnected to a larger sociopolitical context. The leaders of the President's Committee Shared this vision.

The Committee expressed an abiding faith in legal process and envisioned the cause as defending that process against attacks by any group. In one article, Tweed, Segal, and Professor Herbert Packer critically responded to Martin Luther King's "Letter from Birmingham Jail," urging that the solution to the "civil-rights problem" lay not in civil disobedience but,

> by reliance upon the administration of the law through due process in the courts and fair enforcement by the appropriate authorities. Thus the spectacle of repeated violations of law, actual or apparent, by those who are pressing the fight for civil rights is deeply troubling to many thoughtful persons who reject the notion that the ends justifies the means. . . (Tweed, Segal, and Packer 1969: 90).

Yale Law School Dean Eugene Rostow, another force behind the creation of the group, in a letter to the Kennedy Administration, spoke of concerns that "Massive parades in the streets, however disciplined, carry the risk of violence and mob action," and that the Birmingham campaign, "smacks of government by mob-demonstration" (Rostow 1963b). Government belonged in the legislative halls, the courtrooms, and the executive branch, he implied, assuming that the system was basically sound and ignoring the fact that in the South, as in Washington government was whites only.[3]

The group was dedicated to defending the legal system and upholding the duties of the profession. Their cause: to uphold the rule of law and to urge the legal profession to provide counsel to those who needed it. As stewards of the profession, they vowed to "speak out against irresponsible criticism of courts and the judicial process, urge adherence to the rule of law. . . " (LCCRUL 1964). They would urge parties on both sides to abide court orders (Unsigned 1963). The lawyers also aimed to fulfill a professional duty to provide representation to those needing it. From the Committee's perspective it did not matter who provided such representation; even if a lawyer did not support the cause it was their duty to defend their client. To that end, the Committee began reaching out to its bar association brethren in the Deep South, encouraging attorneys to live up to their professional duties and represent individuals arrested in the course of civil rights actions—something virtually no white lawyers in those states had been willing to do up until then.

From the beginning the President's Committee refused to take a position on the civil rights cause. In an open letter to George Wallace regarding his refusal to follow court orders requiring the integration of the University of Alabama, the lawyers who would soon form the President's Committee urged the Governor to submit to the rule of law. From their perspective, the lawyer's duty in such a situation when the courts have made clear their ruling is to urge client and community to honor the decision that has been reached, they wrote (Unsigned 1963). One sentence scratched out of the draft letter sent to signatories is telling: "As members of the bar, as officers of the law, we pledge ourselves to support the civil rights of all citizens, regardless of race or color, to the full extent of the law" (Unsigned 1963). Even such neutral language was too much. They believed supporting civil rights—even when required by law—was too controversial. They were mediators, negotiators, and communicators, not civil rights activists, reflecting the attitude expressed in the sign on the desk of Civil Rights Division head Burke Marshall: "Blessed are the peacemakers, for they shall catch hell from both sides" (Burns 1970; Navasky 1971: 177). When Committee historian Ann Garity Connell asked founding members if they thought of themselves as civil rights lawyers, "The universal response was no" (Connell 2003: 88 n.3).

The President's Committee's vision of the role of the lawyer was similarly proceduralist. The group first undertook direct representation of a movement client in late 1963, when Jack Pratt, counsel to the National Council of Churches' (NCC's) Commission on Religion and Race approached the NCC's attorney, Robert Knight of Shearman and Sterling, in search of legal representation for a group of ministers going South to work with the movement. Knight, a member of the President's Committee, got reluctant Committee approval and sent along a young associate, Robert Lunney. The representation followed the parameters of traditional lawyer–client relationships: the client in need of help approached the attorney and a representation agreement was drafted. Reflecting the Committee's concern with *its* cause—the rule of law—in exchange for representation the ministers agreed not to violate a Mississippi state court injunction barring racial demonstrations, agreeing instead to allow lawyers to test it in the courts. The relationship between attorneys and clients reflected the Committee leaders' notion that there existed "bounds within which the struggle for civil rights may legitimately proceed" (Tweed, Segal, and Packer 1969: 97).

Robert Lunney described his duty while in the South as mediating between "the leadership of the demonstration and the powers that be in the village or city to avoid as much as I could any violence where people could get hurt, because my sense of what was going on was they certainly had rights and privileges that had to be exercised and the powers that be, so to speak, had to recognize that" (Lunney 1992). Lunney saw himself as a clean-cut, reasonable alternative to the civil rights workers who could be "vociferous" and "dressed in a fairly scruffy manner and didn't necessarily deal with the powers that be in a more moderate way" (Lunney 1992). According to Connell, Lunney "went to Mississippi as a representative of the legal establishment... from a major New York firm. His role... was a conventional one, legal counsel. He did not represent any social agenda for change" (Connell 2003: 120).

As plans coalesced for the 1964 Freedom Summer, Jack Pratt of the NCC attended a meeting in the office of Washington lawyer and President's Committee member Lloyd Cutler. According to Pratt the meeting included representatives of many "establishment groups who were active in the South and out of it came the conclusion that thousands of white college students would be coming in from the north in a summer education project and then the question became what should be the role of the establishment" (Pratt 1992).

The President's Committee sought to assure the project conformed to the rule of law. Although continuing to lobby the Mississippi Bar to provide legal counsel to those arrested in civil rights actions, the group also sought lawyers who could provide "objective" legal assistance without succumbing to the "emotionally-charged atmosphere of Freedom Summer" (Unsigned 1964). Lawyers who agreed to spend time in the South were to offer legal counsel to the ministers from the NCC and "where specifically requested to do so, and where possible under the local rules and procedures," offer actual representation. They were to represent individuals, not members of a movement (Hammer 1966: 83). One of the stated goals was to advise the ministers and students working with them "on their rights and responsibilities so as to *prevent* breaches of valid state and local laws and ordinances" regardless of whether such breaches might be an integral part of strategies for change (Bernhard and Doyle 1964). Pratt was giving up on the President's Committee's ability to provide unfettered legal assistance of the type the movement demanded. LCCRUL acted as a professional SMO is presumed to act: substituting its goals for those of the movement, attempting to deradicalize movement actions. Yet the classical SMOs coordinating the fight in Mississippi—primarily SNCC and CORE (Congress of Racial Equality)—were philosophically opposed to such elite control.

Beginning in the early 1960s, SNCC and CORE activists had begun to bristle at the Inc. Fund's cautious and controlled top-down model that was showing too few results too slowly. Furthermore, they did not hold the reverence for law and the legal system that the lawyers at the Inc. Fund or LCCRUL held. Law spoke in terms of "all deliberate speed." Their strategy—forged in the sit-in movement of 1960 that quickly spread across the nation—differed distinctly. "Freedom Now!" was increasingly the dominant slogan of the movement. As Howard Zinn observed at the time, "What had been an orderly, inch-by-inch advance via legal processes now became a revolution in which unarmed regiments marched from one objective to another with bewildering speed" (Zinn 2002: 26).

Reliance on the law, some believed, had proven ineffective in confronting a Southern white supremacist society where the rule of law enjoyed few adherents (Dittmer 1986: 72). The Field Foundation's 1961 report on the Inc. Fund noted that many at the NAACP's annual conference believed the lawyers were "moving too cautiously" (Field 1961). Mississippi activist Amzie Moore encouraged SNCC workers to begin organizing in his state because he was tired of going through legal procedures he had endured for years to no avail (Payne 1995: 105).

Others observed that beyond simple frustration with the legal approach, direct action demonstrated a shift in the nature of the cause. Journalist Ralph McGill noted in the *Atlanta Journal-Constitution* that "The sit-ins were, without question, productive of the most change.... No argument in a court of law could have dramatized the immorality and irrationality of such a custom as did the sit-ins.... Not even the Supreme Court decisions on the schools in 1954 had done this.... The central moral problem was enlarged" (Zinn 2002: 28). The activists had transformed the cause from a legal battle to a moral battle, and because law and morality were not the same, lawyers qua lawyers had no special expertise.

Further driving the move to direct action was the organizing philosophy ascendant in SNCC and CORE that rejected top-down, elite leadership. Instead, activists enacted the "radical democratic vision" of SNCC guru Ella Baker who, according to historian Barbara Ransby, understood that

> laws, structures and institutions had to change in order to correct injustice and op-
> pression, but part of the process had to involve oppressed people, ordinary people,
> infusing new meanings into the concept of democracy and finding their own indi-
> vidual and collective power to determine their lives and shape the direction of history
> (Ransby 2003: 1).

Others adopted the philosophy preached at the influential Highlander Folk School that rejected a movement wherein the leadership told people what to do and provided the thinking for them (Payne 1995: 71). With such a philosophy, the top-down, lawyer-led approach of the Inc. Fund was understandably out of favor. The point of protest and organizing was not necessarily aimed at testing law, but rather sought to get people to challenge authorities directly, to put their own bodies on the line and secure their own liberation. Arguments in federal courts were too far removed and mediated to provide such an experience. As attorney Len Holt described SNCC's approach, the group was dedicated to attacking "again, again, again," the manifestations of Southern racism (Holt 1992: 89). The Inc. Fund either lacked the inclination or the means to back them up in such endeavors (Greenberg 1994: 353). Yet, not all members of the legal profession showed the inclination toward leadership and control manifested by the Inc. Fund and LCCRUL. These lawyers reflected a "grassroots" approach to lawyering.

Civil rights organizers bristled at the Inc. Fund's approach and questioned whether lawyers should head the movement, but did not altogether refuse a place for law and lawyering in social change. Activists gave an enthusiastic reception to those who adopted an approach to lawyering that resembled the movement's radical democratic philosophy. When National Lawyers Guild attorneys began meeting with SNCC workers in the South, discussing the possibility of collaboration between the movement and lawyers, taking activists' ideas for legal action seriously and allowing for the possibility of litigation strategies coordinated with and determined by activists rather than lawyers, the reaction was overwhelming. "Why aren't the NAACP lawyers like you guys?" one SNCC worker reportedly asked (Holt 1992: 89).

Since its inception the National Lawyers Guild had balanced its identity as both a bar association and an advocacy group. Its founding constitution made explicit reference to law as a political system and its belief in human rights, stating its aim to unite lawyers "in a professional organization which shall function as an effective social force in service of the people to the end that human rights should be regarded as more sacred than property rights" (Auerbach 1976, Ch. 7; Ginger and Tobin 1988: 11). Furthermore, it was founded as an integrated organization in considered opposition to the ABA's whites-only policy. Thus, its early involvement in civil rights work is hardly surprising. Guild lawyers began aggressively volunteering help to the various civil rights groups, sending volunteers South on an ad hoc basis (Meier and Rudwick 1975: 270).

Organizations like the American Civil Liberties Union (which had adopted the same top-down, lawyer-led approach as the Inc. Fund but was now led by a brash young legal director named Mel Wulf) did the same, sending New York attorney William Kunstler, a board member whose practice lay primarily in the field of corporate law, to represent Freedom Riders (Langum 1999: 47). Kunstler's vision of the legal system was quickly altered by his experience in the South. He recalled in his memoirs: "In the past, lawyers, myself included, viewed the law as sacred and inviolate. But movement law considered the legal system as something to be used or changed, in order to gain the political objectives of the clients in a particular case" (Kunstler 1994: 105).

"Movement law's" vision—that law was not sacrosanct, but simply another tool for achieving political goals—was increasingly influential, reshaping concepts of lawyering for some, and attracting others who already shared some form of the vision. Carl Rachlin, the legal director for CORE understood his work in moral, rather than legal or constitutional terms: "What we had then was a moral understanding that what we were doing was totally right. . . " (Rachlin 1992). The goal was not to win a legal victory, but to transform southern society.

"Grassroots" lawyers understood that the movement's tactics went beyond simply changing the law, and thus the role of lawyers in the movement required a less litigation-centered approach. The Inc. Fund's modus operandi would not serve the movement, as Rachlin realized.

> I made the decision that it wouldn't work because the NAACP was, as able as it was – and this was in no way to minimize the quality of work they had done – I didn't feel it was capable at that moment in its history of dealing with people in motion. The NAACP had very brilliantly set up a series of activities leading to fine victories in the courts, but they were based upon a program that the NAACP designed (Rachlin: 1992).

The Inc. Fund's model assumed people functioned in a certain way, but CORE (and SNCC) had people "in motion all of the time." Thus, Rachlin believed a new organization of lawyers was needed that would better fit with the activists' approach.[4] "I would not in any way tell people how to behave and I thought that's what the NAACP with all its ability might tend to do. I didn't want in any way to interfere with the spontaneity of the activities that CORE people were engaging in at that time" (Rachlin 1992). Rachlin found other attorneys who agreed with his understanding of movement needs—attorneys who had independently come to the same conclusion. Jack Pratt from the NCC who was exasperated by the President's Committee's moral timidity, and Mel Wulf who due to a strong dose of professional competition was worried that the National Lawyers' Guild's program in the South would make him and his organization look less than committed to the civil rights cause (Pratt 1992; Wulf 1992).

Grassroots lawyering was different from the elite/vanguard or procedural-ist forms of practice. Lawyers for the Guild sought to be "responsive, unaloof, and 'regular,'" seeming to know "*where it was at*" (Holt 1992: 89) (emphasis in original). LCDC expected its lawyers to reject the special status and treatment attorneys often expected, instructing its volunteers, "We try to balance the obli-gation to function effectively as lawyers with the need not to have too great a gulf between our conditions of life and those of the people whose rights and dignity we are committed to serve" (Unsigned 1965). Lawyers acted as collabo-rators rather than directors, even in the realm of litigation (Holt 1992: 89). Thus LCDC's founders envisioned coordinating with protesters in *advance* of an ac-tion to keep people out of jail and out of court through prospective, offensive legal actions—seeking injunctions to prevent arrests, for instance—rather than purely uncoordinated, reactive, defensive legal representation (Kinoy 1983: 191–200).

Under no circumstances were lawyers to direct the movement. In its instructions to attorneys heading South, LCDC made this explicit:

> The volunteer civil-rights lawyer is not a leader of the civil-rights movement. We are there to help the movement with legal counsel and representation, not to tell the movement what it should do. You may, if asked, suggest what the legal consequences of a course of action might be, but you may not tell them whether or not they should embark on it. They have more experience than you at civil-rights work in the South, and they are responsible for the action program. Even if they make mistakes, they are theirs to make; your task is to defend their every constitutional and legal right as resourcefully and committedly as you can, even if they have made a mistake. Until the time comes when they ask us to lead the movement, do not be misled by any advantage of education, worldly experience, legal knowledge, or even common sense, into thinking that your function is to tell them what they should do. The one thing that the Negro leadership in the South is rightly disinclined to accept is white people telling them any further what to do and what not to do, even well-meaning and committed white, liberal Northerners (Unsigned 1965; Wulf 1992).

Succinctly, Guild program director George Crockett wrote, "In the war against injustice in Mississippi, lawyers are not the front line troops" (NLG 1964). Kunstler understood lawyers were "not the heart [of the movement] but merely an appendage." "Marching and protesting, being out on the streets – that was where the strength of the movement lay, and that would be how it would finally prevail" (Kunstler 1994: 105, 126). Lawyers were nonetheless a part of the movement. They were activists, as well.

LCDC's founders had a sense of the role of lawyers within the movement, yet this did not necessarily mean the attorneys they recruited shared that understanding. Lawyers for every group that sent lawyers South in the summer of 1964 came from different places, different professional situations, and possessed different understandings of why they were going. Some went to uphold the rule of law, others to advance the movement cause. Others went because it sounded like a fun (or sexy or dangerous) escape from daily legal drudgery. Regardless, the experience of lawyering in the South had a significant impact on many (if not most) of the attorneys, forcing them to reenvision the legal system, the cause, and the role of lawyers within the cause.

Although one magazine certainly exaggerated when it wrote that the policies set by LCDC and the President's Committee were ignored by the lawyers once they arrived South, the experience of the summer challenged the conceptions of lawyering laid out by the group's leaders (Hammer 1966: 83). Lawyers for the President's Committee spent most of their time that summer visiting with members of the local bar around the state of Mississippi, attempting to persuade them to represent people in need of counsel, as required by the *Canons of Professional Ethics* and as promised by the state bar's resolution affirming "its stand and the time-honored traditions of the Bar" to provide legal assistance to all in need, regardless of cause (Bernhard and Doyle 1964).

LCCRUL volunteers reported meetings with some "rational segregationists" as well as others who questioned the very suggestion that Mississippi had a race problem (O'Connell and Bryan 1964). By summer's end, LCCRUL lawyers expressed frustration with such efforts, reporting to the Committee office that no progress could be made through the existing power structure. They were abandoning the proceduralist ideal of neutral representation. Another labeled the bar resolution a meaningless "perversion" (Hopkins 1964). The assumption that the system was "essentially sound" did not stand up to their experiences.

When they were engaged in legal work, the lawyers for the President's Committee were similarly frustrated, bucking at the restrictions requiring them to represent only ministers. President's Committee lawyers were left idle much of the time because ministers were but a small portion of the activists in the state and (as one lawyer sarcastically reported) were not conveniently arrested at evenly spaced intervals. The President's Committee's lawyers were forced to remain idle while "travesties on the legal process were being committed on others than ministers" (Stone 1964). The Committee's rules did not conform to the reality of the situation in Mississippi, particularly in distinguishing between members of the movement. The President's Committee board may have been concerned about maintaining nonpartisanship or some semblance of a traditional lawyer–client relationship, but many of its emissaries began to see their duty differently. They were not representing individuals, but rather *the movement* (Sullivan 1964). In other words, LCCRUL volunteers increasingly strained against the proceduralist orientation espoused by the Committee's leadership. What the board decided in its meetings in DC and New York did not conform to what lawyers saw on the ground in the Deep South. LCCRUL sent lawyers down to fight for the cause of the rule of law, but many volunteers came to share the movement's vision of their cause.

As a result, some ignored their agreement with the President's Committee and represented nonministers. Others ignored organizational rules barring collaboration with other groups and donated their spare time to LCDC (O'Connell and Bryan 1964; Stone 1964). At summer's end many emphatically urged the

President's Committee to reconsider the "absurd limitation on our jurisdiction." Wrote attorney Bob Ostrow, in an angry missive, "As soldiers in the 'Third Revolution' as someone has categorized it, we must take any and all cases, work with anyone and everyone, deny no one our talents..." (Ostrow 1964; Sullivan 1964). Such battles between attorneys and LCCRUL leadership continued well after the organization established a permanent office in Jackson, MS. Staff attorneys increasingly identified as movement lawyers, while group leaders pushed them to remain nonpartisan mediators, unaffiliated with the civil rights cause (though by 1965 the restriction on representation was lifted).

LCDC attorneys did not suffer from idleness. The summer saw over 1,000 arrests alone and a typical day involved investigations into a church bombing and a separate incident involving the beating of two summer workers, the release of fifteen workers from jail, the arrests of three men accused of looking at a white girl, and the harassment of a voter registration worker (MSP 1964). When arrests did happen, LCDC (and LCCRUL) lawyers often relied on a controversial legal strategy: removal. Using a Reconstruction-era law, lawyers were able to petition to take cases out of state and local courts and into federal courts if they believed that the defendants would not be assured fair treatment at the local level or if the case against them involved a violation of their civil rights (Amsterdam 1965: 2–15). Once the petition was filed the federal judge had to grant habeas corpus, getting activists out of jail and back on the streets within twenty-four hours.

In addition to keeping activists in motion, the technique also threw state prosecutors for a loop. It created in the legal arena a protest technique with many similarities to direct action attempts to fill the jails or stop the functioning of voter registrar's offices. As one summer volunteer recalled, "The intention was to make the point in the federal courts that you couldn't get a fair trial in the state courts and to absolutely clog their dockets" (Weisman 1992). Removal did not resolve the cases themselves (and thus the controversy from the perspective of the Inc. Fund (Greenberg 1992)), but LCDC lawyers were not particularly concerned with such legal victories. They were also looking to the movement's immediate needs: keeping people out of jail was the priority, both for protection—given the fate of Goodman, Schwerner, and Chaney—and for organizing reasons.

Such "fireman" work—as LCDC Executive Secretary Henry Schwarzschild called it—exposed lawyers to "southern justice" and to the movement in ways they had not known before. Local judges (or justices of the peace) ignored basic due process guarantees, convicting defendants in less than thirty seconds (Gutman 1965: 82). Others flagrantly rejected the US Constitution and the Supreme Court, pointing to "local customs" that required segregated

courtrooms (Schulman 1965: 111). Others experienced firsthand the violence
of southern law enforcement. Henry Aronson, an attorney for the Aetna insurance company, was exposed to such brutality on his first day in the South
when Jim Clark, the infamous sheriff of Dallas County, Alabama, threw Aronson down a flight of stairs after Aronson served him with notice of a pending
lawsuit. "Violence wasn't beyond them. That had a large effect on me," Aronson
recalled (Aronson 1992).

The discrimination meted out by legal actors in Mississippi brought one
LCDC volunteer to comment that "the state stood as a working example of
totalitarianism in the United States" (Tonachel 1964). President's Committee
attorneys were similarly impressed by their interactions. Mississippi law of-
fended "the basic instincts of a lawyer," wrote one (Wing 1964). Bob Ostrow
wrote bluntly, "There is *no* law in Mississippi" (Ostrow 1964).

Their experiences with violence and lawlessness left one impression on attorneys; work with the movement left another. George Crockett of the Lawyers'
Guild wrote that "The individual lawyer who worked in Mississippi alongside
the movement almost invariably expressed profound changes in his own outlook and understanding. He had experienced a new set of legal values, a different
system of legal practice and a strange, uncomfortable set of human relations.
His personal beliefs were obviously and deeply affected" (NLG 1964).

Some were struck by their encounters with the movement workers. Bruce
Sullivan of the President's Committee was impressed that the young people
running the campaign in Mississippi had a "general high level of ability." Bob
Ostrow balanced the horrors of Mississippi injustice with his experiences "meeting, talking to, and learning from," movement members. Al Bronstein, an LCDC
volunteer described attending a mass meeting in St. Augustine, Florida as "one
of the most beautiful, exciting, moving, emotional moments of my life." Many
letters concur that while lawyers went South with the belief that they were representing individuals in a traditional way, by the time they returned they knew
that they were defenders of a movement (Stone 1964).

This was perhaps the most significant change, particularly for the President's
Committee volunteers. One volunteer wrote that the "most important lesson"
was:

> the need of a lawyers participating with the civil rights group to become identified in
> the minds of the young civil rights workers, with their objectives in the project. . . . The
> attorneys who go down there to participate. . . must be impressed with the need for
> demonstrating their enthusiasm for the cause, because their restraining counsel is not
> likely to be considered by the young workers in the absence of personal confidence
> in the attorney (Sullivan 1964).

Thus it was not surprising that Bob Ostrow was described (derisively) by one of his President's Committee peers as having "gone SNCC" early in his time in Missisippi. George Crockett of the Guild noted a similar phenomenon among his volunteers: "By mid-week they wanted to be just as militant as the COFO (Council of Federated Organizations) workers and take part themselves in voter registration work" (NLG 1964).

An LCDC volunteer now understood that "grass-roots, everyday legal representation for Negroes is an essential element in the freedom struggle in Mississippi" (Tonachel 1964: 19). Harvard Law Professor Mark deWolfe Howe (who went to Mississippi with LCDC in 1965), in the preface to a collection of essays by lawyers involved in the movement that summer, wrote, "It may be that in existing circumstances the lawyer who finds himself professionally engaged in 'the movement' must see his responsibility as different, almost in kind, from what it has been in other times and other settings. If he is to be true to his profession he must, perhaps, see himself as engaged not by a client but by a cause. . . " (Howe 1965: vii). Professionalism now called for a different conception of lawyering.

At the close of Freedom Summer, eighteen lawyers had gone South with the President's Committee. The Guild sent close to sixty and LCDC approximately 115 (Holt 1992: 275–80). Regardless of organization, lawyers seemed to see their value not in terms of legal victories won or representation provided. Rather, lawyers saw their *presence* as the value. Their presence—in the streets, in COFO Freedom Houses, in jails, in courtrooms—played a role in deterring white Southerners, and particularly state actors, from meting out greater violence and lawlessness against the movement (Freirichs 1964; NLG 1964; Stone 1964). The President's Committee report on the summer project characterized this as a "federal presence" that restrained whites (Bernhard and Doyle 1964; Nevas 1964). Lawyers provided an important morale boost for the movement, showing them that someone was looking out for them (Bernhard and Doyle 1964; Nevas 1964; NLG 1964; Sullivan 1964). They were part of the process of helping people find "their own individual and collective power to determine their lives" (Ransby 2003), helping the movement with their technical abilities rather than telling the movement how to proceed.

None of this is to say that lawyers emerged from the summer having had identical experiences or with uniform notions of what they did and why, as demonstrated in sources such as the writings of lawyers in *Southern Justice* or the reports of President's Committee volunteers. Some seemed to finish their time in the South with many important views and ideas unchanged.[5] Some continued to believe in the professional mission of the President's Committee. Others continued to have faith that the Federal courts were the mechanism best suited to achieve the goal of equality. The available evidence only allows for generalizations. By and large they emerged skeptical of the value of law and litigation, yet with few exceptions remained confident that law, lawyering, and the legal system had a place in the civil rights cause. In this sense they were much like the activists they represented who were simultaneously cynical and optimistic about those things.

What is evident is the existence of a gulf between the visions of the Northern leaders of these organizations and what the volunteers believed after encountering and grappling with the reality of the Southern white supremacy. It is important to distinguish between organizational goals and the actions taken on the ground. It was a long way from Washington and New York to Jackson, MS, and even further to such hamlets as Clarksdale or Philadelphia. The visions of law and professionalism espoused by organization leaders did not necessarily translate into such on the ground in the Deep South.

The experiences of lawyers in the Deep South demonstrated, at their most basic, that not all lawyering was the same. Lawyers were able to distinguish between mainstream practices and cause lawyering practices. Activists recognized distinctions between lawyering approaches that put lawyers in charge and those that helped the movement take the course activists wished. The historical record reveals professionals discussing their work with movement activists, and their visions of the legal system and the cause in starkly different terms. Although professional SMOs may have often exerted a moderating influence on the movement, not all such groups did so. As the example of lawyering in the civil rights movement suggests, the relationship between movements and professional SMOs was at times far more reciprocal—with the movement influencing lawyering as much (if not more) than lawyering influenced the movement. In the case of Freedom Summer, it seems that lawyers actually made protest more possible as a tactic—for legal actors prevented arrests or lessened the impact of those arrests, keeping people on the streets to organize, register, and march.

At the apex of civil rights movement activism—between 1963 and 1966—it was the movement that was exerting greater influence on the actions and views of legal professionals involved in the movement rather than professionals who were on the direction of the movement. Many lawyers came with either their own understandings of lawyering, or with the strictures of the organization that sent them. However, in case after case, interaction with the movement and exposure to the realities of Southern justice and violence changed their understandings of their professional and personal role in the movement. Nonprofessionals challenged and redefined professionalsim in the Lawyering context (a concept that is not uniform in its definition) in ways that the social movement literature must take into account.

Notes

1. These groups supplemented the small number of African American attorneys practicing in Deep South states—in Mississippi there were only three black attorneys admitted to practice in 1964–as well as the smaller number of white attorneys willing to take on cases with civil rights undertones. Chestnut, J. L. and J. Cass (1990). *Black in Selma.* New York: Farrar, Straus, and Giroux; Greenberg, J. (1994). *Crusaders in the Courts.* New York: Basic Books; Porter, A. (1998). "Norris, Schmidt, Green, Harris, Higginbotham and Associates: The Sociolegal Import of Philadelphia Cause Lawyers." *Cause Lawyering: Political Commitments and Professional Responsibilities.* A. Sarat and S. Scheingold. New York: Oxford University Press, pp. 151–80. In this essay, due to the constraints of archival resources, I focus little attention on the National Lawyers Guild and its significant contribution to lawyering in the civil rights movement. I also do not touch on the Law Students Civil Rights Research Council, another group mentioned as part of the professionalization of the movement, Jenkins, J. C. and C. M. Eckert (1986). "Channeling Black Insurgency: Elite Patronage and Professional Social Movement Organizations in the Development of the Black Movement." *American Sociological Review,* 51(Dec.): 812–29. That group has been well covered by Amy Ruth Tobol's history of the group, Tobol, A. R. (1999). "Badge of Honor: The Law Students Civil Rights Research Council." Ph.D. dissertation, Buffalo, SUNY-Buffalo.

2. Greenberg saw the Guild as politically dangerous (as its reputation as a communist-front group could cause problems that would distract from the movement's goals) and both technically and strategically sloppy (Greenberg 1992).

3. Note, however, that Rostow did say in another letter, "We have left this problem to the judges much too long" (Rostow 1963a).

4. Rachlin: 1992 Rachlin was unwilling to associate with the Guild because of the Guild's perceived links to the Communist party (Rachlin 1992).

5. In addition to the report filed by President's Committee volunteers Bryan and O'Connell, another by Morton Klevan reiterates over and over that the Committee is a "conservative" organization dedicated to upholding "law and order" (Klevan 1964).

Bibliographical Note

Archival sources were a major resource in the construction of this paper. The following archives are indicated in the entries below:

Field Foundation Papers, Center for American History, University of Texas

LCCRUL Papers, Wesleyan University Library, Special Collections and Archives, Middletown, CT

Pierre Tonachel Papers, on file with author
Ralph Bunche Oral History Collection, Moorland-Springarn Library, Howard University
Richard Frank Papers, on file with author
Thomas Hilbink Interviews, tapes on file at Columbia Oral History Research Office; Transcripts available from author.

References

Amsterdam, A. G. (1965). "Criminal Prosecutions Affecting Federally Guaranteed Civil Rights: Federal Removal and Habeas Corpus Jurisdiction to Abort State Court Trial." *University of Pennsylvania Law Review*, 113(6): 793–912.

Aronson, H. (1992). Interview by Thomas Hilbink, November 9, 1992.

Auerbach, J. S. (1976). *Unequal Justice: Lawyers and Social Change in Modern America.* New York: Oxford University Press.

Bernhard, B. and J. Doyle (1964). Report on the Mississippi Summer Project, October 20, 1964, Civil Rights—Executive Committee Meetings (1963–67) File, Box 27, LCCRUL Papers (emphasis added).

Bourne, C. (n/a). History of the Field Foundation, Field Foundation Papers.

Branch, T. (1988). *Parting the Waters: America in the King Years, 1954–1963.* New York: Simon and Schuster.

Burns, W. H. (1970). W. Haywood Burns, Interview by Robert Wright, August 19, 1970, transcript, Bunche Oral History Collection.

Chestnut, J. L. and J. Cass (1990). *Black in Selma.* New York: Farrar, Straus, and Giroux.

Connell, A. G. (2003). *The Lawyers' Committee for Civil Rights Under Law: The Making of a Public Interest Group.* Washington, DC: Lawyers' Committee for Civil Rights Under Law.

Dittmer, J. (1986). "The Politics of the Mississippi Movement." In *The Civil Rights Movement in America*, C. W. Eagles, ed. Jackson, MS: University Press of Mississippi, pp. 65–93.

Field Foundation (Field) (1961). Request for Renewal of Grant-in-aid for NAACP Legal Defense Fund, Spring 1961, NAACP Legal Defense and Education Fund, Inc. S.A. 61 File, Box 2T69, Field Foundation Papers.

Freirichs, C. A. (1964). Letter to Lawyers Constitutional Defense Committee, September 1, 1964, Pierre Tonachel Papers.

Ginger, A. F. and E. M. Tobin, eds. (1988). *The National Lawyers Guild: From Roosevelt through Reagan.* Philadelphia: Temple University Press.

Greenberg, J. (1960). *Race Relations and American Law.* New York: Columbia University Press.

———. (1992). Interview by Thomas M. Hilbink, October 15, 1992.

———. (1994). *Crusaders in the Courts.* New York: Basic Books.

Gutman, J. S. (1965). "Oktibbeha County, Mississippi." In *Southern Justice*, L. Friedman, ed. New York: Pantheon, pp. 80–87.

Haines, H. (1984). "Black Radicalization and the Funding of Civil Rights." *Social Problems*, 32: 31–43.

Hammer, R. (1966). "Yankee Lawyers in Mississippi Courts." *Harper's*, (November): 79–88.

Helfgot, J. (1981). *Professional Reforming*. Lexington, MA: Lexington Books.

Hilbink, T. M. (2004). "You Know the Type Categories of Cause Lawyering." *Law and Social Inquiry*, 29(Summer): 657–98.

Holt, L. (1992). *The Summer That Didn't End*. New York: Da Capo Press.

Hopkins, S. (1964). Letter to Berl Bernhard, October 4, 1964, Mississippi Summer Project 1964—Reports File, Box 40, LCCRUL Papers.

Howe, M. D. (1965). "Our Splendid Bauble." In *Southern Justice*, L. Friedman, ed. New York: Pantheon, pp. v–ix.

Hunter, M. (1963). "Lawyers Promise Kennedy Aid in Easing Race Unrest: Leaders of the Lawyers Committee." *New York Times*, June 22: 1.

Jenkins, J. C. (1983). "Resource Mobilization Theory and the Study of Social Movements." *Annual Review of Sociology*, 9: 527–53.

Jenkins, J. C. and C. M. Eckert (1986). "Channeling Black Insurgency: Elite Patronage and Professional Social Movement Organizations in the Development of the Black Movement." *American Sociological Review*, 51: 812–29.

Jones, L. (2006). "The Haves Come Out Ahead: How Cause Lawyers Frame the Legal System for Movements." In *Cause Lawyers*, vol. IV, A. Sarat and S. Scheingold, eds. Palo Alto, CA: Stanford University Press, pp. xxx.

Kalman, L. (1996). *The Strange Career of Legal Liberalism*. New Haven, CT: Yale University Press.

Kinoy, A. (1983). *Rights on Trial: the odyssey of a people's lawyer*. Cambridge, MA: Harvard University Press.

Klevan, M. (1964). Letter to David Stahl, August 5, 1964, Mississippi Summer Project—1964 (June–November) File, Box 40, LCCRUL Papers.

Kunstler, W. M. (1994). *My Life as a Radical Lawyer*. New York: Birch Lane Press.

Langum, D. J. (1999). *The Most Hated Lawyer in America*. New York: NYU Press.

Lawyers Committee for Civil Rights Under Law (LCCRUL) (1964). Report to the Members of the Lawyers Committee for Civil Rights Under Law, March 1964, Report to Members—1964 File, Box 1, LCCRUL Papers.

Lewis, A. (1960). "Do Laws Change the Hearts of Men?" *New York Times*, May 1: BR6.

Lewis, J. (1991). "Original Text of Speech to Be Delivered at the Lincoln Memorial." In *The Eyes on the Prize Civil Rights Reader*, C. Carson, D. J. Garrow, G. Gill, V. Harding, D. C. Hine, eds. New York: Penguin, pp. 163–65.

Lunney, J. R. (1992). J. Robert Lunney, Interview by Thomas Hilbink, October 9, 1992.

Marshall, A. M. (2006). "Social Movement Strategies and the Participatory Potential of Litigation." In *Cause Lawyering*, vol. IV, A. Sarat and S. Scheingold, eds. Palo Alto, CA: Stanford University Press, pp. xxx.

McAdam, D. (1982). *Political Processes and the Development of Black Insurgency*. Chicago, University of Chicago Press.

McCann, M. (2004). "Law and Social Movements." In *The Blackwell Companion to Law and Society*, A. Sarat, ed. Malden, MA: Blackwell Publishing, pp. 506–22.

McCann, M. and J. Dudas (2006). "Backlash: Mapping the Changing Context of Movement Lawyering." In *Cause Lawyering*, vol. IV, A. Sarat and S. Scheingold, eds. Palo Alto, CA: Stanford University Press, pp. xxx.

McCarthy, J. and M. Zald (1973). *The Trend of Social Movements*. Morristown, NJ: General Learning.

———. (1977). "Resource Mobilization and Social Movements." *American Journal of Sociology*, 82: 1212–41.

Meier, A. and E. Rudwick (1975). *CORE: A Study in the Civil Rights Movement*. Urbana, IL: University of Illinois Press.

Mississippi Summer Project (MSP) (1964). Running Summary of Incidents, no date (ca. August 1964), Pierre Tonachel Papers.

Moses, R. (1964). Memorandum to Jack Greenberg, no date (ca. April 1964), NAACP folder, Box 7, LCCRUL Papers.

NAACP Legal Defense and Educational Fund (NAACP-LDF) (1963). 1963 Annual Report, NAACP File, Box 7, LCCRUL Papers.

NAACP Names a White Counsel. (1961). *New York Times*, October 5: 1.

National Lawyers Guild (NLG) (1964). Project Mississippi (pamphlet) (ca. Fall 1964), National Lawyers Guild File, Box 8, LCCRUL Papers.

Navasky, V. S. (1971). *Kennedy Justice*. New York: Atheneum.

Nevas, A. (1964). Letter to Henry Schwarzschild, July 21, 1964, Pierre Tonachel Papers.

O'Connell, J. and L. T. Bryan (1964). Report to LCCRUL on Activities in Mississippi (ca. Fall 1964), Mississippi Summer Project 1964—Reports File, Box 40, LCCRUL Papers.

On Civil Rights Frontier: Jack Greenberg. (1961). *New York Times*, October 5: 31.

Ostrow, R. W. (1964). Letter to Berl Bernhard, October 30, 1964, Mississippi Summer Project 1964—Reports File, Box 40, LCCRUL Papers.

Payne, C. M. (1995). *I've Got the Light of Freedom*. Berkeley, CA: University of California Press.

Perrow, C. (1979). "The Sixties Observed." In *The Dynamics of Social Movements*, M. Zald and J. McCarthy, eds. Cambridge, MA: Winthrop, pp. 192–211.

Piven, F. F. and R. Cloward (1977). *Poor People's Movements*. New York: Pantheon.

Porter, A. (1998). "Norris, Schmidt, Green, Harris, Higginbotham and Associates: The Sociolegal Import of Philadelphia Cause Lawyers." In *Cause Lawyering: Political Commitments and Professional Responsibilities*, A. Sarat and S. Scheingold, eds. New York: Oxford University Press, pp. 151–80.

Pratt, J. (1992). John Pratt, Interview by Thomas Hilbink, September 13, 1992.

Rachlin, C. (1992). Interview by Thomas Hilbink, October 13, 1992.

Ransby, B. (2003). *Ella Baker and the Black Freedom Movement*. Chapel Hill, NC: University of North Carolina Press.

Rostow, E. (1963a). Letter to Deputy Attorney General Nicholas Katzenbach, June 3, 1963, Statement of Policy and Program (Rosenman) File, Box 1, LCCRUL Papers.

———. (1963b). Letter to President John F. Kennedy (draft), May 15, 1963, Statement of Policy and Program (Rosenman) File, Box 1, LCCRUL Papers.

Sarat, A. and S. Scheingold (2005). "The Dynamics of Cause Lawyering: Constraints and Opportunities." In *The Worlds Cause Lawyers Make*, A. Sarat and S. Scheingold, eds. Palo Alto, CA: Stanford University Press, pp. 1–34.

Schulman, R. P. (1965). "Clarksdale Customs." In *Southern Justice*, L. Friedman, ed. New York: Pantheon, pp. 107–11.

Shamir, R. and S. Chinski (1998). "Destruction of Houses and Construction of a Cause: Lawyers and Bedouins in the Israeli Courts." In *Cause Lawyering: Political*

Commitments and Professional Responsibilities, A. Sarat and S. Scheingold, eds. New York: Oxford University Press, pp. 227–57.

Staggenborg, S. (1988). "Consequences of Professionalization and Formalization in the Pro-Choice Movement." *American Sociological Review*, 53: 585–605.

Stone, L. B. (1964). Report to LCCRUL, September 10, 1964, Mississippi Summer Project 1964—Reports File, Box 40, LCCRUL Papers.

Sullivan, B. M. (1964). Letter to David Stahl, July 16, 1964, Mississippi Summer Project 1964—Reports File, Box 40, LCCRUL Papers.

Tobol, A. R. (1999). "Badge of Honor: The Law Students Civil Rights Research Council." Ph.D. dissertation, SUNY-Buffalo.

Tonachel, P. (1964). "There is No Justice, There is No Freedom." *Village Voice*, New York, September 17: 10–11, 18–19.

Tushnet, M. V. (1994). *Making Civil Rights Law: Thurgood Marshall and the Supreme Court, 1936-1961*. New York: Oxford University Press.

Tweed, H., B. G. Segal, and H. Packer. (1969). "Civil Rights and Civil Disobedience to Law." In *Civil Disobedience: Theory and Practice*, H. A. Bedau, ed. New York: Pegasus, pp. 90–97.

Unsigned (1963). Unsigned Letter (Bernard Segal, drafted), June 4, 1963 (draft letter regarding University of Alabama Crisis), Statement of Policy and Program File, Box 1, LCCRUL Papers.

———. (1964). Unsigned memo (likely John Pratt), "Request for Lawyers for Summer Work in Southern States," no date (ca. May 1964), Mississippi Summer Project—— 1964 (April–June 1964) File, Box 40, LCCRUL Papers.

———. (1965). Unsigned Memorandum for LCDC volunteers (likely authored by Henry Schwarzschild) (ca. 1965), Frank papers.

Weisman, L. (1992). Interview by Thomas Hilbink, September 2, 1992.

Wilkins, R. and J. Jones (1965). Memorandum from Roy Wilkins and John Jones (to Field Foundation), March 29, 1965, NAACP (Special Contribution Fund) 3rd 1965, Box 2s416, Field Foundation Papers.

Williams, J. (1998). *Thurgood Marshall: American Revolutionary*. New York: Times Books.

Wing, John (1964). Letter to Berl I. Bernhard, October 7, 1964, Mississippi Summer Project 1964—Reports File, Box 40, LCCRUL Papers.

Wulf, M. L. (1992). Interview by Thomas Hilbink, September 1, 1992.

Zinn, H. (2002). *SNCC: The New Abolitionists*. Cambridge, MA: South End Press.

Cause Lawyers in the First Wave of Same Sex Marriage Litigation

SCOTT BARCLAY AND SHAUNA FISHER

On May 20, 1974, the Court of Appeals of Washington in *Singer v. Hara* (11 Wn. App. 247) rejected a legal claim for same sex marriage initiated in 1972 by Seattle-based, gay rights activist, John Singer. Writing for the court, Chief Justice Swanson (11 Wn. App. 247 at 264) "concluded that the state's denial of a marriage license to [same sex] appellants is required by our state statutes and permitted by both the state and federal constitutions." Although state courts in Minnesota (in *Baker v. Nelson* 191 N.W.2d 185), New York (in *Anonymous v. Anonymous* 67 Misc. 2d 982), and Kentucky (in *Jones v. Hallahan* 501 S.W.2d 588) had previously issued opinions that denied marriage to lesbian and gay couples, the legal claim in *Singer v. Hara* was the first of the legal challenges to state policies prohibiting same sex marriage to rely primarily on state constitutional provisions, rather than rights associated with the US Constitution. Moreover, it did so by extensively referencing the gender equality provision introduced into the Washington state constitution in 1972—a provision that was increasingly present, or determined by state courts to be implied, in many other state constitutions. Thus, the negative decision by the Washington court appeared at the time to preclude the possibility of legal challenges in other states on similar state constitutional grounds. Accordingly, after the 1974 decision in *Singer v. Hara*, no legal claims were pressed directly on same sex marriage in any state court for seventeen years.[1]

The 1991 filing of the claim in the *Baehr v. Lewin* (74 Haw. 530) in Hawaii (see Eskridge 2002, Goldberg-Hiller 2002) ended this extended moratorium by lesbian and gay rights activists on litigating the issue of same sex marriage in state and federal courts. By 2004, in response to cases brought by lesbian and gay rights activists, even state courts in the state of Washington managed to overcome the legal reasoning in *Singer v. Hara*. On August 4, 2004, the Superior

Court of Washington (King County) in *Andersen v. King County* (2004 WL 1738447) found that Washington's prohibition of same sex marriage violated the state's constitution. The finding was reinforced by a similar holding on September 7, 2004 by the Superior Court of Washington (Thurston County) in *Castle v. State of Washington* (2004 WL 1985215), which also explicitly declared unconstitutional the state's 1998 Defense of Marriage Act. These two cases in Washington, and similar cases in other states, signaled clearly that the apparent legal obstacle represented by the 1974 decision was easily able to be broached by 2004.

For sociolegal scholars, this switch in court-defined outcomes in Washington between the 1974 court decision and its 2004 counterparts is enlightening. Clearly, it demonstrates the dynamic nature of legal interpretation in relation to an unchanged set of laws—the key provisions of the Washington constitution did not change in their formal composition during this period, even if the judicial interpretation of these various provisions expanded (especially in relation to the application of equal protection and privacy) during the intervening period.

For their part, the legal claims presented in 1974 and 2004 are remarkably similar. Each claim draws upon the same provisions of the state's constitution and largely eschews federal constitutional provisions. In addition, the 1974 claim, like its 2004 counterpart, constructs its legal argument in the frame of "same sex" marriage; a frame that highlights gender inequality in the current law rather than a focus upon inequality related to the sexual orientation of the claimants. Furthermore, each claim was initiated and litigated by a cause lawyer or cause lawyers after the issue of same sex marriage had been raised publicly both in Washington State and nationally.

The similarity in legal context and the divergence in court-defined outcomes offer a perfect background for consideration of the role of social movements and cause lawyers. Consequently, we use these Washington court decisions on same sex marriage to capture the different roles of litigation by cause lawyers at divergent moments in the development and promotion by social movements of new social definitions.

Cause Lawyers and the Cases

The 1974 Case

Singer v. Hara was initiated on April 27, 1972 on behalf of two men, John L. Singer and Paul Barwick, who unsuccessfully attempted on September 20, 1971 to have the King County Auditor, Lloyd Hara, issue them a marriage license.

At the time, Singer was "the organizer and leader of the Seattle Gay Alliance" (Rivera 1999, n. 138).

The lawyer in the case was Michael E. Withey, who had only graduated from the University of San Francisco's School of Law a few months before Singer and Barwick first attempted to gain a marriage license. Since handling the *Singer* case at the very start of his professional career, Withey has pursued a variety of causes beyond lesbian and gay rights. For example, he has litigated on behalf of native American activists in relation to return of human remains and artifacts; he has pursued personal injury claims for murdered union organizers targeted by the Marcos' regime of the Philippines; and, he has sued a foreign company operating in the United States whose health and safety standards placed workers in danger (Stritmatter et al. Web site 2005). He operates today within a private practice (in the law firm of *Stritmatter, Kessler, Whelan, Withey, Coluccio*) and did so at the time of the *Singer* case (in the law firm of *Smith, Kaplan & Withey*).

Although the idea may surprise many sociolegal scholars who are used to thinking of the same sex marriage debate as a very recent phenomenon, the *Singer v. Hara* case occurred during a period of active discussion of same sex marriage in Washington and the nation. However, most of the national attention concerning same sex marriage in the early 1970s was initially generated by groups opposed to the ratification of the federal Equal Rights Amendment (ERA) and its state equivalents. The ERA sought (unsuccessfully on the national level and successfully in many states, including Washington) to introduce language into the respective constitution enshrining equal rights based on sex and/or gender characteristics. Opponents to the introduction of the federal ERA or a state equivalent used the possibility of forcing states to endorse same sex marriage as a way to denigrate and dismiss the need for such an amendment.

In this context, discussion of same sex marriage occurred regularly throughout the period from 1971 through 1975. For example, the US Senate Committee that promoted the ERA discussed and rejected the possibility that the proposed amendment permitted same sex marriage (see Maitland 1975). The *New York Times* (March 11, 1975: 40) and the *Seattle Post-Intelligencer* (e.g., October 30, 1972: A-4 and November 5, 1972: 10) each had at least one article concerning the legal validity of same sex marriage in light of passage of a state or federal ERA.

In fact, the filed briefs and the Court of Appeals' opinion in *Singer v. Hara* (11 Wn. App. 247 at 250) reference the extensive discussion of the possibility of same sex marriage in the campaign in Washington State in relation to passage of that state's ERA. According to the court's opinion (11 Wn. App. 247 at n.5), the following statement against the proposed constitutional amendment also occurred "in the 1972 Voters Pamphlet published by the Secretary of State: ....

Homosexual and lesbian marriage would be legalized, with further complication regarding adopting children into such a 'family.' "

The 2004 Case

Castle v. State of Washington was filed in Thurston County Superior Court on April 1, 2004 on behalf of eleven romantically committed, same sex couples located throughout Washington. *Andersen v. King County* was filed on May 7, 2004 on behalf of eight romantically committed, same sex couples who had been denied a marriage license by King County. In the briefs in both cases, the couples are presented as ordinary members of the community whose legal and social interactions as parents or as a couple are often hindered by the failure of the State of Washington to officially and legally sanction their relationship.

Based on the expansive lineup of lawyers and organizations represented in initiating these two cases, it is obvious that these claims were widely supported. There were five separate lawyers who signed onto the initial brief in the *Castle* case. Paul Lawrence and Matthew Segal were in private practice with the law firm of Preston, Gates, and Ellis LLP. Paul Lawrence, according to the American Civil Liberties Union (ACLU) Web site (2005), is also "lead ACLU cooperating attorney and national ACLU board member." Roger Leishman was in private practice with the law firm Davis Wright Tremaine LLP. He is a member of the Board of Directors of ACLU Washington and a former Senior Staff Attorney for the ACLU (Davis Wright Tremaine LLP Web site 2005). ACLU Washington was represented directly by their staff attorney, Aaron Caplan. Karolyn Hicks was in private practice with the personal service law firm of Stokes Lawrence, PS.

There were seven lawyers who signed onto the initial brief in the *Andersen* case. Patricia Novotny was associated with the University of Washington Law School and its Women's Studies Department. She has previously represented the Northwest Women's Law Center in legal actions in Washington State and appears to do so in the present case. Lisa Stone and Nancy Sapiro represented directly the Northwest Women's Law Center. Jennifer Divine and Bradley Bagshaw were in private practice with the law firm of Helsell Fetterman LLP. Jamie Pederson was in private practice with the law firm of Preston, Gates, and Ellis LLP. He is also "Co-Chair of the National Board of Directors of Lambda Legal Defense & Education Fund, Inc." (Preston, Gates, and Ellis LLP Web site 2005). Lambda Legal Defense & Education Fund (Lambda Legal) was also represented by Jennifer Pizer.

Like its 1974 counterpart, the 2004 case also occurred in an environment of heightened national awareness on same sex marriage. By the time the case in Washington was initiated in the Summer of 2004, successful litigation strategies had enabled same sex couples to legally marry in Massachusetts as well as in seven Canadian provinces and territories. British Columbia, which shares an extensive land and sea border on the north and west of Washington, was one of the Canadian provinces recognizing same sex marriage. In *Barbeau v. British Columbia (Attorney General)* (2003 BCCA 251), British Columbia's Court of Appeals ordered the province to begin issuing marriage licenses to same sex couples as of July 8, 2003. On Washington's southern border, the Circuit Court of Oregon (Multnomah County) had found on April 20, 2004 in *Li v. State* (2004 WL 1258167) that state's prohibition on same sex marriage to be unconstitutional.[2]

On February 12, 2004, Gavin Newsom, the mayor of San Francisco, authorized the San Francisco city clerk to begin issuing marriage licenses to qualified same sex couples. Jason West, the mayor of New Paltz in New York, and County Commissioners in Sandoval County in New Mexico, each followed suit for a short period. The New York Attorney General announced on March 4, 2004 that New York State would legally recognize same sex marriages celebrated in other locations, even as it contemplated the validity of those marriages celebrated within its own state (Halligan 2004). And, on the national level, President Bush in early 2004 announced his support for a Federal Marriage Amendment to preclude states from introducing same sex marriage.

Cause Lawyering in a Dynamic Social and Movement Context

Given the outcome of the 1974 case and the fact that it appeared at the time to create a substantial legal obstacle to same sex marriage in Washington and nationally, it is easy to presume that it simply represents poor timing or an incorrect legal strategy on behalf of the involved social activist and cause lawyer. Such a claim is not unusual in relation to the legal results of cause lawyering. As Scheingold (1998: 124) notes, "according to some critics of left-activist cause lawyering, legal challenges to the foundations of established authority are counter-productive as well as ineffectual."

Although the litigation activities associated with *Singer v. Hara* appear at first glance to be an example of counterproductive activities, we argue that this view of the 1974 litigation is incorrect on several fronts. First, as amply demonstrated by the actions of two separate state courts in Washington in 2004, the legal precedent established by *Singer v. Hara* did not present a real obstacle to the chances of legal and political success of a united movement for same sex marriage.

But more importantly, we propose that the litigation activities related to the 1974 case have been incorrectly categorized. Instead of being viewed in terms of its subsequent legal outcome—an aspect that has never been considered key to understanding the value of cause lawyering by marginalized groups (e.g., Abel 1998; McCann and Silverstein 1998; Scheingold 1998)—we argue that the litigation activities related to the 1974 case must be redefined consistent with a dynamic view of the relationship between cause lawyering, social movements, and the social context of the relative historical period. Thus, the litigation activities related to the 1974 case represent a different aspect of cause lawyering from the actions undertaken in relation to the 2004 cases. As such, we propose that the 1974 litigation was a necessary predecessor of the cases thirty years later—necessary not only to literally stake a claim upon the validity of the idea in the general public, but also to allow lesbian and gay individuals to decide whether marriage was a path they really wanted to pursue.

Culturally Reclaiming by Legally Claiming

McCann and Silverstein (1998: 281) note that "the more that nonlegalistic tactics are realistic and actionable, the less likely it is that lawyers, litigation, or 'legalism' will come to dominate a movement." Notwithstanding the success of the Stonewall Riots of 1969, nonlegalistic tactics were not realistic and actionable for lesbian and gay rights activists in 1971 when the first marriage cases were initiated in New York, Minnesota, and Washington.

In 1971, there existed no openly gay official in any major elected office. Only four of the fifty states—Colorado, Connecticut, Illinois, and Oregon—had decriminalized prohibitions on consensual sodomy. In the remainder of the states, sodomy laws were predominantly used to target the sexual activities of gay couples. Federal and state courts initially restricted the attempts by Lambda to establish an organization devoted primarily to the use of a litigation strategy to realize lesbian and gay rights (Andersen 2005). More generally, courts defined the creation of lesbian and gay rights organizations as an action akin to criminal conspiracy (*Ratchford v. Gay Lib* 434 US 1080). And, in 1971, the American Psychiatric Association still classified homosexuality as a mental illness.

To a large extent, the individual constituents of the lesbian and gay rights movement in 1971 remained isolated and in fear of social, financial, and even criminal retribution for identifying their sexual orientation. Six years after Singer attempted to obtain a marriage license, the Supreme Court of Washington upheld the dismissal of a gay teacher in Tacoma based only on the teacher's sexual orientation (*Gaylord v. Tacoma School District* 88 Wn.2d 286). Singer himself was dismissed from his federal civil service position for drawing attention to his sexual orientation through his activism around the same sex marriage issue (Eskridge 1996: 128; Rivera 1999: 1040–41). Similarly, Jay Baker, the student activist who initiated the 1971 same sex marriage claim in Minnesota, was

threatened with criminal fraud and restricted temporarily from taking the Minnesota Bar for filing the marriage documents in that case as well as for being
open about being gay (*New York Times* January 7, 1973: 55). As Justice Brennan
in *Rowland v. Mad River Local School Dist* (470 US 1009 at 1014) noted in 1985,
"because of the immediate and severe opprobrium often manifested against
homosexuals once so identified publicly, members of this group are particularly
powerless to pursue their rights openly in the political arena."

In such a social and legal context, it is hard to imagine the 1974 case in
Washington as leading to a legal success. Moreover, all of the public discussion
occurring at this time on same sex marriage was openly dismissive of the real
possibility of such state recognition being extended to encompass lesbian and
gay couples. Instead, same sex marriage was publicly pilloried by legal scholars
and most social activists as a ridiculous and impossible situation raised inap-
propriately by opponents of the ERA to denigrate and obfuscate the true value
of the proposed federal amendment and its state counterparts (see Maitland
1975).

In the social struggle for lesbian and gay rights in the early 1970s, the filing
of the legal claim in the *Singer* case, and its counterparts in Minnesota, New
York, and Kentucky, can be identified as not being primarily about winning a
legal victory that would bring about a commensurate change in social behavior
toward lesbian and gay individuals. Rather, the filing of these legal actions represent an attempt to directly and publicly challenge the socially accepted (and
hence, socially constraining) definitions of sexuality and to reclaim the territory
of same sex marriage on behalf of lesbian and gay couples.

First, the filing of the claim and the associated publicity began the process
of denaturalizing the current notions of sexuality, marriage, love, and commitment. One of the mechanisms for the state's exercise of power is through the
institutions and symbols associated with the law and legal ideology. A significant contribution from scholarship associated with the critical legal studies
movement is the explicit recognition that the law and legal ideology are neither neutral nor egalitarian, but rather support and mask an unequal power
structure that actually disfavors large portions of society (e.g., Smart 1989;
Kennedy 1998). Through the use of law, the state protects certain social, political, and economic configurations (Abel 1998) or, in this case, a certain sexual
configuration—heterosexual couples are defined as the norm. To the extent that
these configurations are accepted as natural and alternative configurations are
unimaginable, legal ideology is hegemonic. The filing of the claim in the 1974
case publicly signals that the sexual configuration associated with marriage was
now contested and that the imposed sexual hegemony was no longer simply

accepted as natural. Like many practices embodied in law, this is not to imply that the dominant sexual configuration associated with marriage was privately accepted by lesbian and gay individuals prior to this historical point, even if there was not always public rejection by such individuals (e.g., Eskridge 1999).

Second, McCann (1994: 10; see also Scheingold 1974; Handler 1978; Olson 1984) notes that litigation of this sort can be important for "building a movement, generating public support for new rights claims, and providing leverage to supplement other political tactics." For the embryonic lesbian and gay rights movement, litigation allowed them to publicly proclaim their presence. Such signals were particularly important because these lesbian and gay communities had previously been rendered largely invisible through social and legal actions.

More consequential than simply facilitating the building of a movement or acting to recognize the presence of a new rights claim is the fact that this litigation publicly reclaims and reappropriates the idea of same sex marriage and returns its "ownership" to lesbian and gay individuals—those individuals who would really have to make the decision whether to endorse marriage or even whether to marry. In the act of litigating, same sex marriage is literally and socially transformed from the ridiculous to the possible (as demonstrated by the fact that the state's highest court must respond to this idea). And, it becomes an idea "claimed" (literally through the filing of a legal claim) by lesbian and gay groups rather than by those who sought to denigrate or dismiss the ERA. The 1974 case cements forever a culturally dominant link between lesbian and gay rights and same sex marriage that easily outlives its original derogatory context.

In this context, reclaiming same sex marriage by the act of legal claiming is a fundamental step in the transformative process of denaturalizing the hegemonic norms associated with marriage. As Bower (1994: 1013) argues, "when marginalized groups creatively appropriate key concepts (including those provided by law) that have accepted ideological meaning, opportunities may be created to engage in community-based struggles that are not merely defensive or reactive." The litigation activities related to *Singer v. Hara* actually reframe the terms of the debate around this issue in terms that continue to define the present boundaries of the same sex marriage discussion.

In contrast to the 1974 case, the 2004 case was filed at a time of serious national discussion on the issue of same sex marriage. Same sex marriage was already a legal reality in one state. The discussion occurred after the elimination of the criminalization of private, consensual sodomy among adults by states and eventually through US Supreme Court intervention. Courts and legislatures in a number of states had begun to alter adoption and custody laws to reflect the "myriad configurations of modern families" (*Matter of Evan* 153 Misc. 2d 844 at

852), including recognizing lesbian and gay couples and individuals as parents. In 2004, a very large number of local and national lesbian and gay rights organizations were also politically active and visible participants in the civic discussion of laws that impact on their lives and their choices. Furthermore, being openly gay no longer automatically precluded election to office and there were a small, but growing, number of openly gay elected officials at all levels of government.

In this context, litigation played a substantially different role than it did for the 1974 case. The 2004 case fits more with an expressed idea of using the successful results of litigation activities to subsequently pressure the elected branches and administrative agencies into the full realization of the desired right—a "politics of rights" perspective (Scheingold 1974). The litigation in 2004 appeared designed to place the state legislature on notice to accept the idea that same sex marriage was about to become a legal and social reality.

Generally, cause lawyering involves participating in practices that aim to change the law in ways that restructure dominant social configurations that marginalize or oppress certain groups. Cause lawyers can engage in a range of legal and political activities to "achieve greater social justice" for marginalized individuals or groups (Menkel-Meadow 1998: 37) and to "challenge prevailing distributions of political, social, economic, and/or legal values and resources" (Sarat and Scheingold 2001: 13). Yet, the opportunities for cause lawyering are shaped by the legal and political context (Menkel-Meadow 1998; Sarat and Scheingold 1998).

For example, in a highly constrained system and hostile political climate, immigration lawyers in Britain make narrow claims through litigation on behalf of individual clients (Sterett 1998). Under a highly repressive Israeli occupation, Palestinian cause lawyering has been reduced to predominantly defensive, "damage control" oriented activities such as plea-bargaining in military courts (Bisharet 1998). Changing political and professional pressures and economic realities in the United States have shaped the feasibility of politicizing legal practice and the opportunities available in the public and private sectors. The levels of political activism or impact litigation associated with cause lawyering in the United States have therefore changed over time (Scheingold 1998; Trubek and Kransberger 1998). All of these activities are related, however, in that they can be characterized as "lawyering for the good" or cause lawyering.

In the 1974 and 2004 Washington cases, we can observe cause lawyers adjusting effectively to the social context of the era and the related social recognition of the relevant cause at each of these points. Thus, the actual success of the litigation activities in the 1974 case is best measured by the fact that the 2004 cases occurred in an environment where lesbian and gay rights, including same sex marriage, were a major national issue and full state recognition of lesbian and gay couples is assumed to be inevitable in many locations.

Emulation and Abandonment

McCann and Silverstein (1998: 283) note that "for the pay equity movement, the narrow legal opportunities were no less a constraint on options than were the internal dynamics of intergroup movement politics.... As a result, litigative strategies competed with several alternative approaches; and it was often this internal competition, rather than external judicial limitations alone, that constrained the turn to more formal legal tactics." Accordingly, social movements often use litigation sparingly in order not to interfere with the larger movement goals. Although these tensions are also readily apparent in the lesbian and gay rights movement (e.g., Levitsky 2006), the 1974 and 2004 same sex marriage cases in Washington also raise an alternative way of viewing the role of litigation in relation to social movements with specific structural characteristics.

In the early 1970s (as in earlier periods), lesbian and gay rights activists, like John Singer in Washington and Jay Baker in Minnesota, were faced with the nearly impossible task of organizing a social movement that was composed of a largely invisible set of members that even they could not readily identify or contact. And, the potential members of lesbian and gay rights social movements were often scattered in the diasporas that constitute the random assignment of sexual orientation and birth.[3]

Accentuating this demographic scattering and social invisibility has been the fact that the laws that attempt to govern, constrain, and punish individuals for expressing their sexuality have been located at the state and local level (Eskridge 1996; Pinello 2003; Andersen 2005). Sodomy prohibitions and same sex marriage proscriptions, for example, are based on state laws. Lewd behavior laws and liquor licensing laws applied to restrict the development of gay bars often differed from city to city. Further, as the sodomy prohibitions demonstrated, even in locations with similar laws, enforcement of the law was often peculiar to the individual location (Eskridge 1999).

These circumstances created a unique set of circumstances for the resultant social movement until recently. The effect of demographic scattering and the fact that lesbian and gay rights organizations were often created in direct response to the peculiar enforcement of local or state laws fostered a large number of geographically and organizationally separate lesbian and gay rights organizations. In direct response to these circumstances, these groups have developed a localized focus to respond to the peculiar law and politics of their location. For example, groups involved in the same sex marriage litigation have been very careful to maintain and project the image that this litigation strategy arises from local groups concerned only with the circumstances of their particular location (e.g., Barclay and Marshall 2005).

Given these two constraints upon the social movement and related lesbian and gay rights organizations, the role of litigation activities can be identified as extending beyond the benefits associated with publicizing the relevant issue and building the larger social movement. We propose that activists, cause lawyers, and, on some rare occasions, ordinary individuals used litigation and its commensurate publicity (especially the publicity such events generated within the relevant lesbian and gay community) as a way to communicate options for possible future directions for the larger movement.

Smart (1989; see also McCann 1994) notes that one of the difficulties of using legal strategies to define or achieve movement goals is that it requires social movements to adopt fixed goals over extended periods of time. This is a constraint that restricts the fluid nature of social movements and the power gained by its members through involvement in collective decision making. Scholars have long noted and argued about the tension between cause lawyers pursuing planned litigation and the fundamental need of a social movement to set its own direction (e.g., McCann and Silverstein 1998).

In the case of the multitude of geographically and organizationally separate lesbian and gay rights organizations, litigation presented to these individual organizations an opportunity in relation to determining its future direction. Each case initiated by a disparate lesbian and gay rights organization presented publicly to the larger movement a possible direction for the larger movement that they could subsequently endorse or reject by their own actions. In this construction, each act of litigation initiated in the various geographically separate locations represented one lesbian and gay rights organization's publicly expressed proposal for the future direction of the larger movement. Similar organizations in other locations could either *emulate*—repeat the litigation or action in their own location with reference to their own peculiar legal circumstances— or *abandon*—reject the idea of pursuing that litigation or action in their locale for either legal, political, or ideological reasons. In this context, cause lawyers literally use the litigation as an instructional manual to offer suggestions for possible use by other distinct and separate lesbian and gay rights organizations (see, e.g., Eskridge 1996; Bonauto, Murray, and Robinson 1999; Robinson 2001). The very public nature of documents associated with litigation facilitates this ability to exchange information with limited direct contact between various lesbian and gay organizations.

From these actions, priorities are established and goals developed for a movement with little need for direct interaction or a single, centralized, national leadership. A new direction for the larger movement is demonstrated by repeated emulation of the same action in new locations by many different local organizations (see also McAdam, Tarrow, and Tilly 2001: 332–35). Actions without support are simply not repeated in other locations and the movement instead pursues other priorities. The semblance of a national agenda on any issue is largely constructed by the aggregation of the choices of each of the multitude of local organizations.

In the case of same sex marriage, an organized litigation in the 1970s occurred in four separate states and achieved a variety of important aspects discussed above. This litigation generated a robust discussion of the role of marriage in relation to lesbian and gay individuals. By 1974, the possible legality of same sex marriage was an active topic in the gay press, including a series of major articles in *The Advocate*. The result of this discussion is that some form of consensus is reached within the larger movement: marriage becomes identified as norming heterosexuality and reinforcing unequal gender roles (e.g., Ettelbrick 1997; Polikoff 2000). Subsequently, the issue of same sex marriage is literally abandoned by the social movement—as evidenced by its failure to be emulated in any location throughout the late 1970s and early 1980s. Instead, lesbian and gay individuals developed definitions of relationships in opposition to or independent of the definitions offered by local and state laws (Bower 1994; Hull 2003).

However in this same period, lesbian and gay rights organizations turned litigation (and related lobbying) strategies to other issues that won the backing of the larger movement as evidenced by their repeated emulation in a variety of locations. These preferred issues included the successful elimination of sodomy laws in thirty-six separate states by 2003, the development of the legal rights associated with coparent and individual adoption and custody (e.g., Connolly 2002), and the expansion literally city by city of antidiscrimination protections (Wald, Button, and Rienzo 1996; Klawitter and Hammer 1999).

In contrast to the earlier abandonment, litigation in the 1990s on same sex marriage was widely and repeatedly emulated. By the end of 2004, litigation had been initiated in eleven separate states (Hawaii, Alaska, New York, Vermont, Massachusetts, California, Oregon, New Mexico, Washington, New Jersey, and Connecticut) as well as the District of Columbia. The legal claims involved a variety of lesbian and gay rights organizations, including Lambda Legal, Gay and Lesbian Advocates and Defenders, Marriage Equality California, ACLU, Basic Rights Oregon, Northwest Women's Law Center, as well as a number of private attorneys.

In fact, the true power for the larger social movements' individual members inherent in the emulation and abandonment approach is demonstrated during these 1990s same sex marriage cases. In the early 1990s, internal divisions over same sex marriage in some lesbian and gay rights organizations, including within Lambda Legal,[4] initially restrained these organizations from acting enthusiastically on this issue. However, individuals in Hawaii decided to pursue such a case, notwithstanding reluctance by Lambda Legal and other organizations (Andersen 2005). We might note that the nature of litigation, which allows a relatively low cost and a fairly easy threshold for initiation of a claim, is a particularly useful signal in such circumstances for individuals to express their preferences (Lawrence 1991). The initial failure to respond to this issue by Lambda Legal appeared temporarily to damage their standing in light of the shifted preferences of the larger social movement. Subsequently, Lambda Legal moved strongly into the issue consistent with the evidence that the claim for same sex marriage was being emulated widely and repeatedly by other lesbian and gay rights organizations.

Finally, the relative unity among organizations and cause lawyers demonstrated in the *Andersen* and *Castle* cases in Washington in 2004 can be interpreted as an important stand in itself. It signals a sense of unanimity by lesbian and gay rights organizations (and presumably the related social movement) in Washington behind the issue of same sex marriage. It contrasts starkly with the position of this movement in the 1980s. This was a message recognized by the courts. But, it also appeared to be a message recognized in the movement by those who had misgivings about this issue that the larger movement had clearly settled on a direction at this historical point (see Levitsky 2006).

Conclusion

The nature of cause lawyering, like the development of causes themselves, is dependent upon the social, legal, and political context apparent in any era and location. In addition, the nature of cause lawyering is shaped by the structure and constraints inherent in any related social movement. As such, it is impossible to define the role of litigation and its influence upon a social movement removed from consideration of the relevant social movement and its context. In this paper, we have used the two occasions—1974 and 2004—in which cause lawyers challenged the prohibition on same sex marriage in Washington as a basis for highlighting the divergent roles of litigation in relation to the movement for lesbian and gay rights.

We proposed that, in the current context, cause lawyers used litigation to effectively reclaim ownership and legitimacy over the idea of same sex marriage at a time when it had been appropriated for ridicule and derision in the general public. In addition, we argued that, given the nature of the lesbian and gay rights movement, litigation pursued by cause lawyers and individuals became one way to develop input into the direction and goals of the larger movement. Such a process adds to the literature (e.g., McCann and Silverstein 1998) that challenges some of the existing assumptions about the likely conflict between the pursuit of litigation strategies by cause lawyers and the power that arises through social movements setting their own agenda and goals.

Notes

1. Although occasional cases raised this issue in the immediate period after the *Singer v. Hara* decision, it is not in the format of a direct claim for same sex marriage. See, for example, *M.T. v. J.T.* (140 N.J. Super. 77) where the claim involves an attempt by a transsexual to validate their marriage based on their gender identification. Similarly, the attempt by gay rights' activists to use US constitutional provisions in relation to same sex marriage claims also appeared to grind to a complete halt by 1982. See, for example, *Adams v. Howerton*, 486 F. Supp. 1119 (C.D. Cal. 1980) and 673 F.2d 1036 (9th Circuit Court of Appeals).

2. According to the Oregon Supreme Court in *Li v. State* (338 Ore. 376), this lower court decision was overturned by the successful introduction by statewide referendum of an amendment prohibiting same sex marriage to the state's constitution in November 2004.

3. We say "often" scattered because there continues to be the question of whether there were at that time high concentrations of lesbian, gay, and bisexual individuals in specific gay-friendly locations. Despite anecdotal evidence, this question is unresolved, especially as identification for demographic purposes still requires "outing." As such, the measure of lesbian, gay, and bisexual (LGB) presence often captures individuals who are "out" rather than reflects a true measure of all LGB individuals based on their own identification of their sexuality.

4. Evan Wolfson of Lambda Legal was an active participant in the Hawaii case and District of Columbia cases as well as other same sex marriage cases. In contrast, Paula Ettelbrick, who was at that stage the Legal Director of LAMBDA, was one of the more outspoken opponents of same sex marriage. Nonetheless, Ettelbrick filed Lambda Legal's amicus curiae brief in the Vermont same sex marriage case, *Baker v. State* (170 Vt. 194), see Andersen (2005).

References

Abel, Richard. 1998. "Speaking Law to Power: Occasions for Cause Lawyering." In *Cause Lawyering: Political Commitments and Professional Responsibilities*, Austin Sarat and Stuart Scheingold, eds. New York: Oxford University Press.

Andersen, Ellen Ann. 2005. *Out of the Closets and into the Courts*. Ann Arbor, MI: University of Michigan Press.

Barclay, Scott and Anna-Maria Marshall. 2005. "Supporting a Cause, Developing a Movement, and Consolidating a Practice: Cause Lawyers and Sexual Orientation Litigation in Vermont," In *The Worlds Cause Lawyers Make*, Austin Sarat and Stuart Scheingold, eds. Palo Alto, CA: Stanford University Press.

Bisharat, George. 1998. "Attorneys for the People, Attorneys for the Land: The Emergence of Cause-Lawyering in the Israeli-Occupied Territories." In *Cause Lawyering: Political Commitments and Professional Responsibilities*, Austin Sarat and Stuart Scheingold, eds. New York: Oxford University Press.

Bonauto, Mary, Susan M. Murray and Beth Robinson. 1999. "The Freedom to Marry for Same-Sex Couples: The Opening Appellate Brief of Plaintiffs Stan Baker et al. in *Baker et al. v. State of Vermont*." *Michigan Journal of Gender and Law* 5(2): 409–75.

Bower, Lisa. 1994. "Queer Acts and the Politics of Direct Address: Rethinking Law, Culture, and Community." *Law and Society Review* 28: 1009–32.

Connolly, Catherine. 2002. "The Voice of the Petitioner: The Experiences of Gay and Lesbian Parents in Successful Second-Parent Adoption Proceedings." *Law and Society Review* 36: 325–46.

Eskridge, William N. Jr. 1996. *The Case for Same-Sex Marriage*. New York: Free Press.

———. 1999. *Gaylaw: Challenging the Apartheid of the Closet*. Cambridge, MA: Harvard University Press.

———. 2002. *Equality Practice: Civil Unions and the Future of Gay Rights*. New York: Routledge.

Ettelbrick, Paula. 1997. "Since When is Marriage a Path to Liberation." In *Same-Sex Marriage: The Legal and Moral Debate*, Robert M. Baird and Stuart E. Rosenbaum, eds. New York: Prometheus Books.

Goldberg-Hiller, Jonathan. 2002. *The Limits to Union: Same-Sex Marriage and the Politics of Civil Rights*. Ann Arbor, MI: University of Michigan Press.

Halligan, Caitlin. 2004. *Opinion of the New York State Solicitor General on the Legality of Same Sex Marriages in New York State*. Issued by the New York State Attorney General's Office, March 3, 2004.

Handler, Joel F. 1978. *Social Movements and the Legal System: A Theory of Law Reform and Social Change*. New York: Academic Press.

Hull, Kathleen. 2003. "The Cultural Power of Law and the Cultural Enactment of Legality: The Case of Same-Sex Marriage." *Law and Social Inquiry* 28: 629–58.

Kennedy, Duncan. 1998. "Legal Education as Training for Hierarchy." In *The Politics of Law: A Progressive Critique*, 3rd edn., David Kairys, ed. New York: Perseus.

Klawitter, Marieka and Brian Hammer. 1999. "Spatial and Temporal Diffusion of Local Antidiscrimination Policies for Sexual Orientation." In *Gays and Lesbians in the Democratic Process*, Ellen D. B. Riggle and Barry L. Tadlock, eds. New York: Columbia University Press.

Lawrence, Susan E. 1991. "Justice, Democracy, Litigation, and Political Participation." *Social Science Quarterly* 72: 464–77.

Levitsky, Sandra. 2006. "To Lead with Law: Reassessing the Influence of Legal Advocacy Organizations in Social Movements." In *Cause Lawyers and Social Movements*, A. Sarat and S. Scheingold, eds. Palo Alto, CA: Stanford University Press.

Maitland, Leslie. 1975. "U.S. Amendment: What Will It Do." *New York Times* March 11, 1975: 40.

McAdam, Doug, Sidney Tarrow, and Charles Tilly. 2001. *Dynamics of Contention.* New York: Cambridge University Press.

McCann, Michael W. 1994. *Rights at Work: Pay Equity Reform and the Politics of Legal Mobilization.* Chicago: University of Chicago Press.

McCann, Michael and Helena Silverstein. 1998. "Rethinking Law's 'Allurements': A Relational Analysis of Social Movement Lawyers in the United States." In *Cause Lawyering: Political Commitments and Professional Responsibilities*, Austin Sarat and Stuart Scheingold, eds. New York: Oxford University Press.

Menkel-Meadow, Carrie. 1998. "The Causes of Cause Lawyering: Toward an Understanding of the Motivation and Commitment of Social Justice Lawyers." In *Cause Lawyering: Political Commitments and Professional Responsibilities*, Austin Sarat and Stuart Scheingold, eds. New York: Oxford University Press.

Olson, Susan M. 1984. *Clients and Lawyers: Securing the Rights of Disabled Persons.*Westport, CT: Greenwood Press.

Pinello, Daniel R. 2003. *Gay Rights and American Law.* Cambridge: Cambridge University Press.

Polikoff, Nancy. 2000. "Why Lesbians and Gay Men Should Read Martha Fineman."*American University Journal of Gender, Social Policy and the Law* 8: 167–76.

Rivera, Rhonda R. 1999. "Our Straight-Laced Judges: The Legal Position of Homosexual Persons in the United States." 50 *Hastings Law Journal*: 1015 (originally published in 1979 in 30 *Hastings Law Journal*: 799)

Robinson, Beth. 2001. "The Road to Inclusion for Same-Sex Couples: Lessons from Vermont." *Seton Hall Constitutional Law Journal* 11(2): 237–57.

Sarat, Austin and Stuart Scheingold. 1998. "Cause Lawyering and the Reproduction of Professional Authority: An Introduction." In *Cause Lawyering: Political Commitments and Professional Responsibilities*, Austin Sarat and Stuart Scheingold, eds. New York: Oxford University Press.

———. 2001. "State Transformation, Globalization, and the Possibilities of Cause Lawyering: An Introduction." In *Cause Lawyering and the State in a Global Era*, Austin Sarat and Stuart Scheingold, eds. New York: Oxford University Press.

Scheingold, Stuart. 1974. *The Politics of Rights: Lawyers, Public Policy and Political Change.* New Haven, CT: Yale University Press.

———. 1998. "The Struggle to Politicize Legal practice: A Case Study of Left-Activist Lawyering in Seattle." In *Cause Lawyering: Political Commitments and Professional Responsibilities*, Austin Sarat and Stuart Scheingold, eds. New York: Oxford University Press.

Smart, Carol. 1989. *Feminism and the Power of the Law.* New York: Routledge.

Sterett, Susan. 1998. "Caring About Individual Cases: Immigration Lawyering in Britain." In *Cause Lawyering: Political Commitments and Professional Responsibilities*, Austin Sarat and Stuart Scheingold, eds. New York: Oxford University Press.

Trubek, Louise and M. Elizabeth Kransberger. 1998. "Critical Lawyers: Social Justice and the Structures of Private Practice." In *Cause Lawyering: Political Commitments and Professional Responsibilities*, Austin Sarat and Stuart Scheingold, eds. New York: Oxford University Press.

Wald, Kenneth D., James W. Button, and Barbara A. Rienzo. 1996. "The Politics of Gay Rights in American Communities: Explaining Antidiscrimination Ordinances and Policies." *American Journal of Political Science* 40:1152–78.

Web Sites

American Civil Liberties Union Web site. <www.aclu-wa.org/Issues/lesbiangay/index. html> Last accessed May 26, 2005.

Davis, Wright, Tremaine LLP Web site. <www.dwt.com/offloc/seattle.htm> Last accessed May 26, 2005.

Preston, Gates, and Ellis LLP Web site. <www.prestongates.com/people> Last accessed January 29, 2005.

Stritmatter, Kessler, Whelan, Withey, Coluccio LLP Web site. <www.skwwc.com/ attorneys/attny_withey.html> Last accessed January 29, 2005.

Cause Lawyering and Political Advocacy

Moving Law on Behalf of Central American Refugees

SUSAN BIBLER COUTIN

> I've decided that I'm no longer going to work to change laws for immigrants.
> — I'm only going to work with immigrants to change laws.
> > Quote from an immigration attorney

> The ABC case actually changed history. — And resulted in the mobilization and increasing space for the mobilization and organizing of Salvadoran refugees.
> > Quote from an immigration attorney

Relationships between "causes," "law," and "lawyering" are complex. Attorneys who take up particular causes may be inspired by or even participate in broad-based social movements. Their experiences within these movements may produce deep commitments to right social and political wrongs and to make law serve justice. Acting on these commitments may entail representing individual clients, filing class action suits, founding organizations, advocating legislative change, organizing particular constituencies, and negotiating with the officials who interpret and enforce law (Sarat and Scheingold 1998, 2001; Scheingold and Sarat 2004). "Law" and "social movements," may, however, have different life courses. Cases that grow out of social movement activity may take years to be adjudicated and may be transformed as they move through successive procedural steps (Mather and Yngvesson 1980–81; Garth 1992). As legal actions are pending, political and historical circumstances can change both the "cause" and the social movement out of which these actions grew. At the same time, legal developments—whether successes or setbacks—define issues in particular terms, create new demarcations, establish new rules, and set new processes in motion. As Michael McCann (2004: 510) notes, "legal mobilization politics typically involves reconstructing legal dimensions of inherited social relations." Law thus has an "embedded" quality—law references prior conditions, dates, and legal language, but law also can redefine agendas, constituencies, and causes. Cause lawyers, in conjunction with social movements, shape (or attempt to shape) the path of law, even as such pathmaking can redefine social reality in ways that, in turn, redefine causes and reshape activism.

Examining the different life courses of social movements and legal actions contributes to the social movement and cause lawyering literatures by revealing how relationships between law and advocacy unfold over time. To understand these shifts, it is important to note that advocacy takes multiple and overlapping forms, including activism, political mobilization, and social movements. Activism consists of ongoing efforts, often by members of nongovernmental organizations, to influence policy in a particular area. Political mobilization refers to the organizing work entailed in recruiting a "base" of individuals who are affected by particular policies, and who are willing to take actions (such as attending a rally) designed to influence policy makers. Social movements entail both activism and political mobilization, but are distinguished by their broad-based, oppositional character, the scope of the legal, political, and social changes that they seek, and ways that they mark history (McCann 2004). Activism, mobilization, and social movements can engage law both formally, through lobbying and lawsuits, and informally, by taking actions that have particular legal significances (Coutin 1993). Both formal and informal legal actions may influence official law, sometimes in ways that neither cause lawyers nor movement members anticipate.

To examine the relationship between cause lawyering and political advocacy, this chapter analyzes legal and political activism on behalf of Salvadoran asylum seekers from the 1980s to the present. Although this period has generally been described as legally conservative (McCann and Dudas, this volume), cause lawyers were relatively successful in securing immigration rights for Central American asylum seekers. During the 1980s, a broad-based Central American solidarity movement was formed in order to counter US support for right-wing regimes in El Salvador and Guatemala, oppose human rights abuses in Central America, and advocate that Salvadorans and Guatemalans who fled civil war and political violence in their homelands be granted asylum in the United States. Religious activists who declared their congregations "sanctuaries" for undocumented Salvadoran and Guatemalan refugees were key components of this movement. Attorneys also played numerous roles. Lawyers represented individual asylum seekers, founded refugee rights clinics, defended religious activists who were indicted on alien-smuggling charges, and filed class action suits on behalf of Central American refugees. By the late 1980s, following the conviction of eight sanctuary activists in 1986, the solidarity movement began to decline; however, legal initiatives launched by cause lawyers were still very much alive. In 1991, a class action suit known as "*American Baptist Churches v. Thornburgh*" or "ABC" was settled out of court, granting Salvadorans and Guatemalans the right to de novo asylum hearings (Coutin 2001b), and in 1990, Congress created

"Temporary Protected Status" (TPS) and awarded Salvadorans eighteen months of this status. Changed circumstances redefined the significance of TPS and the ABC agreement. Peace accords were signed in El Salvador in 1992 and in Guatemala in 1996, making it harder for ABC class members to win political asylum. Moreover, in 1996, revisions to US immigration laws eliminated or restricted many other avenues through which class members could legalize. In this changed context, a new campaign for legal permanent residency was launched. In 1997, a remedy—the Nicaraguan Adjustment and Central American Relief Act (NACARA)—was approved; however, greater immigration benefits were accorded to Nicaraguans who fled left-wing regimes than to Salvadorans and Guatemalans who fled right-wing ones. This disparity gave rise to renewed activism, which in turn resulted in regulations that virtually guaranteed legal permanent residency to Salvadoran and Guatemalan NACARA applicants.

Throughout this policy-making process, political advocacy fueled and was in turn reshaped by cause lawyering. The Central American solidarity movement was comprised of refugees, religious activists, attorneys, and other advocates. In the 1980s, solidarity workers mobilized around a range of issues, including political change in Central America, US foreign policy, peace, human rights, and refugee rights. Only some of these issues—particularly civil and refugee rights— were addressed through cause lawyering, even though cause lawyers may have been motivated by broader political concerns (Coutin 2001a). The legal remedies that cause lawyers (and others) were able to craft in the early 1990s in turn mobilized a somewhat different constituency, consisting of immigrant- and refugee-rights activists, Central American immigrants, and even some Salvadoran government officials. This constituency mobilized more explicitly around immigration rights, although these rights were of course linked to the political and human rights concerns that had motivated the solidarity movement during the 1980s. Legal developments redefined causes, constituencies, and agendas, even as changed circumstances gave legal developments new meanings.

My analysis of the relationship between social movements and cause lawyering derives from three research projects that I conducted from the mid-1980s to the present. From 1986–88, I did fieldwork within sanctuary communities in the San Francisco East Bay and in Tucson, Arizona. My sanctuary research included volunteer work with community groups that represented Central American asylum seekers, interviews with refugees, sanctuary activists, and attorneys who defended indicted sanctuary activists, and an analysis of the transcripts and press coverage of the 1985–86 Tucson sanctuary trial (Coutin 1993, 1995). From 1995–97, I did fieldwork in Los Angeles regarding Salvadoran immigrants' continued efforts to obtain permanent legal status in the United States. I observed the legal services programs of Central American community organizations, attended immigration hearings, followed political advocacy efforts, and interviewed immigrants, attorneys, and activists (Coutin 2000). Most recently, from 2000–2002, I did research in Los Angeles, Washington DC, and San Salvador regarding shifts in US and Salvadoran policies regarding the US Salvadoran population. This project entailed interviews with US and Salvadoran policy-makers, advocates (including cause lawyers) who attempted to shape policy, and Central Americans who were eligible to apply for legal permanent residency under NACARA. Through these three projects, I was able to follow (either through interviews or direct observations) a range of cause lawyering activities and political advocacy—and in transnational contexts (see also Sarat and Scheingold 2001).

I begin by analyzing cause lawyers' and solidarity workers' efforts to obtain political asylum for Central American refugees during the 1980s. I continue by describing how Central American peace accords and US immigration reforms led both advocates and cause lawyers to change strategies. I conclude by delineating the realignments that made NACARA possible and that then produced unprecedented regulations. Throughout, I attend to the shifting relationships between causes, lawyers, and law.

Solidarity and Refugee Rights

Efforts to secure legal protection for Salvadoran and Guatemalan refugees began during the early 1980s, as a solidarity movement composed of religious groups, political activists, and legal advocates sought to establish that the US government was discriminating against Salvadoran and Guatemalan asylum seekers due to foreign policy considerations (Coutin 1993; Smith 1996). Because the US government was supporting the governments of El Salvador and Guatemala in their wars against guerrilla insurgents, granting safe haven to nationals of these countries would have tacitly admitted that a US ally was committing human rights violations. Generally speaking, refugees who fled "communist" regimes were welcomed, and Salvadorans and Guatemalans, who fled right-wing regimes, were not (USCR 1986). Legal advocates were outraged at this seeming violation of the Refugee Act of 1980, which had just established that, in contrast to prior US refugee law, which limited "refugee" status to individuals from Communist countries and the Middle East, persecuted aliens who reached US territory could petition for asylum, regardless of country of origin (Kennedy 1981).[1]

To prevent Salvadorans and Guatemalans from being deported, solidarity workers sought to mobilize law. Volunteers connected Salvadorans and

Guatemalans who were in deportation proceedings with attorneys who were willing to represent asylum seekers without charging for services. Lawyers committees and immigrants rights centers began to proliferate in major US cities such as Washington DC, San Francisco, Los Angeles, Chicago, and Boston, and eventually comprised an infrastructure of organizations that engaged in legal advocacy on behalf of immigrants' rights. Much as death penalty attorneys seek to prolong life (Sarat 1998), attorneys who represented Central American asylum seekers sought to delay deportation. A San Francisco attorney who worked with one immigrants rights center recalled, "Our whole expectation was [that] we were going to represent people and string their cases along as far as we could, hoping that the war would end, or we'd win temporary protected status.... Representing individual refugees was tied to the sanctuary movement, which was tied to political events, which was tied to trying to win temporary protected status."

In addition to representing individual asylum seekers, legal advocates filed class action suits. Although each suit focused on a particular legal issue, these class actions were part of a broad attempt to challenge immigration officials' treatment of Central Americans. *Orantes-Hernandez v. Meese*, which was filed in the early 1980s and decided in 1988 (*Orantes-Hernandez v. Meese* 1988), prohibited immigration officials from coercing Salvadorans into agreeing to depart the United States, required officials to inform Salvadorans of their right to apply for asylum, and prohibited immigration agents from transferring detainees to detention centers that were geographically distant from detainees' attorneys (Churgin 1996). *Mendez v. Reno*, which was decided in 1993, challenged the perfunctory nature of asylum interviews (*Mendez v. Reno* 1993). An attorney involved in the *Mendez* case described his depositions of the officials who conducted these interviews:

I would have them under oath, sitting across the table like this, and say, "Okay. Tell me —" First, asked them about the training. You know, what training? "Well, I watched somebody else do it for ten minutes or an hour, something like that." "Okay. Now tell me the grounds on which someone's eligible for and entitled to get political asylum." And they would say, "What do you mean?" And I'd say, "Well, you know, there's five grounds in the statute on which someone's eligible or entitled to get asylum. Can you name them?" "Uh, no I can't do that right now." "Well, take your time. Think about it." They got through the entire deposition, they couldn't say, they didn't know a single thing.

The so-called "Young Male Case" sought to establish that young Salvadoran men who were at risk of being forcibly recruited by the Salvadoran military deserved political asylum (See Compton 1987; *Sanchez-Trujillo v. INS* 1986). An attorney who was involved described the theory of the case and the resources that it mobilized:

> In 1980 when the Refugee Act was passed, they added a category to the act... membership in a particular social group. And there had never been any definition of what that was and we decided that basically, this was what it was meant for, was people who weren't, who didn't necessarily have their own political opinions but the government suspected them of having a political opinion. And so we developed what was really an imputed political opinion theory but couched it in terms of young men of military age from El Salvador as a social group and who the government suspected of being guerillas or guerilla supporters.

Although it was unsuccessful (cf. Barclay and Fisher, this volume), the young male case is indicative of the growing significance of Central American refugee issues to immigration and human rights networks. As an advocate whom I interviewed in 2001 commented, "Most of us have spent practically all of our careers on this."

In addition to filing class action suits, legal advocates and other activists sought legislative change in the form of "Moakley-Deconcini" (after its sponsors, Joe Moakley and Dennis Deconcini), a bill that would grant Salvadorans a temporary legal status known as "Extended Voluntary Departure" (EVD) (Churgin 1996). The Reagan administration opposed the Moakley-Deconcini legislation, arguing that the asylum system was working, that most Salvadorans had come to the United States in search of jobs rather than safety, and that a grant of EVD would serve as a "magnet" to additional illegal Salvadoran migrants. Proponents of Moakley-Deconcini, in contrast, contended that the asylum system was not able to recognize victims of generalized violence, that EVD would be available only to those already in the United States and not to future migrants, and that no one had proposed that the United States take in the world's poor.[2] Throughout the 1980s, repeated attempts to pass Moakley-Deconcini, including an effort to attach it to the 1986 Immigration Reform and Control Act (IRCA), failed, largely, according to interviewees, due to opposition from the Reagan administration and Senator Alan Simpson, a staunch and influential proponent of restrictive immigration measures.

As the Moakley-Deconcini bill languished in the US Congress, advocates devised a new class action suit on behalf of Central American asylum-seekers. During the 1980s, religious activists had helped Central Americans cross the United States–Mexico border, sheltered these migrants in congregants' homes and congregations, and transported migrants to places of safety around the

United States. US law holds citizens accountable for the immigration status of those they shelter and transport. By treating Central Americans as legal refugees, movement members staked an informal legal claim. Direct action therefore indirectly engaged law (cf. Hilbink; Marshall, this volume). In 1985 the indirect became direct, as the US government filed criminal charges against US religious activists who had declared their congregations "sanctuaries" for Salvadoran and Guatemalan refugees (Coutin 1993, 1995). In response, advocates sued US authorities in civil court. An attorney who was involved in conceptualizing what came to be known as "ABC" (*American Baptist Churches v. Thornburgh*) described the origins of this case:

> ABC in particular was actually conceived of initially as more responsive to the sanctuary prosecutions than it was to the discriminatory treatment of Salvadoran and Guatemalans. When the government started prosecuting church people for assisting Salvadoran and Guatemalans, again, networks of people were talking about how to respond to that and not just always to be put in a defensive position, but to try to do some affirmative litigation to try to stop the prosecutions.... Our central argument was, "You know, Salvadorans were refugees, it was just that the U.S. wasn't recognizing them as refugees. But the U.S. was in violation of both its international and national legal obligations, and consequently, they shouldn't be prosecuting people who were just kind of doing what they were supposed to be doing, which is protecting people from *refoulement* to torture. And persecution." And so we ... decided to do this litigation that would focus both on, you know trying to enjoin the sanctuary prosecutions and trying to stop a discriminatory treatment of the refugees.

Like its predecessor, the Young Male case, the ABC lawsuit mobilized cause lawyers, refugee rights organizations, and even a private law firm that made its resources available to class counsel. Like other "rule-of-law" cause lawyers, the attorneys involved in the ABC case "tend[ed] to identify with rights, legality, and constitutionality as ends in themselves" (Scheingold and Sarat 2004: 19). One attorney said that his organization had joined in this lawsuit out of a concern "that the government was discriminating against individuals based on their nationality in violation of the law.... Whether the system is fair, whether there's undue foreign policy influence on the asylum determination, whether there's a legitimate asylum determination, whether it's a legitimate process; that's critical. Because that's a question of whether the government is complying with the law." The attorneys who litigated the ABC case were motivated by a strong sense that US refugee law was perpetuating injustice:

> The idea that we would discriminate against someone who's fleeing persecution; you know, it was such a complete denial of the principles of the United States, ... of refugee protection, of international law.... Not only were we supporting these human

rights abusers in El Salvador, then we were sort of in a way perpetuating a further terror on that same population in United States by depriving them of their rights under the law. And trying to send them back to the very human rights violators that United States government was supporting. And so that whole sort of system, kind of systematic violation of the law and violation of human rights was just so profoundly offensive. And so at odds with what I think United States ought to be, and how the law ought to operate.... To be a victim of persecution in El Salvador and then a victim of discrimination at the hands of the United States government.

To correct this situation, the ABC lawsuit sought to bar future prosecutions of sanctuary workers, prohibit additional deportations of Salvadorans and Guatemalans, and prevent foreign policy considerations from influencing asylum proceedings. The first two of these claims were dismissed (*American Baptist Churches v. Meese* 1987, 1989), but litigation on the third claim went forward. Then, in 1990, as attorneys in the ABC case prepared for discovery proceedings, the US government suddenly offered to settle. Several factors may have been responsible for officials' change of heart (Blum 1991). First, efforts to reform the asylum unit were already underway. Second, the discovery process was likely to be both financially burdensome and politically embarrassing. Third, this case was connected to a social movement. An attorney involved in the litigation recalled, "Every time we went to court, the courtroom was filled with people from the sanctuary movement. And they would do prayers out front before hand and be there with their habits and collars and everything in court and it was a very powerful statement." Fourth, following the 1989 Salvadoran final offensive, efforts to broker a peace agreement in El Salvador intensified. This changed political scenario may have had repercussions within immigration and asylum policies.

As the ABC settlement negotiations were underway, advocates simultaneously overcame opposition to legislation granting temporary status to Salvadorans. According to a key immigrant rights attorney, advocates persuaded Salvadoran President Napoleon Duarte, who was concerned about the destabilizing effect of deportations, to ask Senator Jesse Helms to support temporary refuge for Salvadorans. At the same time, advocates-related, Senator Simpson agreed to support this legislation in exchange for Senator Moakley's assurance that he would not seek an "amnesty" for Salvadoran TPS recipients.[3] As a result, the 1990 Immigration Act, which was signed by President George Bush, created "Temporary Protected Status" and declared that Salvadorans who had been in the United States prior to September 19, 1991 could receive eighteen months of this status.

TPS was incorporated into the ABC settlement, which established that every Salvadoran and Guatemalan who was in the United States prior to September 19,

1991 (in the case of Salvadorans) or October 1, 1991 (in the case of Guatemalans) had the right to apply or reapply for political asylum and have a de novo hearing on their claims (*American Baptist Churches v. Thornburgh* 1991). Special rules to ensure fair hearings were established, advocates were given the right to train asylum officials regarding conditions in Central America, and immigration officials agreed to publicize the agreement so that Central Americans would be aware of their rights. Salvadoran TPS applicants were deemed to have registered for the benefits of the settlement agreement, and both Guatemalans and Salvadorans were also permitted to register for benefits directly.

The ABC agreement created a new constituency (cf. Gordon, this volume): ABC class members. In order for TPS and the ABC agreement to actually benefit this class, however, eligible Central Americans had to apply for TPS and asylum. Cause lawyers were involved in promoting the application process. One attorney explained that he advised Central American groups

> "Hay que quedarse en el barco grande [You have to stay in the big boat]. You apply for TPS, and when you finish TPS, what happens? Then you apply for ABC. . . . " And I'd call people up from the audience and I'd go place by place by place. "If you stay in the big boat, you're going to be okay. If you don't stay on the big boat, see that sign over there?" And I would point to the exit sign. "Then you get the premio de TACA [the TACA (a Central American airline) prize; presumably a plane ticket home]."

Some 240,000 Salvadorans and Guatemalans did apply, and, when applicants' immediate family members are taken into account, the number of people who benefited from the settlement agreement is actually larger.

Doubts about the wisdom of applying were not unfounded, however, as TPS and the ABC settlement agreement placed Salvadorans and Guatemalans in an ambiguous position: these migrants were granted temporary authorization to remain in the United States, but, as this authorization would evaporate if TPS expired and if asylum claims were denied, ABC class members and TPS recipients remained legally vulnerable. During the 1990s, improved conditions in Central America and legal change in the United States exacerbated this vulnerability.

Peace Accords and Immigration Reform

In the early 1990s, the Central American solidarity movement declined significantly. This decline can be attributed to several factors. By the late 1980s, sanctuary, which had been a key component of the solidarity movement, was no longer perceived as the most appropriate form of advocacy. Increases in the size and stability of the Central American community made it unnecessary for Central Americans to be housed or transported by US activists. Central Americans who immigrated prior to January 1, 1982 were able to get legal permanent residency through IRCA (see Bean, Edmonston, and Passel 1990; Ulloa 1999), while more recent migrants obtained temporary legal status through TPS and ABC. With legal protection, Central Americans had less need of solidarity workers. Moreover, despite sanctuary activists' resolve to be undeterred by the 1986 conviction of key movement members, government surveillance of and legal action against the movement probably took a toll. With the 1992 peace accords in El Salvador, some members of the solidarity movement turned their attention to other causes. Central American community groups found funding sources drying up, and some activists actually became nostalgic for the sense of urgency that the war had created (Coutin 2000).

Although the Central American solidarity movement declined, cause lawyers and Central American activists continued to seek a permanent immigration remedy for ABC class members and TPS recipients. Both Central American activists and the Bush administration faced the immediate question of what to do when TPS expired after the allotted eighteen months, a question that was complicated by the fact that peace accords were signed in El Salvador in 1992. Central American groups lobbied heavily for an extension of TPS, and new groups and coalitions—such as ASOSAL (the Association of Salvadorans of Los Angeles) and the Salvadoran American National Network (SANN)—grew out of this effort. Bush administration officials were less than enthused about granting an extension. At the same time, they recognized that to deport Salvadorans could destabilize postwar El Salvador. Accordingly, rather than renewing TPS, the Bush administration permitted Salvadoran TPS recipients to register for a new status: "Deferred Enforced Departure" or "DED." DED was in turn extended until January 31, 1996, the deadline that the INS eventually set for Salvadoran ABC class members to file for political asylum under the terms of the settlement agreement. The rationale for temporary status had shifted, however, from migrants' need for safe haven to El Salvador's need for remittances and stability.

As TPS was extended, but in the form of DED, the asylum interviews anticipated by the ABC settlement agreement were delayed (cf. Gordon, this volume), and cause lawyers, Central American activists, and administration officials began to explore a possible blanket grant of legal permanent residency to ABC class members. A member of the ABC class counsel recounted, "For a while it looked promising and then I think it just foundered on all the political dynamics in Washington and all that sort of thing. They said ABC was this big new amnesty, and it was pre-'96 before Clinton was going to be up for reelection. And all the anti-immigrant stuff." In contrast to this assessment, one of the INS officials in charge of the ABC caseload attributed the difficulty in granting this request to law rather than politics, saying simply, "the plaintiffs' counsel was pushing the INS to consider the ABC class members' cases in a different way. And we just couldn't do it, because of the limitations of the law."

As efforts to obtain a blanket grant of permanent residency for ABC class members foundered, anti-immigrant sentiment in the United States grew, resulting in legislation that dramatically changed the climate in which ABC class members' cases would be adjudicated. The Illegal Immigration Reform and Immigrant Responsibility Act (IIRIRA) and the Antiterrorism and Effective Death Penalty Act (AEDPA), both of which were approved in 1996, were devastating for ABC class members (Wasem 1997). In the event that their asylum claims were denied, ABC class members had planned to apply for suspension of deportation, a status awarded to aliens who could prove seven years of continuous presence, good moral character, and that deportation would be an extreme hardship. IIRIRA abolished suspension of deportation and replaced it with cancellation of removal, which required proving ten years of continuous presence, good moral character, and extreme and exceptional hardship. Those class members who could not prove ten years of continuous presence or meet the higher hardship standard would not be eligible for cancellation. Moreover, IIRIRA capped the number of suspension or cancellation cases that could be approved in a single year at 4,000. Even if they *were* permitted to apply for suspension or cancellation, the 4,000 cap made these unlikely remedies for the 240,000-plus ABC class members.

In April 1997, in this changed legal context, the INS finally began to interview ABC class members on their asylum claims. As Central American nations braced for what they feared would be mass deportations, Central American advocates and community groups in the United States launched a new campaign for legal permanent residency for ABC class members.

Unlikely Alliances and Unprecedented Regulations

After IIRIRA made it appear that many ABC class members would eventually join the ranks of the undocumented or the deported, Central American advocates sought to establish that in fact, ABC class members were long-term residents whose legal status, though temporary, made them much more like permanent residents than like recent entrants petitioning for the right to stay. At first, this effort seemed doomed to failure. A Los-Angeles-based advocate recalled that shortly after NACARA passed, she and a colleague met with Washington DC attorneys who, she said, had been "aware of these issues for their entire careers and who were very sympathetic," but who advised them that Congress would not approve a remedy for the ABC class. The Clinton administration was not, however, uninterested in creating such a remedy. In May 1997, at a summit meeting with the Central American presidents, Clinton stated that it would be problematic to return Central Americans, who had lengthy ties to the United States and who supported their countries financially through remittances, to countries where they could be a destabilizing force. Clinton remarked, "These Central American countries are in a rather special category. After all, the United States Government was heavily involved with a lot of these countries during the time of all this upheaval" (Clinton 1997: 571).

Following Clinton's 1997 visit to Central America, the INS drafted legislation that restored the suspension eligibility of ABC class members and participants in the Nicaraguan Review Program, and that exempted these migrants from the 4,000 annual cap. In a bipartisan effort, this legislation was introduced by Senators Bob Graham (Democrat) and Connie Mack (Republican) of Florida. As an immigration measure, this legislation faced difficulty. Some, such as Lamar Smith, a staunch proponent of restricting immigration, regarded it as another amnesty (Wasem 1997). Others, who regarded the Contras as "freedom fighters" and the Salvadorans and Guatemalans as illegitimate economic immigrants, were only interested in creating a remedy for the Nicaraguans. So, Salvadorans, Guatemalans, and Nicaraguans (with the support of Cuban activists) joined forces to lobby for this legislation. The Salvadoran government hired Rick Swartz, a Washington DC political consultant specializing in "left-right coalitions" and immigration advocacy. Central American activists organized vigils, fasts, and rallies, and former Contra supporters held joint press conferences with advocates who had participated in the Central American solidarity movement.

These strategies paid off, and NACARA was approved in 1997. Nonetheless, the cold war ideology that secured support from legislators who were lukewarm on immigration matters gave rise to a disparity within the legislation. Nicaraguans who were in the United States prior to 1995 were given the right to automatically adjust their status to that of legal permanent residents, whereas Salvadorans and Guatemalans who had received TPS or had applied for asylum prior to 1991 were given the right to apply for suspension of deportation, a lengthier, more complex, and less certain process. The disparity within NACARA was galling to Salvadoran and Guatemalan activists and officials, who immediately sought to restore parity. Advocates proposed legislation that extended NACARA benefits to Hondurans and Haitians, moved the eligibility date to 1995 rather than 1991, and granted all the same remedy: adjustment of status. Efforts to pass parity legislation were derailed by partisan politics prior to the 2000 presidential elections. There was also considerable pressure to create parity administratively, by interpreting NACARA in ways that would equalize treatment of Salvadoran, Guatemalan, and Nicaraguan NACARA beneficiaries. In fact, during a 1999 trip to Central America, Clinton promised Central American leaders that he would minimize disparity in treatment. A Department of Justice official recalled that when Clinton returned, "he gave us our marching orders. These were to be as equitable as possible in reconciling the disparity but to be consistent with the law."

The process of issuing the regulations that would govern NACARA's implementation created opportunities for advocates to mobilize supporters. During the comment period that followed the approval of NACARA, advocates submitted thousands of recommendations. An attorney who helped to coordinate this effort described the process:

> There was a massive outpouring of comments. They said they'd never received so many . . . .They were looking at thousands! . . . We had comments that were signed by refugees. I'd never seen that happen before. I mean, they didn't write them of course. But they were in English and Spanish, and they signed them, and then we organized mailings. I think we got about, hundreds and hundreds of comments by the refugees themselves.

Through a process that one participant described as "torturous," regulations that created unprecedented solutions to a series of debates were crafted. One debate concerned who should adjudicate NACARA claims. To date, only immigration judges had heard suspension claims. However, most ABC class members had asylum petitions pending with the asylum unit of the INS. ABC class members were more likely to win suspension than asylum, but the only way for them to come before an immigration judge was first to be interviewed by an asylum official on the merits of their asylum claims. Such a cumbersome process could produce lengthy delays. Advocates therefore encouraged the INS to streamline the NACARA process by granting asylum officers the authority to adjudicate applicants' suspension claims. After some debate, the Attorney General did so. One of the regulations' authors explained, "We [the asylum unit] had the files, and asylum had to do the interviews anyway. Most would lose their asylum cases but be granted NACARA. It was a time-saver to do them together. Moreover, the issues in the asylum claim and in the suspension claim were interconnected."

A second debate concerned the enumeration of hardship factors. Like other cause lawyers, who generally oppose leaving matters to officials' discretion

(McCann 2004), advocates urged the INS to specify ways that the ABC class met the hardship criteria. Immigration judges, on the other hand, stressed the importance of adjudicating NACARA claims according to established case law. One of the regulations' drafters summarized this issue: "Should the hardship factors come from the case law that has been developed around suspension cases, or from the particular situation of ABC class members? The NGO community wanted the hardship factors to be defined by the particular situation of ABC class members. And the view that prevailed was that the hardship factors were defined by the relevant case law." The regulations nonetheless took the unprecedented step of *specifying* these hardship criteria. Case law was codified through the NACARA regulations.

Finally, a third debate focused on whether or not the INS could grant a blanket finding of hardship to ABC class members. In their comments on the NACARA legislation and on the first published version of the NACARA regulations (i.e., the proposed rule), advocates urged the INS to find that the ABC class had met the extreme hardship standard according to suspension law. Such a finding would virtually guarantee a grant in almost all NACARA cases (except, for instance, those in which the applicant had become statutorily ineligible, e.g., due to criminal convictions) and could make individual interviews of NACARA applicants unnecessary, thus greatly speeding adjudication. The Department of Justice balked, arguing that case-by-case adjudications were required, and that to grant a blanket finding of hardship would go beyond the authority of the statute. Gradually, however, the idea of granting *certain* NACARA beneficiaries—primarily, the ABC class—a *rebuttable* presumption of hardship emerged. An official who was involved in drafting the regulations recounted, "We felt that most officers could adjudicate without the presumption. But the advocacy community really wanted it. So we looked at it, and we decided we could do it." The interim rule, published on May 21, 1999, stated that "*ABC* class members ... will be presumed to satisfy the requirements for extreme hardship" (Department of Justice 1999: 27866).

The cause lawyers who had represented Central American asylum seekers, filed class action suits, negotiated with US immigration officials, and advised Central American community organizations regarded the NACARA regulations as a victory for Salvadoran and Guatemalan refugees. One attorney, who had worked on Central American refugee issues since the early 1980s, described the regulations as "amazing." During the 1980s, US officials had denounced Salvadorans and Guatemalans as economic immigrants undeserving of political asylum. In contrast, without conceding any wrong-doing on the part of the

INS, the NACARA regulations explicitly recognized the conditions that brought Salvadorans and Guatemalans to the United States:

> These individuals fled circumstances of civil war and political violence in their home-lands during the 1980s, and some applied for asylum in the United States. In 1985, advocates for Guatemalan and Salvadoran refugees, church groups, and refugees themselves brought suit against the United States Government for allegedly discriminatory treatment of Guatemalan and Salvadoran asylum applicants. The Department settled the litigation in 1990, following significant developments in its asylum and refugee law and procedures, including the creation of a professionally trained asylum officer corps and Congress's grant of TPS to Salvadorans (Department of Justice 1999: 27865).

Although the NACARA regulations attempted to minimize disparity between NACARA beneficiaries, NACARA contributed to renewed activism in favor of a broad-based legalization program. One cause lawyer incorporated community organizing within public outreach regarding NACARA. This attorney stated that when he did NACARA trainings, he invited his audience to analyze the case of a nineteen-year-old Salvadoran:

> She doesn't qualify. She was here, didn't file for ABC or TPS. So I've had her speak at NACARA trainings. We do a mock interview. I go through the interview and I say [to the audience], "Well, what's she eligible for?" "Nothing." "I guess we just have to tell her, 'There's nothing you can do.' Is that what you're doing, Gloria?" She says, "No! I'm active in Centro Latino Cuzcatlan. I led a delegation of young people to Washington D.C."

Another advocate commented on the empowering lessons of NACARA: "NACARA...opened a crack for the rest of us.... That made it possible to say, 'If you did it for the Cubans, you can do it for the Salvadorans. If you do it for the Salvadorans, you can do it for the Hondurans. If you do it for the Hondurans, you can do it for the Mexicans.' That opened the door."

Conclusion

Advocacy on behalf of Central American asylum seekers was deeply significant to immigration and refugee rights attorneys. One member of the ABC class counsel described the settlement agreement as "pretty much an overwhelming victory for half a million people.... We got every single decision since 1980 that got denied overturned. And set up a whole process by which people could apply again for asylum."[4] Another attorney, who had argued cases before the US supreme court, described the ABC suit as one that "stands out among a handful that were just profoundly significant." A third attorney described the impact of the ABC case as follows:

> I think that people felt that it was a really important landmark, or sort of you know moment of recognition, a demarcation, I guess, between a whole system that was premised on the use of discriminatory and illegal criteria in the adjudication of claims to a time when you could sort of really start walking down a path where at least there was the hope that adjudications were going to be based on more universal and neutral criteria.

Social movements, political organizing, and cause lawyering on behalf of Central American asylum seekers were integrally connected, yet the nature of these connections changed over time. During the 1980s, cause lawyering grew out of a solidarity movement that was rooted in Central America. Cause lawyers were mobilized by solidarity workers, Central American asylum seekers, and religious activists who were concerned about US military aid to the Salvadoran and Guatemalan governments, human rights abuses in Central America, and the fate of Central American refugees. Cause lawyers were inspired by Central Americans' accounts of persecution and injustice, sanctuary activists' willingness to take legal risks on behalf of refugees, and Central American activists' pursuit of social change in Central America. To make law serve justice, cause lawyers represented individual asylum seekers, established organizations and networks that have continued to advocate for immigrant and refugee rights, filed class action suits, negotiated with US officials, and pursued legislative change. In short, the Central American solidarity movement mobilized and created legal remedies and infrastructures whose significance extends beyond the "cause" out of which they originated.

During the 1990s, the legal remedies—TPS, the ABC settlement, and NACARA—that cause lawyers and others obtained in turn redefined struggles for immigrant and refugee rights. Although the solidarity movement declined in the late 1980s and early 1990s, Central American activists and immigrants themselves mobilized to demand legal permanent residency, equal treatment of people who immigrated for similar reasons, and a permanent legalization program. The ABC case and the NACARA legislation and regulations not only reshaped refugee law and procedures but also empowered immigrants in several senses. By continuing to live and work in the United States, Salvadorans and Guatemalans were able to support postwar reconstruction in their homelands. Organizations and campaigns dedicated to securing legal permanent residency formed in response to TPS, DED, and ABC. Each of these remedies carved out new sets of constituents and established legal precedents to which other immigrant groups could appeal. Finally, NACARA's limitations—for example, the lengthy application process, the need for individual adjudications, and the boundaries around those eligible for this remedy—contributed to calls for a broad-based legalization program. Clearly, law's movements can themselves mobilize.

Acknowledgments

Research for this paper was funded by the National Science Foundation's Law and Social Science program (Award numbers SES-0001890 and SES-0296050) and by a research and writing grant from the John D. and Catherine T. MacArthur Foundation. Earlier drafts of this paper were presented at the 2004 Law and Society Association meeting, and at the March 2005 "Lawyers and Social Movements" conference at UCLA. I am grateful to Austin Sarat and Stuart Scheingold for organizing this conference and panel, and to Rick Abel and the participants in the Lawyers and Social Movements conference for their comments on earlier versions. I am particularly indebted to the individuals who agreed to be interviewed as part of my research.

Notes

1. This neutral adjudication standard was tested almost immediately, with the arrival of large numbers of Cubans, who were paroled into the United States, and Haitians, who were generally denied asylum (see Kennedy 1981; *Haitian Refugee Center v. Smith* 1982; Churgin 1996). According to Gregg Beyer (2000), a "control" orientation characterized initial implementation of the 1980 Refugee Act. Examiners, who had no particular training in asylum or refugee law, were given responsibility for adjudicating affirmative asylum applications at District Offices.

2. For a fuller account of these debates, see House of Representatives (1984).

3. An interviewee who was present during these negotiations stated, "Moakley promised that he would not support an amnesty for the Salvadorans who were getting Temporary Protected Status. And then Simpson agreed to support the bill. I was there when he said it. And then we went out into the hall and there were cheers!"

4. This policymaking process was not without ironies. The ABC case might not have been filed if the US government had not prosecuted sanctuary workers, NACARA would probably not have been proposed were not for IIRIRA, and the NACARA regulations might not have granted applicants a presumption of hardship were not for the disparity between Nicaraguans, Guatemalans, and Salvadorans.

References

American Baptist Churches v. Meese. 1987. No. C-85-3255 RFP, United States District Court for the Northern District of California, 666 F. Supp. 1358.

————. 1989. No. C-85-3255 RFP, United States District Court for the Northern District of California, 712 F. Supp. 756.

American Baptists Churches v. Thornburgh. 1991. No. C-85-3225-RFP, United States District Court for the Northern District of California, 760 F. Supp. 796.

Bean, Frank D., Barry Edmonston, and Jeffrey S. Passel, eds. 1990. *Undocumented Migration to the United States: IRCA and the Experience of the 1980s*. Washington, DC: Urban Institute Press.

Beyer, Gregg. 2000. "Striking a Balance: The 1995 Asylum Reforms." Paper presented at *A Symposium and Celebration: The Fifth Anniversary of the 1995 Asylum Reforms*, February 1, 2000, US Immigration and Naturalization Service, Washington, DC.

Blum, Carolyn Patty. 1991. "The Settlement of *American Baptist Churches v. Thornburgh*: Landmark Victory for Central American Asylum-Seekers." *International Journal of Refugee Law* 3(2): 347–56.

Churgin, Michael J. 1996. "Mass Exoduses: The Response of the United States." *International Migration Review* 30(1): 310–25.

Clinton, William J. 1997. *Public Papers of the Presidents of the United States: William J. Clinton (In Two Books). Book II—July 1 to December 31, 1997*. Office of the Federal Register, National Archives and Records Administration, Washington, DC: US Government Printing Office.

Compton, Daniel. 1987. "Recent Development: Asylum for Persecuted Social Groups: A Closed Door Left Slightly Ajar. *Sanchez-Trujillo v. INS*, 801 F. 2d 1571 (9th Cir. 1986)." *Washington Law Review* 62: 913–39.

Coutin, Susan B. 1993. *The Culture of Protest: Religious Activism and the US Sanctuary Movement*. Boulder, CO: Westview Press.

————. 1995. "Smugglers or Samaritans in Tucson, Arizona: Producing and Contesting Legal Truth." *American Ethnologist* 22(3): 549–71.

————. 2000. *Legalizing Moves: Salvadoran Immigrants' Struggle for US Residency*. Ann Arbor, MI: University of Michigan Press.

————. 2001a. "Cause Lawyering in the Shadow of the State: A US Immigration Example." In *Cause Lawyering and the State in a Global Era*, Austin Sarat and Stuart Scheingold, eds., pp. 117–40. Oxford: Oxford University Press.

————. 2001b. "The Oppressed, the Suspect, and the Citizen: Subjectivity in Competing Accounts of Political Violence." *Law and Social Inquiry* 26(1): 63–94.

Department of Justice. Immigration and Naturalization Service. 1999. "Suspension of Deportation and Special Rule Cancellation of Removal for Certain Nationals of Guatemala, El Salvador, and Former Soviet Bloc Countries; Final Rule." *Federal Register* 64(98): 27856–82.

Garth, Bryant G. 1992. "Power and Legal Artifice: The Federal Class Action." *Law and Society Review* 26(2): 237–72.

Haitian Refugee Center v. Smith. 1982. No. 80-5683, United States Court of Appeals, Fifth Circuit N** Former Fifth Circuit Case, Section 9(1) of Public Law 96-452-October 14, 1980, 676 F. 2d 1023, May 24.

House of Representatives. 1984. "Temporary Suspension of Deportation of Certain Aliens." Hearing before the Subcommittee on Immigration, Refugees, and International Law of the Committee on the Judiciary, House of Representatives, 98th

Congress, Second Session on H.R. 4447, April 12. Washington, DC: US Government Printing Office.

Kennedy, Edward M. 1981. "Refugee Act of 1980." *International Migration Review* 15(1–2): 141–56.

Mather, Lynn and Barbara Yngvesson. 1980–81. "Language, Audience, and the Transformation of Disputes." *Law and Society Review* 15(3–4): 775–821.

McCann, Michael. 2004. "Law and Social Movements." In *The Blackwell Companion to Law and Society*, Austin Sarat, ed., pp. 506–22. Malden, MA: Blackwell.

Mendez v. Reno. 1993. No. CV-88-04995-TJH, C.D. Cal., August 12.

Orantes-Hernandez v. Meese. 1988. No. CV-82-1107 KN, United States District Court for the Central District of California, 685 F. Supp. 1488; 1988 US Dist.

Sanchez-Trujillo v. INS. 1986. 801 F. 2d 1571 (19th Cir. 1986).

Sarat, Austin. 1998. "Between (the Presence of) Violence and (the Possibility of) Justice: Lawyering against Capital Punishment." In *Cause Lawyering: Political Commitments and Professional Responsibilities*, Sarat Austin and Stuart Scheingold, eds., pp. 317–46. New York: Oxford.

Sarat, Austin and Stuart Scheingold, eds. 1998. *Cause Lawyering; Political Commitments and Professional Responsibilities*. New York: Oxford.

———. 2001. *Cause Lawyering and the State in a Global Era*. New York: Oxford.

Scheingold, Stuart A. and Austin Sarat. 2004. *Something to Believe In: Politics, Professionalism, and Cause Lawyering*. Stanford, CA: Stanford University Press.

Smith, Christian. 1996. *Resisting Reagan: The US Central America Peace Movement*. Chicago: University of Chicago Press.

USCR (United States Committee on Refugees). 1986. *Despite a Generous Spirit*. Washington, DC: American Council for Nationalities Service.

Ulloa, Roxana Elizabeth. 1999. *De indocumentados a residentes: Los salvadoreños en Estados Unidos*. San Salvador: FLACSO.

Wasem, Ruth Ellen. 1997. "Central American Asylum Seekers: Impact of 1996 Immigration Law." No. 97-810 EPW. Washington, DC: Congressional Research Service, Library of Congress. Available at http://countingcalifornia.cdlib.org/crs/pdf/97-810.pdf.

Consumer Cause Lawyers in the United States

Lawyers for the Movement or a Movement unto Themselves?

STEPHEN MEILI

The consumer movement is top-heavy with lawyers.[1]

Introduction

At the conclusion of his 2004 essay on law and social movements, Michael McCann suggests four new directions for research on the topic of law and social movements: additional empirical and theoretical inquiry that connects sociological and social movement theory; comparative cross-national and transnational study of legal mobilization; the relationship between legal mobilization politics and courts, judges, and legal professions; and the efficacy and effects of legal mobilization (McCann 2004). In analyzing the role of cause lawyers in the US consumer protection movement over the past fifty years, this chapter explores the first and last of those suggested new directions: First, it uses empirical data in the form of surveys and follow-up interviews with lawyers and non-lawyers active in the movement, as well as law professors, to connect sociological theory (specifically cause lawyering theory) and social movement theory in the context of consumer protection. Second, it examines the efficacy and legacy of legal mobilization strategies in the consumer protection movement in order to determine whether they affirm the observation in the critical literature that "legal mobilization produces a relatively feeble form of politics ... [and] tends to generate countermobilizations of unique scale and success" (McCann 2004). Through this analysis, the chapter examines one of the questions central to the cause lawyering literature: For what purpose do cause lawyers occupy a particular social field?

Social Movement Theoretical Underpinnings

The most useful and arguably most accurate social movement model through which to view the modern US consumer protection movement (i.e., since the mid-twentieth century) is the Political Process Model propounded by McAdam

(1982) and others.[2] According to this model, a social movement is a political phenomenon wherein the factors that influence institutionalized political processes are seen as accounting for social insurgency. Under this model, a social movement is characterized by a continuous process from generation to decline, rather than a onetime reaction to a social strain or a discrete series of developmental stages (McAdam 1982). McAdam contrasts the Political Process Model with two earlier models of social movement theory. The first is the Classical Model, which described a social movement as an emergent group of discontented individuals whose motivation for participation is not the desire to attain political goals, but the need to manage the psychological tensions of a stressful social situation; for such movement members, participation in the movement is more therapeutic than political. By contrast, the Political Process Model, as the name suggests, posits that social movements are rational attempts by excluded groups to mobilize sufficient political leverage to advance collective interests through noninstitutional means. Social movements are about collective political power, not individual therapy.

McAdam also contrasts the Political Process Model with the Resource Mobilization Model, under which social grievances are relatively constant and pervasive (as opposed to sudden spikes of discontent or stress under the Classic Model) and thus insufficient to create a social movement by themselves. Instead, the key variable for movement creation is the amount of social resources available to unorganized but aggrieved groups, which make it more or less possible to launch an organized demand for change. As Corey Shdaimah has recently observed, the resource mobilization theory helps to explain how shifting funding dynamics for public interest causes over the past three decades have influenced cause lawyer activists and the roles that they play within social movements (Shdaimah 2005).

Unlike the Resource Mobilization Model, the Political Process Model emphasizes the ebbs and flows of political forces, rather than resource allocation, which create (or close off) spaces within which movements can evolve, flourish, or wither. Under the Political Process Model, movements are particularly successful if their members have contacts with movement organizations, because these contacts help individuals counteract the "fundamental assumption that wealth and power are concentrated in America in the hands of a few groups, thus depriving most people of any real influence over the major decisions that affect their lives" (McAdam 1982).

The general contours of the Political Process Model have been supported by numerous scholars since the early 1970s (Jenkins and Perrow 1977; Tilly 1978; McAdam 1982; Tarrow 1983). These scholars see "the timing and fate of movements as largely dependent upon the opportunities afforded insurgents by the shifting institutional structure and ideological disposition of those in power" (McAdam, McCarthy, and Zald 1996). Thus, according to the Political Process Model, leaders of social movements are pragmatic actors whose strategic decisions about how best to achieve movement goals are influenced by the continuing evolution of political obstacles and opportunities.

A threshold question is whether the consumer protection movement in the United States qualifies as a social movement at all. Some, including McAdam himself, are skeptical. They liken consumer and environmental advocacy to public interest lobbies or formal interest groups, rather than true social movements, because they have access to State decision makers and rely almost exclusively on institutionalized strategies, rather than collective action, for change (McAdam 1982). Moreover, according to McAdam, these "movements" are controlled by elite members of society with access to powerful individuals and institutions (McAdam 1982) . Others have criticized the consumer movement as having a middle class bias whose agenda is fixed by self-appointed advocates with no connection to the consuming public and, therefore, little accountability to their members (McCann 1986; Herrmann and Mayer 1997). Still others question whether the collective identity necessary for a true social movement exists when certain of its members (i.e., wealthy consumers) can simply purchase their way out of many of the problems plaguing the majority of members (Barclay 2005). Even some current consumer advocates and cause lawyers question whether the consumer movement is a social movement in the generally accepted way that term is used:

"I don't think there is a 'rank and file' in the consumer movement"(Interview 1).

"The consumer movement, compared to many others, has not been a mass movement. It has largely been a movement among reformers"(Interview 2).

"[There is not] some sort of carefully orchestrated 'movement' [in consumer protection]" (Interview 3).

In a similar vein, McCann observes that the modern consumer protection movement, like other liberal public interest movements that proliferated in the wake of the civil rights and antiwar movements of the 1950s and 1960s, is more accurately described as a "checkbook affiliation," most of whose members do little to support the cause at hand beyond making monetary donations to one or more advocacy organizations (McCann 1986). According to McCann, such organizations provide only the illusion of participation for most citizen contributors, because they rarely, if ever, directly interact with each other (McCann

1986 citing Topolsky 1974). Instead of exhortations to collective action, these organizations appeal to political individualism and legal "self-help" as antidotes to current problems (McCann 1986). As a result, consumer advocacy groups (and the cause lawyers often at their helm) have generally emphasized legal strategies such as litigation, administrative rulemaking, and legislative advocacy that, as many have noted, are the most distant and alienating forums for political and economic redress (McCann 1986 citing Black 1973; Handler 1978). Hilbink characterizes the type of lawyering in which these cause lawyers engage as "Elite-Vanguard Lawyering," which privileges law as a "superior form of politics" (Hilbink 2004). McCann concludes that this style of lawyering, with its focus on high-level policy battles, limits the ability of liberal organizations to create real change in culture, social structure, and personal character (McCann 1986).

Despite these observations, the post-World War II US consumer movement exhibits many characteristics of a social movement under the Political Process Model. For example, individual consumers, perceiving themselves to be excluded from political and economic power, staged grassroots protests such as boycotts against grocery stores and other merchants that charged exorbitant prices (Herrmann and Meyer 1997). Many of these protests, as well as other citizen-based calls for reform, were energized by journalistic interpretations of industry practices in a variety of areas, including meatpacking, advertising, pesticides, and automobiles (Herrmann and Meyer 1997). In the 1960s and 1970s numerous organizations, many based at the grassroots level, were able to put together temporary coalitions to advance the cause of consumers in state legislatures (Herrmann and Meyer 1997). More recently, state and local consumer organizations have organized around a host of issues (e.g., privacy protection, food and auto safety, predatory lending to lower income consumers) by engaging in lobbying and media campaigns (Interview 7). At least some of these efforts are carried out as the Political Process Model stipulates; that is through noninstitutional means such as public protests, media campaigns, etc. What makes the Political Process Model particularly applicable to the US consumer protection movement, as well as to the cause lawyers within it, is that those cause lawyers have constantly adapted to changes in the political climate in order to achieve their goals. The following section of this chapter explores this phenomenon in more detail.

Consumer Cause Lawyers as Pragmatic Actors

The behavior of consumer cause lawyers over the past several decades verifies Scheingold's recent observation that cause lawyers do not, in fact, privilege litigation over other forms of legal and social mobilization (Scheingold 2004). Rather, consumer cause lawyers have altered their strategy depending on a variety of factors, including the existing political climate. Indeed, according to all of the consumer lawyers I interviewed for this chapter, it is only within the past decade (i.e., since the early 1990s) that litigation has become the primary legal mobilization strategy in the consumer movement. Prior to that time, consumer lawyers were a far less prominent force in the overall movement, and those who were involved focused their efforts more on community organizing (albeit sometimes in the context of class actions or impact litigation), coalition building, and legislative advocacy. Among those cause lawyers at the forefront of these forms of legal mobilization were legal services lawyers funded by the federal government, as well as the National Consumer Law Center (NCLC), an NGO originally funded by the federal government that shaped and supported the delivery of legal services by storefront neighborhood offices (Ogburn 1997).

According to one legal services attorney who specializes in consumer protection issues:

In the 1960s the lawyers in the consumer movement concentrated quite heavily on legislation, drafting the consumer protection code that became the federal Consumer Credit Protection Law, as well as various state laws. I think that until the mid to late 1980's the consumer movement was not primarily lawyer-driven, and that litigation was a very small part of the social movement. More significant were product safety and other issue campaigns. I began my own practice in 1983 . . . when a coalition of groups had just persuaded the sheriff and the courts to stop mortgage foreclosure sales. It was a time when litigation was very much an annex to a movement largely of unemployed workers and non-lawyer advocates. We had similar experiences with challenges to mass transit and utility price increases (Interview 4).

In a similar vein, one consumer law professor notes that consumer advocates, including lawyers, actually prefer legislation to litigation, and that during the late 1960s and early 1970s there was much success in the legislative arena (Interview 5). Indeed, a brief, ten-year window witnessed the creation of most of the federal consumer protection laws on the books today, including the Truth in Lending Act (TILA), the Fair Credit Reporting Act, the Equal Credit Opportunity Act, the Magnuson-Moss Warranty Act, the Fair Packaging and Labeling Act, the Fair Debt Collection Practices Act, and many state statutes dealing with fraud and deception (Silber 1997). Consumer cause lawyers were instrumental in the passage of these and other consumer protection statutes. But because the consumer movement is not radical by any measure (it is more about market efficiency than wholesale transformation), these movement lawyers were never in danger of crossing "the nethermost boundaries of the professional project" (Scheingold 1998).

The strategy of consumer cause lawyers began to change during the 1980s. Amid the ascendancy of free market conservatism within all three branches of the federal government and, somewhat later, many statehouses, legislative advocacy on behalf of consumers became much more difficult (McCann and Dudas 2005). This backlash against the advances achieved by the movement in the 1960s and 1970s took many forms. For one, the federal government drastically reduced funding for, and otherwise restricted the activities of, legal services programs around the country: "The Republican right targeted Legal Services programs explicitly because of [their] organizing activity.... As a result, legal services programs receiving federal funds were barred from bringing class actions, and funding cuts also resulted in consumer litigation being curtailed" (Interview 4). Indeed, budget cuts compelled many local legal services offices to abandon consumer advocacy altogether, both on behalf of individuals and groups. They were forced to focus their efforts on the most urgent problems of the poor, such as evictions and termination of public assistance benefits.

Second, it became virtually impossible to enact new laws that would in any way regulate the private sector. Indeed, not one landmark piece of consumer legislation was promulgated in the entire decade. Instead, as one consumer lawyer observed, market deregulation was exalted: "I think that the 'Market as God' theology [has met] with increasing success since the dawn of the Reagan Era.... Therefore, no new laws dealing with reform or new issues [were enacted]" (Interview 1).

Third, the Reagan Administration appointed leaders to consumer protection agencies who were either hostile or indifferent to those agencies' underlying mission. As a result "government enforcement of existing laws [was] starved" (Interview 1). For example, the Federal Trade Commission, which had been very aggressive in prosecuting corporate fraud and misrepresentation in the 1960s and 1970s, became nearly dormant in the 1980s (Whaley 2002). One non-lawyer activist for a national consumer protection organization noted that because of the lack of resources available for state and local consumer protection agencies, many consumer laws would go unenforced but for private attorneys (Interview 8).

Finally, and in many ways because of the trends noted above, the nature of the enemy changed during the 1980s. In the 1960s and 1970s, consumer cause lawyers focused much of their energy at State actors, that is, legislators and agency bureaucrats. Legislators needed to be lobbied (and at times publicly embarrassed) in order to pass legislation at the forefront of the consumer agenda. Bureaucrats needed to be monitored to ensure that they were properly overseeing the industries they were charged with regulating. Indeed, a large part of the agenda of the Nader organizations of the era was "watching the watchdogs." But as deregulation opened the door to more egregious and widespread exploitative business practices, consumer cause lawyers shifted their attention to battling private corporations.

In order to effectively confront this newly reempowered adversary, leaders in the consumer movement, including consumer cause lawyers, adopted new strategies. Ralph Nader's network of consumer lawyers and other advocates established citizen groups on the state and local level that were funded by small individual contributions. These organizations, primarily the Public Interest Research Groups in numerous states, focused on grass roots and media campaigns (Herrmann and Mayer 1997; Mierzwinski 1997; Interview 7).

The second important strategic move by consumer cause lawyers in response to the political realities of the 1980s and early 1990s was the decision by the NCLC to consciously "grow the private bar" of consumer litigators, that is, to enlist private attorneys in the cause of consumer protection (Interview 6). According to one cause lawyer active in the NCLC, the founders of NCLC wanted to show private members of the bar that they could simultaneously help people and make a living (Interview 6).

How did NCLC do this? By encouraging individual private attorneys—most of whom would not have defined themselves as cause lawyers previously—to use the array of state and federal consumer laws passed in the 1960s and 1970s to advance the cause of consumer protection by representing consumers in private lawsuits. Most of these laws have fee-shifting provisions that permit prevailing plaintiffs to recover their attorney's fees from the defendant. In a popular phrase, these individual attorneys act as "private attorneys general," complementing and in some cases completely replacing the state-employed attorneys who had previously enforced consumer protections laws. The NCLC promoted this new model of consumer cause lawyering in four significant ways: it helped create the National Association of Consumer Advocates (NACA), a membership organization whose mission is to protect consumers through the private enforcement of consumer protection statutes. Second, beginning in 1992, NCLC, together with NACA, organized an annual conference during which experts in various subfields of consumer protection lawyering (automobile fraud, unfair debt collection practices, disclosure law, predatory lending, and the like) lead how-to panels with the explicit aim of encouraging attorneys to sue offending corporations. Third, the NCLC published a series of manuals for lawyers describing applicable causes of action in a variety of consumer law contexts. These manuals have achieved the status of sacred text among many consumer cause lawyers. And fourth, NACA established a series of e-mail listserves that facilitate networking among consumer cause lawyers. Like the network of solo and small firm practitioners studied by Blom (2005), the consumer cause lawyers who participate in these listserves form a "virtual law firm" where lawyers otherwise disconnected can share substantive legal expertise, information about defendants, and strategy.

Litigation is, of course, a convenient vehicle for attacking corporate behavior in such a political and social environment, because (1) procedural rules help to create an arguably level playing field on which to confront the adversary, (2) fee shifting provisions in most consumer statutes make it economically feasible to pursue claims even where the monetary damages at stake are marginal, and (3) with the exception of one identifiable plaintiff (in either an individual case or a class action), it is not necessary to engage the public. Of course, for the same reason, a litigation strategy entails little public accountability.

By a variety of numerical measures, NCLC and NACA have met their original goals. The number of private attorneys practicing consumer law has increased tenfold in the past decade (Interview 6). The NCLC has sold over $2 million worth of its manuals in the same period (Interview 6). Attendance at NACA's annual conference of lawyers has risen from approximately eighty in 1992 (its first year) to 611 in 2004. Similarly, NACA's membership has grown from its original fourteen to over 1,000 today.

This cadre of consumer law litigators recruited by NCLC and NACA suggests an addition to the list of four "ideal types" of cause lawyers identified by McCann and Silverstein (1998). To staff technician, staff activist, hired gun, and nonpracticing lawyer, we might add "free agent litigators"; that is lawyers in private practice loyal to a movement cause (and attracted by the attorneys' fees such loyalty can generate) but with no formal (i.e., employment) relationship to movement leaders other than through the yearly membership fee they must pay to belong to the organization. Like the leaders of many "checkbook" affiliations, these cause lawyers have little accountability to the consumer movement generally; they are, by and large, almost exclusively accountable to their individual clients.[3]

Other contributors to the cause lawyering literature have noted that lawyers in private practice arguably qualify as cause lawyers (Kilwein 1998; Bloom 2001; Blom 2005). But unlike the private lawyers in those studies, who tend to practice in a variety of substantive areas (personal injury, family law, labor law, employment law, civil rights and criminal law) against different types of adversaries (insurance companies, spouses, employers, unions, private corporations, and the State), the private attorneys within NACA focus on a relatively narrow set of substantive issues and are almost always aligned against private businesses. This limited set of issues and a common enemy contributes to a sense of collective identity among consumer cause lawyers. It also suggests, as noted later in this chapter, that consumer cause lawyers may be a social movement unto themselves.

Although the cause lawyers I interviewed saw the shift to litigation as inevitable, given the political and economic realities of the 1980s, many nevertheless decried litigation's limiting impact on social movement development that has been noted by several observers (Scheingold 1974; McCann and Silverstein 1998; McCann 2004). As one consumer lawyer observed:

"[consumer] litigation is still closely tied in to legislative efforts, but not so much to grass roots organizing and public opinion campaigns.... Lawyers have been effective in unraveling the more elaborate ways in which merchants and lenders are exploiting consumers. On the other hand lawyers have not been very effective at increasing the consciousness of the consuming public of these new forms of exploitation, or at educating through the media so as to help galvanize a broader movement" (Interview 4).

A non-lawyer consumer advocate for a national organization noted that sometimes lawyers "are blind to the potential that media campaigns, citizen power and other advocacy techniques have to win effective social change and new consumer protection laws"(Interview 7).

Another way in which the conscious emphasis on litigation as a cause lawyering strategy has hampered the consumer movement is through the kind of backlash noted by McCann (2004). Much of this backlash reflects the success of litigation, particularly class action lawsuits, carried out on a state-by-state basis by the growing number of consumer lawyers. Large corporations, including credit card companies, telecommunications giants, and debt collection firms fought back. Yet rather than simply employ more aggressive litigation tactics (a traditional way in which well-funded defendants have an edge), many of these corporations sought to change the rules under which the battle is fought. Perhaps the most effective such change, and the one least noticed by the public or the mass media, has been federal preemption of state laws (Interview 6). Because many of the fee-shifting statutes under which consumer cause lawyers experienced success were state laws (particularly in states with strong consumer protection traditions like California), corporations convinced Congress to preempt those state laws that offer stronger protections than federal statutes. Thus, in recent years Congress has preempted numerous state laws in areas such as banking and telecommunications.

Large corporations have also employed the strategy of forcing their customers to arbitrate, rather than litigate, disputes. Mandatory arbitration clauses now appear in all manner of standard form consumer contracts, including those for insurance, credit cards, mortgages, cell phones, and payday loans (Bland et al. 2004). These clauses prevent cause lawyers from entering the forum where they feel most comfortable and can achieve the greatest financial reward for themselves and their clients.

Corporations have also succeeded in demonizing consumer cause lawyers by including them within the broad sweep of so-called tort reform. As one consumer law professor observes "I think the success [of the consumer movement] has been hampered by a well organized and funded 'tort reform' movement which often picks up consumer issues in its wake" (Interview 5). Of course, some misguided lawsuits (or legitimate lawsuits misinterpreted by the media) have made this corporate strategy easier: consumer lawyers have brought class actions based on hyper-technical violations of disclosure laws that result in minimal monetary recovery for individual class members (the proverbial twenty-five cent check) but hefty attorneys fee awards that make powerful fodder for corporate lobbyists and newspaper columnists (Interview 2; Interview 8). And according to one nonlawyerconsumer advocate, the movement has been hurt by lawyers who negotiate so-called "coupon settlements" in class actions; that is in lieu of cash, class members receive a coupon for the defendant's goods or services (e.g., one free month of called I.D.) interview 8 from a telephone company. Such settlements help the lawyers, who receive large attorney's fee awards, and the corporate defendants, who are likely to retain many customers after the expiration of the normally brief period of free service covered by the coupon, but not the consumer class members, who receive no monetary award for the defendant's violation of their rights.

Nevertheless, such legal advocacy setbacks have sometimes advanced the overall cause. This phenomenon is consistent with observations from other social movements, including the pay equity movement (McCann 1994; Scheingold 1994). Two examples cited by the cause lawyers and other advocates I interviewed were in the area of ATM surcharges and predatory lending practices. For example, although court challenges to ATM surcharges by banks and credit unions have been generally unsuccessful, the publicity generated by these cases has compelled many financial institutions to offer no-charge ATM services (Interview 7). Although most lawsuits challenging predatory lending practices have failed in court, they have attracted the kind of public outcry and media attention that has led to legislation prohibiting abusive lending practices in individual states like North Carolina and Wisconsin (Interview 4). Perhaps not surprisingly, however, there are now plans in Congress to introduce legislation preempting state and local antipredatory lending laws.

Of course, as McCann and Silverstein caution, it is important not to "overstate the centrality of lawyers and legal tactics in social movements" (McCann and Silverstein 1998). As one non-lawyer activist noted:

> I have been part of an ongoing non-litigation effort to build institutional con-
> sumer power, which has been quite effective, if spotty in some places. There
> are a whole set of [non-lawyer] advocacy-based specialization consumer
> groups working in the area of health care reform, privacy, media reform,
> etc. . . . I think the consumer movement has many leaders who are non-
> lawyers, and who are equal in stature to the lawyers. I think the rank and file
> consumer advocates and rank and file consumers themselves support most
> of the tactics of the movement's leadership, except for the tactics one elder
> statesman has recently chosen: running for President (Interview 7).

The Rise and Fall of Rights Consciousness Among Consumer Cause Lawyers

One of the most striking aspects of the rise in prominence of consumer cause lawyers within the US consumer protection movement has been the concomitant de-emphasis on consumer rights within the movement as a whole. This is consistent with McCann's speculation that law may matter most at the *earliest* phases of a social movement's organizational and agenda setting, because it is at this time that the law can give a movement a legal frame (McCann 2004). In the case of the consumer movement, the focus on rights may have reached its zenith in terms of exposure and acceptance when President Kennedy articulated a set of four consumer rights in 1962: the right to be heard, the right to know, the right to safety, and the right to choose (Bannister 1997). That the articulation of such rights would rise to the highest levels of the US government is testimony both to the strength of the consumer movement up to that point and to the power of rights consciousness generally in US society at that time (Scheingold 1974; McCann 2004).

Whether it is attributable to Kennedy's speech or other factors, it is undeniable that the following decade witnessed the creation by statute of numerous rights that had not existed before, including the right to be free of abusive debt collection practices and discrimination in the extension of credit, the right to know about product ingredients and the financial terms of a transaction, and the right to enforce a product's express and implied warranties. The establishment of these rights provided the consumer movement with a focus and a frame around which to build public support and thus exert further pressure for progressive change on government elites (Tarrow 1994; Scheingold; 1998; McCann 2004). Of course, as one consumer cause lawyer noted, many of these "rights" were the codification of well-established common law doctrines (Interview 2). But because many of the statutes contained fee-shifting provisions, they opened the door to far more litigation on behalf of consumers (including class actions) than had previously been the case.

Despite the consumer movement's success in creating rights in the mid-twentieth century and the rights consciousness that success engendered, many of the consumer lawyers and advocates I interviewed downplay the importance of rights work in the movement:

> I don't think notions of rights are as critical in the development of consumer protection as in civil rights and other progressive movements. It is more akin to the environmental movement, where the organizing ideas are to redress the balance of power and limit the damage done by unrestricted corporate greed. Rather than thinking in individualistic rights-based terms, I think the area lends itself more to a collective norms approach that regards bad behavior as something to restrain, not just to protect individual victims but for the broader good (Interview 4).

> Giving consumer rights has been and remains a legitimate movement goal, but I think the consumer movement aspires to higher goals, such as equalizing the power of producers and consumers to make the economy work more competitively (Interview 7).

Some consumer advocates, both lawyers and non-lawyers alike, view the focus on rights as actually harming the overall movement. In making this argument, they single out one of the most significant rights created during the 1960s heyday, the right of consumers to full disclosure of credit terms. The primary federal statue in this area is the TILA, which requires creditors to conspicuously disclose relevant credit terms such as the finance charge, annual percentage rate, and total of payments. The point of this statute was to prevent creditors from disguising the true cost of credit. Indeed, TILA is the preeminent statutory symbol of the mid-twentieth century shift from "let the buyer beware" to "let the seller disclose."

According to one consumer cause lawyer, disclosure laws like TILA have not been particularly effective at protecting consumers (Interview 4). Another consumer cause lawyer says that they have been used as a smokescreen to thwart more important consumer protections (Interview 2). One consumer law professor suggests that proponents of disclosure laws falsely assumed that such laws would solve all problems (Interview 5). As a non-lawyer consumer advocate puts it:

> disclosure is not enough if you can't act on the information to protect yourself... more protection is needed for vulnerable consumers who lack market clout to protect themselves and for all consumers when the risk cannot be perceived or prevented by personal action (such as airplanes with faulty controls or cars that don't withstand crashes or food that contains contaminants) (Interview 8).

Another consumer cause lawyer believes that rights such as disclosure are (1) malleable by corporate interests and (2) more of a means to effective consumer protections (at least as utilized by cause lawyers) than as ends in themselves:

> Business has figured out that a blur of fine print disclosures is an easy way to avoid giving consumers information that they can really put to good use. Disclosure requirements usually have been the necessary tool for eventually demonstrating that more compensatory and punitive remedies are needed to deter consumer abuses. (Interview 3).

A further reason why the consumer movement has been less concerned with rights than other social movements, such as the civil rights and womens' rights movements, is the sheer breadth of all of the issues and concerns that fit within the umbrella of "consumer protection." In part because of the movement's success in establishing numerous rights forty years ago, "consumer protection" now includes everything from safe toys to fair lending practices. As one non-lawyer consumer advocate notes, this breadth has made the consumer movement less focused on one specific reform than other movements:

> While in the mid-60s it had a Nader-inspired push for reforms that may have accomplished a lot in a short time and thereby paralleled some of the short-term intensive efforts of the civil rights, environmental or womens' movements, I think it has been both a strength and weakness of the consumer movement that we've been less focused on one specific reform that everyone works on all at the same time. Strands of the movement focus on predatory lending, on privacy, on health care, on legal rights, on banking reforms broadly, on product safety, on communications, etc. This has given us a broad reach, but the sheer breadth of the number of issues we work on means that protecting

consumers means different things to different people. We are fighting many battles on many fronts rather than focusing all our efforts on one consumer protection initiative. To some extent, that means that while some consumers have subscribed to Consumer Reports for 30 years or more, they may not consider themselves consumer advocates. You see a lot more Greenpeace or Sierra Club bumper stickers than Consumer Now! Bumper stickers (Interview 7).

In a similar vein, another non-lawyer consumer advocate noted that "consumer groups work more on solving specific problems than on building support for a consumer movement per se. This had led to disjointed efforts as groups fade when the problem has been resolved or they hit a brick wall" (Interview 8).

The lack of focus on—indeed, even the avoidance of—rights work by recent consumer cause lawyers has probably cost the consumer movement the kind of media attention so critical to the advancement of objectives in other social movements (Zald 1992; Tarrow 1994). As McCann observes, the mass media has a propensity to publicize legal rights claims and thereby strengthen the power of legal mobilization pressure tactics such as litigation and legislative advocacy (McCann 2004). But issues like fundamental fairness, market efficiency, and corporate greed suggest the kind of "class warfare" that the US media tends to avoid, particularly in the current political climate. This is particularly true in the current era of media concentration and timidity in the face of corporate control. As one consumer lawyer noted: "the media has been harder to reach with complicated issues, and as its ownership has been concentrated under corporate ownership, it's getting harder to get sustained and intelligent media coverage" (Interview 1).

Moreover, several of the advocates interviewed for this chapter, lawyers and non-lawyers alike, noted that most consumer protection issues are not "sexy" enough to garner much media attention (Interview 5; Interview 6; Interview 7). Reflecting on a recent television drama episode concerning depression and student suicide, one consumer lawyer asked, tongue firmly in cheek, "Can you see a predatory loan [episode] on 'Law and Order' " (Interview 1). Some advocates also attribute the lack of public attention to consumer issues to the fact that, as one consumer cause lawyer put it, "with some of the consumer [issues] even the victims don't always know they've been victims. And it can be very hard to explain.... It is not at all hard to explain 'driving while black' or employment discrimination" (Interview 1).

Many cause lawyers also note that, unlike other social movements, the consumer movement has been opposed by an extremely well-funded and sophisticated opposition, that is, wealthy corporations wishing to maintain their advantage over consumers. This opposition can use and manipulate the media at least as well as cause lawyers and other consumer advocates. The campaign to "demonize" trial lawyers (including consumer lawyers) within the "tort reform" campaign was identified as one example (Interview 1). So was the well-circulated idea that consumers must bear some responsibility for protecting their own interests in the marketplace, signaling a return to "let the buyer beware":

> The civil rights movement didn't have to deal with the "victim has to take some responsibility" [argument. The consumer movement must deal with arguments such as] "they signed it didn't they", and "they are deadbeats anyway" that minimize the harm to the affected people. Figuratively, the civil rights movement was more black and white on where the moral high ground lay, and on where the right response lay. . . . My take on the philosophy of the radical right—both corporate right and theocratic right, is that responsibility is something other people must take; for example, it is the consumer's responsibility not to get cheated; it's not the businessman's responsibility not to cheat in the first place (Interview 1).

Indeed, one of the strengths of a rights discourse is that it makes it easier to determine where the "moral high ground" lies when it comes to social movements. However, large corporations, supported by over two decades of deregulatory zeal in both federal and state government, have succeeded in muddying the moral high ground when it comes to consumer protection. Indeed, they have succeeded in parlaying an unfettered market into something of a moral imperative (President Bush's emphasis on "freedom" in recent speeches strikes a similar tone). This has made the role of consumer cause lawyers more difficult and frustrating—and sometimes confusing—than in other social movements. In movements such as civil rights, cause lawyers were nearly universally perceived as possessing the morally superior argument; victory was only a matter of time. But one senses from conversations with consumer cause lawyers that the battle is far more difficult and there is no light at the end of the tunnel:

> We are losing ground, consistently and continually. Every once in a while we put a stake in the ground, but then the stake gets pulled up . . . we are still at the point of arguing the worthiness of consumer protection (Interview 6).

> So, I'd say that some of the concentration in litigation is simply that it's been harder to make progress legislatively than it was, say, in the late 1960s and early 70s, when state legislatures and Congress were actually interested in doing something affirmative, and when Rupert Murdoch and Fox News weren't

driving the caliber of the media debate. I'd also say, though that if the radical right continues its agenda into the judiciary, we're going to be losing that avenue, as well (Interview 1).

These pessimistic comments bring to mind Abel's yardstick for measuring the success of cause lawyers: they are "most successful when a confident government is engaged in social change and most often frustrated when a frightened government is desperately scrambling to retain power" (Abel 1998). "Confident" may not be the first word that springs to mind when one recalls the US government of the mid 1960s to the mid 1970s, given Vietnam and Watergate; and yet, when the President himself articulates a series of consumer rights, it certainly *sounds* like the government was confident at least about consumer protection and its place in state policy. And cause lawyers active in the movement at that time, most notably Ralph Nader, met with great legislative success and reaped the benefits of the broad public consensus about rights generally. On the other hand, one could reasonably conclude that the US government of the post-Cold War era, despite its macho bearing, is actually quite frightened and desperately trying to retain the power it feels it lost during the reforms of the 1960s and 1970s. Against such a frightened State that has been aggressively lobbied by powerful corporations, consumer cause lawyers as a group appear to feel less successful than in the past.

A Social Movement of Consumer Cause Lawyers?

The tremendous expansion in consumer cause lawyering over the past decade (particularly in the litigation forum) exhibits the trappings of a social movement unto itself. Although no one would mistake plaintiffs' lawyers as a traditionally unrepresented or excluded group, the active recruitment of previously traditional lawyers into the practice of consumer law exhibits some of the same characteristics of the Political Process Model of social movements. By the early 1990s, the leaders of one of the country's premier consumer lawyering NGO (NCLC) viewed themselves as excluded from the position of influence over policy they had previously enjoyed. Their recruitment of litigating attorneys was a mobilization strategy in response to the political realities of the 1980s and was consciously designed to obtain leverage over corporations and, by extension, the political process, while simultaneously advancing the collective interests of consumers generally.

Yet perhaps more important than whether a group of cause layers are, in fact, a social movement is whether they exhibit some of the characteristics of a social movement. And consumer cause lawyers certainly do, particularly because of the distance between consumer cause lawyers and those citizens out of power for whom the cause lawyers purport to speak. Without the constraints of a mobilized, vocal, and demanding citizen base, consumer cause lawyers and their leaders in elite organizations are freer to pursue their own movement agenda than lawyers who work in other social movements. And the divide between cause lawyers and rank and file movement members is only exacerbated by the legal mobilization strategy of litigation, which excludes all but the most active non-lawyers (such as the representative plaintiffs in class actions) from the decision-making process of movement elites. Moreover, as illustrated by the movements in support of same sex marriage (Barclay and Fisher 2005) and reform of the child welfare system (Shdaimah 2005), cause lawyers play a more pivotal role when there seems to be no movement "out there" and/or during periods of dormancy within an otherwise active movement. Moreover, as Shdaimah observes, it can be difficult to maintain commitment to a latent social movement, particularly from the more distant role of elite adherent assumed by many left-activist cause lawyers (Shdaimah 2005).

What seems to have emerged over the past decade of lawyers dominating the consumer movement is a kind of submovement of consumer cause lawyers, featuring a rank and file cadre of litigating private lawyers (many of whom were recruited by NCLC and NACA) and a movement leadership, that is, veteran consumer cause lawyers who occupy leadership positions in national consumer and consumer law organizations. Moreover, although those rank-and-file cause lawyers are largely responsible for the movement's success through their litigation of scores of victorious lawsuits against corporations that violate state and federal consumer protection laws, they are sometimes a source of frustration for the movement leadership, who decry ill-considered lawsuits that set back the movement either through harmful appellate decisions, "gotcha" technicalities or the demonization of plaintiffs' lawyers generally (Interview 1; Interview 2). This kind of conflict within the hierarchy of lawyers working for the same cause has rarely been examined within the cause lawyering literature (which tends to view lawyers within one movement as somewhat monolithic) and bears further research.

An alternative framework for the increased importance of cause lawyers in the consumer protection movement is as a reflection of the growing power of NGOs as a political force in the United States and throughout the world (Shamir and Ziv 2001). The consumer cause lawyers I studied for this chapter became a political force meriting a sustained countermobilization by business interests only after they had formed their own NGO, that is, NACA. As individual attorneys litigating the occasional consumer protection case, they had little impact beyond the result of the immediate lawsuit. Yet once coalesced within an NGO, their numbers grew and their litigation strategy was influenced by leaders of that NGO. This development created a more unified attack on corporate excess, leading both to significant courtroom victories and the counterattack of dramatic legislative restrictions on consumer rights.

Conclusion

In their chapter in the first Cause Lawyering volume, McCann and Silverstein ask "What explains the varying approaches and characters of different legal activists?" (McCann and Silverstein 1998). Using the examples of the pay equity and animal rights movements, they identify four principle factors: (1) the formal roles and relationships of cause lawyers in movement organizations, (2) the general organizational structures of the movements within which lawyers act, (3) the systemic opportunities for tactical legal success, and (4) the lawyers' own historically developed experiential knowledge and insights about political lawyering (McCann and Silverstein 1998). Although each of these factors helps explain the role of cause lawyers in the US consumer protection movement at any given time over the course of its history, the Political Process Model of social movements provides a particularly compelling frame for viewing the changing role of cause lawyers in that movement. At its most basic level, the theory argues that social movements are political, rather than personal, and that from their generation to their decline they (and their members and leaders) react to changing political and social realities. So has it been with consumer protection cause lawyers. In the first half of the twentieth century, lawyers played little, if any, organized role in the US consumer protection movement. The leaders of the movement were typically non-lawyer directors of consumer protection organizations and trade unions. Much of the movements' advances were attributable to groundbreaking books and articles that aroused sufficient public concern to compel political elites to institute reforms. In the mid-twentieth century, consumer lawyers, riding the crest of a rights-based wave created by the dominant social movements of the day, joined with non-lawyer activists to press for legislative reforms in a number of areas. Political and social conditions created an opening for rights-based legislation (as well as substantive protections in food and product safety), and consumer cause lawyers took advantage. Then, in the late 1970s, when deregulation gained a foothold both politically and socially, consumer cause lawyers found themselves less able to affect reform through state or federal legislation. They also found, during the 1980s, that fewer resources were being devoted to state-based enforcement of consumer protection laws (both by governmental agencies and by publicly funded poverty lawyers). As a result, these lawyers (led by a few consumer advocacy organizations) made a very conscious decision to focus their efforts on litigation as a means of vindicating the rights that the laws enacted two decades earlier were designed to protect. As McCann and Silverstein observed with respect to the animal rights and pay equity cause lawyers in their study, and as the Political Process Model would predict, these consumer cause lawyers did not choose to emphasize litigation in the 1990s because they somehow prefer it on a professional level. Rather, they saw it as the only effective method remaining to them within a movement stalled by deregulatory zeal amid government elites, hostility to consumer protections by corporate elites, and a fragmented consumer movement that had little awareness of, or interest in, many of the abuses that private lawyers sought to battle.

This leads to the second of McCann's suggested areas for future research: the efficacy of legal mobilization strategies in the consumer protection movement and whether those strategies have generated countermobilizations of unique scale and success. Based on the foregoing study, the answer to this question would appear to be a definite yes. On the one hand, consumer cause lawyers have, over the past forty years, been remarkably successful in both creating and enforcing a host of consumer rights that either did not exist, or were weakly enforced, under the common law. It is safe to say that statutes covering areas such as warranties, credit disclosures, debt collection, and fraud and misrepresentation would not exist today had it not been for the efforts of a cadre of consumer cause lawyers who worked with local, state, and national consumer organizations to obtain passage of those laws. And yet, their very success has led to the kind of "equal and opposite reaction" that now has left consumer cause lawyers on the defensive and in a uniformly depressed mood. Landmark legislation has been eviscerated by deregulation, lack of funding for enforcement, preemption by existing or subsequently enacted federal law, and anticonsumer interpretation by conservative judges. The countermobilization, a product of consumer cause lawyers' own success, has been strong and multifaceted, and shows no signs of abating.

Notes

1. Interview 6.

2. For references to other social movement theoretical frameworks, see Staggenborg (1996).

3. Although class action settlements must be approved by the presiding judge, that judge normally confines his or her consideration of the fairness of the settlement to the interests of the members of the class, not the general public.

References

Secondary Sources

Abel, Richard. 1998. "Speaking Law to Power." in *Cause Lawyering: Political Commitments and Social Responsibilities*, ed. A. Sarat and S. Scheingold.New York: Oxford University Press.

Bannister, Rosella. 1997. "Consumer Education." in *Consumer Encyclopedia*, ed. Stephen Brobeck. Santa Barbara, CA: ABC-CLIO.

Barclay, Scott. Comment at Cause Lawyering and Social Movements Conference, Los Angeles, March 5, 2005.

Barclay, Scott and Shauna Fisher. 2005. "Cause Lawyers and Social Movements, Failure and Success: Comparing the Two Waves of Same Sex Marriage Litigation." Draft paper presented at Cause Lawyering and Social Movements Conference, Los Angeles, March 4–5.

Black, Donald. 1973. "The Mobilization of Law." *Journal of Legal Studies* 2: 125–50.

Bland, F. Paul, Michael J. Quirk, Kate Gordon, and Jonathan Sheldon. 2004. *Consumer Arbitration Agreements: Enforceability and Other Topics*. Boston: National Consumer Law Center.

Blom, Barbara. 2005. "Cause Lawyering and Social Movements: Can Solo and Small Firm Practitioners Anchor Social Movements?" Draft paper presented at Cause Lawyering and Social Movements Conference, Los Angeles, March 4–5.

Bloom, Anne. 2001. "Taking on Goliath: Why Personal Injury Litigation May Represent the Future of Transnational Cause Lawyering." in *Cause Lawyering and the State in a Global Era*, ed. A. Sarat and S. Scheingold.New York: Oxford University Press.

Handler, Joel. 1978. *Social Movements and the Legal System: A Theory of Law Reform and Social Change*. New York: Academic Press.

Herrmann, Robert and Robert N. Mayer. 1997. "U.S. Consumer Movement: History and Dynamics." in *Consumer Encyclopedia*, ed. Stephen Brobeck. Santa Barbara, CA: ABC-CLIO.

Hilbink, Thomas M. Summer 2004. "You Know the Type . . . : Categories of Cause Lawyering." *Law and Social Inquiry* 29(3): 657–98.

Jenkins, J. Graig and Charles Perrow. 1977. "Insurgency of the Powerless: Farm Worker Movements (1946–1972)." *American Sociological Review* 42: 249–68.

Kilwein, John. 1998. "Still Trying: Cause Lawyering for the Poor and Disadvantaged in Pittsburgh, Pennsylvania." in *Cause Lawyering: Political Commitments and Social Responsibilities*, ed. A. Sarat and S. Scheingold.New York: Oxford University Press.

McAdam, Doug. 1982. *Political Process and the Development of Black Insurgency, 1930–1970*. Chicago: University of Chicago Press.

McAdam, Doug, John D. McCarthy, and Mayer N. Zald, eds. 1996.*Comparative Perspectives on Social Movements*, Cambridge: Cambridge University Press.

McCann, Michael. 1986. *Taking Reform Seriously: Perspectives on Public Interest Liberalism.* Ithaca, NY: Cornell University Press.

——. 2004. "Law and Social Movements." in *The Blackwell Companion to Law and Society.* Malden, MA: Blackwell.

McCann, Michael and Jeffrey Dudas. 2005. "Backlash: Mapping the Changing Context of Movement Lawyering." Draft paper presented at Cause Lawyering and Social Movement Conference, Los Angeles, March 4–5.

McCann, Michael and Helena Silverstein. 1998. "Rethinking Law's 'Allurements': A Relational Analysis of Social Movements Lawyers in the United States." in *Cause Lawyering: Political Commitments and Social Responsibilities,* ed. A. Sarat and S. Scheingold. New York: Oxford University Press.

Mierzwinski, Edmund. 1997. "Public Interest Research Groups." in *Consumer Encyclopedia,* ed. Stephen Brobeck. Santa Barbara, CA: ABC-CLIO.

Ogburn, Willard P. 1997. "National Consumer Law Center." in *Consumer Encyclopedia,* ed. Stephen Brobeck. Santa Barbara, CA: ABC-CLIO.

Scheingold, Stuart. 1974. *The Politics of Rights: Lawyers, Public Policy, and Political Change.* New Haven, CT: Yale University Press.

——. 1998. "The Struggle to Politicize Legal Practice: A Case Study of Left-Activist Lawyering in Seattle." in *Cause Lawyering: Political Commitments and Social Responsibilities,* ed. A. Sarat and S. Scheingold. New York: Oxford University Press.

——. 2004. *Preface to the Second Edition of the Politics of Rights,* 2nd edn. Ann Arbor, MI: University of Michigan Press.

Shamir, Ronen and Neta Ziv. 2001. "State-Oriented and Community-Oriented Lawyering for a Cause: A Tale of Two Strategies." in *Cause Lawyering and the State in a Global Era,* ed. A. Sarat and S. Scheingold. New York: Oxford University Press.

Shdaimah, Corey S. 2005. "Intersecting Identities: Cause Lawyers as Legal Professionals and Social Movement Actors." Draft paper presented at Cause Lawyering and Social Movements Conference, Los Angeles, March 4–5.

Silber, Norman I. 1997. "Consumer Law." in *Consumer Encyclopedia,* ed. Stephen Brobeck. Santa Barbara, CA: ABC-CLIO.

Staggenborg, Suzanne. 1996. "The Survival of the Women's Movement: Turnover and Continuity in Bloomington, Indiana." in *Mobilization: An International Journal* 1(2): 143–58.

Tarrow, Sidney. 1983. *Struggling to Reform: Social Movements and Policy Change During Cycles of Protest.* Western Societies Program Occasional Paper No. 15. New York Center for International Studies, Cornell University, Ithaca, NY.

——. 1994. *Power in Movement: Social Movements, Collective Action and Politics.* Cambridge: Cambridge University Press.

Tilly, Charles. 1978. *From Mobilization to Revolution.* Reading, MA: Addison-Wesley.

Topolsky, Mary. 1974. "Common Cause?" *Worldview* 17: 35–39.

Whaley, Douglas J. 2002. *Problems and Materials on Consumer Law.* New York: Aspen Publishers.

Zald, Mayer N. 1992. "Looking Backward to Look Forward: Reflections on the Past and Future of the Resource Mobilization Research Program." in *Frontiers in Social Movement Theory,* ed. Aldon D. Morris and Carol McClurg Mueller. New Haven, CT: Yale University Press.

Interviews

Interview 1—Lawyer employed by a state-based consumer advocacy organization, January 2005.

Interview 2—Lawyer employed by a national consumer law organization, January 2005.

Interview 3—Legal services lawyer specializing in consumer law issues, January 2005.

Interview 4—Legal services lawyer specializing in consumer law issues, January 2005.

Interview 5—Consumer law professor, January 2005.

Interview 6—Lawyer employed by a national consumer law organization, January 2005.

Interview 7—Non lawyer consumer advocate employed by a national consumer advocacy organization, January 2005.

Interview 8—Non lawyer consumer advocate employed by a national consumer advocacy organization, January 2005.

Lawyers and Activists/Lawyers as Activists: Professional Identities and Movement Politics

To Lead with Law

Reassessing the Influence of
Legal Advocacy Organizations in Social Movements

SANDRA R. LEVITSKY

The NAACP's early successes with test case litigation created a model for using law as a social movement strategy that has since been replicated by advocates for such wide-ranging interest groups as consumers, environmentalists, gays and lesbians, economic libertarians, and the poor. Today, organizations that specialize in planned litigation continue to proliferate, despite critiques from both the political left and right about the efficacy of litigation as a tool for social reform (Horowitz 1977; Handler 1978; Rosenberg 1991). Indeed, the proliferation of legal advocacy organizations across social movements suggests that litigation must provide *some* benefits to social movements; otherwise the prevalence of these groups makes neither organizational nor political sense (see Morag-Levine 2001).

And, in fact, a growing literature on cause lawyering has identified a litany of ways in which litigation strategies can benefit social movements. Within this literature, a number of sociolegal scholars emphasize the *heterogeneity* of social movements (Olson 1984; Hunt 1990; McCann 1998). Contemporary American social movements are collective challenges by organizations engaging in a wide range of strategies and tactics, but with common purposes and social solidarities (cf., Tarrow 1998). Sociolegal researchers have stressed the importance of *complementarity* among these various organizations, arguing that successful legal mobilization depends on deploying legal strategies in conjunction with other forms of collective action (Scheingold 1974; McCann 1994). And yet we know very little about the network of ties that connect organizations specializing in different approaches to social reform (but see Levitsky 2005), or in particular, how legal advocacy organizations integrate their expertise with the tactics of other organizations in the movement.

Researchers have also invoked the heterogeneity of social movement organizations to refute the longstanding contention that lawyers and legal strategies tend to dominate social movement activity (Olson 1984; Hunt 1990; McCann 1998). Here the argument is that because litigation strategies are just one form of social movement activity among many, lawyers cannot unduly influence agenda setting in the movement. But this characterization of social movement organizations as equivalently positioned actors, each specializing in their own approach to social reform, has tended to occlude important differences in the resource capacities among organizations. Organizations that specialize in test case litigation often have access to specific kinds and quantities of resources not available to most grassroots organizations. Yet, the question of how such resource disparities affect the capacities of organizations to influence the direction of movement activity has received little direct empirical attention.

This chapter uses a case study of interorganizational relations in the Chicago gay, lesbian, bisexual, and transgender (GLBT) movement to examine (1) how legal advocacy organizations integrate their legal expertise with other organizations in the movement and (2) how disparities in resources affect the relative capacities of legal advocacy and grassroots organizations to promote their goals and interests. I argue that while legal advocacy organizations do assist other organizations in the movement, interorganizational relations are not defined by reciprocal but by *unilateral* cooperation. As a result, many activists in the movement perceive legal advocacy organizations as operating independently from the rest of the movement, imposing their agendas without consultation with grassroots activists and with few opportunities for input from the rest of the GLBT community. And while there was no evidence that legal advocacy groups dominated the movement by steering others toward litigation strategies, their considerable organizational resources nevertheless had a significant impact on agenda setting for the movement.

Cause Lawyering as a Social Movement Tactic

After the relative success of the initial waves of legal advocacy organizations in the 1950s and 1960s, the value of litigation as a tactic for social change was called into serious question. In addition to being expensive and time consuming, critics contended that litigation tactics produce inadequate remedies that are rarely self-enforcing (Handler 1978; Rosenberg 1991); they deradicalize social conflict, reducing real demands and grievances to abstract legal concepts (see, e.g., Gabel and Kennedy 1984; Tushnet 1984; Bumiller 1988); they impoverish political and public debates about relevant issues (Glendon 1991); and they shift "ownership" of the grievances from the movement community to elite professionals, who are often somewhat removed from the source of the conflict (White 1987; Menkel-Meadow 1998).

Although few sociolegal scholars dispute the limitations of litigation strategies and legal discourse more generally, a growing cadre of researchers has argued that legal mobilization strategies can nevertheless benefit social movements in a number of important ways: Litigation can raise expectations, spark indignation and hope, and stimulate a rights consciousness among movement constituents and supporters; it can help legitimize a movement's goals and values, publicize the movement's causes, and provide leverage in bargaining with powerful elites (Gusfield 1967; Scheingold 1974; Handler 1978; O'Connor 1980; Galanter 1983; Schneider 1986; McCann 1994, 1998). These scholars suggest that cause lawyers today do not naively cling to law's transformative potential, but hold a sophisticated understanding of the limitations of legal action and the "liberal" biases of legal norms (McCann and Silverstein 1998). Indeed, many cause lawyers spend just a fraction of their time practicing traditional law—preparing and arguing cases—and instead devote most of their schedules to educating the public, rallying existing or potential supporters, coalition building, and political strategizing (Olson 1984; McCann and Silverstein 1998; Barclay and Marshall 2005). Some cause lawyers actively participate in other forms of collective action—including direct action or street protest activity—in addition to, or outside of, their legal practices (Kilwein 1998; Scheingold 1998; Coutin 2001; Scheingold and Sarat 2004).

But if sociolegal scholars have produced an impressive body of evidence demonstrating the sophistication with which individual cause lawyers use their legal expertise in social reform efforts, less attention has been given to formal interactions between social movement groups at the *organizational* level. I argue that understanding the nature of these interorganizational relations would help to illuminate at least two key questions about the role of cause lawyering in social movements. First, in acknowledging that legal tactics alone cannot successfully bring about social change, sociolegal scholars have repeatedly highlighted the importance of using legal strategies *in conjunction with* other forms of collective action. But how do legal advocacy groups actually cultivate cooperative relationships with nonlegal movement organizations?

"Cooperative" relationships might involve specific collaborations on events or issues, or it might involve sharing specialized knowledge, skills, information, and other organizational resources. Theoretically, organizations that specialize in test case litigation are poised to both contribute to and benefit from such relationships: their familiarity with law, legal venues, and the discourse of rights are potentially useful resources for a range of social movement activities, including public education, protest activity, lobbying, and consciousness raising (Marshall 2006). But, importantly, interactions with nonlegal organizations could also serve as *information conduits* for legal advocacy groups, opportunities for GLBT constituents of widely varying ideologies to communicate their concerns or grievances to those actors who seek to represent "the movement" in judicial arenas. Thus, an analysis of how legal advocacy organizations actually deploy their expertise to complement the activities of nonlegal movement organizations, and, conversely, how legal advocacy organizations rely on the expertise or tactics of other organizations, will help to illuminate the extent to which legal advocacy groups actually integrate their work with the rest of the movement.

Second, sociolegal scholars have suggested that in social movements constituted by a diverse field of organizations, lawyers rarely play a central leadership role or command the authority to steer the movement in any particular direction (Olson 1984; Hunt 1990; McCann 1998; McCann and Silverstein 1998). These theorists conceptualize social movements as *pluralistic* enterprises in which no one organization disproportionately influences the movement's agenda. But social movement researchers have long observed that the capacity of social movement organizations to pursue their goals and represent their constituents depends in large part on their capacity to mobilize resources, and that these resource capacities vary among movement organizations (McCarthy and Zald 1977).

Organizations that adopt a bureaucratic or "professionalized" organizational form—characterized by a formal division of labor, paid professional staff, a "paper" membership (mostly names on mailing lists), and reliance on foundation or grant support for funding (McCarthy and Zald 1973, 1977)—tend to be larger, wealthier, more stable, and have considerably more influence with elites than their grassroots counterparts (Zald and Ash 1966; Gamson 1975; Staggenborg 1989; Minkoff 1997).[1] Groups that specialize in legal advocacy frequently adopt this organizational form as a way of meeting the unique resource demands of planned litigation (O'Connor 1980; Epstein 1985; Epp 1998; den Dulk 2001). Indeed, sociolegal scholars have documented the institutionalization of the professionalized legal advocacy organizations in social movements of widely varying political ideologies (Albiston and Nielsen 2003). Yet, despite the prevalence of these organizations, few sociolegal researchers have considered how resource disparities affect the relative capacities of legal advocacy organizations and other movement groups to promote their organizational goals and strategies. Indeed we would expect, contrary to recent claims in the cause lawyering literature, that legal advocacy organizations would have *considerable* influence in agenda setting, given their advantages with respect to organizational resources.

This chapter seeks to interrogate the nature of interorganizational relations between legal advocacy organizations and nonlegal movement organizations in the Chicago GLBT movement. After a brief summary of the methods used in case selection and description of the Chicago GLBT movement, the analysis proceeds in two parts. First, I analyze the complementarity of social movement tactics in the Chicago movement, focusing in particular on how legal advocacy organizations integrate their expertise with other organizations. I then consider how organizational structure and resources affect the relative capacities of GLBT groups to pursue and promote their organizational goals. The chapter concludes with a discussion of the implications of these findings for cause lawyering more generally.

Methods and Case Background

Chicago is currently home to several GLBT legal and political advocacy organizations, a flourishing gay press, a gay chamber of commerce, numerous associations for GLBT professionals, and a wide-ranging network of grassroots organizations. The heterogeneity in GLBT social movement organizations thus allows for an analysis of how activists with diverse ideologies and agendas view interorganizational relations and the role of legal advocacy organizations within the movement.

I conducted thirty-one in-depth interviews with the founders and past or present leaders from fifteen GLBT organizations in Chicago during the Summer of 2000. Following Minkoff's (1999) typology, I selected groups that specialized in four social movement tactics, broadly defined as: (1) *advocacy organizations* (i.e., groups that rely on lobbying and litigation to influence policy and public opinion in institutional settings), (2) *protest organizations* (i.e., groups that use outsider tactics or disruptive means such as demonstrations, sit-ins, and marches to influence policies, public officials and public opinion), (3) *service organizations* (i.e., groups that provide tangible goods or services, such as health care, counseling or individual legal representation, as well as intangible goods such as information about legal issues, hotlines for victims of gay bashing, and support or consciousness-raising), and (4) *cultural organizations* (i.e., groups that emphasize cultural or ideological activities such as sponsoring film festivals, challenging homophobia in schools, and media monitoring and production). I also interviewed editors from *The Chicago Free Press*, a gay and lesbian newspaper, and from Lambda Publications, which produces several newspapers and magazines for the Chicago GLBT community. Together, these organizations may be said to represent the movement's "repertoire of contention" (Tilly 1978), providing a range of perspectives on movement objectives, strategies, and organizational resources.

There are two organizations in Chicago's GLBT movement that specialize in test case litigation: Lambda Legal Defense and Education Fund, and the American Civil Liberties Union (ACLU) of Illinois's Gay and Lesbian Rights Project. Both of these organizations are formal, bureaucratic organizations with considerable resources at their disposal. At the time of this study, Lambda's Midwest Regional office had two full-time paid attorneys, a regional director responsible for coordinating fundraising, public education, and outreach efforts, a development officer, a program assistant, and two legal and administrative assistants. The Midwest office also draws on resources from the national headquarters in New York City for public education/public relations. The ACLU of Illinois is also a formal, bureaucratic organization with a professional staff. Its Lesbian and Gay Rights Project has access to the considerable resources of the ACLU's eight-person development team and public education department as well as two full-time staff attorneys.

The Complementarity of Litigation and Other Social Movement Tactics

Sociolegal scholars have argued that successful legal mobilization strategies depend on deploying legal skills in ways that specifically complement other forms of movement activity (Scheingold 1974; McCann 1994). An analysis of interorganizational relations in the Chicago GLBT movement finds that most legal advocacy organizations regularly deployed their legal expertise to assist nonlegal movement organizations in their efforts. But the complementarity of expertise was in most cases *unidirectional.* There was little evidence that law organizations in turn relied on the expertise of, or input from nonlegal GLBT organizations.

All of the activists interviewed for this study shared a sophisticated understanding of social reform. Viewing social change as resulting from a combination of political, legal, and cultural reform, activists regarded all social movement strategies and tactics as *necessary but not sufficient* tools for social change (cf., McCann and Silverstein 1998). Rather than spread organizational resources and expertise thin by trying to engage in multiple venues or strategies, activists felt that organizations should develop expertise in just one aspect of social reform, deploying their specialized focus on behalf of the overall movement (Levitsky 2005). Juanita Crespo[2] of Amigas Latinas, an organization for Latina lesbians and bisexuals, relied on the metaphor of the body in making this point: Each part of the body does specific, often very different tasks, but they are all connected. For the body to work effectively, the individual parts must work together. Within the Chicago GLBT movement, there was in fact a great deal of interaction among organizations specializing in different strategies, including legal reform. Interviews suggested five specific ways in which wide-ranging constituencies had been assisted by the expertise of legal advocacy groups.

First, some organizations relied on legal advocacy organizations as a source of legal expertise. Amigas Latinas, for example, organized a number of enormously popular legal workshops for its members in which attorneys from Lambda Legal Defense provided information on custody and other family law issues. Similarly, the ACLU worked with the Gay, Lesbian, Straight Educational Network of Chicago (GLSEN/Chicago) to publish and distribute an informational brochure on school nondiscrimination and harassment policies.

Second, some organizations pointed to specific cases that have directly helped their constituencies. Renee Olgetree of Chicago Black Lesbians and Gays, described being "forever indebted" to Lambda for its assistance in suing on behalf of local gay and lesbian African Americans to march in Chicago's Bud Billiken parade, one of the country's largest African American parades. Evette Cardona of Amigas Latinas noted that the clients in Lambda's second-parent adoption success were two Latina lesbians. Staff members at AIDS Legal Council applauded Lambda's efforts in cosponsoring a suit against Mutual of Omaha for capping HIV insurance coverage in violation of the Americans with Disabilities Act.

Third, activists across all organizations expressed a deep appreciation for the public education achieved from well-publicized lawsuits (cf., McCann 1994). Some asserted that press coverage not only makes more people aware of GLBT issues, but it also helps people suffering from discrimination to realize they are not alone, that the issues with which they are wrestling are collective, rather than individual problems. Other activists noted that lawsuit publicity helps put a human face on an otherwise abstract issue. Note that in these cases it is not the litigation itself that activists perceived as valuable, but the publicity associated with the litigation. Susan Curry, former Executive Director of AIDS Legal Council of Chicago, articulated this distinction well:

> [I]t's the publicizing of litigation or litigating in tandem with public relations... [that] can be a powerful social reform tool. Obviously, if you just litigate quietly and get the best outcome for your client or clients, that's great. But that's not going to have any of the impact you'd desire for the greater class without any kind of spin.... [People] have to read the *Chicago Tribune*, see it on the news, and it has to be in their face for them to get used to it, to learn.

The fourth way in which activists valued legal advocacy involved its mobilizing potential, even around litigation campaigns that have *not* been successful. For example, a number of activists noted the responses around the country to the Supreme Court's ruling in *Boy Scouts of America v. Dale*, in which the Court upheld the Boy Scouts' exclusionary antigay membership policy. In response to the court ruling, demonstrations occurred around the country, and many schools and city governments (Chicago included) voted to deny Boy Scouts access to funds and facilities. These in turn increased visibility for the movement and publicized the issue of GLBT discrimination.

The fifth and final way in which activists integrated the work of legal advocates with their own, involved the role of legal rights in fostering a sense of pride and self-confidence in one's sexual identity. Many activists believed that the most effective way of achieving fundamental social change on issues relating to sexual orientation is to "come out." To the extent that antidiscrimination legislation and lawsuits protect people from some of the negative consequences of coming out, legal rights were perceived to be a critical prerequisite. In this regard, Lambda Legal Defense and Education Fund and the ACLU worked closely with Equality Illinois, a statewide lobbying organization, in drafting antidiscrimination legislation at the city, county, and state levels, and in subsequently *defending* newly enacted legislation against legal challenges. Art Johnston, cofounder of Equality Illinois, commented on the empowering effects of these legal protections:

> When I go to the gay and lesbian association in Decatur who meet in a church basement on a Saturday night after dark, and park their cars blocks away so nobody can see them walking to this place, even though it doesn't say "gay meeting" on it. When I see what they go through, when I see them wearing name tags that say "Joe M." and "Mary C." and usually those names aren't even the truth.... That's when I know that this stuff changes things.... [I]f you carry the burden for a certain amount of time, you don't even know you're carrying the burden anymore. You don't even know it. But when it's lifted, suddenly I mean, I've got to tell you what happened in [Chicago] in the six, eight, nine months after we passed [the antidiscrimination ordinance]. It was like watching everybody suddenly stand up straight. It was a remarkable experience.

The ways in which activists describe legal advocacy organizations as being valuable then—as sources of legal expertise or organizational assistance, as vehicles for public education, and as tools for mobilization and coming out—suggest that legal activity plays an important role in a wide variety of social movement strategies. Yet, if there is evidence that attorneys and staff members from legal advocacy groups deployed their expertise in ways that assisted other forms of movement activity, it is notable that they rarely solicited assistance or advice from protest, service, or cultural organizations in their own legal efforts. Those cases in which legal advocacy groups assisted nonlegal organizations typically involved lawyers doing work *for* rather than *with* other activists. One consequence of the one-sidedness in cooperative relations was a perception among many activists that law organizations operated *independently* of the rest of the movement.

Many of the activists in the study, for example, mentioned they thought that the agendas of legal advocacy organizations were formulated in an insular, exclusionary way, without consultation with other organizations in the movement. Chris Smith, cofounder of Affinity, an organization for African American lesbians, described the "disconnect" between the agendas of legal advocates and her organization's constituents: "Not that the work isn't good, not that the people involved aren't passionate, but it feels very removed." Indeed, *all* of the respondents from five of the most notable Chicago GLBT service organizations organized around racial and ethnic identities, as well activists from more radical protest organizations such as Queer to the Left and the Chicago Anti-Bashing Network, spoke of feeling "removed" from the legal rights strategies that had been articulated by legal advocacy organizations in the movement.

Lawyers themselves acknowledged that Lambda and the ACLU had a reputation in some GLBT constituencies as being "white" or "elitist" organizations. The perception of racial bias, attorneys noted, was partly based on demographics— all of the attorneys and staff principals at Lambda and the ACLU of Illinois at the time of this study were white. Lawyers attributed the "elitist" reputation of their organizations largely to processes of case selection and development. The former head of the ACLU's Gay and Lesbian Project noted for example that lawsuits provide few opportunities for grassroots or client participation: "The strategy calls are being made between the plaintiffs and lawyers...mostly the lawyers." Another attorney from the ACLU observed that there are sometimes good reasons for attorneys to avoid seeking input from other organizations in the movement:

> Lawyers being lawyers believe that there are two classes of people in this world. And one class is lawyers and the rest is the vast serf class out there, and I think there is some real snobbery towards activists and some idea that we ought to exclude the views of those who aren't lawyers. And you know, it's not wholly unwarranted. You can't have a group like Act-Up picking your litigation strategy for you because you may be getting some places you don't want to go very quickly. And that's not to pick on Act-Up. It's just that...litigation really is kind of incremental. You know, it creeps along and activists generally are not comfortable with a creep-along model, and lawyers generally are not real comfortable with a "Hey, I'm going to show up and throw pig blood at the Pope."

Attorneys and staff members at legal advocacy organizations insisted that before they take on any case, they take the time to generate input from the community. Pat Logue, supervising attorney at Lambda Legal Defense: "I think what's important is having a sense of responsibility as a lawyer that you represent the community, you don't represent yourself. You represent Lambda, you represent a client, but you also really represent the community, and . . . it's incumbent on you to know what's going on in that community." Matthew Roberts, also of Lambda Legal Defense, concurred: "We don't operate like . . . on-high authorities. The attorneys will look really hard and carefully to identify other attorneys, other community groups, anyone that can sort of help fill in the picture so we really know whether it makes sense to pursue a case." When, for example, Lambda was debating whether to bring a second-parent adoption appeal to the Ohio Supreme Court, Logue solicited input from lawyers all over Ohio who specialize in gay rights work to get a sense of the political pros and cons in bringing the case. It is notable, however, that the outreach efforts of legal advocacy groups tended to focus first and foremost on other *attorneys* and not on local grassroots organizations.

The perception among many organizational leaders that the priorities of their constituencies were not reflected in the litigation agendas of advocacy organizations can be attributed in part to the organizational structure of legal advocacy organizations: there are few opportunities for the grassroots GLBT community to meaningfully articulate their views or influence the decision making of formal, bureaucratic organizations such as Lambda or the ACLU. And the limited formal mechanisms that do exist for community outreach do little to overcome racial/ethnic or class divisions in Chicago. One important gauge of community concerns at Lambda, for example, is the number of intake calls they receive on any given issue. At the time of this study, the Lambda office received approximately 600 intake calls a year, and attorneys used these calls to identify the recurring problems in the community. Yet, interviews with other attorneys and activists in the community suggested that Lambda has poor name-recognition and visibility in communities of color in Chicago. As a consequence, the intake calls received by Lambda are unlikely to represent the concerns of the nonwhite, nonmiddle class GLBT community. As one staff member at Lambda tellingly noted, "Our community is so diverse, there are certainly areas of concern that we might not be attacking and might not be tackling, that people think well, you guys are behind. And I can't tell you what those are."

Thus there is evidence to support the claim that legal advocacy organizations are committed to deploying their skills and expertise in ways that complement and support the work of other social movement activities. But the nature of these cooperative relationships was in this case strikingly unidirectional; as a consequence, many activists voiced concern that legal strategies were being formulated and implemented independently of the rest of the movement. Some grassroots leaders also expressed concern that in trying to promote and publicize their constituents' interests and the actions of their organizations, they simply could not compete with the financial and professional resources available to Lambda and the ACLU. The following section considers the issue of resource disparities in light of the debate over whether lawyers and litigation strategies disproportionately influence the direction of movement activity.

Leading the Movement with Law

Responding to the contention that litigation strategies tend to dominate social movement efforts, some sociolegal scholars have argued that lawyers in heterogeneous social movements rarely occupy leadership roles in the movement or command the authority to lure others toward litigation strategies (Hunt 1990; McCann and Silverstein 1998). The analysis of interorganizational relations in the Chicago GLBT movement suggests that legal advocacy organizations can and do occupy an influential role in the movement due largely to the organizational resources of these groups relative to the rest of the GLBT community. Indeed, many activists in this study, particularly activists of color and self-identified radical leftists, expressed considerable resentment over the tendency of legal advocacy organizations to set the agenda for the rest of the movement without grassroots participation. This dynamic is perhaps most clearly illustrated with the issue of gay marriage.

In 1990, three gay couples applied for marriage licenses in Hawaii to challenge the state's ban on same-sex marriages.[3] According to Pat Logue, supervising attorney at Lambda Legal Defense, both the ACLU and Lambda initially tried to discourage the individual plaintiffs from filing lawsuits. It was only when the plaintiffs chose to go forward anyway, that Lambda took up their case. When the Hawaii Supreme Court issued a decision in 1993 in favor of the plaintiffs, Lambda initiated a nation-wide Marriage Campaign among GLBT organizations to prepare for the political backlash. It was this publicity and organizing campaign—more than the litigation itself—that engendered controversy in the Chicago GLBT community.

Nearly all of the activists of color and self-identified radical leftists in this study independently brought up the subject of the gay marriage campaign sponsored by Lambda Legal Defense as an example of a *top-down strategy*, conceived of and implemented by attorneys with little attention to the needs and desires of the greater GLBT community. "I don't remember Lambda ever consulting anybody about a strategy," remarked Jeff Edwards of Queer to the Left. "I don't remember any community-wide discussion about where Lambda should be going." Another member of Queer to the Left observed that Lambda's role in the marriage campaign was much more than representing three couples in Hawaii: "[I]t wasn't just about we're going to represent these three people and we're going to make an issue of this in Hawaii. This was we are going to make a national campaign, this is going to be the lead issue and this is why people need to come out in support. I mean, they completely hijacked the movement for quite a while and I think we still face the remnants."

Renee Ogletree, cofounder of Chicago Black Lesbian and Gays also brought up the issue of gay marriage: "What seems to drive the rights issue is . . . gay [marriage.] You go into the black lesbigay community and ask them what are the most important things to you and you will not hear marriage. . . . What you will hear are employment and housing. . . . " Neena Hemmady, cofounder of Khuli Zaban, an organization for South Asian and Middle Eastern lesbians and bisexuals, echoed this sentiment: "[F]ighting for marriage rights, for example, is something Lambda has definitely put resources into. Now, from my perspective, you know, marriage is not the number one priority for us as a community. I feel like marriage is important, and yes it would give validation in huge ways, but if there's people that don't have enough food to eat, you know, where is our sense of priority?"

Although all of these activists generally spoke very positively of the work of legal advocacy organizations, they returned again and again to the point that these organizations have "forced" their issues onto the rest of the movement. One activist noted she felt like the legal advocacy organizations were trying to "create" issues for the movement:

> It's like the litigation's put first and then the movement's needs are put second. . . . [N]ow the issue is if we could just get marriage. And that's what we think gay people really need. If we could just get marriage, then we would stop facing discrimination and blahblahblah. Let's put all our money, let's put all our effort in and then oh we lose that. You know, and then what are we left with now?

Another activist echoed this: "[T]he bottom line is that I don't think [legal advocacy organizations] are part of a larger . . . community-wide talk about what's the next step. Sort of like marriage is on the agenda, great. Let's do it." Interestingly, even staff members at the legal advocacy organizations suggested that the way they publicize their work sometimes involves a top-down approach.

"One of the things we continually have to do . . . is to get people to think well, this isn't just something that lawyers get worried about. Or even worse, that this isn't just something that gay lawyers get worried about. . . . So it's continually a challenge of . . . trying to articulate why are these issues broadly important."

The perception among grassroots activists that Lambda "hijacked" the movement with its sponsorship of the Marriage Campaign grew largely out of the *structural* fact that legal advocacy organizations, like most formal, bureaucratic organizations, have considerably more resources than the grassroots organizations that make up the bulk of the movement. With budgets that dwarf those of the rest of the GLBT community and a full-time professional staff, the legal advocacy organizations in this study were able to achieve a high degree of visibility for their actions relative to other organizations in the movement. In particular, the legal advocacy organizations had both financial and human resources to devote exclusively to the media, and this had an effect on how their goals and activities were portrayed in the press. Two editors of the *Chicago Free Press*, the city's largest gay newspaper, noted that professionalized organizations tend to be more press savvy than grassroots organizations, and their press savviness tends to lead to better—and often more frequent—stories. Louis Weisberg, the Editor-in-Chief of *Chicago Free Press* explains:

> [Professional organizations] know how to respond to the press, they understand our deadlines and things like that, they know what kind of information we need. . . . [W]ith a paper like ours that has a very small staff, we don't have someone who's covering [the] city and the courthouse. . . . We rely on those organizations to get us the news. . . . So organizations that are regularly faxing us and emailing us what they're doing, they do get a lot more coverage.

The ease with which these organizations access the gay and mainstream media stands in stark contrast to the smaller grassroots organizations in Chicago. With the exception of the direct action/agitprop groups (whose activities, according to gay journalists, tend to disproportionately attract media attention for their visuals), most of the grassroots organizations in this study struggled with the issue of media access, finding they had neither the money nor the human resources to actively court the media for attention.

The resources of legal advocacy organizations, then, and the way they are wielded in the media, reinforced the perception among activists that these organizations dominate the movement in terms of size, sophistication, and visibility. Such findings suggest that the sociolegal characterization of social movements as a field of differently specialized, but equivalently positioned organizations may underestimate the influence that legal advocacy organizations have on movement activity. Legal advocacy organizations were perceived by many activists as not only selecting issues to litigate without grassroots participation, but also promoting those issues in ways that "crowded out" other GLBT interests. This form of movement "domination" is accomplished not by individual lawyers who command the authority to steer the movement in any particular direction, but by the kinds and quantities of resources available to legal advocacy organizations relative to their grassroots peers.

The Consequences of Leading with Law: Conclusions

What then are the consequences of leading with law? Why does it matter that legal advocacy organizations choose not to consult with or rely on the expertise and tactics of other movement organizations, so long as they are deploying their own expertise in beneficial ways? This chapter concludes by briefly considering two ways in which the dominance of legal advocacy organizations in social movements compromises—or tempers—the emancipatory potential of cause lawyering as a social movement strategy.

One consequence of the perception that legal advocacy organizations are "going it alone" or "hijacking the movement" is that legal strategies will become disconnected from the movement's political/cultural strategies, leaving the movement vulnerable not only to political backlash, but also to legal victories that cannot be translated into social reform. This is again illustrated with the issue of same-sex marriage. After the initial court victory in Hawaii, the political backlash sustained by the GLBT movement was substantial: By 1998, Hawaii citizens had not only voted to amend its constitution to ban same-sex marriage, but also twenty-six state legislatures had passed statutes banning recognition of same-sex marriages, and President Clinton had signed into law the Defense of Marriage Act. Five years later, history repeated itself: Following another legal victory in Massachusetts,[4] in which the state supreme court held the prohibition against same-sex marriage to be unconstitutional, the GLBT movement again felt the brunt of political backlash: In the November 2004 election, eleven states overwhelmingly voted to amend their constitutions to prohibit same-sex marriage. Although GLBT litigation groups, both in Chicago and nationally, have done a remarkable job coordinating their *legal* efforts (resulting in a series of legal victories on same-sex marriage), many leaders and grassroots activists have speculated that the lack of coordination between litigation groups and the rest of the movement has cost the movement dearly. In the weeks after the November 2004 election, Matt Foreman, executive director of the National Gay and Lesbian Task Force, a national gay rights organization, reflected on the co-ordination problem: "There is no putting lipstick on this pig," he told *The New York Times*. "Our legal strategy is at least 10 years ahead of our political and legislative strategy" (Liptak 2004).

It is this separation between legal and political/cultural strategies that led to the initial critique of planned litigation as a social movement tactic (Scheingold 1974). That we can find such stark evidence of this legal/political disconnect in social movements today, despite evidence that attorneys are quite cognizant of the limitations of legal strategies (see, e.g., McCann and Silverstein 1998), suggests that the division may be more a result of *interorganizational* dynamics than the misguided legal consciousness of individual attorneys and activists.

A second consequence of the lopsidedness of interorganizational relations between legal advocacy groups and other organizations in the movement re-lates to the capacity of legal advocates to represent the movement's diverse constituencies. Bureaucratic, "professionalized" organizations have long been vulnerable to the charge that without grassroots participation, they cannot know—or represent—the concerns of the movement's diverse constituencies.[5] For the legal advocacy organization, whose responsibility it is to litigate cases designed to make law for an entire "community," this is an especially potent critique (see Bell 1975–76; Rubenstein 1997). With few opportunities for GLBT constituents to participate in the organizational activities or decision making of litigation groups beyond checkwriting, placing intake calls, or filing lawsuits (Barclay and Fisher 2006), how can attorneys in these organizations effectively collect information on the needs and interests of their "client"? And, conversely, what mechanisms are available to grassroots activists for holding cause lawyers accountable for their strategic decisions (Marshall 2006)? As the professional-ized legal advocacy organization becomes institutionalized across social move-ments, these concerns about accountability and representation warrant further scrutiny, as they have important implications for not only how, but also on whose behalf litigation strategies are deployed.

Notes

1. This is not to say that there are not limitations to the professionalized organi-zational form: *non* bureaucratic organizations are often more effective at mobilizing grassroots participation (Zald and Ash 1966; Robnett 1997), providing movements with a source of tactical innovation (Staggenborg 1989), and creating long-term commitments (Gamson 1991; Polletta 2002).

2. All activists quoted in this study gave permission to use their real names.

3. For an excellent account of the Hawaii same-sex marriage case and its political aftermath, see Goldberg-Hiller (2002).

4. *Goodridge v. Department of Public Health* (November 18, 2003).

5. Thus, the largest women's movement organizations have been accused of ignoring the interests of women of color, working class women, and lesbians and bisexuals (Travis 1986; Ryan 1992; Seidman 1993). The leading black civil rights advocacy groups and leadership have been accused of silencing gays and lesbians (Hemphill 1991; Phelan 1993; Cohen 1996) and those with biracial or multiracial identities (Gamson 1995).

References

Albiston, Catherine R. and Laura Beth Nielsen. 2003. "Mapping Law and Social Reform in the New Millennium: Results from a National Random Sample of Public Interest Law Organizations in the United States." Paper presented at the 2003 Law and Society Meeting.

Barclay, Scott and Shauna Fisher. 2006. "Cause Lawyers in the First Wave of Same Sex Marriage Litigation." in *Cause Lawyers and Social Movements*, edited by Austin Sarat and Stuart A. Scheingold. Stanford: Stanford University Press, pp. XXX.

Barclay, Scott and Anna-Maria Marshall. 2005. "Supporting a Cause, Developing a Movement, and Consolidating a Practice: Cause Lawyers and Sexual Orientation Litigation in Vermont." in *The Worlds Cause Lawyers Make: Structure and Agency in Legal Practice*, edited by Austin Sarat and Stuart A. Scheingold. Stanford: Stanford University Press, pp. 171–202.

Bell, Derrick A. 1975–76. "Serving Two Masters: Integration Ideals and Client Interests in School Desegregation Litigation." *Yale Law Journal* 85: 470–516.

Bumiller, Kristin. 1988. *The Civil Rights Society: The Social Construction of Victims*. Baltimore: Johns Hopkins University Press.

Cohen, Cathy J. 1996. "Contested Membership: Black Gay Identities and the Politics of AIDS." in *Queer Theory/Sociology*, edited by Steven Seidman. Oxford: Blackwell Publishers, pp. 362–94.

Coutin, Susan Bibler. 2001. "Cause Lawyering in the Shadow of the State: A US Immigration Example." in *Cause Lawyering and the State in a Global Era*, edited by Austin Sarat and Stuart A. Scheingold. New York: Oxford University Press, pp. 117–40.

den Dulk, Kevin. 2001. *Prophets in Caesar's Courts: The Role of Ideas in Catholic and Evangelical Rights Advocacy*. Unpublished doctoral dissertation, University of Wisconsin.

Epp, Charles R. 1998. *The Rights Revolution: Lawyers, Activists, and Supreme Courts in Comparative Perspective*. Chicago: University of Chicago Press.

Epstein, Lee. 1985. *Conservatives in Court*. Knoxville, TN: University of Tennessee Press.

Gabel, Peter and Duncan Kennedy. 1984. "Roll Over Beethoven." *Stanford Law Review* 36: 26.

Galanter, Marc. 1983. "The Radiating Effects of Courts." in *Empirical Theories About Courts*, edited by Keith O. Boyum and Lynn Mather. New York: Longman, pp. 117–42.

Gamson, Joshua. 1995. "Must Identity Movements Self-Destruct? A Queer Dilemma." *Social Problems* 42: 390–407.

Gamson, William A. 1975. *The Strategy of Social Protest*. Homewood, IL: Dorsey Press.

———. 1991. "Commitment and Agency in Social Movements." *Sociological Forum* 6: 27–50.

Glendon, Mary Ann. 1991. *Rights Talk: The Impoverishment of Political Discourse*. New York: Free Press.

Goldberg-Hiller, Jonathan. 2002. *The Limits to Union: Same-Sex Marriage and the Politics of Civil Rights*. Ann Arbor, MI: University of Michigan Press.

Gusfield, Joseph. 1967. "Moral Passage: The Symbolic Process in Public Designations of Deviance." *Social Problems* 15: 175–88.

Handler, Joel F. 1978. *Social Movements and the Legal System*. New York: Academic Press.

Hemphill, Essex (ed.). 1991. *Brother to Brother*. Boston: Alyson.

Horowitz, Donald L. 1977. *Courts and Social Policy*. Washington, DC: Brookings Institution.

Hunt, Alan. 1990. "Rights and Social Movements: Counter-Hegemonic Strategies." *Journal of Law and Society* 17: 309–28.

Kilwein, John. 1998. "Still Trying: Cause Lawyering for the Poor and Disadvantaged in Pittsburgh, Pennsylvania." in *Cause Lawyering: Political Commitments and Professional Responsibilities*, edited by Austin Sarat and Stuart A. Scheingold. New York: Oxford University Press, pp. 181–200.

Levitsky, Sandra R. 2005. "Niche Activism: Negotiating Organizational Heterogeneity in Contemporary American Social Movements." Paper presented at the 2005 American Sociological Association Meeting.

Liptak, Adam. 2004. "Caution in Court for Gay Rights Groups." *The New York Times* November 12: 16.

Marshall, Anna-Maria. 2006. "Social Movement Strategies and the Participatory Potential of Litigation." in *Cause Lawyers and Social Movements*, edited by Austin Sarat and Stuart A. Scheingold. Stanford: Stanford University Press, pp. 164–181.

McCann, Michael. 1994. *Rights at Work: Pay Equity Reform and the Politics of Legal Mobilization*. Chicago: University of Chicago Press.

———. 1998. "How Does Law Matter for Social Movements?" in *How Does Law Matter?: Fundamental Issues in Law and Society*, edited by B. Garth and A. Sarat. Evanston, IL: Northwestern University Press, pp. 76–108.

McCann, Michael and Helena Silverstein. 1998. "Rethinking Law's 'Allurements': A Relational Analysis of Social Movement Lawyers in the United States." in *Cause Lawyering: Political Commitments and Professional Responsibilities*, edited by Austin Sarat and Stuart Scheingold. New York: Oxford University Press, pp. 261–92.

McCarthy, John D. and Mayer N. Zald. 1973. *The Trend of Social Movements in America: Professionalization and Resource Mobilization*. Morristown, NJ: General Learning Press.

———. 1977. "Resource Mobilization and Social Movements: A Partial Theory." *American Journal of Sociology* 82: 1212–41.

Menkel-Meadow, Carrie. 1998. "The Causes of Cause Lawyering: Toward an Understanding of the Motivation and Commitment of Social Justice Lawyers." in *Cause Lawyering: Political Commitments and Professional Responsibilities*, edited by Austin Sarat and Stuart A. Scheingold. New York: Oxford University Press, pp. 31–68.

Minkoff, Debra C. 1997. "Organizational Mobilizations, Institutional Access, and Institutional Change." in *Women Transforming Politics: An Alternative Reader*, edited by Cathy J. Cohen, Kathleen B. Jones, and Joan C. Tronto. New York: New York University Press, pp. 477–96.

———. 1999. "Bending with the Wind: Strategic Change and Adaptation by Women's and Racial Minority Organizations." *American Journal of Sociology* 104: 1666–703.

Morag-Levine, Noga. 2001. "The Politics of Imported Rights: Transplantation and Transformation in an Israeli Environmental Cause-Lawyering Organization." in *Cause Lawyering and the State in a Global Era*, edited by Austin Sarat and Stuart A. Scheingold. New York: Oxford University Press, pp. 334–53.

O'Connor, Karen. 1980. *Women's Organizations' Use of the Courts*. Lexington, MA: Lexington Books.

Olson, Susan M. 1984. *Clients and Lawyers: Securing the Rights of Disabled Persons*. Westport, CT: Greenwood Press.

Phelan, Shane. 1993. "(Be) Coming Out: Lesbian Identity and Politics." *Signs* 18: 765–90.

Polletta, Francesca. 2002. *Freedom is an Endless Meeting: Democracy in American Social Movements*. Chicago: University of Chicago Press.

Robnett, Belinda. 1997. *How Long? How Long?: African American Women in the Struggle for Civil Rights*. New York: Oxford University Press.

Rosenberg, Gerald N. 1991. *The Hollow Hope: Can Courts Bring About Social Change?* Chicago: University of Chicago Press.

Rubenstein, William B. 1997. "Divided We Litigate: Addressing Disputes Among Group Members and Lawyers in Civil Rights Campaigns." *Yale Law Journal* 106: 1623–81.

Ryan, Barbara. 1992. *Feminism and the Women's Movement*. New York: Routledge.

Scheingold, Stuart A. 1974. *The Politics of Rights: Lawyers, Public Policy, and Political Change*. New Haven, CT: Yale University Press.

———. 1998. "The Struggle to Politicize Legal Practice: A Case Study of Left-Activist Lawyering in Seattle." in *Cause Lawyering: Political Commitments and Professional Responsibilities*, edited by Austin Sarat and Stuart A. Scheingold. New York: Oxford University Press, pp. 118–48.

Scheingold, Stuart A. and Austin Sarat. 2004. *Something to Believe In: Politics, Professionalism, and Cause Lawyering*. Stanford: Stanford University Press.

Schneider, Elizabeth M. 1986. "The Dialectic of Rights and Politics: Perspectives from the Women's Movement." *New York University Law Review* 61: 589–652.

Seidman, Steven. 1993. "Identity and Politics in a 'Postmodern' Gay Culture: Some Historical and Conceptual Notes." in *Fear of a Queer Planet: Queer Politics and Social Theory*, edited by Michael Warner. Minneapolis, MN: University of Minnesota Press, pp. 105–42.

Staggenborg, Suzanne. 1989. "Stability and Innovation in the Women's Movement: A Comparison of Two Movement Organizations." *Social Problems* 36: 75–92.

Tarrow, Sidney. 1998. *Power in Movement*. Cambridge: Cambridge University Press.

Tilly, Charles. 1978. *From Mobilization to Revolution*. Reading, MA: Addison-Wesley.

Travis, Toni-Michelle. 1986. *Women as an Emerging Power Bloc: Ethnic and Racial Considerations*. Madison, WI: University of Wisconsin.

Tushnet, Mark. 1984. "An Essay on Rights." *Texas Law Review* 62: 1363.

White, Lucie. 1987. "Mobilization on the Margins of the Lawsuit: Making Space for Clients to Speak." *New York University Review of Law and Social Change* 16: 535–64.

Zald, Mayer and Roberta Ash. 1966. "Social Movement Organizations: Growth, Decay, and Change." *Social Forces* 44: 327–341.

Social Movement Strategies and the Participatory Potential of Litigation

ANNA-MARIA MARSHALL

Cause lawyering research is generating an increasingly detailed picture of the working conditions of attorneys who pursue political projects through their legal work. This research has asked and answered questions about cause lawyers' legal education, their ideological commitments, and the organization of their legal practices. More broadly, this work has explored the role of cause lawyers in the profession—how they experience tension between their roles as attorneys and activists—and the place of these lawyers in political and social struggles. This chapter, however, adopts a movement-centered perspective that focuses on the ambivalent role played by cause lawyers in social movements. Although attorneys pursue legal and political strategies, movements do not unquestioningly welcome their contributions. Rather, the tension between the myth of rights to the politics of rights runs through many social movements, generating debates about the effectiveness of legal strategies and the wisdom of hiring lawyers.

These debates are prevalent in the environmental justice movement. Environmental justice activists want to reclaim environmental decision making from the politicians, lawyers, and scientists who dominate the policy processes to make those processes more receptive to public participation. Legal strategies compromise those goals because they depend on lawyers who are often considered movement outsiders and on the courts that are seen as formal channels of political influence, captive of hostile corporations and government agencies. In spite of this skepticism, environmental justice movements continue to pursue lawsuits based on civil rights, environmental, and tort claims. Yet litigation in the environmental justice movement is characterized by high levels of grassroots participation, both in the preparation for the case and in the mobilization surrounding the lawsuit. In this chapter, I argue that cause lawyers in the environmental justice movement are largely responsible for unleashing the participatory potential of this litigation.

Cause Lawyers and Social Movement Strategies

Social movements face conflicting demands when choosing their strategies and tactics. "The ideal movement strategy is one that is convincing with respect to political authorities, legitimate with respect to potential supporters, rewarding with respect to those already active in the movement, and novel in the eyes of the mass media. These are not entirely compatible demands" (Rochon 1998: 109). Movements reconcile these competing demands by drawing on "repertoires of contention"—the familiar forms of collective action that are culturally available. Although susceptible to innovation over time, these repertoires constrain the choices of movement activists (Tarrow 1998).

Movement repertoires often include extrainstitutional strategies, such as demonstrations, sit-ins, boycotts, and civil disobedience. Marginalized groups pursue these forms of direct action because they do not enjoy access to conventional channels of political activity (Piven and Cloward 1977; Cress and Snow 2000). Such tactics are disruptive, aimed at creating conflict to pressure elites. These more confrontational strategies appeal to loyal activists, whose participation in these struggles strengthens their bonds to the movement and helps create collective identity (Gamson 1975; Piven and Cloward 1977). Yet these disruptions risk alienating the public and policymakers whose support is often necessary to make the changes the movement seeks.

Movements also draw on more conventional strategies by interacting with powerful elites in institutional arenas where elites themselves feel most comfortable (Galanter 1974; Piven and Cloward 1977). These tactics include legislative lobbying, participating in the electoral process, and litigation (Jenkins and Eckert 1986). By invoking legitimate institutions, these tactics can broaden the appeal of a movement's message and sometimes result in policy concessions (Jenkins and Eckert 1986; Staggenborg 1988). Ironically, the availability of these institutional tactics is often the result of successful protest, but the policy concessions rarely remedy the structural problems that gave rise to the movement. Moreover, incremental policy changes can be short-lived, often withdrawn when the protests stop (Piven and Cloward 1977: 30).

In addition, institutional tactics can be demobilizing for the movement itself. Piven and Cloward noted that when protests become too threatening, elites begin offering concessions to radical groups, hoping to "channel the energies and angers of the protestors into more legitimate and less disruptive forms of political behavior . . . " (Piven and Cloward 1979: 30; Jenkins and Eckert 1986). Rather than knocking on doors and organizing protests, activists begin directing their efforts at elites, often using the complex language of law, science, urban planning, and other forms of expertise that amount to foreign languages removed from the daily lives of ordinary movement constituents (Cable, Hastings, and Mix 2002). Movements investing scarce resources in institutional strategies are much less likely to organize the direct action tactics that develop a movement. Moreover, more disruptive strategies can undermine conventional activities, which may depend on the appearance of political respectability of the movement (Piven and Cloward 1977; Cable, Hastings, and Mix 2002).

A movement's choice of tactics is shaped, in part, by its activists. First, professionals formalize movement organizations (McCarthy and Zald 1977; Staggenborg 1988). For example, their emphasis on fund-raising requires that they get grants and other financial assistance. Funding organizations, in turn, require grant recipients to keep financial records and generate reports on their activities. To respond to these requirements, social movement organizations must hire staff and develop record-keeping routines and procedures (Staggenborg 1988; Markowitz and Tice 2002). Second, professional activists tend to direct activists toward moderate, institutional strategies and away from broad demands for sweeping change (Jenkins and Eckert 1986; Staggenborg 1988). When they appeal to elites for funds, social movement organizations effectively turn away from more disruptive protest tactics that might jeopardize their funding (Jenkins and Eckert 1986). Professional activists are less likely to make broad demands for sweeping change and are more likely to settle for symbolic victories, which in turn demobilize moderates who are satisfied with symbolic achievements and much less interested in the way those achievements are implemented (Scheingold 1974 [2004]; Jenkins and Eckert 1986).

Because of their elite training and expertise, cause lawyers are often considered movement professionals who, like other professional activists, direct social movements toward institutional arenas and away from direct action. Because of their legal training, cause lawyers come to believe that most social problems have legal cures, but litigation is expensive and time-consuming (Scheingold 1974 [2004]; Menkel-Meadow 1998). In addition, litigation translates conflict into rarefied and unfamiliar jargon that must be managed and negotiated by legal professionals, such as lawyers and judges. Thus, it displaces ownership of the conflict from ordinary people, who are potential activists, and places it in the hands of elites who are often remote and distant from the struggle itself (McCann and Silverstein 1998; Menkel-Meadow 1998).

This account of movement activists and the strategies they favor relies on two different sets of assumptions that are problematized by the involvement of cause lawyers in a social movement. The first questionable assumption is that social movement strategies can be easily divided into categories of institutional and extrainstitutional, disruptive and nondisruptive tactics. Legal strategies reveal the tension in such conceptual dichotomies. Obviously, litigation relies on institutional channels of political influence and provides social movements with direct access to official policymakers—access that they might not otherwise enjoy (Burstein 1991). On the other hand, legal strategies are also inherently confrontational. Lawsuits are based on injuries and therefore can provide a forum for the direct articulation of grievances—often by ordinary people who can participate by telling their stories directly to policymakers. In addition, litigation casts those responsible for the injuries, often identifiable corporate and state elites, as wrongdoers and lawbreakers. Moreover, legal strategies—such as bailing protestors out of jail—sometimes support more disruptive tactics (Hilibink this volume). And for some social movements, all they can do is provide legal services to their poor and dispossessed constituents (Fleury-Steiner 2006; Shdaimah this volume).

The second set of problematic assumptions is that activists themselves fall neatly into categories with elites and professionals in one camp and grassroots activists in another. Yet the most recent research on cause lawyers demonstrates that such lawyers often balance competing identities as both professionals and activists (Jones 2005, this volume). As they adopt identities as grassroots activists, cause lawyers recognize that few social problems are cured with legal solutions alone. Thus, they deploy their legal skills, but only at the direction of movement leaders, preferring political mobilization and grassroots organizing to litigating cases (McCann and Silverstein 1998; Barclay and Marshall 2005; Fleury-Steiner 2006; Jones 2005, this volume; Hilibink this volume). In adopting these strategies, cause lawyers are in a better position to give voice to their clients and to members of marginalized groups (Shdaimah this volume).

Cause lawyers' identities—and the strategies they pursue—are influenced by their practice settings (McCann and Silverstein 1998; Scheingold and Sarat 2004; Barclay and Marshall 2005). Scheingold and Sarat (2004: 73) have observed: "Where one practices influences how one practices, whether one can push beyond conventional types of lawyering work to politicize practice, what one can accomplish, and—when considered in the aggregate—the capacity of cause lawyering to contribute to democracy." Given their ideological commitments and their access to broader social movement networks, salaried cause lawyers working for legal rights organizations are thought to be most likely to devote their time to political strategies other than litigation (McCann and Silverstein 1998; Scheingold and Sarat 2004). On the other hand, attorneys doing pro bono work in large law firms rarely engage in transgressive lawyering (Scheingold 1974 [2004]: xxxix; Scheingold and Sarat 2004). Cause lawyers working in small law firms may organize their practices in political ways and pursue legal strategies that reflect a more political agenda, but because of financial constraints they may have less time to pursue grassroots strategies, such as participating in protests or community organizing. Moreover, such lawyers may not have the experience with activism or connections to social movement organizations that would support a commitment to encourage more participatory strategies (McCann and Silverstein 1998).

In this chapter, I draw on examples of activists in the environmental justice movement and the strategies they choose to challenge prevailing assumptions about cause lawyers and the social movements they serve. First, I show that legal strategies in the environmental justice movement do not fit neatly into the dichotomous "institutional" and "extrainstitutional" categories. Rather, activists have developed more participatory legal strategies that are confrontational even as they seek access to conventional political channels of influence. Second, I show that the adoption of these legal strategies is only weakly related to the practice settings of the cause lawyers who pursue them.

This chapter is based on case studies of environmental justice campaigns across the United States compiled by Scott Sherman at the University of Michigan's Department of Natural Resources and Environment (Sherman 2003). Sherman's data set consists of sixty particular movements challenging environmental injustice, which Sherman defined as "the disproportionate exposure of poor communities or communities of color to environmental hazards," and not simply so-called "Not in My Backyard" (NIMBY) disputes, which could occur in any community. The cases were chosen because they were prominent campaigns that received a great deal of attention in the mass media and scholarly research. The cases were coded for a number of variables, including the type of environmental hazard in dispute, the types of strategies used, the number and nature of political allies, and the outcomes of the movement efforts. In addition to Sherman's data, I collected information about the lawyers involved in each campaign, including the practice settings in which they worked.

This data set of environmental justice campaigns is not a representative sample; such a sample would be almost impossible to compile.[1] Given the prominence of the cases, the data set consists of cases that are notable in some way, thus limiting the ability to make generalizations about the environmental justice movement based on these sixty cases. Still, there are revealing patterns—and in some cases, a lack of patterns—among these cases that can be useful in developing hypotheses about the role of legal strategies and cause lawyers in the movement.

The Movement for Environmental Justice

Grievances and Frames

Ample evidence demonstrates that environmental hazards are most likely to be located in communities where structural barriers block residents' access to the political resources necessary to protect themselves from such hazards (Bullard, 2000; Roberts and Toffolon-Weiss, 2001). Although some argue that property values are the primary explanations for the location of environmental hazards, other researchers have shown that race also influences siting decisions (Szasz 1994). Rather than isolating either race or class as a source of discrimination, at least one researcher has concluded that discrimination in environmental hazards is an "ambiguous and complicated entanglement of class, race, educational attainment, occupational patterns, relationships between the metropolitan areas and rural or non-metropolitan cities, and possibly market dynamics" (Been 1995; Bullard 2000).

The environmental justice movement is decentralized, actually made up of many individuals and small, grassroots organizations that are fighting environmental degradation in their immediate communities (Szasz 1994). Environmental justice activists tend to be poor or working-class individuals and families whose homes, jobs, or schools are located near sources of pollution. As a result of this proximity, these individuals develop serious health problems or the value of their homes dramatically declines. These problems constitute the grievances around which the movement initially mobilizes (Szasz 1994; Bullard 2000). At least one national environmental organization works primarily on environmental justice issues—the Center for Health, Environment and Justice (CHEJ). But the CHEJ's primary focus is to provide support and resources to the grassroots groups engaged in local struggles against environmental degradation (Szasz 1994).

Although the movement is by its very nature dispersed, environmental justice struggles have several common frames (Capek 1993; Szasz 1994). First and most obviously, environmental justice campaigns challenge the health and safety risks posed by environmental hazards, such as landfills and incinerators, located in poor and minority neighborhoods (Capek 1993; Szasz 1994; Cole and Foster 2001;). Second, environmental justice movements promote democratic participation in the important public decisions that affect the ordinary lives of communities. In this regard, activists in the movements aim to exercise greater control over the technical expertise and legal procedures that govern decision making (Szasz, 1994; Cable, Hastings, and Mix 2002). Finally, because these threats often materialize in poor and minority communities, activists connect environmental quality to broader issues of civil rights and social justice, including demands for better jobs, education, health care, and housing (Capek 1993; Bullard 2000).

Environmental Justice Strategies

Given this political context, environmental justice organizations deploy a variety of tactics in their efforts to challenge local pollution. Grassroots activists favor direct action tactics. Community organizations sponsor protests and civil disobedience, sometimes laying down in front of the tractors and bulldozers intended to build new facilities. The civil disobedience, in particular, has its roots in the civil rights movement (Bullard 2000). Some of these organizations also become very savvy in attracting media coverage of their protests. These tactics attract public attention to policymaking that usually occurs in secret (Szasz 1994; Cole and Foster 2001; Roberts and Toffolon-Weiss 2001). In addition, these organizations often sponsor self-education projects about science, law, and government. They even get involved in doing some of the scientific testing themselves (Szasz 1994). In addition to being judged politically effective, direct action reflects a general skepticism in the movement about the role of experts (Cable, Hastings, and Mix 2002).

However, in seeking access to official decision makers, environmental justice activists go to the sites where decisions are made by participating in institutional political channels (Roberts and Toffolon-Weiss 2001). Citizen groups may organize during political campaigns to elect sympathetic politicians (or to remove politicians who are too friendly with polluters). They also organize around the formal proceedings on the siting of environmental hazards. For example, they conduct research, file documents, and fill public hearings with local residents offering testimony about the effects of both actual and potential environmental hazards (Roberts and Toffolon-Weiss 2001). Some organizations engage in direct negotiations with corporations in "consensus-based decision making" to achieve some concessions, such as promises to devote resources to cleaning up communities. When these political channels fail to bring about desired results, some environmental justice organizations have filed lawsuits seeking enforcement of environmental laws or compensation for injuries (Cole and Foster 2001).

When using these institutional tactics, environmental justice groups must often rely on the technical expertise of others in the scientific and legal communities. Scientists and engineers measure existing levels of contaminants and make estimates about the effects of actual or proposed facilities (Cable, Hastings, and Mix 2002). Lawyers get involved by educating activists about the obscure regulatory and administrative procedures that characterize environmental decision making and by litigating disputes among activists, corporations, and the government (Cole and Foster 2001). But scientific and legal expertise is rarely free, and environmental justice organizations can find themselves raising money to hire scientists and lawyers rather than engaging in more productive and participatory oppositional strategies (Cable, Hastings, and Mix 2002). Moreover, retaining experts interferes with the movement goal of claiming power over the knowledge needed to participate in democratic decision making (Cable, Hastings, and Mix 2002).

Scholars studying the environmental justice movement portray lawyers as outsiders. Cable and her colleagues report that environmental justice activists think of lawyers as independent hired guns, not necessarily tied to the movement (Cable, Hastings, and Mix 2002). And as hired guns, lawyers are perceived as being more concerned about collecting fees than about the goals or the success of the movement. Because of their extensive education, lawyers often seem elitist, especially in their interactions with the poor and working-class activists who make up the ground troops of the movement. According to activists (and the academics who study them), lawyers are unskilled, even inept at doing the organizing necessary to build a movement (Cable, Hastings, and Mix 2002).

Even so, environmental justice organizations turn again and again to litigation to pursue their goals. This choice does not necessarily reflect a false rights consciousness, a misguided belief in the myth of rights. Rather, some environmental justice activists have tried to transform legal strategies and adapt them to the broader purposes of the movement. In the section that follows, I outline the ways in which several environmental justice campaigns have incorporated direct action into their legal strategies.

The Participatory Potential of Legal Action

Environmental justice activists and scholars often warn about the dangers in the "lure of litigation." For example, one lawyer in the movement, Ron Simon, cautioned activists: "The most common mistake I have seen is that people believe they can hire a lawyer and stop all the work (reading, organizing, speaking, going to meetings) that has brought the cause along. Too many times, hiring the lawyer is the death knell to all other activities—a terrible mistake" (Simon 1985). In these accounts, litigation crowds out other social movement strategies, demobilizing the grassroots efforts and establishing the lawyers as the decision makers for the movement.

On the other hand, many environmental justice movement campaigns include litigation as one of many strategies. In many of these struggles, movement organizations were led not by lawyers but by the grassroots activists most directly affected by the environmental hazards being challenged, who opted for political tactics and direct action in addition to legal strategies. Indeed, the litigation proceeded in the midst of media campaigns, citizen research projects, as well as protests and demonstrations. And behind the litigation were committed attorneys who did not relegate themselves to courtroom activities but who took an active part in developing and contributing to the movement's other tactics.

Mass Media Campaigns

Many have observed that social movements use litigation to draw public attention to their struggles (Scheingold 1974 [2004]; Olson 1984; McCann 1994). In this long tradition, environmental justice campaigns often seek to publicize the plight of ordinary citizens whose health and safety are being endangered by corporate greed and governmental indifference. These media campaigns are designed to win favorable public opinion and support and to shame public officials into being more protective of the environment in poor and minority communities. Although lawyers may sometimes try to dissuade activists from seeking too much publicity to avoid antagonizing judges and prospective juries, cause lawyers in the environmental justice movement have used the mass media to publicize corporate and governmental wrongdoing uncovered in the course of litigation.

For example, in St. James Parish, Louisiana, Shintech Corporation wanted to build a plastics manufacturing plant on the banks of the Mississippi River. The plant would have joined a large number of other industrial plants, all of which were contributing to the pollution in the area. The plan to build the factory there immediately created a political conflict in the parish, pitting supporters of development against those concerned by increased water and air pollution. This cleavage also divided the largely poor African-American community in the area. Some African-Americans believed that the plant would bring much-needed jobs to their community, while others worried about the health risks associated with increased pollution levels (Roberts and Toffolon-Weiss 2001; Sherman 2003).

The citizens' group, St. James Citizens for Jobs and the Environment (SJCJE), was a coalition of many of the poor citizens of St. James parish and included both black and white residents. Its leaders consisted largely of middle-aged and elderly women who did not want to engage in civil disobedience or protests, so their strategies consisted largely of gathering powerful political allies, lobbying political officials, and pursuing administrative remedies and lawsuits. Although they worked with Greenpeace, they warned the environmental organization that they would not participate in any confrontational or unconventional tactics. Early on, however, they decided that they wanted legal representation and finally got the Tulane University Environmental Law Clinic to file lawsuits and environmental complaints (Roberts and Toffolon-Weiss 2001; Sherman 2003).

In the discovery phase of the legal proceedings, the Clinic uncovered evidence that exposed the many connections between the Louisiana Department of Environmental Quality (DEQ) and Shintech. The Clinic hired private investigators to follow DEQ officers and Shintech executives and found that they had secret meetings late at night. In the course of discovery, the Clinic found memoranda where Shintech public relations officers offered to assist the DEQ in creating the best possible record justifying the location of the plant. The SJCJE and the Law Clinic publicized this cozy relationship between the DEQ and the polluters, generating an enormous amount of adverse publicity for the many state actors, including Governor Mike Foster (Roberts and Toffolon-Weiss 2001; Sherman 2003). Thus, the discovery stages of a lawsuit can bring to light facts that vividly illustrate corporate and governmental wrongdoing, but cause lawyers and activists must work closely together through all stages of litigation to publicize those facts.

Citizen Research

Environmental justice campaigns try to empower ordinary people to take control over the decision making that affects their lives. Resisting the scientific and legalistic jargons in which environmental policymaking is conducted, environmental justice advocates struggle to master these forms of knowledge so that they can understand and challenge public officials and corporate agents who adopt rules and issue permits to polluters. This mastery is vital to effective participation in the democratic process surrounding environmental policies. Thus, citizen research in science and law is crucial to ongoing environmental justice campaigns.

For example, in Anniston, Alabama, community residents demanded relocation and clean up of PCB contamination spread by a nearby Monsanto plant. Residents collected soil and water samples in the neighborhood and helped scientists conduct basic testing of those samples. The studies they helped produce were used to undermine Monsanto's claims that the PCB levels in the community were at safe levels. In addition, the studies were used in several lawsuits filed against Monsanto. Monsanto finally relocated the neighborhood in settlement of some of these cases (Sherman 2003).

Ordinary citizens also engage in legal research when they do not have resources to pay lawyers. In Jacksonville, Arkansas, People Against Chemically Contaminated Environment challenged an incinerator operating in a rural, poor, white neighborhood. Working with Greenpeace and the National Toxics Campaign, residents did research on all the different federal laws that the incinerator was violating. In addition, local citizens cooperated with scientific tests of the air in the vicinity of the incinerator. Their research revealed that the incinerator was generating more pollutants than it was burning, and the EPA finally closed down its operation (Sherman 2003).

Protests and Demonstrations

Protests are a prominent tactic in environmental justice campaigns. Drawing on a repertoire of direct action developed in the civil rights movement, activists have practiced civil disobedience and staged demonstrations to protest the siting of environmental hazards. Many of these protests occur in the context of public hearings required by law and held by governmental agencies, sometimes disrupting the proceedings (Gibbs 1982; Bullard 2000). Thus, environmental justice activists both participate in conventional political channels even as they engage in confrontational challenges to the process. In this context, the line between direct action and participation in institutional forums is difficult to discern.

In Homer, Louisiana, Louisiana Energy Services (LES) hoped to locate a uranium enrichment plant on a tract of land sitting between two African-American communities. LES promised that the plant would bring jobs to an economically depressed area, and had the full support of local, pro-development politicians. Before building the plant, LES had to submit to a permitting process before the Nuclear Regulatory Commission (NRC), but company officials expected little opposition. However, African-American residents living near the proposed plant site were alarmed when they heard of the plans for the uranium enrichment plant. The promise of more jobs was not appealing to people who were already living amidst some of the worst pollution in the country (Bullard 2000; Roberts and Toffolon-Weiss 2001; Sherman 2003). Local residents formed an organization named Citizens Against Nuclear Trash (CANT) to oppose the construction of the plant.

CANT activists tailored their strategies to the local political environment. They were concerned that protests would alienate other residents—and potential sympathizers—in a conservative Louisiana county. Thus, they favored more institutional, less threatening strategies, such as attending public hearings, lobbying local officials, and conducting extensive research into the environmental hazards posed by uranium enrichment and the questionable practices that led to the facility's proposed siting. Although its members actively pursued these strategies themselves, CANT also hired EarthJustice, a public interest firm in New Orleans to pursue legal remedies before the EPA and the NRC. (Earth-Justice was previously the Sierra Club Legal Defense Fund and now has offices around the country to assist in local environmental justice disputes.) (Bullard 2000; Roberts and Toffolon-Weiss 2001; Sherman 2003.)

EarthJustice attorneys filed a complaint before the NRC, alleging among other things that the siting decision was based on racist considerations. When the NRC finally scheduled a hearing on the complaint, it was an occasion for a massive demonstration against the plant. CANT arranged to have at least seventy-five people in the courtroom each day. They bussed in schoolchildren who were ushered into the courtroom ten at a time. Greenpeace, the National Association for the Advancement of Colored People (NAACP), and the Southern Organizing Committee, a civil rights group, brought demonstrators to protest on the courthouse steps. And of course, television and print reporters were there to cover the proceedings. Although the formal legal and scientific arguments being made were obviously important, the hearings also provided an opportunity for broader movement participation (Roberts and Toffolon-Weiss 2001). Eventually, the NRC denied LES the permit—the first time that the NRC had ever issued such a denial.

Cause Lawyers for Environmental Justice

Environmental justice activists have shown that grassroots participation can be consistent with institutional strategies led by professionals. But what kinds of cause lawyers are most likely to adopt participatory legal tactics? Research on cause lawyers suggests that legal activists working for social movement organizations would be most likely to seek out opportunities to synthesize direct action and legal strategies (McCann and Silverstein 1998; Scheingold and Sarat 2004). Yet in these illustrations—as in the rest of the case studies of environmental justice movements—there is no discernible pattern connecting the lawyers' practice settings to their choice of tactics.

Indeed, EarthJustice played an important role in the campaign in Homer, Louisiana against the uranium enrichment plant. EarthJustice is a legal rights organization affiliated with the Sierra Club, and as such, it has extensive connections with other mainstream environmental organizations. Although its litigation docket enforces environmental regulations and protects wilderness areas, EarthJustice's branch offices in places like Louisiana (as well as Alaska, Montana, California, and other locations) work closely with grassroots organizations dedicated to environmental justice. Their participation in these grassroots networks made them sensitive to the needs of the local activists and respectful of their choice of strategies. In Homer, for example, EarthJustice lawyers were happy to accept a secondary role, leaving most of the organizing and strategizing to local activists (Roberts and Toffolon-Weiss 2001; Sherman 2003).

Yet another legal rights organization, the California Rural Legal Assistance Project (CRLAP), presided over an environmental justice campaign where activists relied almost exclusively on legal strategies that in the end demobilized local movement (Cole and Foster 2001). Laidlaw was a toxic waste company that was proposing an expansion of a landfill near a Latino community in Buttonwillow, California. The working-class residents got notice of the proposed expansion almost by accident, and formed Padres Hacia Una Vida Mejor—a small, grassroots organization to resist it. The Padres received assistance from a number of larger organizations, including Greenpeace and CRLAP. CRLAP even had community organizers to help mobilize the community to participate in political strategies (Cole and Foster 2001; Sherman 2003).

The central issue in the campaign was the fact that public hearings were all being conducted in English although the community most affected was Latino. However, most of the challenges to this practice were raised in court, using civil rights claims. During the long delays so often associated with litigation, the Padres had little to do. Their organizing efforts and their political work came to a halt, and when they started losing in court, they had little to fall back on (Cole and Foster 2001). In addition, Laidlaw filed lawsuits against the members of Padres for interfering with the expansion plans. The working-class farmworkers had to pay damages to the corporation (Cole and Foster 2001; Sherman 2003). Like EarthJustice, CRLAP is a legal rights organization that combines community organizing with its more traditional legal strategies. Its staff attorneys, like Luke Cole, are self-conscious about the importance of mass-based political mobilization in social movements. Yet CRLAP's strategies at Buttonwillow did little to incorporate grassroots activists.

Another prominent practice setting for cause lawyers in the environmental justice movement are law clinics affiliated with law schools. For example, in the challenge to Shintech, the Tulane University Environmental Law Clinic pursued most of the legal strategies on behalf of the SJCJE (Allen 2003; Sherman 2003). The development of an environmental law clinic at Tulane reflected the region's serious set of environmental problems. The students and faculty in the clinic routinely pursued aggressive legal arguments in a variety of formal proceedings. Moreover, Tulane's clinic employed activists who acted as liaisons between community organizations and the students and faculty who worked on their cases. In the Shintech case, those community organizations planned and carried out direct action strategies in the shadow of the legal proceedings (Sherman 2003). But the clinic's ability to work on these cases was seriously curtailed in the aftermath of the Shintech case. Irked at the clinic's interference with the Shintech plans, the governor of Louisiana, Mike Foster, encouraged the Supreme Court to issue new rules that limited the ability of clinics to represent community groups like that formed by the residents of St. James (Sherman 2003).

Finally, private practitioners are also represented among the environmental justice campaigns in the case studies that rely on participatory strategies. For example, Donald Stewart, a lawyer in a small firm, filed the class action lawsuit against Monsanto on behalf of the citizens of Anniston, Alabama. He got involved when Monsanto offered to purchase the Mars Hill Missionary Baptist Church. Church officials were skeptical of the offer and asked for his assistance (Sherman 2003). After doing some research, he discovered that the church property was contaminated by PCBs and Monsanto was trying to acquire the church as part of its cleanup effort. Stewart attended a meeting at the church to answer questions, and afterward fielded many phone calls from other members of the community telling him about health problems. He eventually filed a class action lawsuit that ended in a $42 million settlement (Sherman 2003). In addition to individual awards, the settlement proceeds also created a charitable foundation to continue to monitor the health of community residents and to conduct public education on the dangers of PCBs (Sherman 2003).

Stewart's pursuit of the lawsuit did not interfere with the community's pursuit of many other political strategies. A community organization, the Sweet Valley Cobb Town Environmental Task Force, continued to work with politicians and state agencies. In addition, Stewart, a former politician, assisted the Task Force with their media strategy that attracted a great deal of favorable attention in the national and international press. This media strategy often featured the voices of actual residents talking about Monsanto's actions and their resulting health problems (Sherman 2003).

These case studies of the environmental justice movement suggest at best a tenuous relationship between environmental justice movement strategies and the practice settings of cause lawyers who work in those movements. As these brief illustrations show, salaried cause lawyers working for rights-based advocacy organizations can be ideologically committed to the broader movement and can acknowledge the importance of a broad range of political strategies, but may nevertheless use litigation in ways that demobilize a movement. On the other hand, private practitioners and their deference to clients can provide legal support to activists without interfering with other movement strategies and may, in fact, be making contributions to grassroots mobilization.

Conclusion

Environmental justice movements are skeptical of institutional strategies because these official channels of policymaking are so often the captives of opponents of environmental justice, most notably corporate actors who seek to locate hazardous waste sites in politically vulnerable poor and minority communities. Moreover, these institutional arenas often require the use of elites and their inaccessible discourses, thus risking demobilization. It is little wonder that activists question the power of conventional strategies such as litigation to overcome their problems.

Still, conventional political strategies are not necessarily demobilizing. Rather, institutional strategies have participatory potential. Activists can pack courtrooms and public hearings in a show of public support. Ordinary citizens can master the procedural and substantive requirements of various legal regimes. Movements can publicize their litigation efforts to educate the public about the impending hazard. And through this interaction with the legal system, citizens learn how to gain control over the political processes that govern their lives.

Cause lawyers are in a position to tailor legal strategies to fulfill this participatory potential, but cause lawyers' efforts do not necessarily depend on their practice settings. This chapter suggests looking beyond the practice settings to the funding sources of those settings. For example, staff attorneys in legal rights organizations may enjoy a level of independence, but their sources of funding and other institutional constraints may pressure them to temper more radical strategies. On the other hand, when the activists themselves are footing the bill, private practitioners may be more likely to take orders from the clients, even when those orders demand support for disruptive tactics.

This analysis also places cause lawyers squarely in the movements that they serve. The work that they do and the choices they make affect not just the legal profession or political outcomes. Rather, cause lawyers can shape the direction of the movement itself. Far from being resolved, the debate between the myth of rights and the politics of rights is in full swing in the environmental justice movement, where activists need lawyers but are seeking ways of keeping them under control.

Acknowledgments

The author thanks all the participants in the Conference on Cause Lawyering and Social Movements at the UCLA School of Law for their thoughtful comments, especially Scott Barclay, Shauna Fisher, Benjamin Fleury-Steiner, Liora Israel, Lynn Jones, Sandra Levitsky, Michael McCann, Steve Meili, and Austin Sarat. The author also thanks the participants in the Law and Social Movements seminar at UIUC, whose discussions helped sharpen the arguments in this chapter.

Notes

1. There is no authoritative list of the number or nature of environmental justice organizations in the United States or the world. Such organizations are difficult to count because, by their very nature, they are small community groups made up of ordinary people. The organizations also come from marginalized communities that are so often ignored by policy makers and the mass media. Their efforts against the government and corporate polluters are likely to be invisible, particularly when their efforts are unsuccessful.

References

Allen, Barbara L. 2003. *Uneasy Alchemy: Citizens and Experts in Louisiana's Chemical Corridor Disputes.* Cambridge, MA: MIT Press.

Barclay, Scott W. and Anna-Maria Marshall. 2005. "Supporting a Cause, Developing a Movement, and Consolidating a Practice: Cause Lawyers and Sexual Orientation Litigation in Vermont." In *The Worlds Cause Lawyers Make,* Stuart Scheingold and Austin Sarat, eds. Palo Alto, CA: Stanford University Press.

Been, Vicki. 1995. "Analyzing Evidence of Environmental Justice." *Journal of Land Use and Environmental Law* 11: 1–36.

Bullard, Robert D. 2000. *Dumping in Dixie: Race, Class, and Environmental Quality,* 3rd ed. Boulder, CO: Westview Press.

Burstein, Paul. 1991. "Legal Mobilization as a Social Movement Tactic: The Struggle for Equal Employment Opportunity." *American Journal of Sociology* 96: 1201–25.

Cable, Sherry, Donald W. Hastings, and Tamara L. Mix. 2002. "Different Voices, Different Venues: Environmental Racism Claims by Activists, Researchers, and Lawyers." *Human Ecology Review* 9: 26–42.

Capek, Stella M. 1993. "The 'Environmental Justice' Frame: A Conceptual Discussion and an Application." *Social Problems* 40: 5–24.

Cole, Luke W. and Sheila R. Foster. 2001. *From the Ground Up: Environmental Racism and the Rise of the Environmental Justice Movement.* New York: New York University Press.

Cress, Daniel M. and David A. Snow. 2000. "The Outcomes of Homeless Mobilization: The Influence of Organization, Disruption, Political Mediation, and Framing." *American Journal of Sociology* 105: 1063–1104.

Fleury-Steiner, Benjamin. 2006. "'Different Approaches Need to be Taken in Different Settings'—Situating Activist Prison Lawyering: The Struggle for HIV-Positive Prisoner's Rights." *Studies in Law, Politics, and Society* 38: 3–24.

Galanter, Marc. 1974. "Why the 'Haves' Come Out Ahead." *Law and Society Review* 9: 95–160.

Gamson, William A. 1975. *The Strategy of Social Protest.* Homewood, IL: Dorsey.

Gibbs, Lois Marie. 1982. *Love Canal: My Story.* Albany, NY: State University of New York Press.

Hilbink, Thomas. 2006. "The Profession, the Grassroots, and the Elite: Lawyering for Civil Rights in the Direct Action Era." In *Cause Lawyers and Social Movements*, Stuart Scheingold and Austin Sarat, eds. Palo Alto, CA: Stanford University Press.

Jenkins, J. Craig and Craig Eckert. 1986. "Elite Patronage and the Channeling of Social Protest." *American Sociological Review* 51: 812–29.

Jones, Lynn C. 2005. "Exploring the Sources of Cause and Career Correspondence Among Cause Lawyers." In *The Worlds Cause Lawyers Make*, Austin Sarat and Stuart Scheingold, eds. Palo Alto, CA: Stanford University Press.

———. 2006. "The Haves Come Out Ahead: How Cause Lawyers Frame the Legal System for Movements." In *Cause Lawyers and Social Movements*, Stuart Scheingold and Austin Sarat, eds. Palo Alto, CA: Stanford University Press.

Markowitz, Lisa and Karen W. Tice. 2002. "Paradoxes of Professionalization: Parallel Dilemmas in Women's Organizations in the Americas." *Gender and Society* 16: 941–58.

McCann, Michael W. 1994. *Rights at Work: Pay Equity Reform and the Politics of Legal Mobilization.* Chicago, IL: University of Chicago Press.

McCann, Michael W. and Helena Silverstein. 1998. "Rethinking Law's 'Allurements': A Relational Analysis of Social Movement Lawyers in the United States." In *Cause Lawyering: Political Commitments and Professional Responsibilities.* Austin Sarat and Stuart Scheingold, eds. New York: Oxford University Press.

McCarthy, John D. and Mayer N. Zald. 1977. "Resource Mobilization and Social Movements: A Partial Theory." *American Journal of Sociology* 82: 1212–41.

Menkel-Meadow, Carrie. 1998. "The Causes of Cause Lawyering: Toward an Understanding of the Motivation and Commitment of Social Justice Lawyers." In *Cause Lawyering: Political Commitments and Professional Responsibilities.* Austin Sarat and Stuart Scheingold, eds. New York: Oxford University Press.

Olson, Susan M. 1984. *Clients and Lawyers: Securing the Rights of Disabled Persons.* Westport, CT: Greenwood Press.

Piven, Frances Fox and Richard Cloward. 1977. *Poor People's Movements: Why They Succeed, How they Fail.* New York: Pantheon Books.

Roberts, J. Timmons and Melissa M. Toffolon-Weiss. 2001. *Chronicles from the Environmental Justice Frontline.* New York: Cambridge University Press.

Rochon, Thomas R. 1998. *Culture Moves: Ideas, Activism, and Changing Values.* Princeton, NJ: Princeton University Press.

Scheingold, Stuart. 1974 [2004]. *The Politics of Rights: Lawyers, Public Policy and Political Change.* New Haven, CT: Yale University Press.

Scheingold, Stuart and Austin Sarat. 2004. *Something to Believe in: Politics, Professionalism, and Cause Lawyering.* Palo Alto, CA: Stanford University Press.

Shdaimah, Corey. 2006. "Intersecting Identities: Cause Lawyers as Legal Professionals and Social Movement Actors." In *Cause Lawyers and Social Movements*, Stuart Scheingold and Austin Sarat, eds. Palo Alto, CA: Stanford University Press.

Sherman, Scott D. 2003. *Strategies for Success in the Environmental Justice Movement.* Ph.D. Dissertation, University of Michigan, School of Natural Resources and the Environment.

Simon, Ron. 1985. "Legal Corner." *Everyone's Backyard* 3(2):5.

Staggenborg, Suzanne. 1988. "Consequences of Professionalization and Formalization in the Pro-Choice Movement." *American Sociological Review* 53: 585–605.

Szasz, Andrew. 1994. *Ecopopulism: Toxic Waste and the Movement for Environmental Justice.* Minneapolis, MN: University of Minnesota Press.

Tarrow, Sidney G. 1998. *Power in Movement: Social Movements and Contentious Politics.* New York: Cambridge University Press.

The Haves Come Out Ahead

How Cause Lawyers Frame the Legal System for Movements

LYNN JONES

Although research on movement framing processes has explored the ways in which activists frame a cause or the opportunity structure at large, there has been less theoretical and empirical investigation of how cause lawyers frame the law and legal structures as part of the movement process. This interview-based project explores the ways in which cause lawyers frame the legal system and the law, and how particular framing activities by cause lawyers affect the potential course of movements. This work includes two components: (1) I am drawing on what I see as the theoretical link between the "naming, blaming, and claiming" conceptualization in the sociology of law literature and the broader "collective action framing" processes in the social movement literature; and (2) I present evidence of cause lawyers' ideologies about the law as examples of framing, showing that cause lawyers do move beyond the narrower legal claiming.

This chapter challenges assumptions made by scholars in both law and social movements arenas that cause lawyers act in movements according to their professional identities and skills as lawyers. Here, I consider cause lawyers to act like other "ordinary" activists, expressing the theme of "the haves come out ahead" and impacting movements in terms of mobilization, securing resources, and whether strategic choices by movements include legal strategies or extrainstitutional activities. By sustaining the ideology of the "haves" winning, lawyers influence movements who may use, or be constrained by, a dominant collective action frame and a set of collective identities.

Recent social movement scholarship[1] has criticized traditional theoretical conceptions of political opportunity as vague or poorly developed as a model to explain social movement processes (Einwohner 1999; Sawyers and Meyer 1999) and as structurally biased (Goodwin and Jasper 1999). In addition, the traditional macrolevel focus on opportunity concepts ignores the important role of perception, or recognition of opportunities, as movements and their activists must decide whether conditions are ripe for certain issues and strategies. This chapter will focus on cause lawyers as one type of movement activist, and examine the ways in which these lawyers impact movement framing processes.

Lawyers are thought to undermine a movement's goals by acting as professionals who co-opt movement strategies and goals in line with their own elite interests (McCarthy and Zald 1973, 1987; McCarthy, Britt, and Wolfson 1991). Or, because of their professional role, lawyers may be inclined to think of litigation apart from other political tactics or broad movement goals (Scheingold 1974; McCann 1986). This can be problematic for movements as resources are redirected to litigation strategies at the expense of other potentially successful strategies (Rosenberg 1991; McCann and Silverstein 1998). Examining the ideological commitments of cause lawyers provides insight into whether lawyers are engaging as professionals, as activists, or are somewhere in-between.[2] This chapter extends the study of movement lawyers in this direction, considering cause lawyers as providers of key signaling functions for movements: pointing out ripeness of opportunities, framing the injustices, and blaming state/corporate sources of harm.[3] The lawyers in this study demonstrate a range of actions, a commitment to causes comparable to ordinary activists, and, for some, an oppositional positioning vis-à-vis the state.

Cause lawyers are typically judged in movements according to their professional identity. In the tradition of resource mobilization theory (McCarthy and Zald 1973, 1987), there has been much research on the role and impact of professionals on social movements (Zald and Ash 1966; McAdam 1982; Jenkins and Eckert 1986; Staggenborg 1988, 1991; McCarthy, Britt, and Wolfson 1991; Morris and Staggenborg 2004). According to this approach, professionals bring two things to movements. First, they provide some set of resources linked to professional skills, prestige or status, leadership and organization, or simply money. Secondly, professionals are said to be carriers of a set of interests, usually thought to supplant the movements' interests or goals and channel the movement away from disruptive tactics or goals. I argue for further analytic division of movement professionals, particularly lawyers. By doing this, I question the assumption that professionals act as a cohesive set of actors, or in a consistent manner, in interactions with movements. For example, although lawyers and scientists might act differently within movements, we still assume that they act according to their professional role *as* scientists or *as* lawyers, not as *activists*. Rather than viewing lawyers as framing externally or "professionally," I suggest that cause lawyers play an important *internal* role in the framing processes of movements.

From the side of legal scholarship, Joel Handler (1978) argued that social reform groups that turn to the legal system *must* use lawyers and that the relationship between lawyer and client (cause) varies in that "lawyers dominate the relationship when clients are poor, or deviant, or unsophisticated" (p. 25). This view is quite similar to that of social movement scholars in the expectation that lawyers are acting like "hired guns" who help movements accomplish particular goals, or who steer a movement away from its political activities. Instead of viewing lawyers as necessarily constraining movements, they may be seen as framers helping to initiate a positive course of action by movements.[4] It seems possible that *cause* lawyers may fall into this framing role, while other nonactivist lawyers may retain their role as state actors with elite interests.

Lawyers as Framers: Naming, Blaming, and Claiming

One way to unpack the role of lawyers in social movements is to focus on their interpretive activities within legal or social movement organizations. Scholars have long understood that some cognitive mechanism is required for individuals to break away from their ordinary state of passivity and to act collectively. Such mechanisms include classical ideas of Marxist "class consciousness" rooted in material relations, or Weberian ideas about status consciousness linked to market positions. More recently, McAdam (1982) has discussed "cognitive liberation," and Snow and colleagues (1986) defined *frame alignment processes.* Frame alignment processes provide the necessary link between the interests, goals, and interpretations of individuals to those of social movement organizations (Snow et al. 1986: 464; Snow 2004). Building on Goffman's (1974) conception of frames as "focusing and punctuating," collective action frames also function "as modes of attribution and articulation" (Snow and Benford 1992). This function of collective action frames occurs as activists single out an existing social condition and redefine as unjust what was previously viewed as unfortunate, yet tolerable (Snow and Benford 1992). Activists now interpret conditions as intolerable and deserving of corrective action (Turner 1969; Piven and Cloward 1977; McAdam 1982; Snow et al. 1986).

For movements, the framing process is the production and maintenance of meaning, including "diagnostic," "prognostic," and "motivational" framing (Snow et al. 1986; Tarrow 1992; Benford and Snow 2000; Snow 2004). Diagnostic frames specify the problem and identify who is to blame. Prognostic frames define what needs to be done to address the problem. Motivational framing is the call to action that encourages people to take the actions defined during the framing process (Snow et al. 1986). The motivational component of framing includes some articulation of potential efficacy or success—mobilization to act collectively will occur when activists believe such action to be "both potentially effective *and* necessary" (Eisinger 1973, as cited in Meyer and Staggenborg 1996).

In sociology of law, scholars use *disputing concepts* to describe legal mobilization, but they do not fully extend these ideas to social movement lawyers or consider nonlegal framing. Also, lawyers are viewed as involving themselves in legal mobilization, but not more radical political mobilizations.[5] These concepts, however, coincide very well with the framing concepts outlined above. "Naming" is the first stage of the transformation, in which a particular experience is defined as injurious. After naming the problem, individuals then typically attribute fault to some set of social actors with "blaming," which is the transformation of a perceived injurious experience to a grievance. By holding another responsible, blaming also includes a call for some remedy. "Claiming" occurs when the grievance is communicated to those believed to be responsible and a remedy is requested. Each stage of the transformation to a claim is a necessary part of the legal process (Felstiner, Abel, and Sarat 1980–81).

There are obvious links conceptually between naming, blaming, claiming, and collective action framing. For two reasons, I prefer the framing conceptualization for explanation and discussion of cause lawyers: (1) sociolegal scholars do not extend their concepts to explain the ideologies and behaviors of lawyers involved in social movements; and (2) the legal claiming process may be just one part of the ideological work in which cause lawyers engage. Framing is broader and allows for a range of potential remedies—not just legal claiming action. Theorizing the behavior of cause lawyers with framing concepts is more robust because legalistic claiming may not resonate with radical groups or with moderate groups at particular stages of the movement, that is, activists may prefer direct action strategies to legal ones at particular stages. Collective action framing processes typically include extrainstitutional means as remedies and allow for the possibility that cause lawyers frame *beyond* litigation strategies or law.

McAdam (1983) argued that tactical innovation was a necessary task of social movements if they wanted to maintain an edge. The implication is that movements that become institutionalized by going through "proper channels" are destined to fail. Burstein (1991) counters with evidence that legal mobilization or use of the proper channels can still be innovative and does not alone predict failure of movements. He argues that movements may be able to innovate by turning to legal channels and by developing new approaches to legal doctrine. Because lawyers are professionally trained in helping clients with naming, blaming, and claiming, it seems very likely that they will act in a similar capacity in movements, helping to frame grievances into legal disputes and construct a remedial plan of *legal* action. The rights frame, which has been ubiquitous in American movements since the civil rights movement, can be construed as legally based because rights are defined by law. However, the rights frame may not necessarily be used institutionally or to call for a legal remedy.[6] For example, a rights frame can lead to both an attempt for legal remedies and a violent, illegal action that may have a more radical goal. The attempts by feminists to achieve equal pay for equal work are specific activities based in a frame of equal rights for men and women. The animal rights movement, including several radical groups, may invoke a frame of rights while bombing labs that conduct research on animals.

Frames and tactics are linked, and it seems that lawyers, if invoking a legal frame, will possibly "deradicalize" a movement. However, *cause* lawyers, unlike other lawyers, have a view of the courts and the law that does not lessen a movement's power. The lawyers in this sample seem to hold a "schizophrenic" view that the courts *should be* a source for remedy; yet, the law and the courts do not always work to benefit those who need it most. In this chapter, I suggest that *cause* lawyers frame the courts and law: (1) as benefiting the rich or the powerful; (2) as potentially dangerous because a "bad precedent" may be set; and (3) as restricting rights rather than protecting them, both in principle and in practice. Thus, cause lawyers in their talk about courts and law are framing the ideological field for movements.

What Lawyers Think They Bring to Social Movements

It should be noted that the data used for this chapter consist of interviews with lawyers who are active in causes, and not interviews with activists in movements. A number of other chapters in this volume[7] do consider lawyers and movement activists in interaction. My data demonstrate that lawyers are aware that they often bring legitimacy to a movement, and they know this can be both a blessing and a curse. Lawyers also see the specific legal technical skills and resources they may bring; yet many do not see their role in movements to be limited to the legal. Finally, and most important, the lawyers in this study continually referred to the importance of framing and recognizing opportunity for change. I present data to illustrate cause lawyers' understanding of their potential role in saving a movement from strategic mistakes or self-destruction.

Framing the Opportunity: Recognition of Timing and Potential Impact of Legal Strategies

The cause lawyers in this study talked about the possible negative impact of legal strategies for a movement, and those most "core"[8] to the cause-lawyering community talked about the broader impact on a movement over time, including the importance of timing of strategies. For example, the core cause lawyers emphasized organizing and grassroots mobilization, and they articulated the impact that a particular case might have on future mobilization. They also were likely to mention how litigation, or the involvement of lawyers as legal strategists in movements, was best understood in the context of the broader movement activities. One cause lawyer explained:

> I think lawyers are not usually that effective in the process if there isn't grassroots movement to begin with. (come in at different phases, but if come in too early...) Yeah, yeah. What kind of movement can you do when it's just the case by itself? When it's the whole situation to build up—some kind of pressure cooker builds up to the point where there needs to be a lawsuit, or there's some avenue through which you can channel the lawsuit, then that could work.

Note the use of the word "need" with "lawsuit"; cause lawyers do not automatically turn to litigation, but work to recognize a point where a lawsuit might work best or is the only solution. As noted by McCann (1994) the contexts of struggle shape the activists' constant efforts to fit and refit the frame, in that case the remedial frame of equity reform. Another cause lawyer who works in poverty and housing issues described that he is "as interested in political change outside of the court system" and that he considers lawsuits in the larger context of "The Movement":

> What is the movement potential for it? Is it going to motivate people to protest around it? Are people going to organize around it? Is a particularly oppressed group going to get fired up because of this lawsuit? ... before I even litigate a case ... you need to flex your political muscles first and see how far that will go.

This lawyer is demonstrating awareness of framing and timing—that defining things in certain ways may help or hinder mobilization. It appears that the lawyer recognizes the potential dangers of "taking over" by channeling a movement into legal strategies and goals, again a concern of resource mobilization scholars (McCarthy and Zald 1987). See also Marshall (2006) for discussion of the participatory potential of litigation—how it might be used to mobilize the broader movement. The framing capacity of lawyers again becomes relevant. They may not be acting as lawyers, yet they may be the *activists* who define the efficacy of particular strategies in particular "windows of political opportunity" (McAdam 1982; Snow and Benford 1992).

Framing Against the "Haves"

The previous discussion of timing and opportunities considered the way cause lawyers think about the potential of law or litigation strategies. This discussion can be further contextualized in the work of Galanter (1974) who showed that repeat players in courts have considerable advantages before the law, including resources for filing and carrying out expensive and time-consuming lawsuits, hiring experts, and reputation.[9] Galanter described the limitations that the "have-nots" face in securing social change and justice, primarily due to their status as "one-shotters" fighting against the more powerful "haves." Galanter points to the potential power in achieving change if the powerless are able to organize into some semblance of repeat-player status. The lawyers in my study indicate awareness of these issues, and cause lawyers may be the very mechanism allowing the powerless to tap into such repeat-player resources. Movements and issues cycle, but cause lawyers and activist communities may endure, thus allowing for the organizational readiness to frame and act on injustices.

Another common theme among the cause lawyers was their criticism of the system of inequality that is perpetuated in this society. Included in this critique were Marxist and anticapitalist claims, injustice and inequality frames, and recognition that the powerful typically come out ahead in all structures, including the law. What was interesting, however, was that cause lawyers continued to claim that the law *should* or *ought* to offer protection or remedies from injustice, while at the same time cause lawyers cautioned that the law *in action* often favors those who "need it the least." With the "haves come out ahead" frame, cause lawyers are articulating the problems inherent to institutions, and thus, they might steer social movements into more radical actions. One radical cause lawyer framed structured inequality:

> Society is inherently unjust. Capitalist system is inherently unjust and must be changed drastically to one that is built on equality and not one that's built on . . . I mean, the capitalist system we live in is built on inequality. That's how it functions. The inequity is what keeps it going. . . . I also think there are a block of lawyers out there whose basic goal is to prop up and propitiate the capitalist system because they're making damn money out of it and they're protecting their class interests.

He goes on to describe how cause lawyers "see the light" and do not carry such oppressive ideologies.

An environmental cause lawyer further illustrates this framing against inequality inherent to institutions and their processes:

> . . . it's particularly egregious, how well you do in the legal system, the justice system, depends on how much money you have, to a very large degree. How many rich people do you see on death row? Big corporations can go out and hire as many lawyers as they want. . . . Cases that you and I wouldn't dream of bringing because of the cost—these guys can bring everyday. So, our justice system is still a very inequitable one.

He continues:

> ... the more of this kind of work you do, the more of the inequities and outrages you
> see in society, the more you see how much imbalance there is in resources available
> to the haves as opposed to the have-nots. Not just money resources but what that
> means in terms of access to the basics of life.

This type of view, if articulated in the context of movements and activists,
might be characterized as the articulation of blame, as well as the articulation of
whether litigation would be an effective strategy for the movement. It becomes
important to know whether this view is, in fact, articulated by cause lawyers to
other members of the cause. If cause lawyers, instead, articulate that success in the
courts is potentially effective and this resonates, then a movement organization
might steer its actions into litigation. If cause lawyers' frames do not resonate,
then the strategic actions of the movement result from resonant framers more
central to the movement than are lawyers. Thus, researchers must investigate
conditions explaining whose frame succeeds.

Another lawyer who works with housing, homelessness, and poverty causes
described how the structural inequality itself is what will ultimately mobilize the
people. This compares to a political opportunity argument, of which a cognitive
or framing process is key—conditions worsen so much that people will begin
to define the problem with urgency and clear attribution of who is to blame.
Lawyers might help this framing process:

> Now in the nineties we have the welfare reform and, you know, the Republican
> Congress is just nuts ... taking away housing benefits ... every sort of public bed.
> What they don't understand, if they would read their history, they would see what
> quelled the movements in the sixties and thirties was government programs because
> you give people a little bit and it quiets them down. In the nineties, you are removing
> the safety net, and when the people hit the ground? Man, they are going to be madder
> than shit, and they're going to get up, and ... I'm certainly not looking forward to the
> misery that will be caused by it, but I certainly think the potential for organizing,
> especially among poor people and working people, is increasing.

Here, the cause lawyer is framing the structural inequality in a way that speaks
of the inevitability that the powerless will come together. The passion with
which this lawyer speaks indicates the potential for this frame to be influential
in nonlegal mobilization.

Counterframing by Cause Lawyers

Related to these ideas about "the haves," we also see cause lawyers engage in
counterframing, defined as attempts to rebut or neutralize an opposing collective
action frame or an articulation made by an opposing movement organization
(Snow 2004).[10] A homeless rights cause lawyer described (angrily) the "false

use" of rights claims by those who already have privilege and power extended to them structurally. This is a clear critique of how the law is being used to further benefit "the haves." He argues:

> Right now what is concerning me is a lot of the organizing we see is like *regressive* organizing in neighborhoods. 'Let's get the homeless people to get the fuck out. Let's turn back the clock.' That bothers the hell out of me. I certainly wouldn't support that form of organizing, you know, that's backwards moving. 'Let's fuck with homeless people so that my property value isn't screwed.' And a lot of people that we see that are held up as these 'people's movements' now are actually people with money and power already [saying] 'Goddamn it, we've got to assert our rights once again'—that's disturbing.

The framing is evident here as he clearly distinguishes rights claims and the different groups using them; he points out that such use of rights frames and "people's" designations may successfully fool people into mobilization. His attempt to distinguish the work of cause lawyers for the power*less* indicates his understanding of the importance of framing politically, rather than legal claiming, for mobilizing the people.

Framing Chance of Success

Finally, cause lawyers engage in prognostic and motivational framing as they describe the chance of success in courts and whether using the courts is even appropriate action for the movement to take. Should a cause lawyer operate only in terms of disputing processes such as claiming, the goals of the movement might be lost. Previous research[11] has demonstrated that some lawyers are aware of legal potential in the context of political potential, and it is these lawyers who may offer the necessary collective action frame (rather than "claiming" or legal disputing) to the movement.

An immigration lawyer described how the law could be limiting, and this particular framing of immigration issues might direct movements to pursue extrainstitutional options or legislative change rather than pursuing litigation strategies:

> For example, in immigration law there is only so much you can do because the Constitution has a limited role, and immigrants have no Constitutional rights. But in a lot of ways their rights are due process—whatever the Congress says is due— and so it's important that people know who are immigrants what impact these laws have. . . . laws box you in and the only thing to do is change the laws.

Although this lawyer may be continuing to frame issues legalistically, she is steering action away from lawsuits by framing that existing law offers no remedy.

This framing could lead a movement to save precious resources by *not* pursuing a lawsuit that would have minimal impact but tremendous resource spending.

Cause lawyers also described how litigation strategies should be avoided. Such lawyers are experts not in legal disputing but in collective action framing, pointing out the potential harms for the movement and not steering a movement into harm:

> A lot of the solutions that used to be in law are not anymore. And the solutions are more political now. It used to be that all kinds of injustices were done, and you could go to the law and see great victory in the federal courts. There's more and more conservatism among the courts, having been passed by Reagan and Bush. So now, the laws are going to be interpreted more likely than not against the poor and against the minorities. The better way to go might be the legislature, or politically.

McCann's study of pay equity reform activists similarly illustrates that mobilization of law can constrain the power in movement (1994: 217–22). Another cause lawyer in my study echoed McCann's findings concerning use of courts for change:

> There also has been a move of conservatism in the courts in a way that many people no longer believe that bringing certain types of lawsuits is the best vehicle for social change. The federal courts in the '70s and perhaps into the early '80s were seen as a protector of rights. I'm not so sure people would see law as doing that now.

Both of these views illustrate that cause lawyers are *cautious* about turning to the courts, not anxious or ambitious in that direction. As McCann's activists noted, there should not be a jump to "blaming" lawyers for failures before the courts. Cause lawyers, particularly those most centrally involved as activists, do frame the potential negative outcome. So, theories of collective action framing provide explanatory power for the behavior of these lawyers.

Core cause lawyers expressed the concern typical of the social movement critique of professionals, in this case lawyers, taking over:

> I think that there's a tendency of lawyers who want to take over and direct. And make the decisions. And that is something that we should not do. Because, law is a funny thing. It's very narrow. It's got causes of action, and it's got particular remedies. And you may WIN a case, only to find out the whole movement's dissolved, or that it's split, or that nothing has really been accomplished except for years and years of litigation. So that, it's just easy for the lawyer to think of himself of herself as the expert who knows what should be done. And it's much harder and more draining to get the decisions, especially depending on the client, to get decisions made by the people if there's a particular movement.

This quote provides evidence that cause lawyers consider the dangers of law, legal strategies, and channeling by professionals. By distinguishing between types of lawyers, theoretical arguments about the inevitability of legal channeling are challenged. She recognizes the dilemma of wanting to get something accomplished, but also not wanting to kill the movement or its resource base. She points out how "success" in a case can actually mean "failure" for the movement, a concern that compares to "putting all your eggs in one basket." Scholars have also pointed out how successful litigation can be "symbolically" dangerous, as people believe the movement's job is done. For example, following *Roe v. Wade*, the pro-choice activists felt secure that reproductive rights were guaranteed and the issues "rested," while their opponents in the pro-life movement mobilized quickly and with great passion to counter the loss they had suffered (Luker 1984; Staggenborg 1991). Not only can long courses of litigation drain the resources of movements, but they can also impact countermovements and public supporters who witness and respond to the outcome in the public arena.

In sum, it is important to distinguish between lawyers as claimers and lawyers as framers, and between cause lawyers and lawyers as "outside elites." By viewing cause lawyers through the lens of framing processes in social movements, cause lawyers are seen as ordinary activists internal to movement decision making. Framing, rather than disputing, also explains the conditions under which lawyers in movements act beyond their professional roles and skills. Future research should consider cause lawyers at various stages of movements and across different movement contexts or causes. Lawyers may be part of the framing process, or they may be hired "after" framing is complete and the movement desires a lawyer to help with a legal strategy. If lawyers are part of the framing process, there needs to be further exploration of the conditions under which they offer legal frames versus more radical frames. Cause lawyers may enter into framing processes at different times for different causes. Cause lawyers might frame differently for right movements and left movements, or for movements in countries other than the United States. These issues help set the stage for future research on ideologies of cause lawyers in the context of movements. Framing concepts are an important theoretical framework for explaining the link between movement ideologies, tactical choice, and cause lawyers, in any movement or national context.

Notes

1. See Chapter 1 of Snow, Soule, and Kriesi (2004) for a recent summary discussion of social movement terminology. These authors note that most definitions of "social movement" include the common elements of "collective or joint action; change-oriented goals or claims; some extra- or noninstitutional collective action; some degree of organization; and some degree of temporal continuity" (2004: 6).

2. See McCann and Silverstein (1998) for the concept of "flexible lawyering," which allows lawyers to consider litigation, while at the same time viewing the larger repertoire of tactics available to movements; see Jones (2001, 2005) for a discussion of "core" cause lawyers who engage with movements as activists, not lawyers. This concept of "core" might also be compared to McCann and Silverstein's "flexible lawyering" and to McCarthy and Zald's "cadre" participants (1973). Hilbink (2006) emphasizes the significance of lawyers' ideological commitments in understanding movement activities. Finally, Scheingold and Sarat (2004) elaborate definitional issues and cause lawyers' identification with liberal democracy.

3. Scheingold (2004: xxx), referencing McCann (1994) and Epp (1998), highlights the importance of preexisting organizational conditions as necessary to the successful pursuit of rights. Specifically, he mentions the value of a "preexisting leadership cadre of political activists and a supportive political and legal ethos." Political opportunity models of social movements have demonstrated similar theoretical and empirical significance to prior organization and leadership, yet the organizational factors are discussed in conjunction with the cognitive processes: for instance McAdam's (1982) political process model emphasizes "organizational readiness" and "cognitive liberation" or insurgent consciousness as central to the emergence of collective action. What the movement models show more clearly is that organizational readiness and political opportunity alone do not mean mobilization of rights or of movements; the discursive framing is a necessary third element, in which *recognition* by activists of the collective potential for takes place.

4. See Morris and Staggenborg (2004: 177–78) on the important distinction between inside and outside leaders. In this work and in another article (Jones 2005), I further explore whether lawyers act as leaders or as part of the masses, and whether their participation in movements is necessarily linked to their professional status as lawyers. See also Coutin (2001, 2006) for an important empirical illustration of immigration cause lawyers "in the shadow of the state" rather than necessarily "of" it.

5. Scheingold (2004: xxxviii–xix) notes how McCann and Silverstein (1998) and Coutin (2001) provide important empirical evidence of cause lawyers going beyond the expected legal mobilization.

6. See Francesca Polletta (2000) for an examination of rights talk and the ways in which rights claims were extended beyond purely legal limitations. Similarly, Scheingold (2004) argues for a new politics of rights in which he challenges his own earlier assumptions about lawyers and legal mobilization.

7. See, for instance, chapters by Levitsky, Marshall, Meili, and den Dulk.

8. See Jones 2001 and 2005 for further explanation of core cause lawyers. Essentially this term refers to the subgroup of lawyers in one community of cause lawyers that is most involved and committed across multiple issues, multiple organizations, and defines himself or herself to be an activist primarily, with "lawyer" being a less salient part of his or her identity.

9. Please note that this paper emphasizes the signaling functions among movement participants with the potential frame or *perception* that outcomes will favor

the "haves" and does not attempt to explore the *actual* outcomes. For empirical evidence about whether the "haves" continually succeed in the law, see the essays in the edited volume *In Litigation: Do the "Haves" Still Come Out Ahead?* (2003), Herbert M. Kritzer and Susan Silbey, eds., Stanford University Press.

10. Although Scheingold (2004) might define counterframing in terms of the backlash to the progressive mobilization of rights, the broader social movement literature would allow for counterframing to occur on "either side."

11. Scheingold and Bloom (1998) and Jones (2001; 2005) demonstrate the differences among lawyers and among work settings. Also, these previous studies of cause lawyers, as well as McCann and Silverstein (1998) further explain the conditions under which lawyers will be more likely to emphasize mobilization for the cause (as opposed to or beyond legal mobilization). See also Marshall (2006) on litigation and participatory potential for movements.

References

Benford, Robert D. and David A. Snow. 2000. "Framing Processes and Social Movements: An Overview and Assessment." *Annual Review of Sociology* 26.

Burstein, Paul. 1991. "Legal Mobilization as a Social Movement Tactic: The Struggle for Equal Employment Opportunity. "*American Journal of Sociology* 96: 1201–25.

Coutin, Susan Bibler. 2001. "Cause Lawyering in the Shadow of the State: A U.S. Immigration Example." In Austin Sarat and Stuart Scheingold eds., *Cause Lawyering and the State in a Global Era*, 117–40. New York: Oxford University Press.

———. 2006. "Cause Lawyering and Political Advocacy: Moving Law on Behalf of Central American Refugees." In Austin Sarat and Stuart Scheingold eds., *Cause Lawyers and Social Movements*, pp. 101–119. Stanford: Stanford University Press.

Einwohner, Rachel L. 1999. "Practices, Opportunities, and Protest Effectiveness: Illustrations from Four Animal Rights Campaigns." *Social Problems* 46, 2: 169–86.

Eisinger, Peter. 1973. "The Conditions of Protest Behavior in American Cities." *American Political Science Review* 67: 11–28.

Epp, Charles R. 1998. *The Rights Revolution: Lawyers, Activists, and Supreme Courts in Comparative Perspective*. Chicago: University of Chicago Press.

Felstiner, William L. F., Richard L. Abel, and Austin Sarat. 1980–81. "The Emergence and Transformation of Disputes: Naming, Blaming, and Claiming . . . " *Law and Society Review* 15, 3–4: 631–54.

Galanter, Marc. 1974. "Why the Haves Come Out Ahead: Speculations on the Limits of Social Change." *Law and Society Review* 9: 95–160.

Goffman, Erving. 1974. *Frame Analysis: An Essay on the Organization of Experience*. New York: Harper.

Goodwin, Jeff and James M. Jasper. 1999. "Caught in a Winding, Snarling Vine: The Structural Bias in Political Process Theory." *Sociological Forum* 14: 27–54.

Handler, Joel. 1978. *Social Movements and the Legal System: A Theory of Law Reform and Social Change*. New York: Academic Press.

Hilbink, Thomas. 2006. "The Profession, the Grassroots, and the Elite: Lawyering for Civil Rights in the Direct Action Era." In Austin Sarat and Stuart Scheingold eds., *Cause Lawyers and Social Movements*, pp. 60–83. Stanford: Stanford University Press.

Jenkins, J. Craig and Craig Eckert. 1986. "Elite Patronage and the Channeling of Social Protest." *American Sociological Review* 51: 812–29.

Jones, Lynn. 2001. "Career Activism by Lawyers: Consequences for the Person, the Legal Profession, and Social Movements." In Jerry Van Hoy ed., *Legal Professions: Work, Structure, and Organization*, 181–206. Amsterdam: Elsevier Science Ltd.

———. 2005. "Exploring the Sources of Cause and Career Correspondence Among Cause Lawyers." In Austin Sarat and Stuart Scheingold eds., *The Worlds Cause Lawyers Make*, 203–38. Stanford, CA: Stanford University Press.

Kritzer, Herbert M. and Susan Silbey. 2003. *In Litigation: Do the "Haves" Still Come Out Ahead?* Stanford, CA: Stanford University Press.

Luker, Kristin. 1984. *Abortion and the Politics of Motherhood*. Berkeley, CA: University of California Press.

Marshall, Anna Maria. 2006. "Social Movement Strategies and the Participatory Potential of Litigation." In Austin Sarat and Stuart Scheingold eds., *Cause Lawyers and Social Movements*, pp. 164–181. Stanford: Stanford University Press.

———. 2003. "Injustice Frames, Legality and the Everyday Construction of Sexual Harassment." *Law and Social Inquiry* 28: 659–89.

McAdam, Doug. 1982. *Political Process and the Development of Black Insurgency, 1930–1970*. Chicago: University of Chicago Press.

———. 1983. "Tactical Innovation and the Pace of Insurgency." *American Sociological Review* 48: 735–54.

———. 1988. *Freedom Summer*. New York: Oxford University Press.

McCann, Michael. 1986. *Taking Reform Seriously: Perspectives on Public Interest Liberalism*. Ithaca, NY: Cornell University Press.

———. 1994. *Rights at Work: Pay Equity Reform and the Politics of Legal Mobilization*. Chicago: University of Chicago Press.

McCann, Michael and Silverstein, Helena. 1998. "Rethinking Law's 'Allurements': A Relational Analysis of Social Movement Lawyers in the United States," In Austin Sarat and Stuart Scheingold, eds., *Cause Lawyering: Political Commitments and Professional Responsibilities*. New York: Oxford University Press.

McCarthy, John D., David W. Britt, and Mark Wolfson. 1991. "The Institutional Channeling of Social Movements by the State in the United States." *Research in Social Movements, Conflicts, and Change* 13: 45–76.

McCarthy, John D. and Mayer N. Zald. 1973. *The Trend of Social Movements in America: Professionalization and Resource Mobilization*. Morristown, NJ: General Learning.

———. 1987. "The Trend of Social Movements in America: Professionalization and Resource Mobilization." In Mayer N. Zald and John D. McCarthy eds., *Social Movements in and Organizational Society*, 337–91. New Brunswick, NJ: Transaction.

Meyer, David S. and Suzanne Staggenborg. 1996. "Movements, Countermovements, and the Structure of Political Opportunity." *American Journal of Sociology* 101: 1628–60.

Morris, Aldon D. and Suzanne Staggenborg. 2004. "Leadership in Social Movements," In David A. Snow, Sarah A. Soule, and Hanspeter Kriesi eds., *The Blackwell Companion to Social Movements*, 171–96. Malden, MA: Blackwell Publishing.

Piven, Frances Fox and Richard Cloward. 1977. *Poor People's Movements.* New York: Vintage.

Polletta, Francesca. 2000. "The Structural Context of Novel Rights Claims: Southern Civil Rights Organizing, 1961–1966." *Law and Society Review* 34: 367–406.

Rosenberg, Gerald N. 1991. *The Hollow Hope: Can the Courts Bring About Social Change?* Chicago: University of Chicago Press.

Sawyers, Traci M. and David S. Meyer. 1999. "Missed Opportunities: Social Movement Abeyance and Public Policy," *Social Problems* 46, 2: 187–206.

Scheingold, Stuart A. 2004. "Preface to the Second Edition: The New Politics of Rights," In *The Politics of Rights: Lawyers, Public Policy, and Political Change,* xvii–xlvii. 2nd edn. Ann Arbor: The University of Michigan Press.

———. 1974. *The Politics of Rights: Lawyers, Public Policy, and Political Change.* New Haven, CT: Yale University Press.

Scheingold, Stuart A. and Anne Bloom. 1998. "Transgressive Cause Lawyering: Practice Sites and the Politicization of the Professional." *International Journal of the Legal Profession.* 5: 209–54.

Scheingold. Stuart A. and Austin Sarat. 2004. *Something to Believe In: Politics, Professionalism, and Cause Lawyering.* Stanford, CA: Stanford University Press.

Snow, David A. 2004. "Framing Processes, Ideology, and Discursive Fields," In David A. Snow, Sarah A. Soule, and Hanspeter Kriesi, eds., *The Blackwell Companion to Social Movements,* 380–412. Malden, MA: Blackwell Publishing.

Snow, David A., and Robert D. Benford. 1988. "Ideology, Frame Resonance, and Participant Mobilization." *International Social Movement Research.* 1: 197–217.

———. 1992. "Master Frames and Cycles of Protest." In Aldon D. Morris and Carol McClurg Mueller, eds., *Frontiers in Social Movement Theory.* New Haven: Yale University Press.

Snow, David A., E. Burke Rochford, Jr., Steven K. Worden, and Robert D. Benford. 1986. "Frame Alignment Process, Micromobilization, and Movement Participation." *American Sociological Review* 51: 464–81.

Snow, David A., Sarah A. Soule, and Hanspeter Kriesi, eds. 2004. *The Blackwell Companion to Social Movements.* Malden, MA: Blackwell Publishing.

Staggenborg, Suzanne. 1988. "Consequences of Professionalization and Formalization in the Pro-Choice Movement." *American Sociological Review* 53: 585–605.

———. 1991. *The Pro-Choice Movement: Organization and Activism in the Abortion Conflict.* New York: Oxford University Press.

Tarrow, Sidney. 1992. "Mentalities, Political Cultures, and Collective Action Frames: Constructing Meaning through Action." In Aldon D. Morris and Carol McClurg Mueller, eds., *Frontiers in Social Movement Theory.* New Haven: Yale University Press.

Turner, Ralph. 1969. "The Public Perception of Protest." *American Sociological Review* 34: 815–31.

Zald, Mayer N. and Roberta Ash. 1966. "Social Movement Organizations: Growth, Decay, and Change." *Social Forces* 44: 327–41.

In Legal Culture, but Not of It

The Role of Cause Lawyers in Evangelical Legal Mobilization

KEVIN R. DEN DULK

In the 1960s, most observers would not have predicted that Jerry Falwell, the fundamentalist preacher, was destined to lead a political movement. Even Falwell was dubious about the prospect. "I would find it impossible," he declared in a 1965 sermon, "to stop preaching the pure saving gospel of Jesus Christ, and begin doing anything else—including . . . participating in civil-rights reforms" (FitzGerald 1981: 63). But by 1979 Falwell had established a political presence as a leader in the Moral Majority, and in that role he helped to spearhead the creation of the Moral Majority Legal Defense Foundation, a short-lived attempt in 1981 to pursue the parent organization's goals in court. For many of Falwell's supporters, the name of the organization was filled with symbolic meaning. Just as the NAACP Legal Defense Fund had combated legal discrimination against African Americans and sought to redefine the value of equality in America, the Moral Majority Legal Defense Foundation would defend believers from abridgements of their freedoms and help reclaim a Judeo-Christian heritage that had been lost in thirty years of "secularist" interpretations of the Constitution. What he had once declared impossible had now become quite real: Falwell was participating in the politics of rights.

In this chapter I seek to explain why and how cause lawyers associated with groups like Falwell's became part of the broader evangelical movement into public life that began in the late 1970s and 1980s and continues (albeit in different forms) to the present day. Although studies of rights mobilization suggest that lawyers working with or within the civil rights movement tended to privilege litigation at its outset, evangelical activism, like other more recent movements, took the opposite trajectory. Although a mass-based moralist campaign preceded and in fact fostered evangelicalism's eventual development of legal expertise and litigation strategies, evangelical leaders and grassroots activists in

the movement initially used the manifold tactics of public protest. Nevertheless, the movement itself was always intimately linked to the politics of rights.
Indeed, the moral grievances that generated the evangelical political resurgence
quickly became wedded to specific rights-claims in the late 1970s and early
1980s—the *right* to life or the *right* to practice one's faith, among others—to
such an extent that the distinction between moral/religious grievances and legal
rights was blurred.

This embrace of the politics of rights was uneasy but real. On the one hand,
conservative evangelicalism, with its historical tendency to withdraw from a
broader culture perceived as decadent and impure, was in considerable tension
with various rights-based movements of the mid- to late-twentieth century. On
the other hand, unlike other conservative groups that have been skeptical about
or even antagonistic toward rights-based politics (Hatcher 2005), evangelicals
overcame their apolitical stance partly by developing new conceptions of rights
as a means of countermobilization. Their innovative use of rights fits with what
sociolegal research on rights mobilization has suggested about the "constitutive"
nature of legal norms and discourses (McCann 1994; Brigham 1996). Indeed,
while evangelical cause lawyers developed ways of understanding their ideological commitments through a distinctive rights discourse, that discourse itself
began to shape their perception of the cause.

I examine two key elements of the rights mobilization of cause lawyers in the
evangelical movement. First, I argue that these lawyers were remarkably adaptive
and appropriating; they were not wholly oppositional to or uncompromising
about rights. To be sure, conservative evangelicals fervently opposed many
aspects of the women's rights movement and certain elements of church-state
jurisprudence in the 1970s and 1980s, much as they have led the fight against
same-sex marriage more recently (see, e.g., Barclay and Fisher this volume). But
rather than simply reject rights-claims altogether, they refigured the strategic
terrain by appropriating the language of "equal" rights and putting it to their
own purposes. Second, I suggest the key mechanism for this appropriation was
the influence of certain intellectuals within the evangelical movement itself. Although the growing cause lawyering literature has yielded a host of insights into
the professional tensions, motivations, and political obstacles that cause lawyers
face, there is relatively little scholarly attention to how the leadership norms
and structures—including intellectual resources—within social movements
that generate and shape these attorneys' motivations and tactics. I suggest that
such structures were decisively important to evangelical cause lawyers.

Although I examined major evangelical firms and other groups through elite
interviewing, observation, and content analysis of organizational documents,

my focus here is less on common organizational imperatives (e.g., fundraising, recruiting experienced attorneys, networking) than on the power of the religious ideas that animate legal mobilization. I explore specifically two policy areas that have been consistent objects of evangelical attention: abortion rights and church-state law pertaining to educational rights.

Evangelicals and Conservative Rights Mobilization: Some Theoretical Preliminaries

Religious and other socially conservative groups have been heavily involved in litigation over abortion, pornography, and education at least since the late 1970s (Ivers 1998; Brown 2002; den Dulk 2001), and groups associated with economic conservatism have argued their cause in courts since the turn of the century (Epstein 1985; Hatcher 2005). Sociolegal research has often assumed that these forms of conservative advocacy, religious or otherwise, are by definition a reactionary and inherently antiegalitarian phenomenon. In the preface to the new edition of *The Politics of Rights*, for example, Stuart Scheingold (2004: xxiv) suggests that the "backlash against progressive rights strategies" implies that rights serve as "double agents—amenable to *antiegalitarian* as well as egalitarian purposes" (emphasis in original). Scheingold identifies two characteristics of this important (though understudied) form of the politics of rights: (1) the "backlash" itself, a collective effort at legal *counter* mobilization against a progressive politics of rights; and (2) the motivation for this countermobilization, which he suggests is a kind of "antiegalitarianism" (see also Goldberg-Hiller 2002).

Scheingold's understanding of conservative countermobilization is an expected outgrowth of the foundational scholarly work on legal mobilization and cause lawyering. These studies tend to share a common assumption: to mobilize law is to use rights-claims to confront nefarious forms of hierarchy and subordination. As Michael McCann points out in his survey of law and social movements scholarship, members of conservative movements *can* be—and often are—motivated by perceptions that they are in a position of social disadvantage and subordination (McCann 2004: 509). Yet scholars of social movements—particularly law and social movements—have largely ignored conservatives as a potential core constituency of these movements, focusing instead on progressivist or left-liberal activism. Rosenberg's (1991) widely discussed judicial impact study, for example, asks broadly whether court decisions can bring about social change by catalyzing social movements and encouraging groups to form, but he focuses exclusively on proponents of abortion rights, desegregation, and greater environmental protection. Scholars who focus less on the impact of judicial decisions and more on law "as a system of cultural and symbolic meanings" (Galanter 1983: 17) also link legal mobilization to progressive rights-claiming. Although many of these scholars are skeptical about the capacity of rights-claims to fulfill their latent promise, suggesting instead that activists and lawyers are often co-opted by the unavailing "myth of rights" (Scheingold 1974), most agree that under certain conditions rights-claiming can encourage the development of social movements and other forms of political resistance to the status quo (see, e.g., Merry 1990; Sarat 1990; Ewick and Silbey 1992; McCann 1994; Silverstein 1996).

For many sociolegal scholars, then, conservative countermobilization is simply a status quo reaction to these egalitarian rights-claims. Interpreted through this theoretical frame, the evangelical movement appears to fit the image of reactionary anti-egalitarianism—a key source of cultural backlash, as McCann and Dudas put it elsewhere in this volume. Evangelicals mobilized the law over the past three decades partly out of a profound rejection of the very basis of modern rights-claims—claims of individual autonomy that these religious groups perceive as "secularist," immoral, and inattentive to the importance of institutions like the family or the church. They envisioned the Supreme Court's legalization of abortion (*Roe v. Wade* 1973) and a cluster of church-state decisions on education (particularly school prayer) as anathema to their worldview; they also believed that legal trends would eventually lead down a slippery slope into a breakdown of Judeo-Christian order, if the slide had not already occurred.

Yet the story of evangelical rights mobilization is more complex than a straightforward account of reactionary conservatism. Evangelical rights mobilization *was* a response to certain progressive rights-claims, but it did not so much reflect an opposition between egalitarianism and antiegalitarianism as it revealed a conflict over different understandings of equality itself. Put another way, evangelicals accepted the basic terms of political debate, but reframed their arguments to reflect an alternative understanding of rights and equality—a competing "myth," to use Scheingold's term. As I discuss below, this co-optation of progressive "rights-talk" (Glendon 1991) had a powerful resonance with movement activists, including cause lawyers.

Evangelical cause lawyers, however, were not the primary legal mythmakers at the outset of the movement. Like other cause lawyers (Sarat and Scheingold 1998; Scheingold and Sarat 2004), evangelical lawyers found ideological and tangible support not only within the legal profession but also in their broader community, and they were particularly influenced by evangelical intellectuals who directly targeted lawyers for rights-based activism. Recent research on the influence of public intellectuals contends that they possess decreasing societal influence (see. e.g., Posner 2001), but these studies focus on intellectual appeal to a monolithic national "public" rather than to a relatively small, religiously bounded community. Moreover, while Posner (2001) and others suggest that increasing specialization of knowledge has diminished the importance of conventional public intellectuals, I would suggest that specialization has *heightened* the influence of evangelical intellectuals within the tradition, who have provided religious context for the bewildering array of technological advancements, new ideas, and moral controversies endemic in modern life. Intellectuals in the evangelical tradition have been particularly adept in explaining and evaluating such concepts as "rights," "equality," "freedom," and "rule of law" through the eyes of religious worldview. Indeed, evangelical intellectuals have developed relatively coherent notions of "legality," as Ewick and Silbey (1998) understand the term, which have shaped evangelical cause lawyers' motivations and tactics.

Evangelicals and the Religious Vocation of Law

It is somewhat surprising, however, that evangelicals have paid so much attention to legal ideas and activism. As noted earlier, evangelical belief about public life is peculiarly ambivalent, a simultaneous attraction to and repulsion from political and social engagement. George Marsden (1991: 110), a leading historian of evangelicalism, calls this structure of belief a "tension between . . . revivalism and polemics," an inclination to shift focus between spiritual regeneration of the individual and of society as a whole. Modern "evangelicalism" (from the Greek for "gospel") is a legacy of episodic revivalist fervor in Britain and the United States during the eighteenth and nineteenth centuries. In the present day, it is best characterized neither by a specific institutional manifestation (compared to the Catholic Church, evangelicalism is highly decentralized and schismatic) nor a set of demographic characteristics (e.g., the average evangelical today shares roughly the same socioeconomic status as the average American). Instead, evangelicalism's primary unifying feature is a passionate commitment to a set of ideas, particularly the tenets of traditionalist Protestant Christianity: the overwhelming sin of the individual, eternal salvation through Christ's death and resurrection, the final authority and historicity of the biblical text, and personal spiritual transformation (e.g., the once-in-a-lifetime "born again" experience).

Spiritual transformation implies moral transformation as well. For evangelicals, personal piety is a response to salvation that marks an individual as part of the believing community. Society reflects each individual's piety in the aggregate—and often in the breach. To hold the sinner accountable, historically evangelicals have used broader institutions, including the state, to enforce rules of personal piety. At the same time, evangelicals believe change can only occur when "hearts and minds," not outward behaviors, are fundamentally altered, and that alteration only comes through a spiritual conversion that the state cannot coerce. Hence for many evangelicals there is a tension between fostering individual redemption and using the state as a barrier to sin.

This tension leads to a familiar pattern of cyclical political engagement (e.g., Bruce 1988; Jelen 1991). It begins with a set of grievances, often rooted in an evangelical understanding of society's moral failures: alcohol or dancing, creeping socialism, or, more recently, abortion, pornography, secularized schools, and same-sex marriage. Leaders mobilize the grassroots, participants intensify their efforts, and then the process comes to an abrupt halt when the "world" does not conform to heightened expectations. The name "Moral Majority" epitomized these expectations in the 1980s. Many evangelicals envisioned the United States as divided into two: the majority of citizens, who were devoted to Judeo-Christian values, and the powerful secular minority trying to foist its will on the rest of society. Evangelical leaders hoped that they could mobilize the silent majority to redeem culture, but when some leaders recently came to believe that the majority itself was corrupt, they no longer saw a redemptive edge to politics and urged withdrawal (Weyrich 1999; Thomas and Dobson 1999). Ironically, mobilization under the claim of moral consensus exposed the illusion of that consensus.

The law is often a catalyst for this "fight or flight" politics. The paradigmatic case is the famous "Monkey Trial" of 1925, in which Tennessee officials prosecuted John Scopes for violating a state ban on teaching evolution in public schools. The ban was a product of fundamentalist politics in the South, and the battle over the prosecution became a very public clash between these conservatives and their modernist opposition. Conservatives won the courtroom battle, but lost the war of public perception. The trial took on largely mythic proportions (Larson 1997) and is still widely regarded as having dealt a severe blow to the public image of conservative Protestants. Indeed, fundamentalists shared this view and seemed to withdraw from the broader culture in the aftermath of the case. But they did not wither away. On the contrary, they plowed their resources into an impressive subculture, complete with separate educational institutions and mission camps from which leaders continued their critique of modern society, while protecting their own cultural space (Marsden 1991; Carpenter 1999). These institutions became a base of support for evangelical resurgence in the past few decades.

Evangelicals avoided courts as a place for cultural contestation well into the 1970s. Despite three decades of separationist efforts in church-state law led by the American Jewish Congress, American Jewish Committee, and Americans United (Sorauf 1976; Ivers 1995), as well as a burgeoning and increasingly organized push by NOW, NARAL, and the ACLU to secure abortion rights through litigation, evangelical legal advocates were virtually nonexistent. Not only was there no serious effort to sponsor cases, threaten litigation, or file *amicus* briefs to influence abortion or education litigation at the federal appellate level; there was also no evangelical movement or organization in existence at the time that could engage in the politics of rights in any venue. Extrajudicially, some individuals pushed a rights agenda through proposals for legislation or constitutional amendments, especially in the area of school prayer. But these proposals were so rare and their support so weak and diffuse that they can hardly be taken as an indicator of the legal mobilization of evangelicals as a group.

The lack of legal mobilization over education or abortion rights was reflected in intellectual currents among evangelical elites. Against a backdrop of battles in New York and elsewhere for outright abortion law repeal (Nossiff 2001), evangelical intellectuals and opinion leaders in magazines like *Christianity Today*, the most prominent voice of conservative evangelicalism, had little to say about the abortion issue leading up to the *Roe v. Wade* decision in 1973. In 1972, only one out of nearly two hundred *Christianity Today* editorials addressed abortion directly, and there was no discussion of developing a coherent legal response to the mounting efforts of abortion-rights groups to reform the law.[1] *Christianity Today*'s immediate editorial response to *Roe* was almost politically fatalistic, illustrating that perceived social threat does not lead inevitably to legal mobilization or other forms of social action. After declaring that the Court had ruled for "paganism" and decrying "what remains of the democratic process," the magazine suggested that "Christians should accustom themselves to the thought that the American state no longer supports, in any meaningful sense, the laws of God, and prepare themselves *spiritually* for the prospect that it may one day formally repudiate them and turn against those who seek to live by them" (Anonymous 1973). Although highly critical of the Court, the editors responded with legal resignation and urged readers to nurture their spiritual lives in anticipation of worsening conditions in the future. For very different reasons, others in the evangelical community also provided little intellectual ammunition for an attack on new abortion law. A few leaders in the Southern Baptist Convention, the largest evangelical denomination, even gave their lukewarm support to *Roe* as a tolerable expediency for protecting religious beliefs about the issue.

Furthermore, though opinion leaders were apparently more interested in education issues than abortion at the time (e.g., editors at *Christianity Today* were much more likely to address education issues than abortion prior to 1973), their analysis of the law underlying education policy, such as it was, supported a fairly robust separation between the church and the state. Many evangelicals rejected arguments for such proposals as a constitutional amendment to reintroduce prayer in schools and public funding for private religious education (Anonymous 1971b, c, 1972a). *Christianity Today* even objected to providing the Amish a religious exemption from compulsory education requirements, though that position was controversial among evangelicals at the time (Anonymous 1971a, 1972c).

It was not until intellectuals and other elites within the broader world of evangelicalism became convinced that "secular forces" must be confronted in terms of a theology of activist politics that evangelical cause lawyers emerged and rights-advocacy groups began to form in the mid-1970s. To foster this mobilization, elites had to do more than merely publicize grievances and opportunities for redress (McCann 1994); they had to provide a religious justification for why progressive rights-mobilization was a threat at all and why their fellow evangelicals ought to mobilize to combat it. As evangelical leaders began to nudge their fellow religionists out of apolitical isolation, a small group of evangelical attorneys began to see cause lawyering as a distinctively religious vocation. Although they served clients, their underlying commitment was to advance a set of "transcendent" values (see Sarat and Scheingold 1998).

Figure 9.1 suggests the relationship between elite attention to legal matters and organized activism. From 1967 to the late 1970s, major evangelical publishers were producing very few books addressing church-state law or the rapid changes occurring over abortion-rights at the time. After this time period, however, the number of books climbs steadily to its peak in the late 1980s. Meanwhile, one indicator of evangelical rights mobilization—*amicus* participation in Supreme Court abortion rights and education cases—grew at a parallel rate, but with a lag of several years behind evangelical publishing patterns. The data on book publishing are only suggestive of changing beliefs about the specific tactic of legal advocacy, but these patterns are evidence that evangelical intellectuals were beginning to pay attention to the politics of rights prior to the emergence of a cadre of activist lawyers.

Changes in the substance of evangelical ideas were sometimes quite dramatic. By 1980, for example, *Christianity Today* announced a "radical 180-degree reversal" of its earlier opposition to tax support for Christian colleges. The trigger was the magazine's belief that public universities were no longer "neutral"

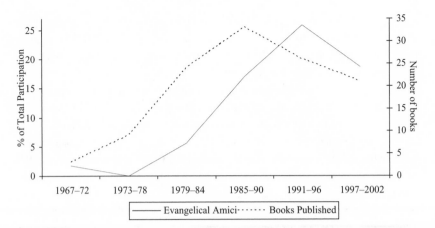

FIG. 9.1. Evangelical amicus participation and books by evangelicals on public life, 1967–2002

institutions, but rather homes for a "religion of secular humanism" that place human beings rather than God at the center of the moral and legal universe. The growth of this "religion" on public campuses was therefore an unconstitutional establishment of religion. Continued denial of tax support would also prohibit free exercise by "penalizing" those who pay tuition costs at religious schools, forcing them to fund two religions. "The American way of free enterprise," the editors at *Christianity Today* declared, required that religions compete free from government intrusion; in the case of secular humanism, however, a religion was being propped up by the power of the state (Anonymous 1972b). Although their separationist adversaries insisted that breaking ties between religion and state would allow all religious expressions equal acceptance, evangelicals argued the contrary position that the value of equality *demanded* greater state accommodation of religion in public life.

For evangelicals, the secular humanists were also hard at work in the abortion battles, "profaning" religious convictions by claiming that human choice trumps the will of God. Leaders at *Christianity Today* began to view evangelicalism's lack of active resistance to abortion as an affront to the "sacredness" and "dignity" of human life. Evangelicals were "apathetic" and "self-absorbed," raising some unappealing comparisons. "Christians no longer need to puzzle about the absent witness of the church in Nazi Germany," *Christianity Today* wrote in 1979. "Unless there is a Christian outcry against man's diminished dignity, history may once again repeat itself" (Anonymous 1979).

Meanwhile, other evangelical opinion leaders and activists were raising the specter of abortion and issuing even more explicit calls for Christian cultural (and particularly legal) engagement. In 1975, several prominent evangelicals, concerned that abortion had become a "Catholic issue," formed the Christian Action Council "to remind non-Roman Catholic Christians that virtually all Christians from the beginning have been against permissive abortion and for the protection of human life" (Anonymous 1976). Francis Schaeffer, an American pastor and writer who operated L'Abri Fellowship in Switzerland as a ministry to young evangelical academics and intellectuals, provided another bridge between ideas and action. He authored widely read books, such as *How Shall We Then Live?* (1976) and *Whatever Happened to the Human Race?* (1979), both accompanied by popular film series. These works, as well as Schaeffer's *Christian Manifesto* in 1981, argued that the *Roe* decision was a culmination of the steady movement of American constitutionalism away from its traditional bedrock in biblical principles. Echoing *Christianity Today*'s fears about the encroachment of secular humanism, Schaeffer claimed that *Roe* symbolized the arbitrary humanistic (or what he also called "sociological") foundation of contemporary law. Schaeffer reminded his audience repeatedly of the biblical theme that government received its ultimate authority from God and no one else. To reinforce his point, he was particularly fond of invoking the seventeenth-century Scottish theologian Samuel Rutherford, whose declaration of the rule of law (*lex rex*, or "the law is king") against the arbitrary "divine right of kings" provided a framework for Schaeffer's overall critique. For Schaeffer, the courts, not the rule of law, had become king (1981)—a perspective whose resonance has only deepened among evangelicals since Schaeffer's time.

Schaeffer's influence extended to a number of fronts in the burgeoning pro-life movement and beyond. For some, his teachings led inexorably to unconventional—and even unlawful—tactics. Randall Terry, leader of the abortion protest group Operation Rescue, suggested that Schaeffer's *Manifesto* was required reading for anyone who wanted to understand his group's work (Wills 1999: 324). This stands to reason: Schaeffer had called for active resistance to the new abortion regime, even to the point of civil disobedience. The analogy between civil disobedience in the civil rights and pro-life movements was always beneath the surface of Schaeffer's calls for social action. But civil disobedience was not the only means of resistance to the perceived humanistic trends in the law. Schaeffer would hearken back to another legacy of the civil rights movement, namely, the use of courts. He struck directly at the heart of evangelical apathy in the legal arena, chiding the attorneys in his audience for ignoring the dramatic change in recent decades:

> Where were the Christian lawyers during the crucial shift from forty years ago to just a few years ago? Surely the Christian lawyers should have seen the change taking place and stood on the wall and blown the trumpets loud and clear. A nonlawyer like myself has a right to feel somewhat let down because the Christian lawyers did not blow the trumpets clearly between, let us say, 1940 and 1970 (1981: 47).

Coupled with the exhortations of other evangelical elites, Schaeffer's explicit challenges to attorneys represented an important evangelical experience: the *calling* to law. For evangelicals, to respond to a call is to spiritualize vocation, that is, to begin to discern a divine plan for one's life and, especially in the legal realm, to respond with obedience to a religious obligation that is bound up with a political cause. To discern a call is neither a static nor an unambiguous experience. To be sure, some evangelical interviewees recall moments during this era in which they perceived an explicit—even literally audible—command to take a particular action. One church-state attorney I interviewed believed he heard a divine voice say, "I am your client," which led him to rethink his vocational plans,[2] but most evangelical attorneys described receiving a call as a dynamic process that requires an attentive and dutiful mind and a confirming environment. The changes at *Christianity Today*, the creation of the Christian Action Council, the teachings of Schaeffer and others, not to mention the emergence of the Moral Majority and other social movement groups—all of these factors, among many others, enabled evangelical attorneys to see cause lawyering as a legitimate vocational aspiration. Before the 1970s, as one attorney recalled, evangelicals "weren't hearing anything from the pulpit that politics is an area where you can incarnate the Gospel."[3] Rather, as another evangelical attorney noted, pastors would preach that law should be left to "civic-minded people" and that evangelicals "need to be concerned with the gospel and missionaries and things like that."[4] Coming out of that environment, one can appreciate the change when, in 1981, *Christianity Today* issued a challenge to evangelical leaders and political activists: "Encourage Christian young people ... to consider a calling to a *ministry* in law" (Anonymous 1981).

The role of religious leaders and activists is built into the process of discerning the call to a legal vocation. Some evangelical attorneys, like John Whitehead, founder of one of the first evangelical firms in 1982, fell under the direct tutelage of pastors and religious intellectuals. Indeed, his choice for the firm's name—the Rutherford Institute—was an obvious paean to Schaeffer's influence.[5] Many others sought guidance from "spiritually mature" colleagues in the legal profession. The Christian Legal Society institutionalized this kind of religious mentorship and helped channel the call of some of its members into church-state law through its own public interest firm, the Center for Law and Religious Freedom (CLRF), founded in 1975. Many interviewees traced their first experiences with answering a call to CLS.[6] For example, after describing his dissatisfaction with his corporate work at a prestigious Baltimore firm, one respondent noted the CLS connection at a particularly distressing moment in his career:

> By God's providence that year [CLS's annual convention] was in Sandy Cove, Maryland. [My wife and I] went to that conference—I had never been involved with CLS at all—and I met [the head of CLS] and shared with him briefly what I was struggling with. And he really affirmed that we weren't total idiots to walk away from all this if that was what God was calling us to do. By the end of that weekend I was convinced that I needed to leave the firm.[7]

Later, he joined the CLRF as a staff attorney. Such responses illustrate how the structure of organizations—in this case, CLS's dual role as a providential spiritual fellowship *and* a church-state firm through its subsidiary, CLRF—facilitated the recognition of distinctly religious obligations. This attorney's experiences, echoed in the responses of most other evangelical respondents, illustrate McAdam's (1986: 64) observation that "integration into supportive networks acts as a structural 'pull' encouraging the individual to make good on his or her strongly held beliefs."

Evangelical intellectuals and opinion leaders also passed on their concern with the *legitimacy* of ideas to the new class of evangelical attorneys. Scholarship through law reviews and law-related books served as an outlet to help validate evangelical ideas in the secular legal community by showing the consistency between legal norms and values and evangelical ideas. It was a vehicle for taking part in the debate over progressive rights-claims, while attempting to redefine the terms of that debate (Scholzman and Tierney 1986: 362–64). Figure 9.2 displays estimates of the number of books and articles written under the auspices of evangelical organizations from 1967 to 2002.[8] There is virtually no evangelical scholarship on legal ideas in the 1970s and then a surge in the 1980s that continues more or less unabated to early 2000s. John Whitehead alone published at least eighteen books and several articles from 1977 to the present, and attorneys for other groups have added many of their own.

By the early 1980s, then, the CLRF, Rutherford, and several other movement law firms had been created to answer the call to cause lawyering. Many more were on the way, including most notably the American Center for Law and Justice (founded in 1990) and Alliance Defense Fund (1994). Movement elites were

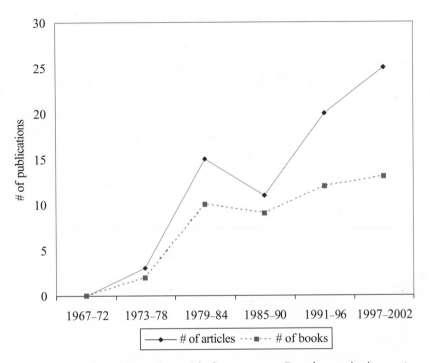

FIG. 9.2. Books and law review articles by attorneys at Evangle organizations, 1967–2002

directly involved in establishing this second wave of rights-advocacy groups. Pat Robertson founded the ACLJ, drawing from the resources of his media (Christian Broadcasting Network), electioneering and mass mobilization (the Christian Coalition), and academic (Regent University) interests. A group of many other prominent evangelicals, including James Dobson of Focus on the Family and the late Bill Bright of Campus Crusade for Christ, founded the Alliance Defense Fund.

The callings pursued by these various groups took many different forms. Many advocates mobilized law for defensive purposes by protecting the autonomy of churches and religious schools; others used advocacy to transform the culture as a whole by focusing on abortion, same sex relations, and other matters of morality policy. The extent of evangelical mobilization is too great to give comprehensive treatment here (den Dulk 2001; Brown 2002; Hacker 2005), but two case examples—one focused on education, and the other on abortion— illustrate how evangelical cause lawyers appropriated and redefined the terms in the politics of rights.

Rights Mobilization and Equality in Education

In the late 1970s and 1980s, evangelical attorneys began an effort to carve out cultural space in public educational institutions, where evangelism was particularly widespread. To national parachurch organizations like InterVarsity Christian Fellowship or Campus Crusade for Christ, not to mention myriad local fellowships, Bible studies, and campus churches, access to public facilities, or other campus resources is a tool to help them evangelize secular universities. From the beginning, such groups as the Rutherford Institute, the CLRF, and later the ACLJ and ADF were at the forefront of battles over "equal access"—the principle that religious and nonreligious individuals and groups alike ought to have the same opportunities to public goods. In fact, the CLRF pioneered the principle: it helped take the seminal equal access case, *Widmar v. Vincent* (1981), to the Supreme Court; it led the intriguing coalition of evangelical and civil liberties groups that pushed through the Equal Access Act in 1984 (Hertzke 1988: ch. 6), applying the equal access principle to public high schools across the country; and it provided leadership in *Widmar's* progeny in federal and state courts, including *Board of Education v. Mergens* (1990), *Lamb's Chapel v. Center Moriches Union Free School District* (1993), and *Rosenberger v. University of Virginia* (1995).

But what motivates the Center's involvement in this body of case law? The CLRF's *amicus* brief in *Widmar* provides a hint. Declaring its concern over "the core values of religious liberty," CLRF describes the "nature of the religious command and obligation" that motivated the Christian students who were denied access to facilities at a public university. In particular, the CLRF invoked biblical mandates, including the Great Commission,[9] to suggest that evangelism was a central part of the students' expression of faith. Because the Court had upheld the right of other religious groups to evangelize in certain public fora, CLRF reasoned that the students in this case should have the same protection. Basic legal equality demanded it.

Of course, CLRF presented this argument to a judicial audience, but linking student evangelism to religious exercise was not simply a legal strategy. The CLRF advocates for equal access because its attorneys believe that evangelism is part of their calling. One of the earliest directors of CLRF characterized the issue this way:

> Our mission [was] to prepare and preserve the ground [for evangelism] through law. The window *is* law. . . . I once asked [several prominent evangelists], "What are you doing to keep the window open?" And they said, "We're praying, Sam." And I said, "Not enough. If my wife had a brain tumor and I said all we are doing is praying

because my God is a mighty God and he can save and heal and he can take care of that tumor, you would say to us, 'We admire your faith, but go to the doctor.'" So when it comes to religious liberty this idea of just praying without going to a lawyer is inadequate, superficial, and unbiblical.[10]

The reference to the Bible here points to a religious idea underlying equal access lawyering. Without exception, CLRF respondents claimed that their approach to equal access is a direct result of institutionalizing the biblical command to "do unto others as you would have them do unto you."[11] In fact, without prompting, a recent director of CLRF said in an interview that a consistent application of the Golden Rule is "the single most important thing in my strategic decision-making."[12] The comment, reiterated in nearly every other interview with CLRF staff, illustrates a convergence between the normative imperatives of evangelicals and their mobilization of law. A biblical mandate affected both whether and how CLRF would get involved in the issue of equal access.

One might question how deep this commitment to *equal* access runs. Although CLRF's motive for advocating equal access was to open the public square to other Christians, the group has been careful to tolerate other uses of the principle. By focusing on equal access, the CLRF itself attempts to "witness" through the legal process by not claiming any special constitutional protections. Using an evangelical moral calculus, this may appear a costly strategy: advocates open the door to beliefs and practices that are anathema. For example, several gay and lesbian organizations that seek to establish chapters in high schools around the country have used the equal access doctrine. But CLRF, rather than working out legal distinctions to exclude these groups, has not opposed the principle's wider application. One attorney described CLRF's willingness to support equal access for all groups as an opportunity for evangelism because it presents Christians as sincere, consistent with principle, and fair.[13] The evangelistic priority served as a strategic bar to exclusionary legal tactics.

Rights Mobilization, Freedom, and Abortion Protest

It is one thing to defend one's slice of culture, as equal access efforts attempted to do for evangelicals; it is another to attempt to transform the culture as a whole. Intellectuals and activists at the outset of the evangelical movement envisioned cultural transformation as a Christian ideal, but some cause lawyers faced a theological problem. "To be a Christian," says Rutherford's Whitehead, "you have to be redemptive. [But] how is a legal group redemptive in the true Christian sense? Redemption is a personal, individual thing, so how do we get into corporate redemption? It depends on your theology."[14] Whitehead's use of "redemption" is a provocative rhetoric to evangelicals. To "redeem" is "to be set free," and the religious meanings that evangelicals attach to "redemptive" forms of freedom influence how they understand the use of legal advocacy for transformative purposes.

Underlying much of evangelicalism's legal advocacy is a presumption that a certain form of freedom is indispensable, a precondition of an individual "accepting Christ as a personal Lord and savior" and living a virtuous life. On the surface, this evangelical emphasis on individual freedom seems at home within one strand of liberal theorizing on law that places a value (at least abstractly) on maximizing the range of individual choices. Indeed, one of the key arguments in favor of the Religion Clauses of the First Amendment has been to formalize autonomy for the benefit of religious believers. Yet the evangelical is less sanguine about the liberal understanding. Liberal theory and practice have often assumed that religionists may enjoy their freedom as long as they keep religious practice a private affair. Many evangelicals, however, cannot abide such an arrangement. They seek more than cultural space to practice religion in private; they wish to transform the culture as a whole by using public means to influence individual behavior and direct others toward their understanding of God's will.

Their notion of freedom is more positive than negative: it is freedom *to be* a certain kind of person, not simply freedom *from* constraints. Freedom is therefore bounded, as we see in this broadly representative statement from Michael Farris, a prominent evangelical cause lawyer:

> I believe in the maximum amount of freedom possible within the boundaries of protecting life, liberty, and property founded on the moral law of God. That's it. I would view myself as a Christian libertarian. Saying that the moral law of God has to be honored and enforced means we don't kill little babies. We don't turn sex into a spectator sport and so on.[15]

Of course, Farris' self-description would make most libertarians cringe. But his examples of abortion and pornography provide an insight into a broader point that motivates many evangelicals: true freedom needs limits, and the source of these limits must be outside the individual's will.

With this view in mind, many evangelical firms expanded their agendas to include matters that are not directly related to the autonomy of religious practices and institutions. Among their various efforts, abortion was—and continues to be—a high priority. Abortion restrictions of all kinds in the post-*Roe* era have faced constitutional challenges, but the primary responsibility for litigating these cases fell to lawyers for the states that passed the restrictions. This placed some limitations on the participation of evangelical cause lawyers in litigation over abortion policy—they were involved primarily as amici or occasional inter-veners and consultants—but they were nevertheless very active in facilitating protest politics against abortion at a grassroots level, among other things.

From the late 1970s, several activist groups—mostly evangelical and Catholic—used civil disobedience and other unconventional tactics in an ef-fort to shut down selected abortion clinics, culminating in Operation Rescue's "Summer of Mercy" in 1993. Abortion providers and abortion-rights groups responded to these efforts through a series of high profile lawsuits that were ultimately settled in the US Supreme Court (see also Van Dyk 1998). With mixed success, they used the so-called Ku Klux Klan Act of 1871 (which for-bids conspiracies against a "class" of people) and the RICO antiracketeering statute as a basis for lawsuits against the abortion protestors (*Bray v. Alexandria Women's Health Clinic* 1993; *NOW v. Scheidler* 1994). They also attempted to ex-tend the power of courts to enjoin some protestor activities (*Madsen v. Women's Health Center* 1994). In these and many other cases, a cluster of evangelical law firms—among them Christian Advocates Serving Evangelism (CASE) and the ACLJ—sponsored the pro-life defense.

CASE and ACLJ were strongly linked by their shared leadership under Jay Sekulow. Sekulow founded CASE in 1991, as he puts it, to "defend the legal rights of individuals and organizations who are telling the gospel" (Sekulow 2005), a mission he brought to ACLJ when Robertson hired him in 1992 as the head of firm. But the "gospel" here meant something more than preaching individual salvation through Christ's death and resurrection, though that was clearly one of these organizations' goals. "Gospel" also encompassed an evangelical vision of the good society, a fulfillment of an understanding of God's intentions for human interaction. For evangelical groups like CASE and the ACLJ, abortion was a particularly clear violation of those intentions.

CASE and the ACLJ abortion litigation used law instrumentally to pursue their opposition to abortion. As one advocate involved in each of these groups put it, "The reason I'm doing what I'm doing now is because of the pro-life movement. . . . I went to law school because I felt very much like I wanted to do something I believed in, and I certainly wasn't in it for the money, and I certainly wasn't in it because I loved the law."[16] His claim exemplifies the priorities of a cause lawyer—his primary commitment is to the cause, not to professional development or even the law itself (Sarat and Scheingold 1998).

Pursuit of the cause can yield intriguing ways of thinking about and acting on the law. Like the CLRF addressing equal access, the groups litigating abortion protest cases see their work in distinctly religious terms. The name "Christian Advocates Serving Evangelism" is telling: the chief aim of the organization is to advance the spread of the Christian message, broadly understood to include conservative Christian teaching on abortion. Litigators in abortion protest cases view themselves as "defenders of the defenders, advocates for the advocates of the unborn," as an attorney for both CASE and ACLJ put it; their job, at least in the first amendment context, is to "clear away obstacles that can stifle the transmission of truth."[17] But the desire to encourage the "transmission of truth" is also reflected in decidedly liberal ways of thinking about the law. The "marketplace of ideas" metaphor is embedded in the language of advocates for CASE and ACLJ. Sekulow is particularly responsive to the metaphor, as we see in this statement: "If we put our message out on the marketplace, if we really believe what the gospel says, our light will outshine the others' darkness. Truth will prevail" (Stafford 1993). The problem for these groups is the perception that the marketplace is captured by a secularist monopoly, which evangelicals see as a worldview that is not neutral with respect to other sets of ideas. Hence the repeated claim by evangelicals, as exemplified in Schaeffer's teachings about the rule of law, that religionists must engage the public square to ensure that political institutions remain open to faith.

Conclusion

These experiences of cause lawyers for the evangelical movement may appear unique. Few religious traditions have mobilized—or countermobilized—law in quite the same way. Cognizant of a long history of anti-Semitism, for example, Jewish groups have worked toward a separation of the religious and political spheres, fearful that the combination of the two threatens their own communities. The "secular" self-definition of the most prominent Jewish rights-advocacy groups—the American Jewish Congress, American Jewish Committee, and Anti-Defamation League—embodies this desire to distinguish the religious from the political (Sorauf 1976; Ivers 1995). Jehovah's Witnesses and the Amish overcame their aversion to political and legal engagement only to carve out their own space for religious freedom; their aim was protection from the broader culture, not redemption of it (Manwarring 1962; Auerbach 1983). Mainline Protestant denominations have engaged the political process on a range of issues, often with opinion leaders preaching a "social gospel" orientation that favors a left-liberal political message. But except for a couple of denominational associations—the Baptist Joint Committee and National Council of Churches—their rights advocacy does not compare to the growth and intensity of evangelical rights advocacy groups over recent decades.

The experience of African American Christianity in the civil rights era is in some ways a more useful comparison to the recent efforts of white evangelical rights advocates. In the 1950s, many intellectuals and opinion leaders in the black church began to take a prophetic posture against various forms of racial discrimination. Their theologies began to speak of liberation in this world and the next (Lincoln and Mamiya 1990). But their social thought and activism were not always welcomed within their own community; many believers in black churches avoided politics altogether. Prompted by painful memories of repercussions for social activism in the past, their theologies focused on the world hereafter rather than the world here and now (Paris 1985). These divergent streams of African American political thinking reveal a tension in the movement between resistance and accommodation, between protest and conformity. The NAACP Legal Defense Fund, as the leading movement organization, reflected the tension quite clearly. On the one hand, the organization was created as a secular alternative to "otherworldly" black churches, where leaders had trouble mobilizing apolitical believers. On the other hand, it is hard to imagine that the NAACP's efforts as a whole could have succeeded without the leadership and other resources of the black churches (see Kluger 1976; Morris 1984; Garrow 1986).

To be sure, the white evangelical experience over the past few decades is different from that of the black churches during the civil rights era, both in terms of the causes the two traditions pursued—one progressive, the other conservative—and the resources and organizational arrangements at their disposal. Black churches did not cultivate a set of explicitly *religious* law firms or cause lawyers, as evangelical elites have developed. But evangelicals have shared ambivalence with African Americans from this era, a moving back and forth between accommodation of the culture around them and resistance to it. In addition, like the translation of a black liberationist theology into the language of civil rights, evangelical intellectuals reframed their religious beliefs into a public rhetoric that in different ways and at different times enabled cause lawyers to pursue their tradition's goals through the politics of rights.

To what extent we can generalize from this analysis is an open empirical question, but the African American example suggests that the experience of evangelical groups is not entirely unique. To be sure, environmental groups, advocates for free markets, groups litigating over tobacco or same-sex marriage, or other efforts at organized rights advocacy will have different mixtures of opportunities and motivations for mobilizing law. But the intensity and coherence of these groups' ideas on rights and social activism, the role of law and government, and the nature of their cause may factor into their decisional calculus. If evangelical rights advocacy is any indication, their decisions are likely mediated—and often preempted—by both legal and extralegal ways of explaining and evaluating the social and political world.

Notes

1. Author analysis of all the nearly two hundred editorials *Christianity Today* published in 1972.

2. Interview with Samuel Ericsson, formerly with CLRF.

3. Interview with Steven McFarland, formerly with CLRF.

4. Interview with Michael Farris, HSLDA.

5. In addition to Schaeffer, Whitehead sought out the late Rousas John Rushdooney, a Christian "reconstructionist" who believed that the Old Testament law is still in universal effect. Whitehead never wholly subscribed to reconstructionism, but Rushdooney did provide "intellectual focus" and a network of other evangelical elites when Whitehead was beginning his career (Whitehead 1999).

6. Interviews with McFarland; Ericsson; Bradley Jacobs, HSDLA (formerly CLRF); and Gregory Baylor, CLRF.

7. Interview with Jacobs.

8. I derived the book figures in Table 2 by running a Library of Congress author search on General Counsels (or equivalents) employed by the major evangelical firms from the 1970s to the present. The figures for legal periodicals were derived from a computer search of the Legal Periodicals Index for articles on abortion, right-to-die, or education that contain the name of any major evangelical organization. I examined the author's institutional affiliation and the acknowledgements, both customarily provided in law review articles, to determine if the author was on staff with an evangelical group.

9. In the New Testament passage of Matthew 28: 18–20, Christ is recorded as leaving his disciples with these words: "All authority in heaven and on earth has been given to me. Therefore go and make disciples of all nations, baptizing them in the name of the Father, and of the Son, and of the Holy Spirit, and teaching them to obey everything I have commanded you. And surely I am with you always, to the very end of the age" (NIV).

10. Interview with Ericsson.

11. Interviews with Jacobs, Baylor, Ericsson, and McFarland.

12. Interview with McFarland.

13. Interview with Ericsson.

14. Interview with John Whitehead, The Rutherford Institute.

15. Interview with Farris.

16. Interview with Walter Weber, ACLJ.

17. Interview with Weber.

References

Anonymous. 1971a. The Amish in Court. *Christianity Today*, October 22: 24.

———. 1971b. "Making No Amends for Prayer." *Christianity Today*, December 3: 31–2.

———. 1971c. "The Prayer Amendment." *Christianity Today*, October 10: 32.

———. 1972a. "Paying for Education." *Christianity Today*, May 12: 27.

————. 1972b. "Tax Support for Christian Colleges." *Christianity Today*, November 7: 10–11.

————. 1972c. "Using the Amish." *Christianity Today*, January 7: 36–7.

————. 1973. "Abortion and the Court." *Christianity Today*, February 16: 33.

————. 1976. "Is Abortion a Catholic Issue?" *Christianity Today*, January 16: 30.

————. 1979. "Beyond Personal Piety." *Christianity Today*, November 16: 13.

————. 1981. "The Contemporary Civil Climate Threatens Religion Freedom." *Christianity Today*, February 6: 16.

Auerbach, Jerold S. 1983. *Justice Without Law? Resolving Disputes Without Lawyers.* New York: Oxford University Press.

Brigham, John. 1996. *The Constitution of Interest: Beyond the Politics of Rights.* New York: New York University.

Brown, Steven P. 2002. *Trumping Religion: The New Christian Right, the Free Speech Clause, and the Courts.* Tuscaloosa, AL: University of Alabama Press.

Bruce, Steve. 1988. *The Rise and Fall of the New Christian Right.* Oxford: Claredon.

Carpenter, Joel. 1999. *Revive Us Again: The Reawakening of American Fundamentalism.* New York: Oxford University Press.

den Dulk, Kevin. 2001. Prophets in Caesar's Courts: The Role of Ideas in Catholic and Evangelical Rights Advocacy. Ph.D. dissertation, Political Science, University of Wisconsin—Madison, Madison.

Epstein, Lee. 1985. *Conservatives in Court.* Knoxville: University of Tennessee.

Ewick, Patricia, and Susan S. Silbey. 1992. "Conformity, Contestation, Resistance: An Account of Legal Consciousness." *New England Law Review* 26: 731–49.

————. 1998. *The Common Place of Law: Stories from Everyday Life.* Chicago, IL: University of Chicago Press.

FitzGerald, Frances. 1981. "A Disciplined, Charging Army." *The New Yorker*, May 18: 63.

Galanter, Marc. 1983. "The Radiating Effects of Courts." In K. D. Boyum and L. Mather eds., *Empirical Theories of Courts.* New York: Longman.

Garrow, David J. 1986. *Bearing the Cross: Martin Luther King, Jr. and the Southern Christian Leadership Conference.* New York: Morrow.

Glendon, Mary Ann. 1991. *Rights Talk: The Impoverishment of Political Discourse.* New York: Free Press.

Goldberg-Hiller, Jonathan. 2002. *The Limits of Union: Same-Sex Marriage and the Politics of Civil Rights.* Ann Arbor: University of Michigan Press.

Hacker, Hans. 2005. *The Culture of Conservative Christian Litigation.* Lanham, MD: Rowman and Littlefield.

Hatcher, Laura. 2005. "Economic Libertarians, Property and Institutions: Linking Activism, Ideas, and Identities among Property Rights Advocates." In A. Sarat and S. Scheingold eds., *The Worlds Cause Lawyers Make: Structure and Agency in Legal Practice.* Stanford, CA: Stanford University Press.

Hertzke, Allen. 1988. *Representing God in Washington.* Knoxville: University of Tennessee.

Ivers, Gregg. 1995. *To Build a Wall: American Jews and the Separation of Church and State.* Charlottesville: University of Virginia Press.

————. 1998. "Please God, Save This Honorable Court: The Rise of the Conservative Religious Bar." In P. S. Herrnson, R. G. Shaiko, and C. Wilcox eds., *The Interest Group Connection.* Chatham, NJ: Chatham House.

Jelen, Ted G. 1991. *The Political Mobilization of Religious Beliefs.* New York: Praeger.

Kluger, Richard. 1976. *Simple Justice: The History of Brown v. Board of Education and Black America's Struggle for Equality*. New York: Knopf.

Larson, Edward. 1997. *Summer for the Gods: The Scopes Trial and America's Continuing Debate Over Science and Religion*. Cambridge, Mass: Harvard University Press.

Lincoln, C. Eric, and Lawrence Mamiya. 1990. *The Black Church in the African American Experience*. Durham, NC: Duke University Press.

Manwarring, David. 1962. *Render Unto Caesar: The Flag Salute Controversy*. Chicago: University of Chicago.

Marsden, George. 1991. *Understanding Fundamentalism and Evangelicalism*. Grand Rapids, Mich: Eerdmans.

McAdam, Doug. 1986. "Recruitment to High Risk Activism: The Case of Freedom Summer." *American Journal of Sociology* 92: 64–90.

McCann, Michael. 1994. *Rights at Work: Pay Equity Reform and the Politics of Legal Mobilization*. Chicago: University of Chicago.

McCann, Michael W. 2004. "Law and Social Movements". In A. Sarat ed., *The Blackwell Companion to Law and Society* Oxford: Blackwell.

Merry, Sally Engle. 1990. *Getting Justice and Getting Even: Legal Consciousness Among Working-Class Americans*. Chicago: University of Chicago.

Morris, Aldon D. 1984. *The Origins of the Civil Rights Movement*. New York: Free Press.

Nossiff, Rosemary. 2001. *Before Roe: Abortion Policy in the States*. Philadelphia, PA: Temple University Press.

Paris, Peter J. 1985. *The Social Teaching of the Black Churches*. Philadelphia: Fortress.

Posner, Richard A. 2001. *Public Intellectuals: A Study of Decline*. Cambridge, MA: Harvard University Press.

Rosenberg, Gerald. 1991. *The Hollow Hope: Can Courts Bring About Social Change?* Chicago: University of Chicago.

Sarat, Austin. 1990. ". . . The Law Is All Over": Power, Resistance, and the Legal Consciousness of the Welfare Poor." *Yale Journal of Law and the Humanities* 2: 343–80.

Sarat, Austin, and Stuart Scheingold, eds., 1998. *Cause Lawyering*. New York: Oxford.

Schaffer, Francis A. 1976. *How Should we Then Live*. Old Tappan, NJ: Revell

Schaeffer, Francis A. 1981. *A Christian Manifesto*. Westchester, Illinois: Crossway Books.

Schaeffer, Francis A. and C. Fverett Koop 1979. *Whatever happened to the Human Race?* old Tappan, NY: Revell.

Scheingold, Stuart. 1974. *The Politics of Rights: Lawyers, Public Policy, and Political Change*. New Haven: Yale University Press.

———. 2004. *The Politics of Rights: Lawyers, Public Policy, and Political Change*. Ann Arbor, MI: University of Michigan Press.

Scheingold, Stuart A., and Austin Sarat. 2004. *Something to Believe In: Politics, Professionalism, and Cause Lawyering*. Stanford, Calif.: Stanford Law and Politics.

Scholzman, Kay L, and John T. Tierney. 1986. *Organized Interests in American Democracy*. New York: Harper and Row.

Sekulow, Jay. 2005. *How a Jewish Lawyer from Brooklyn Came to Believe in Jesus*. Available at http://www.jewsforjesus.org/answers/lifestories/jay_sekulow

Silverstein, Helena. 1996. *Unleashing Rights: Law, Meaning, and the Animal Rights Movement*. Ann Arbor: University of Michigan Press.

Sorauf, Frank. 1976. *The Wall of Separation: Constitutional Politics of Church and State.* Princeton, NJ: Princeton University Press.

Stafford, Tim. 1993. "Move Over, ACLU." *Christianity Today,* October 25: 20–24.

Thomas, Cal, and Ed Dobson. 1999. *Blinded by Might: Can the Religious Right Save America?* Grand Rapids, Mich: Zondervan.

Van Dyk, Robert. 1998. "The Pro-Choice Legal Mobilization and Decline of Clinic Block-ades." In D. A. Schultz ed., *Leveraging the Law: Using the Courts to Achieve Social Change.* New York: Peter Lang.

Weyrich, Paul. 1999. "The Moral Minority." [Reprint]. *Christianity Today,* September 6: 43.

Whitehead, John. 1999. *Slaying Dragons: The Truth Behind the Man Who Defended Paula Jones.* Nashville: Thomas Nelson.

Wills, Garry. 1999. *Under God: Religion and American Politics.* New York: Touchstone.

Intersecting Identities

Cause Lawyers as Legal Professionals and Social Movement Actors

COREY S. SHDAIMAH

Introduction

The role of professionals is a frequent theme in social movement literature. Cause lawyering scholarship suggests that cause lawyers involved with social movements or social movement organizations derive meaning and professional satisfaction from assisting causes as professionals (Menkel-Meadow 1998). Further, their drive to participate in social movements often stems from identification with or empathy for the motives and goals of the movement (Sarat and Scheingold 2004). Relying on intensive interviews with "left activist" (Scheingold 1998) cause lawyers from a variety of nonprofit public interest law firms, this chapter explores the meanings of lawyers' intersecting identities. In contrast to many other explorations of the role of lawyers in social movements, this chapter focuses on lawyers' own perceptions and understanding of their roles rather than lawyers' impact on a given social movement.

First, I provide a brief outline of methods and a description of the lawyers interviewed in this research. In the following section, I outline lawyers' motivations in choosing the law, showing that this choice was motivated primarily by a desire for social change (however defined). Next, I examine the role that lawyers see for themselves at a time when the movements with which these particular lawyers identify are in abeyance, or in a latency phase (Melucci 1994; Robnett 1997). Lawyers' connections to movements at such stages are even more tenuous than when movements are in active phases. I argue that this can both amplify lawyers' importance to a movement and isolate lawyers. Last, I explore the possibility that left activist cause lawyering (and perhaps analogously right wing cause lawyering) itself is usefully viewed as a social movement: it reflects the attempts of a group of like-minded, marginalized individuals to effectuate social change through collective action (Snow, Soule, and Kreisi 2004). Considering themselves participants in a cause lawyering social movement helps lawyers to cope with the sense of alienation from social movements in latency phases. It also may serve an important role in revitalizing movements, creating and sustaining movement networks, and maximizing social change potential in otherwise hostile political climates.

A Note on Methods and Participants

The data for this chapter are drawn from two sources. The first explored the client-professional relationship in a legal services setting. For the purposes of this chapter, I rely on twenty-one interviews with eleven legal services lawyers working in a large legal services firm that I call "Northeast Legal Services" (NELS). These lawyers worked in a variety of practice areas and combined individual representation with other legal tools including legislative advocacy, outreach and community education, and class action litigation. The second was an exploratory study of the Philadelphia public interest law community, in which Sue Wasserkrug and I interviewed sixteen lawyers in the nonprofit public interest sector.[1] These lawyers practiced in a variety of nonprofit professional settings, some of which focused on specific issues (such as education), while others served specific populations (such as juveniles). Interviews lasted between one and two hours; all were tape-recorded and then transcribed changing identifying information.

Neither of these projects was originally intended to explore social movement issues, thus the questions were not formulated to elicit answers that neatly fit into existing social movement paradigms. However, as analysis on both projects progressed it became clear that the lawyers saw themselves as part of broader movements for social change and measured themselves against such movements. They did so whether the movements are currently active or not, and regardless of whether others viewed the movements as real or merely the product of wishful thinking.

All the lawyers interviewed perceived their work as part of something larger. Although the "something larger" may be rather amorphous, like "the Movement" described by one of the lawyers in Scheingold and Bloom's study (1998, cited in Scheingold and Sarat 2004), it exerts a strong influence on career choices and practice. Indeed, most of the lawyers in these studies work in what can be described as social movement organizations (McCarthy and Zald 1977) that were spawned from or began as part of movements: the women's movement, poor people's movements, AIDS activism, and others. At the time of the interviews, as now, there was a general pessimism on the left as to the efficacy of law as a tool for social change. However, these left-activist lawyers saw a role for themselves in the pursuit of social change as lawyers, even if such is limited to incremental change or to keeping the proverbial flame alive. The mythological heyday of "progressive" social movement activity during the 1960s and the 1970s exemplified by the civil rights movement, the black power movement, and the feminist movement seem long past, even as incipient models of social change are emerging (see Snow, Soule and Kreisi 2004). Veteran lawyers in these interviews began to practice in the 1970s and saw themselves as part of the social movement efforts of that time. However, even more recent law school graduates drew their inspiration from these heady days. They compared their work using the yardstick of widespread changes that were once imaginable (if not attainable in fact), against which they view current efforts as "pie in the sky." It is often their connection to real or imagined social movements that shapes lawyers' choices of tactics and, perhaps more importantly, sustains them in their work.

Cause or Law as Anchor?

Without exception, lawyers explicitly chose the legal profession as a means to promote social change. For most, it is the cause rather than the law that is the centrifugal force. Ruben, who represents parents in child welfare proceedings, summed it up:

> The public interest part came before the lawyer part. I wanted to do something that involved advocacy for poor people and marginalized people and somehow I decided that I wanted to pursue law to do that, so when I applied to law school that was my intention.

Some identified with the needs of imagined or actual constituents. Arthur spoke of growing up poor and how that influenced his career choice.

> I grew up in New York City, came from a poor family in public housing my first 15 years. And I think [I] grew up with a healthy respect for poor people and the needs of poor people and the fact that they don't get the same kind of treatment... that others in our society get and... when I went to college and was active in politics and political science... Then in law school it was always with the idea that law would be a powerful tool for change and for ensuring that everyone in society had access to certain basic things and certain protections under the law.

Perhaps even more compelling than the perception of need were lawyers' own values and sense of obligation. Vicki, a recent graduate of an elite law school (and an elite college before that) who worked in the area of employment, put it this way:

> If I'm at this point, then it's my obligation and my duty to then look back and make sure that I'm doing something for people that are trying to come the same way or that haven't been given the same advantages or the same privileges. 'Cause I—I totally consider it luck that I am where I am, and that if someone isn't given as, the same kind of luck that I use my luck to help them out.... And that's the fundamental core of—'cause I'm not a religious person and so I think that's sort of my religion...I think it's a tiny redistribution of resources is how I see it. That I have a huge amount of resources invested in me and so I want to go invest it in other people as well.

Most lawyers' expressed a long-held commitment to social justice. A number of lawyers were influenced by transformative experiences, often as young adults or teenagers in high school or college. Ben taught in the prison system as a college student during the civil rights era:

> I was teaching in prison, which I had started while I was an [Elite College] undergrad.... After I graduated, the school board hired me as a teacher to teach in...a maximum security prison.... The experience in jail was...a massive growing experience. I grew up in the suburbs in a fairly protected world and it was a real shock for me to sort of, sort of confronting the humanity of society's damned. And I had a lot of good relationships there and felt very engaged.... I was a philosophy major at [Elite College], which was sort of at the opposite end of the world I guess in some ways, I mean very, very remote by definition. And I remember being in a panic at the end of college feeling that this is all wonderful and exciting and fun but I felt sort of disconnected from the world like I was floating around in summer camp for privileged children. And so the experience in jail kind of, was a really wrenching, sort of grounding in the realities of the world.

JoAnn, a lawyer in the family advocacy unit, was influenced in her career choice by a mixture of personal trauma, popular media images of lawyering, and a desire to effect lasting change in people's lives. JoAnn explains how she went from a focus on biology to wanting to help others through legal services practice at NELS:

> It was really a wake-up one day.... It was a combination of [being] date-raped during my senior year of college, and although I really wasn't dealing with it yet, in May of that year I'm sure it was in the back of my mind. But I also had spent most of college watching LA Law. And a lot of my friends in college were going off to law school and it just occurred to me that that's really the path I wanted to be taking. So a year later when I really started dealing with the after-affects of the date rape and I was in grad school for biology and was very, very unhappy that's when I kind of decided what type of law I wanted to do, which is not at all what I'm doing but I wanted at that point to do, to prosecute criminal law. And I left grad school and eventually applied to law school.

For a number of lawyers, a career in the law was not, in fact, their first choice, and they decided to practice law only after weighing the instrumental value of a law degree and the leverage that comes with it. Like Suzanne, a family advocacy lawyer who began law school in her late twenties, some worked in the nonprofit sector and decided that they could not advance their career or social change goals without a professional degree. They considered law a good choice because of the prestige and flexibility of a law school education:

> I realized that the work that I did had to have some sort of importance to me personally.... So I started working for a non-profit organization. And then I realized that just having a BA, you know being at the bottom of a rung in a non-profit can be a really horrible, frustrating experience (laughs). So I needed an advanced degree and then it took me a couple more years to sort of think, like, well maybe law was the way to go... I wasn't sure I wanted to practice when I went in but... it's a relatively prestigious advanced degree and I can take it off in different directions depending on what kind of public interest I wanted to do.

More than one had been involved in social movement activities before becoming lawyers. Dolores, the director of a women's advocacy program, chose law as the best way to contribute to the women's movement. Rather than *turning* to lawyers for help in advocacy, she *became* one:

> I was sort of tired of deferring my judgment to lawyers. Because I knew virtually in any advocacy or policy discussion... everyone would turn to a lawyer.... And in terms of advancement of women it was very clear to me—I mean this was the '70s—that things were changing rapidly and the changes were all legal.

This is not just the attitude of veteran lawyers. Allison began her career in 1989 as a paralegal, "exploring" the possibility of a career in the law at a legal services firm.

> I think what really pushed me to go to law school was ... [the] first year [that I worked as a paralegal], there were three US Supreme Court cases going on in my little office and it was just an amazing thing ... to watch what a tool the law could indeed be as a— "Good God!" You know? "Look at this!" And for me that's what going to law school has been about. How can I use it as a tool? I don't have any particular faith in the justice system necessarily, but I know as a practical matter it can get things done.

Others initially chose law only after considering (and in some cases attempting) careers that they regarded as promising avenues for social change such as journalism or community organizing. Marjorie, a consumer advocacy lawyer, wanted to be a teacher:

> I wanted to go to law school because I wanted to save the world (laughs)...So I didn't have good abilities to become a doctor or become a teacher, so it just seemed like a good fit for my capabilities.

> I taught for a couple of years and I thought I wanted to be a teacher because I thought that's really what this world needs, is effective teachers, and I learned that I'm not the most effective teacher. So, I mean, but it was really I think kind of looking at what I could do to help people with my skills.

Harold, director of an education law program, joked about discovering an "unfortunate aptitude" for law. In all cases, lawyers looked for means to maximize their personal efficacy to best serve their chosen social change agendas and constituents. Martin, a public housing lawyer, acknowledged a long-standing interest in social change and in the law, "[Legal services] was a nice fit. I was always interested in social justice and social change." Later, when asked about job satisfaction, Martin summed up what appears to be true for most of the lawyers, "I tell anybody who will listen that if I couldn't be a legal aid lawyer I wouldn't be a lawyer. I don't know what I'd be, but I wouldn't be a lawyer." Martin's identity as a lawyer is inextricably connected to the kind of work he does. The exact form that this assistance takes is less relevant to Martin and other cause lawyers than the desire to work for their vision of a better society.

Lawyers' Assessment of Law as a Tool for Social Change

Social movement literature provides a helpful framework for making sense of how lawyers view their work as social movement actors. Nearly all of the lawyers interviewed here worked in what is best described as a latency phase of the social movement cycle.[2] For most, law has always been a tool to further other goals, and the choice of profession and legal strategies are secondary to the desire for social change. In order to stay relevant and active, they adapt their practice and goals to suit changing structures and opportunities (McCann and Dudas 2006).

Many lawyers, particularly those who had been practicing since the 1970s, saw law as one means of tapping into power among many (Davis 1993). Despite the initial optimism expressed by left activist cause lawyers who started their practice in a political and social climate that augured hope, most had less impact than they imagined they would. This did not necessarily translate into disillusionment. As Ben said:

> I viewed my becoming a lawyer as being somehow at the cutting edge of social change, which I think in a lot of ways made sense given the early 1970s, '60s. I mean it was this little blip in legal history where the courts were actually a vehicle of social change as opposed to their historic role, which has now been reestablished as keeping order on the plantation.... I certainly don't have any illusion any longer about my role being in some sort of vanguard or cutting edge of social change. At the same time I don't feel disillusioned at all.

Younger lawyers started out with more cynicism and were more pessimistic about the potential of the law (or any other tool) for social change. Still, they were no less committed or passionate about their work. Steve, a legal services lawyer in practice since the late 1980s, described his decision to become a lawyer during college when he worked as a residential tutor for disadvantaged youths:

> I was attending a conference on racism, I think. And so I'm in the middle of this conference—the light bulb went off in my head that the revolution was not happening and that the best way for me to attempt, in my highfalutin way, to effectuate social change, is to become a lawyer.

When questioned further on whether his initial assessment still held, he explained:

> I mean, am I changing the world? No. But the revolution still isn't happening and at some basic level this office, legal aid programs, and myself personally make a difference in people's lives on basic bread and butter issues. And, yeah, we're still playing at the margins in terms of the social- I mean we're not changing the political/social system, but we make things less worse for people. Which, and you know, there are people in this office who have a lot of trouble with what we do not in terms of they don't like their jobs, but it bothers them more that we're playing at the margins, that we are not fermenting [*sic*] the revolution. And we're not. We're not. We really are not. And that's fine. I mean I can live with it. But no, I love this job, this is a great job. And we do make a difference, both individually and on issues that affect our client population. And *but for* the work we did, things would be considerably worse for our clients.

Steve's initial expectations were quite different from Ben's. Not only did he not expect to effectuate the broad change that Ben had anticipated, but his vocational choice was also formed precisely because of his perception that no broad social change was on the horizon. Cause lawyers who enter or remain in practice have to focus their practices and expectations to make them compatible with the existing (and often limited) opportunity structures. When there is no hope for a desired social change and there seems to be no movement "out there," the work of elites (McCarthy and Zald 1977) or core lawyers (Jones 2005) is even more important.

Marcia's somewhat contradictory assessment of what it means to do impact work shows the challenges of working in a political climate that is at odds with her understanding of social justice:

> I'm not sure I made the right decision [to become a lawyer].... Now it's really dangerous.... When I first graduated I was working for the Public Advocate in [a neighboring state] and that was a cabinet level departmental position. And I did right to habilitation—'cause my clients were mentally retarded—class actions in Federal Court. And then now (laughs), if you could stay out of Federal Court on a lot of issues it's better. It's safer to stay out [because] the decisions are just so conservative . . .

For Marcia, bringing work out of the realm of the individual to try to shape broader policy is downright dangerous. If the likelihood of what she considers "good" decisions is minimal (and the likelihood of "bad" decisions maximal), then work that has far-reaching effects is better avoided. When questioned further, Marcia noted that although her work carried with it the danger of making things worse for her clients she feels that she must persevere in order to hold ground:

> I don't really wish I hadn't [become a lawyer] because I think it's all a matter of keeping the pressure on. And even though I think we're in a really conservative time, the pendulum- you know people talk about it swinging back. It won't swing back if there's not a whole bunch of us working for it.

Marcia's ambivalent assessment makes it clear that lawyers who value social change recognize both the importance of and the danger with the work they do. They must take account of strategic contingencies, not the least of which is the inability to predict favorable outcomes. This balancing act is not the same for all lawyers or all fields. Variations depend not so much on philosophical outlook but more on whether the lawyer perceives a particular practice venue (such as the Federal courts) as receptive to the kind of change she or he envisions. Movements go through phases; as Marcia's assessment of her career attests, sustaining commitment to a social movement over time requires versatile skills, staying power, and an ability to spot political opportunities as well as to cope with frustration. As Diane says of the different forms her own activism has taken:

> I was active in the civil rights movement, primarily, and then the anti-war movement. And the issue came up about how one could continue to be useful, particularly in the civil rights movement, over time. And it seemed to me that the only way to do that was to have the skills that would be helpful.

Lawyers use a diverse array of legal skills and strategies. Some have largely individual client caseloads, while others focus on "impact" work consisting of class action suits, representation of and collaboration with community groups, participation on various committees or task forces, legislative and administrative advocacy, and/or educational outreach and training. All show a willingness to adapt their methods to changing political and social climates, demonstrating that their social change commitments are stronger than adherence to particular practice techniques or specialties.

Jeanine, who devotes most of her efforts to lobbying, considers defensive work an important part of cause lawyering. She is proud of her successes in thwarting conservative attempts at countermovement social change.

> Over the years (now I have an opportunity to brag!) what are our finest accomplishments are things that we stopped. But that's the nature of the work we do and the nature of having the [state] legislature that we have. Three times in five years we helped defeat a proposal to push tuition vouchers in this state. We helped defeat one constitutional amendment that would have eviscerated the search and seizure provision of the Pennsylvania Constitution, which the Pennsylvania Supreme Court has interpreted more strictly than the 4th amendment. The prosecutors got frustrated and wanted to get rid of it and say the 4th amendment is all that applies, and we helped stop that. We worked to help stop the abolition of the insanity defense . . . [and for] the restoration of family planning funding after all the years when there was no money in the state budget for family planning.

In contrast, Dolores finds being on the defensive a bleak prospect, particularly compared to her initial expectations and experiences, and she cautions young women to think carefully before choosing a career in law.

> I'm frequently called upon to advise young (women particularly) about their futures. . . . I think there's a lot of work that needs to be done . . . that doesn't take a lawyer . . . and I think the opportunities unfortunately are kind of limited, but that people can find ways to do it, but I don't think it's quite what it was. You know I mean we just had one rolling success after another in the '70s, and thought about fundamental, not incremental changes. And an awful lot of what we're doing now is trying to maintain more than expand. There are huge areas where there haven't been any real enforcement of legal rights. It's pretty hard for me. So I think I would maybe stay in this position myself but . . . advise people to think real carefully about it and understand its usefulness as a tool maybe more than as a whole career in itself.

Many were frustrated with their inability to bring about more systemic changes. The benefits that they are able to secure through the legal processes seem meager and inconsequential. Pete, who has since left the practice of law for other social justice work, was disheartened:

> Particularly in the setting in which I work, welfare stuff, the law only guarantees the most minimal level of safety net. So even if you're looking at things in terms of what is social justice from an economic perspective or what is the minimum kind of financial stability that you think any person who lives in an affluent society should have. The best lawyers here—in my practice, welfare law—are not going to accomplish anything approximating that. You know, if I do a great job on trying to get somebody who's being kicked off of welfare I've gotten them—let's say a single mother and 2 kids, $403 a month to live on—that's abhorrent. It's a joke, it's a farce . . . and we spend almost none of our time trying to advocate the grant level to be increased because we've decided it's a complete dead end. I mean we're doing conservative work of trying to fight back even worse changes. So that's kind of the dilemma and the irony in all this. It's hard to figure out, well what am I doing, in terms of the broader vision?

Many lawyers, including Pete, cope with this frustration by keeping in mind that what are perhaps "objectively" inadequate victories can be meaningful for their clients.

When larger systemic change is not possible through direct challenges, lawyers attempt other means of change. Lawyers like Ben view some of the work with individuals as impacting systems, if in a circuitous route.

> I work in systems that before I was a lawyer the poor had absolutely no rights whatsoever. For example a lot of my work deals with mortgage problems and homeownership and preserving home ownership. Before we came along, if you were behind in your mortgage and you're poor, you lost your house . . . So we came along and sort of figured out that people shouldn't lose their houses and there's ways of protecting their ownership and keeping them in and developed a legal practice that essentially didn't exist before. . . . in the trenches, primarily in the context of individual cases, but also in the context of taking on the systems as a whole, we have managed to alter the balance of power fairly significantly I think at least in this little geographic blip.

Lesnick (1991) describes how lawyers' worldview or orientation, including their rejection of the status quo, informs their practice. This influences their work with clients, often in ways that contribute to the formation of a critical consciousness that is necessary for the incubation of a social movement (Melucci 1994). Helping clients (and each other) recognize problems as systemic fosters the understanding that problems are not lodged within the individual, thus shifting the locus of blame and the type of action required to rectify the situation.

According to Lesnick, a liberal perspective accepts the basic premises of the legal (and economic) status quo and acknowledges the rules and roles it dictates (1991: 7–9).[3] In contrast, a radical perspective challenges prevailing legal, social, and economic structures (1991: 9–11). Lawyers and clients who challenge the premises of the legal system are radical by definition, even if they choose to play by its rules when they perceive that as the best (or only) available strategy. In a political and social environment perceived as hostile, "realistic radicals" may adopt nominally liberal practices. This is a contingent strategy with an eye toward a longer term radical agenda. Lesnick describes what a radical perspective tempered by "reality checks" might look like, urging that we:

> Struggle to overcome the dichotomy ... between the liberal and radical perspectives, seeking to infuse the day-to-day choices of "liberal" practice with the insights suggested by a radical perspective. Such an effort tries to steer clear of two polar hazards: to avoid adopting—falling prey to, some would say—the "nothing can change until everything changes" consciousness of a pure radical view, and to avoid succumbing (more than momentarily, at least) to the strong pull that the practice of law has toward regarding "radical" insights as just too counter-productive to hold on to. (1991: 11)

A realistically radical orientation should not be confused with a liberal perspective that not only uses but also *accepts* dominant norms and values, even if it is unclear precisely how this difference plays out in actual situations and what it means to the participants. Lawyers, like other strategic social movement actors, must weigh available resources and the given social and political context. Such an assessment respects clients' and lawyers' choices, and may result in preferring individual tactics, even when problems are understood as structural or systemic. It is also significant for lawyers attempting to sustain a view of themselves as part of a larger social movement—a view that presents a challenge.

Schram's "radical incrementalism" (2000: 178–82), like Lesnick's realistic radicalism, posits the necessity and potential of incremental change. Schram adds an explicit aspect of compassion grounded in recognition of the pressing and immediate needs of those who cannot wait until fundamental changes may eventually be realized, underscoring the need for diffuse action when movements are latent. To forego available but imperfect avenues of action in the here and now would be to ignore people who experience need in pursuit of theoretical integrity; many cause lawyers are unwilling to give up on what they can achieve through incremental work even if there is no visible social movement activity within which this resonates.

For caring individuals with a radical perspective, working within existing systems in order to be relevant is dangerous but necessary. This is a political consideration that assesses the success of different social change strategies and an ethical stance that recognizes that immediate needs should not be ignored, even as social change seekers work toward building a movement to advocate for a more perfect system. Steve told me that if there were a viable movement out there, then he would be in the streets rather than working as a legal services lawyer. In its absence, he relishes any opportunity to snipe at the system:

> My view of social justice in my job is getting as much as I can from a system which I think is fundamentally flawed. I think the welfare system's terrible. It may be more or less terrible than it was 5 or 10 years ago, but it's still fundamentally wrong. However, my clients have to live in it. And what I view my job in terms of social justice is getting the best or the least bad deal I can for my clients out of that system because I have concluded, and it's probably a combination of (a) I don't have the strength and skills to revamp the system and (b) I don't think it's happening. And the best that I can do is work to try and reform it at some level incrementally but realize, you know, give me break. And at the practical level work within its framework to manipulate it as best I can to get the most I can for my clients. That's what I do.

Left activist cause lawyering can also give voice to individuals who would otherwise not be heard. Although such voices may be compromised by the legal process and the professional-client relationship, it can foster a greater sense of citizen participation in forums where marginalized citizens are rarely heard (Minow 1996), particularly if they are not part of an existing network or group. Although many of the lawyers interviewed do work with one or more social movement organizations, the majority of clients are not members of such groups. Ruben notes, for example, that the child welfare system isolates individuals from each other in a way that works against the formation of collective grievances. They are not able to discover the problems they have in common.

> Well, the problem in this area is there aren't really any community groups. . . . In child welfare I think it's the nature of the kind of the problem. It's frustrating, because parents are so disserved by the way the systems works, and one of the things that would help would be a parents group to advocate for change, but the system tends to isolate parents into their individual problems and cases.

As a result of this, Ruben often finds himself as the spokesperson of a larger group of real or imagined constituents as well as his individual clients' lawyer. He gave this example:

> I'm going to be participating in [a state legislative advisory committee]. There I'm not representing any individual clients; it's a committee to discuss possible changes in the state's child welfare legislation. And there I see my role as representing the interest of the class of people who are parents who have or might have some involvement in the system.

In addition to representing a group of people who may have no other access to policy makers, lawyers can also act as hubs on a metaphoric wheel, with individual clients as the spokes. Clients who believe their problems are unique learn from lawyers that there are others experiencing similar problems; this can help them find each other and foster a collective consciousness and motivate activism. Ben tells of Valerie, who learned that she was the victim of a predatory loan (rather than the victim of her own poor judgment). Once Ben told her that she was one of many victims of the same loan company, Valerie framed her problem differently. Although embarrassed at first, she spoke out about the problem, approaching her neighbors and eventually speaking publicly in the media and with city and state legislators.

Individual legal actions expose unfairness by helping clients express their dissatisfaction in legal forums. Law and the language of rights that emerges from public legal challenges and rhetoric can rally and energize movements, whether or not they are enforced or even recognized legally (McCann 1994; Engel and Munger 2003). They also provide opportunities to form and maintain consciousness and identity as well as shape the debate around which social movements coalesce (Hunt and Bernfeld 2004; Barclay and Fisher 2006).

Lawyers work with clients to create shared narratives of responsibility and injustice that legitimate grievances and indict oppressive and unfair systems. Lawyers can help reinforce a client's tenuous or budding understanding of his/her problem as one that is more systemic than individual. The individual changes wrought in this process can be meaningful for clients, improving their lot materially, validating their perspective, giving them a sense of vindication, and creating a basis for collective action.

> I feel like if this person gets a little more power on an individual level, you know, to me there's social change in creating confidence for someone who has been living a very difficult . . . kind of life. So hopefully there is this perception that even someone with limited education, with limited money can go to (thumps on the desk) legal services, can get some help and get a problem resolved and that gives them connection, a feeling that their society is serving them . . . I don't know if there's a lot of social change in (individual relief), except for a sense of, in the person that, yeah, you know the government thought that, I mean this—whatever it was, you know the corporation-whatever- thought that they could just roll over this person and then the person got some legal assistance.

Legitimating grievances is particularly important when individual and collective experiences are not otherwise validated publicly (Gould 2002). However, as I have described in this section, it can be difficult to maintain commitment to a latent social movement in a way that lends coherence and meaning to incremental work.

Cause Lawyering as a Movement to Grow a Movement

When the movement with which lawyers identify is latent, many feel the deep frustrations and ambivalence of working for a cause in a hostile political climate. I have highlighted some of the ways in which cause lawyers, *as social movement actors*, are able to reconcile their work as necessary, if disappointing, in the absence of an obvious and active social movement. In addition to these strategies, most cause lawyers need to see themselves as part of a larger collective with a shared agenda in order to keep social movement fires burning or to nurture incipient social movements. Jon, a lawyer who works in the local branch of a civil rights organization, tries to keep sight of his vision of a just society to sustain him in his work:

> [A] value that's important, maybe not every day I can see it or sense it, but in the bigger scheme, [is] knowing that we are making a more just society.... We just need to remember ... what we're here to do. We're not here just to win cases and get good publicity and put on a good fundraising banquet. It's putting it all together so that next year we'll be able to look back and say: society, from our perspective, is better because we did x, y and z.

When the movement they identify with (poor peoples' movements, women's rights) has not yet coalesced or has dissipated, what is the larger collective? What is the shared agenda? Even when movements are strong, as Arthur notes, lawyers largely function as elite actors with outsider status.[4]

> You had to recognize that you were not a part of the community and it was wrong to think that you were a part of the community. You were this outside professional coming in and although *you* thought of yourself differently as a professional than perhaps other lawyers downtown. But reality was that you were a stranger in that community. And a stranger in a lot of ways.

I propose that left activist cause lawyers may themselves constitute a social movement. Left activist cause lawyers see themselves as a larger collective of individuals with a shared agenda who are marginalized both in their profession (Scheingold and Sarat 2004) and in their role as elite actors, and who are distanced from the movements they support (Polikoff 1996). My contention is arguable. However, I am less concerned with whether or not it is objectively true than with using the social movement theory to better understand the self-conception of left activist cause lawyers and the motivation and material support they draw from their collective identity (see also Meili's profile of consumer lawyers, 2006).

Left activist cause lawyers are a group of professionals, working in a variety of practice settings and substantive fields using a variety of tactics, who share a belief that we live in an inequitable and unjust society and that the law is an appropriate tool to change that. Left activist cause lawyers, and cause lawyers in general (Hatcher 2005; Southworth 2005), share the ideal of using the law for social change, and of being engaged with, indeed committed to, their causes in a way that goes against traditional notions of lawyers as detached, objective officers of the court. In this sense they are not just lawyers, but *cause* lawyers whose activities and ideals are oppositional to what López (1992) calls "regnant lawyering" and cuts across substantive borders (Scheingold and Sarat 2004). Cause lawyers are aware that traditional law practices reflect and reinforce inequities and injustices. They realize that this requires that they challenge not only the inequitable social system, but also the professional norms to which they are socialized, their colleagues, and the legal system, which, as described by Ben, is basically charged with the role of "keeping order on the plantation."

Challenging and changing the existing political and legal order is not only a tool in the service of a larger goal, but also a goal in and of itself. This helps to explain why lawyers who knew that they wanted to go into some sort of public interest work often did not have a firm commitment to a particular issue or social movement. Others were drawn to cause lawyering through identification with particular areas such as disability rights or the women's movement, but were unable to find jobs that suited these interests. The experience of JoAnn is typical. Once she decided on a career in civil legal services JoAnn was willing to be flexible in order to work at a legal services program:

> I liked helping out people in [a] one-on-one way...That was something I wanted to get out of biology but you're so far removed from the people you're helping when you're doing biological research that I never felt that. And I was feeling that with [criminal] defense work. But it also felt like I was just patching up problems...That's what led me to apply to civil legal services...feeling that that was a better place for me to be helping people do something better with their lives. And I knew that [NELS] was one of the best places to work in the country for legal services. And I thought I was going to come here and do welfare work or something and I didn't even know that dependency, the work I do...existed when I started (laughs). They just kind of put me [here]...They needed so many people in so many slots it's where I ended up.

JoAnn, like many others, sees connections in the various substantive areas of left activist cause lawyering. For her, it is all of a piece, and many of her individual clients and the constituents of her policy work are in fact clients and constituents of fellow left activist lawyers. The problems they experience are also related: health, poverty, housing, family issues, and more. This not only makes the choice of substantive specialty flexible, but it also paves the way for the creation of integrated networks among left activist cause lawyers.

The Dynamics of Funding, Legal Services Jobs, and the Reproduction of Hierarchy[5]

When McCarthy and Zald first formulated their resource mobilization theory, it was as much the response of theorists who were attuned to the politics of their times as it was a scholarly contribution to the work of social movements (McCarthy and Zald 1977). One of the benefits of viewing left activist cause lawyering as a social movement is that it avails cause lawyers of analytical and strategic tools used in social movement literature.

For example, the insights of resource mobilization theory are helpful in understanding the funding dynamics that influence left activist cause lawyering and to formulate a response that is more likely to succeed in garnering and conserving resources. Viewing cause lawyers as movement activists and the organizations in which they work as social movement organizations that work in the same social movement sector also encourages viewing resources constraints through social movement lenses. One lawyer saw the existence of a large number of different organizations working toward similar goals and sharing similar (and in many cases, the same) client base as a bank of sorely needed resources. As she put it, "I'm glad there are other organizations around, because we have more than enough work to do."

In the conservative political and funding climate that has persisted since the 1980s, funding cuts have plagued left activist cause lawyering organizations. The scarcity of resources has made left activist law organizations compete to divvy up an ever-shrinking pie among organizations with different substantive goals or that employ different legal tools. However, there are advantages to understanding this scarcity as a broader attack on left activist lawyering requiring a collective, more systematically focused response. In this section I provide hiring practices as an example of individual response to a problem of scarcity that has systemic roots and consequences, which I then contrast to a local, collective response to federal funding cuts.

The difficulties of staying committed to a career in public interest law through law school and then obtaining work in this field are well documented (Jones

2005; Thompson 2005). Vicki was employed via a fellowship sponsored by the corporate law firm she agreed to practice with upon completing a year at a public interest firm. According to Vicki, this arrangement was the only way she could pursue public interest work:

> One of the measures of a law school is how many of their graduates have jobs. Finding a public interest job is much more difficult than finding a corporate job so of course [my top-tier school] is going to track people into corporate. And I think one of the things that I benefited from was knowing what I wanted right when I walked in...Even so it was still hard for me to stay committed. It's so much easier to find another kind of job. And really it was a compromise to say, "Okay I'm going to go to this firm in order to do public interest work," when public interest work was probably what I really want to do. And yet to be able to do it, I'm going to have to go to a firm. So...it's hard to keep the focus on that as you're going through law school. Mostly because at the end of it you have all these loans and you're like well, I'm going to need a job (laughs)...And it's going to be easier to find it in the private sector.

As Vicki underscores, it is not just lack of funding for legal services and the corresponding paucity of job opportunities but the (not unconnected) norms, values, and finances of legal education that work against careers in public interest law.

Funding considerations also constrain employment practices in more insidious ways. At the time of my interviews, NELS could only hire new attorneys through sponsorship; it was forced to either cut services to clients or to hire in conformity with funding organizations' criteria. All of the recently hired attorneys at NELS attended top tier law schools. A number of lawyers expressed concern that this elitist hiring pattern, whatever the cause, contradicts the norms and values that guide lawyering for social justice. Such patterns reinforce existing power differentials and hierarchical practices within the profession as well as between lawyers and clients (Auerbach 1976; Guinier, Fine and Bailin 1997). Lawyers from elite schools are less likely to be drawn from the communities they serve or to resemble members of those communities in even superficial ways. As funding continues to be cut, gutting legal services programs around the country, jobs have become more and more scarce.

Marcia discussed the dilemma that NELS faced when they tried to address these concerns by choosing what they viewed as excellent candidates who did not graduate from elite law schools. When I asked Marcia whether students from top tier schools stand a better chance of winning fellowships, she told me how NELS' loss of autonomy in choosing potential employees hit home for her and the organization:

> Well not only do they have a better chance . . . ! I was on the attorney hiring committee and I was really pushing [to hire qualified attorneys who did not graduate from top-tier schools]. But the foundations just won't take these folks. . . . And then when we didn't get an attorney that year, *boy*! I mean . . . , I've changed my mind. Because we really need those attorneys. . . . And it's a self-fulfilling prophecy.

Public interest programs are caught within a system that through limited re-sources reinforces existing power relations. NELS ascertained through trial and error that in order to remain viable and balance other commitments (chiefly its mission to provide clients with legal representation) it must make a trade-off and conform to funding exigencies. Although this tradeoff was a conscious decision, it left many feeling compromised and reveals some of the more sub-tle conserving pressures of the legal profession (Sarat and Scheingold 2004). It also demonstrates the difficulty of taking on systems as isolated organizations working through existing channels.

In contrast, when federal funding threatened the viability of Philadelphia's Community Legal Services (CLS), the Philadelphia public interest bar treated this as a general attack. Arthur described it as part of the conservative response to the success of lawyering for marginalized populations.

> Republicans when they got into power one of their primary objectives was: How can we cut the funding? Can we defund legal services? And when they weren't successful-at least let's . . . restrict what they can do and let's taint all of their money so that if they accept one dollar of federal money, every dollar of their money wherever it may come from, from foundations or state money or whatever will be tainted with these restrictions. We'll take away their ability to do class actions, to do legislative advocacy. We won't allow them to represent disfavored populations like aliens and prisoners, we won't let them do welfare reform and challenge our efforts there. We won't let them . . . represent poor people in public housing accused of drugs or criminal activity. And you go right down the list.

Although these actions largely affected one local provider, CLS, the public interest law community viewed the restrictions through the broader frame-work of an attack on left activist cause lawyering. Such a framing resulted in a response that drew on existing networks and collective resources that local left activist cause lawyering organizations and the private bar had cultivated over twenty years. Drawing on Gerald López (1992), Arthur sees such coalition building as one of many "rebellious lawyering" tools, which include all kinds of activities that left activist cause lawyers use to further their social change goals.

> Poor people are really isolated and to the extent they remain isolated it only perpetuates poverty. Legal services programs were once isolated. Everybody was the enemy. You didn't link with anybody else. You viewed everybody in a skeptical [and] in some ways a hostile way. That, unfortunately, diminished the effectiveness of legal services. And I think by building these coalitions and socializing others to understand legal services we've created a network of powerful allies on behalf of the poor that is ever expanding.

The Philadelphia left activist cause lawyering community viewed the possible loss of its largest member organization as a blow to the movement rather than just the organization, a view that made a community response the logical choice. The Philadelphia collaborative response to the federal funding restrictions led to the creation of a new organization (Philadelphia Legal Assistance) and substantial changes in infrastructure to CLS that were made possible by support outside the organization affected (Carr and Hirschel 1998). Diane, who worked at another organization, recalled that when the public interest bar decided together that CLS would give up the restricted federal funding, they all realized that CLS would need more funds for the transition:

> Well once you gave up the money you had to figure out how to survive. How did we get legal services firmly funded? We all agreed that the emergency priority should be for legal services that year, in terms of the Bar funding. They say a number of people gave up various awards and let the money flow to legal services. Because—of course. They were hurting, and their mission was crucially important, so of course they have to be supported. It never occurred to anyone to do anything else.

According to Harold, this is typical for Philadelphia left activist cause lawyers:

> The greyheads have created a model of leading and sharing. I've also raised a lot of money for other offices. Often shared projects, and in helping people find funders. . . . When it comes down to dollars, it is usually the most honest sign (laughs).

The interviews are replete with examples of collaborative projects, which draw on each organization and individual's expertise in an attempt to increase funding and to leverage resources. Although substantive missions are incompatible and lead to possible clashes, collaboration helps to ensure that left activist cause lawyering organizations are considerate of each other, when possible. Speaking about joint efforts to reform the Philadelphia Family Court, Harold said:

> Not everybody . . . has Family Court issues, but a significant number do, and we come at it in different ways. And we want to make sure that we're not pushing our problems

to other areas. For example, if you want to get a judge out of the (Protection from Abuse) Court, the Dependency Court doesn't want bad eggs either. So how do we make recommendations that don't just push the problems to our colleagues but are real solutions? And how do we act in concert to have the most influence?

It is clear that when the cause lawyers and cause lawyering organizations see themselves as a social movement sector made up of different social movement organizations that have a common agenda, this can be helpful in garnering resources. Understanding left activist cause lawyering against a backdrop of social movement literature also provides fertile direction for self-reflection and future research. If we view cause lawyers and cause lawyering organizations not as isolated players but as social movement actors and organizations occupying a shared social movement field, it raises a host of strategically and analytically useful questions. For example, how are individual SMOs (and the social movement as a whole) altered or shaped by other SMOs? Are these different from the trade-offs SMOs make with institutional opponents or with countermovement SMOs?

Searching for Identity, Support and Meaning

Although social movement theory is a lens that helps theorists and practitioners make sense and evaluate what they see, perhaps more importantly it helps actors give meaning to the work they do and understand their shared identity. The data suggest that viewing themselves as a part of a larger collective is an important ideological resource for left activist cause lawyers. What Rubin (2000) has noted about the function of conferences to the community-based development movement can also be said of community building attempts for shoring up the strength of the left activist cause lawyering movement, including: "training, networking, socializing and socialization." Further:

> [A]ctivists learn[] they c[an] depend upon each other for help and through extended discussions worked out a shared, understanding—a framing- for both themselves land their supporters... the latent function of conferences is to turn a disparate, and potentially competitive set of community builders into a community that both provides help for its members and works out a shared ideology of what should be accomplished. (Rubin 2000: 36).

Networks of activist lawyers support each other through the provision of concrete advice. The sharing of novel legal strategies and basic "how-to" information as Meili describes among consumer lawyers (2006) was echoed by lawyers in this study. Advice is requested and proffered locally and through national networks (see Blom 2005 on virtual cause lawyer networks).

Practical advice is not the only kind of support that left activist cause lawyering networks provide. Much of the literature on lawyers and social movements focus on the danger of lawyer-domination or of lawyers being out of touch with grassroot activists or their constituents (Hilbink 2006; Levitsky 2006). It does not address how lawyers can continue to work when they are distanced from the movement that they serve (Polikoff 1996) or when the social movement landscape to which they look is barren, as is the case for most of the lawyers in this study. As the idea of radical incrementalism discussed above suggests, lawyers in direct service remain committed to their work through the provision of needed services to very real individuals (if not social movements or SMOs) who come to them with immediate and very real needs, and provide lawyers with immediate feedback (see also Shdaimah 2005). However, left activist cause lawyering networks also provide encouragement and support.

Most of the lawyers here spoke of feeling beleaguered. At various times they have felt the hostility of the private bar to left activist cause lawyering, an unreceptive political climate, and the fears they have in challenging the system as inexperienced lawyers or using novel techniques. The pervasive nostalgia that "progressive" lawyers here and elsewhere express for an imagined heyday of lawyering in the 1960s and 1970s serves as a touchstone, or what Battaglia (1995) calls a "powerful force for social reconnection." It is the left activist cause lawyers' story of a glorious (or at least interesting) past that mitigates the frustration of defensive lawyering. It gives a sense of shared history, a sort of foundation myth, for progressive lawyering as they imagine it can be. Such a history helps left activist cause lawyers identify each other as part of the same movement through tracing their shared political heritage and mission. It also provides left activist cause lawyers with the hope that goals that may seem unattainable on behalf of movements that may or may not (re)materialize one day are realistic, rather than quixotic.

Left-activist cause lawyering networks provide significant emotional and professional support, and often the two are combined. Allen practiced in a "small town in the coal fields . . . for a year and that local bar would have been happy to run us out of town and in fact in many ways they tried to." When I asked Allen about people whom he thinks about in his practice, he spoke of the importance of Mark Weiner, a central figure in the local bar, as a role model in terms of the way he treats people.

[Mark Weiner] is a person who combines really good hard work, high quality work, and treats people with respect. And . . . that is a big one for me personally, and I try to work on it myself . . . No matter what he's thinking about people, he treats people with respect and a certain kindness actually.... And I do remember him, because even when I was in the wilds of [a coal mining area], being fairly isolated in one office with one other new attorney, I could call him up. He would take the phone call, knowing me or barely knowing me and give advice.

Allen's example shows not only how left activist cause lawyers look to other left activist cause lawyers as models for practice, but also the kinds of qualities that help them stay committed through the creation of a professional and emotional support network of the kind that is crucial for continued social movement work, particularly in a hostile or isolating environment (Gould 2002). When the circle of support is widened to include local bar associations that nurture the work of public interest lawyering, left activist lawyers feel empowered and derive significant social capital from such support. Judith, an attorney who works in domestic violence counseling and has worked elsewhere, compared the support she derives from the network she has in Philadelphia to what was lacking in her previous practice setting:

There IS a community here, there is an identified community, and people know each other and people are generous with their time. People are interested in other people's kinds of cases, and the problems they run into, there's a feeling here that you're a full fledged lawyer, and that you're doing something that's worthwhile, and that people aren't looking at you like you're a crackpot because they know that you've got a law degree and probably you're working for a lot less money than you could make if you were in private sector....[Here] there is a sense that what you are doing is valued in the community. And that's important, I think, and that gives people an extra sense of energy and urgency about doing the work.

Diane echoes Judith and emphasizes what all the participants in that study made clear: this approach strengthens the lawyers' and the organizations' morale and helps them to continue their work.

One of the things that is unique about us is we're a community... And one aspect of that community is a certain number of us have... spent the last 30 years going from baby lawyers to middle aged lawyers working together and... I think that there is, certainly among most of us, a sense that... we're really part of one enterprise that has the same mission and has the same clients, and we just have different areas of expertise in relation to them.... And that our mission is no better or more important, and our clients are, as I say, not even any different. So we're one community of people who are trying to accomplish a common goal.... So it would make no sense to any of us to do anything but be supportive of each other, whether it's a funding effort, space, a loan to meet payroll until their next fee award comes in. I think that that sense that we're all one family engaged in the same enterprise is something that—I can't imagine how anyone could have a different view of it.

Recognizing the coordinated actions of the different social movement actors and social movement organizations that make up a putative cause lawyering movement, social movement theory helps to understand how they work together to achieve shared goals and the heterogeneity of (sometimes conflicting) agendas and tactics they employ. Perhaps more importantly, it endorses their actions as important political actors rather than lone wolves acting on a private sense of justice.

Intersecting Identities

In this chapter I have suggested that many cause lawyers in general, and left activist cause lawyers in particular, view themselves as important social movement actors who work with and on behalf of marginalized groups. Indeed, they generally identify more with their causes than with their professional role as lawyers. It can be difficult, however, to sustain a commitment to a movement that appears to be on the decline, underground, or more imagined than real. Even when social movements are vibrant, lawyers by virtue of their elite professional roles often stand at some distance from the movement or from other movement actors. In the interviews conducted here, it is clear that left activist cause lawyers derive important material resources as well as a strong source of identification and meaning from the more "horizontal" association with a movement of like-minded cause lawyers. In the tradition of politically engaged social movement theories, this research suggests that this is not only a helpful way of understanding cause lawyers but also might be a helpful way for cause lawyers to think of themselves in order to sustain their morale and enhance their material and ephemeral resources.

Acknowledgments

Thanks to Judie McCoyd, Jim Baumohl, and Roland Stahl for their comments on various sections and incarnations of this chapter. I am also grateful to all the participants in the Cause Lawyering and Social Movements Conference held at UCLA in May 2005, especially to Stuart Scheingold and Austin Sarat for their continued inspiration, encouragement, and energy. My greatest debt is to the lawyers who generously shared their time and their experiences.

Notes

1. A number of the ideas presented here, particularly those that relate to the public interest bar as a community, were first developed with Sue Wasserkrug in a

paper we presented at the Annual Meetings of the Law and Society Association in Pittsburgh in 2003 (Shdaimah and Wasserkrug 2003).

2. Although the lawyers viewed themselves as adherents to different (if not always unconnected) movements, most of the movements are connected to left-activist agendas that they consider currently disfavored.

3. Lesnick's definition of the liberal perspective is informed by what Kaufman (1968) describes as a hollow liberalism, which has been exploited by conservative politicians and thinkers and is not truly grounded in the classic liberal perspective, which is "the belief that the ultimate aim of public policy is the protection and promotion of each person's equal opportunity to develop his potentialities as fully as possible" (1968, p. 4); and a conviction of the necessity of "political democracy to the realization of a good society" (1968, p. 5).

4. As Polikoff (1996) describes, this may be the case even if the lawyers identify with the movements and their goals directly and personally.

5. Duncan Kennedy (1982) applies the term "reproduction of hierarchy" to law school education.

References

Auerbach, Jerold. 1976. *Unequal Justice: Lawyers and Social Change in Modern America.* New York: Oxford University Press.

Barclay, Scott, and Shauna Fisher. 2006. "Cause Lawyers in the First Wave of Same Sex Marriage Litigation." In A. Sarat and S. Scheingold eds.,*Cause Lawyers and Social Movement.* Stanford: Stanford University Press.

Battaglia, Debbora. 1995. "On Practical Nostalgia: Self-Prospecting among Urban Trobrianders." In Battaglia ed., *Rhetorics of Self-Making.* Berkeley: University of California Press.

Blom, Brenda Bratton. 2005. "Cause Lawyering and Social Movements: Can Solo and Small Firm Practitioners Anchor Social Movements?" Unpublished conference paper. Conference on Cause Lawyering and Social Movements, March 4–5, UCLA School of Law.

Carr, Catherine C. and Alison E. Hirschel. 1998. "The Transformation of Community Legal Services, Inc., of Philadelphia: One Program's Experience Since the Federal Restrictions." *Yale Law and Policy Review* 34: 319–35.

Davis, Martha F. 1993. *Brutal Need: Lawyers and the Welfare Rights Movement, 1960–1973.* New Haven: Yale University Press.

Engel, David M., and Frank W. Munger. 2003. *Rights of Inclusion: Law and Identity in the Life Stories of Americans with Disabilities.* Chicago: University of Chicago Press.

Gould, Deborah B. 2002. "Life During Wartime: Emotions and the Development of ACT UP." *Mobilization: An International Journal.* 72: 177–99.

Guinier, Lani, Michelle Fine, and Jane Balin, J. 1997. *Becoming Gentlemen: Women, Law school, and Institutional Change.* Boston: Beacon Press.

Hatcher, Laura. 2005. "Economic Libertarians, Property, and Institutions: Linking Activism, Ideas, and Identities among Property Rights Lawyers." In A. Sarat and

S. Scheingold eds., *The Worlds Cause Lawyers Make: Structure and Agency in Legal Practice*. Stanford: Stanford University Press.

Hilbink, Thomas. 2006. "The Profession, the Grassroots, and the Elite: Cause Lawyering for Civil Rights and Freedom in the Direct Action Era." In A. Sarat and S. Scheingold eds., *Cause Lawyers and Social Movement*. Stanford: Stanford University Press.

Hunt, Scott A. and Robert D. Bernfeld. 2004. "Collective Identity, Solidarity, and Commitment." In D. Snow, S. Soule and H. Kriesi eds., *The Blackwell Companion to Social Movements*. Malden: Blackwell Publishing.

Jones, Lynn C. 2005. "Exploring the Sources of Cause and Career Correspondence Among Cause lawyers." In A. Sarat and S. Scheingold eds., *The Worlds Cause Lawyers Make: Structure and Agency in Legal Practice*. Stanford: Stanford University Press.

———. 2006. "The Haves Come Out Ahead: How Cause Lawyers Frame the Legal System for Movements." In A. Sarat and S. Scheingold eds., *Cause Lawyers and Social Movement*. Stanford: Stanford University Press.

Kaufman, Arnold S. 1968. *The Radical Liberal: The New Politics: Theory and Practice*. New York: Simon and Schuster.

Kennedy, Duncan. 1982. "Legal Education and the Reproduction of hierarchy." *Journal of Legal Education* 32:591–615.

Lesnick, Howard. 1991. "The Wellsprings of Legal Responses to Inequality: A Perspective on Perspectives." *Duke Law Journal* 1991: 413–14.

Levitsky, Sandra R. 2006. "To Lead With Law: Reassessing the Influence of Legal Advocacy Organizations in Social Movements." In A. Sarat and S. Scheingold eds., *Cause Lawyers and Social Movement*. Stanford: Stanford University Press.

López, Gerald. 1992. *Rebellious Lawyering*. Boulder: Westview.

McCann, Michael. 1994. *Rights at Work: Pay Equity Reform and the Politics of Legal Mobilization*. Chicago: University of Chicago Press.

McCann, Michael and Jeffrey Dudas. 2006. "Retrenchment . . . and Resurgence? Mapping the Changing Context of Movement Lawyering in the United States." In A. Sarat and S. Scheingold eds., *Cause Lawyers and Social Movement*. Stanford: Stanford University Press.

McCarthy, John D. and Mayer N. Zald. 1977. "Resource Mobilization and Social Movements: A Partial Theory." *American Journal of Sociology* 82: 1212–41.

Meili, Stephen. 2006. "Consumer Cause Lawyering in the United States: Lawyers for the Movement or a Movement unto Themselves." In A. Sarat and S. Scheingold eds., *Cause Lawyers and Social Movement*. Stanford: Stanford University Press.

Melucci, Alberto. 1994. "A Strange Kind of Newness: What's New in New Social Movements." In E. Larana, H. Johnston, and J. Gusfield eds., *New social movements: From ideology to identity*. Philadelphia. Temple University Press.

Menkel-Meadow, Carrie. 1998. "The Causes of Cause Lawyering: Toward an Understanding of the Motivation and Commitment of Social Justice Lawyers." In A Sarat and S. Scheingold eds., *Cause Lawyering: Political Commitments and Professional Responsibilities*. New York: Oxford University Press.

Minow, Martha. 1996. "Political Lawyering: An Introduction." *Harvard Civil Rights-Civil Liberties Law Review* 31: 287–96.

Polikoff, Nancy D. 1996. "Am I My Client? The Role Confusion of a Lawyer Activist." *Harvard Civil Rights-Civil Liberties Law Review* 31: 443–71.

Robnett, Belinda. 1997. *How Long, How Long?: African American Women in the Struggle for Civil Rights*. New York: Oxford University Press.

Rubin, Herbert J. 2000. "What Conferences Accomplish for Social Change Organizations: Illustrations from the Community-Based Development Movement." *Journal of Community Practice* 74: 35–55.

Scheingold, Stuart and Austin Sarat. 2004. *Something to Believe In: Politics, Professionalism, and Cause Lawyering*. Stanford: Stanford University Press.

Scheingold, Stuart. 1998. "The Struggle to Politicize Legal Practice: A Case Study of Left activist Lawyering in Seattle." In A. Sarat and S. Scheingold eds., *Cause Lawyering: Political Commitments and Professional Responsibilities*. New York: Oxford University Press.

Schram, Sanford F. 2000. *After Welfare: The Culture of Postindustrial Social Policy*. New York: New York University Press.

Shdaimah, Corey S. 2005. "Dilemmas of "Progressive" Lawyering: Empowerment and Hierarchy." In A. Sarat and Scheingold eds., *The Worlds Cause Lawyers Make: Structure and Agency in Legal Practice*. Stanford: Stanford University Press.

Shdaimah, Corey S. and Sue Wasserkrug. 2003. *"Consciously Creating Community: The Philadelphia Public Interest Law Community."* Paper presented at the 2003 Annual Meetings of the Law and Society Association.

Soutworth, Ann. 2005. "Professional Identity and Political Commitment among Lawyers for Conservative Causes." In A. Sarat and Scheingold eds., *The Worlds Cause Lawyers Make: Structure and Agency in Legal Practice*. Stanford: Stanford University Press.

Snow, David A., Soule, Sarah A., and Hanspeter Kreisi. 2004. "Mapping the Terrain." In D. Snow, S. Soule and H. Kriesi eds., *The Blackwell Companion to Social Movements*. Malden: Blackwell Publishing.

Thomson, Douglas. 2005. "Negotiating Cause Lawyering Potential in the Early Years of Corporate Practice." In A. Sarat and Scheingold eds., *The Worlds Cause Lawyers Make: Structure and Agency in Legal Practice*. Stanford: Stanford University Press.

Beyond Litigation: Other Roles, Other Styles for Cause Lawyers in Social Movements

The Movement Takes the Lead

The Role of Lawyers in the Struggle for a Living Wage in Santa Monica, California

KATHLEEN M. ERSKINE AND JUDY MARBLESTONE[1]

Introduction

Since 1994, a series of legislative initiatives called living wage ordinances (LWOs) have taken effect in cities throughout the United States.[2] These initiatives vary greatly, but most require companies contracting with city governments or receiving public money to pay their employees a wage higher than either federal or state minimum wages. A living wage is often defined as a wage that provides an income sufficient to raise a family of four with one wage earner above the poverty line.[3]

Proponents laud the living wage as a means of eliminating corporate welfare, organizing workers, and broadening the national discourse by raising the notion of economic justice for the working poor, locality by locality. Detractors argue LWOs inhibit development, interfere with the play of free market forces, and drive businesses and jobs away from municipalities. At its heart, the living wage movement and the opposition to it are about wages, jobs, and the best way to obtain economic prosperity for a municipality's low-wage constituents as well as who has, and who should have, the power to set standards regarding wages and benefits. These goals and dynamics affect the ways both proponents and opponents of the living wage frame the issues.

In many cases, LWOs are passed only after campaigns of political mobilization and activism put significant pressure on legislators.[4] The movement to pass an LWO in Santa Monica, California illustrated just such community activism and political pressure. From its roots as a small group of community activists supporting workers engaged in a fight to keep a union at one major luxury hotel and a handful of staff members at a nonprofit organization, the movement grew to encompass scores of community volunteers, Santa Monica resident activists, clergy, union members and leaders, Santa Monica City Council (City Council) members, attorneys, educators, law students, and workers in a broad coalition called Santa Monicans Allied for Responsible Tourism (SMART).

This chapter focuses on the role of lawyers in a "localized movement"—a series of connected campaigns in Santa Monica from 1996 through the fall of 2002, during which an LWO was both passed and repealed—and it pays particular attention to how lawyers participated in this dynamic fight. Through a brief chronological narrative in "A Brief History of the Santa Monica Living Wage Movement," we look at the various facets of this localized movement. "The Santa Monica Living Wage Struggle as 'Social Movement'?" discusses our working definition of a "social movement." "Cause Lawyering and the Santa Monica LWO" discusses cause lawyering literature and the role of cause lawyers in the Santa Monica LWO movement. In "The Santa Monica Living Wage Movement and the Framing of Social Movements," we consider how both the proponents of the Santa Monica LWO framed the issue as well as how the opposition distorted the proponents' message and also created "countermessages" in a way that, many believe, harmed the democratic process in the battle over the living wage.

A Brief History of the Santa Monica Living Wage Movement

The SMART Coalition and the Initial Shaping of a Santa Monica LWO

Santa Monicans Allied for Responsible Tourism (SMART), the coalition responsible for mobilizing support for and drafting the Santa Monica LWO, was formed in June 1996.[5] The coalition stemmed from joint efforts of community activists, the Hotel Employees and Restaurant Employees Union (HERE[6]) Local 814, and the Los Angeles Alliance for a New Economy (LAANE), a nonprofit research and community action organization working closely with HERE. The vision of HERE and LAANE was to mobilize community allies to build a base of strength for workers. HERE and LAANE leaders believed in building a new kind of labor movement in which community involvement and support were critical to advancing the rights of low-wage workers.[7]

Early on, SMART consisted primarily of community leaders and clergy, and its initial goal was to help workers fight a union decertification effort at what was then the Fairmont Miramar. Beth Leder-Pack, a founding member of SMART, commented: "... we actually didn't start with the living wage ordinance as our agenda. That's not why SMART was formed. We began as a community group ... mainly to support the efforts of the unionized workers at the Miramar-Sheraton hotel...."[8]

In 1997, in an effort spearheaded by LAANE, the Los Angeles City Council passed an LWO in Los Angeles. Soon after, SMART, with the help of LAANE, started conceiving a plan to propose a living wage to cover the low-wage workers at Santa Monica's luxury beachfront hotels. SMART leaders would also recruit a successful legal team similar to one that had assisted LAANE in the Los Angeles living wage campaign.[9]

Although SMART's base grew largely out of support for workers' rights to unionize and have a voice on the job, SMART was a broader coalition than those involved in the traditional labor movement.[10] Through various rallies, community events, and one-on-one communication, SMART successfully mobilized a broad-based community coalition of longtime community activists, college students, law students, hotel workers, lawyers, and community residents new to activism.

In the fall of 1999 and spring of 2000, SMART began shaping its proposed LWO. SMART's proposal required all firms in the "Coastal Zone," a 1.5-square-mile strip along Santa Monica's coastline, and all other businesses contracting with the city that employed more than fifty people to pay those employees a living wage, designated at $10.69/hour.[11] It was estimated that this proposal would cover over 2,000 workers in Santa Monica.[12] SMART's primary arguments for an LWO were that businesses in the Coastal Zone had benefited from the City's financing and subsidizing of the tourist zone, that hotels in the Coastal Zone had reaped a significant benefit from the passage of a proposition precluding any further development of new hotels in the zone, and that an LWO should be directed at those businesses having the greatest proportion of low-wage employees.[13]

The City Council responded to SMART's proposed LWO by issuing a nationwide request for proposals and commissioning an economic study, completed in August 2000.[14] The Chamber of Commerce commissioned its own study.[15] The two studies came to radically different conclusions.[16] However, the City Council did not have an opportunity to act on either study. Opponents preempted the City Council by placing a so-called "living wage" measure on the ballot for the upcoming November 2000 election.

The First Challenge to the Santa Monica LWO: Proposition KK

The first challenge to the LWO came with Proposition KK (Prop KK or KK), an initiative placed on the city's November 2000 ballot. This initiative is the first example of many in the history of the Santa Monica living wage movement in which the opposition co-opted the message of living wage supporters. In an attempt to preempt SMART's proposed living wage, a business coalition calling itself Santa Monicans for a Living Wage (SMFLW) hired a large law firm to draft a ballot measure that would enact a living wage at $8.32 an hour with benefits and divest the City Council of the power ever to enact another LWO. The SMFLW ordinance also covered only the city's own employees and full-time employees of businesses receiving more than $25,000 in city contracts—or about sixty-two employees.[17] The hotel-financed signature-gathering process to qualify this measure for the ballot was extremely controversial.[18]

SMART responded by organizing "Truth Teams" to discourage Santa Monicans from signing ballot petitions and encourage those who had been misled into doing so to rescind their signatures.[19] Despite SMART's efforts, in August 2000 SMFLW succeeded in qualifying its proposition for the November 2000 ballot. The business coalition and SMFLW intensified their efforts to pass Prop KK, sending mailers reading, "Santa Monica's Living Wage should be set by the voters, not the politicians. Yes on Proposition KK. Because it's Fair."[20]

During the ensuing weeks, SMART volunteers and staffers conducted a get out the vote campaign through mailers, newspaper ads, phone banks (calling more than 20,000 voters), and door-to-door campaigning.[21] Twenty-five full-time walkers, including some attorneys active in SMART, canvassed Santa Monica neighborhoods.[22] SMART also combated SMFLW's rhetoric with a mailing campaign, denouncing Prop KK as "deceptive," part of "dirty politics," and a "sham living wage."[23] SMART's efforts were successful; on election day, 78 percent of Santa Monica voters voted no on KK.[24]

Drafting and Passage of the Santa Monica LWO

Prior to the Prop KK campaign, SMART had called upon lawyers to research legal issues and draft memos to persuade the City Council and Marsha Jones Moutrie, the Santa Monica City Attorney (City Attorney), that various aspects of the proposed LWO would withstand legal scrutiny. Much of the pre-KK legal research resumed after Prop KK was defeated as SMART again prepared to convince the City Council to enact an LWO.

The primary groups responsible for drafting the ordinance were the SMART Task Force (Task Force) and the SMART Legal Team (Legal Team). The Legal Team attended to the details of the ordinance and researched various legal issues and language in other ordinances. It then reported to the Task Force, which made final decisions.[25] Although the Legal Team was responsible for identifying and researching legal issues, the entire Task Force developed strategies and voted on questions about major provisions of the proposed ordinance.

The Task Force met approximately monthly from December 2000 through May 2001 to define the central provisions of the ordinance, discuss potential political and legal opposition with the Legal Team, and agree on what recommendations SMART would propose to the City Attorney and City Council. Several issues required careful consideration during the drafting phase, including the wage and benefits provisions, the geographical boundaries of the covered area, the definition of covered employees and employers, an antiretaliation provision, enforcement and penalties, and whether any part of the ordinance would be preempted by federal or state laws.

SMART's March 2001 LWO proposal to the City Council included a wage level of $10.69, plus health benefits of $2.50 per hour and would apply to employers in the city's Coastal Zone. This feature of the Santa Monica proposed LWO made it somewhat unique: although other cities had limited their LWOs to geographical zones, no previous LWO had defined the zone in such a way that it would primarily affect a particular industry. The city staff's report on the proposed ordinance reflected the cautionary position of the City Attorney. Several portions of the report admonished the City Council that it was unclear the city had the power to enact a minimum wage nearly "double" the state minimum wage and require that other employment benefits be provided by private sector employers. The city staff predicted a constitutional challenge to the ordinance's application to private employers in a particular geographical zone, as well as other legal challenges.[26]

The Legal Team delivered to the City Council a comprehensive legal memorandum outlining possible legal challenges to the proposed ordinance and arguing that there would be "no legal impediments to the City['s] enacting the LWO with all the provisions proposed by SMART."[27] City Council members had major concerns about passing the first LWO in the nation applying to private employers in a particular area of a city.[28] One Council member, Herb Katz, asked repeatedly how the ordinance could be constitutional when it treated some workers differently from others.[29] Katz, who ultimately voted against the ordinance, stated that he thought the law was discriminatory.[30]

Despite these concerns, the City Council voted 5-2 to direct the City Attorney to draft an LWO, working with SMART and the business community. On July 24, 2001, after a two-year struggle and months of fine-tuning the ordinance, the City Council passed the Santa Monica LWO.[31]

The Second Challenge to the Santa Monica LWO: Measure JJ

After the City Council passed the LWO, the opposition coalition, calling itself Fighting Against Irresponsible Regulation (FAIR), immediately mobilized a referendum campaign. FAIR had thirty days to gather signatures from 10 percent of voters, or about 5,700 signatures, in order to place the LWO on the ballot for repeal. SMART counterattacked by sending volunteers to grocery store parking lots to alert voters to the opposition's tactics and urge them not to sign any petitions in the coming weeks.[32] In the end, FAIR collected 8,856 signatures, enough of which were valid to place the ordinance on the ballot.[33]

In the weeks before the election, the "No on JJ" campaign sent mailers to Santa Monica residents. One posited, "If Measure JJ is about a 'living wage,' why are luxury union hotels exempt?" A door hanger flyer urged voters to "Save city services," "Protect local jobs," and "Fight discrimination." Another group of mailings projected the LWO would cost the city $3 million and divert funds away from senior citizens centers, schools, and libraries.

Most notably, in the third week of October and within two weeks of the election, the opposition created three "committees" under the California Political Reform Act.[34] Because they were formed after a mid-October filing deadline provided in the Act, these committees were not required to file disclosure statements until January 31, 2003, well after the election. The committees were called the "Quality Schools Coalition," the "Pro-Choice Voters Committee," and the "Democratic Voters Ballot Guide."

The committees sent slate mailers to Santa Monica residents the weekend before the election, making it appear as though democratic candidates, pro-choice leaders, and educators were opposed to JJ. In fact, SMART had won endorsements from the Los Angeles County Democratic Party, the Santa Monica Democratic Club, and leading Democrats in the state. The "Democratic Voters Ballot Guide" mailer displayed photographs of state and local democratic leaders, representing that they endorsed a No vote on JJ. None of these individuals had taken a stand against Measure JJ, and more than one had specifically endorsed the measure.[35] Polling prior to the election showed a solid margin of support for JJ.[36] However, SMART had no time to wage a countermeasure to these deceptive mailers, which very likely tipped the balance toward Measure JJ's defeat. On election day, Measure JJ failed.[37]

In response to the opposition's deceptive tactics, the SMART Task Force voted to organize a public hearing on the election, presided over by leading civil rights scholars, lawyers, and community leaders, to expose the opposition's deceptive practices. SMART wanted to regain control over the message, in part by not remaining passive in the face of what it believed were truly deceptive practices and a hijacking of the political system in order to defeat a popular measure.

Lawyers played a large role in the public hearing. A majority of commissioners were law professors, leading civil rights attorneys, and former California Supreme Court Justice Cruz Reynoso. Three key witnesses were attorneys, including Steve Ury of the Legal Team, who made one of two closing arguments.

The hearing illuminated the deception of the LWO opposition, and resulted in a report of the commission's findings, concluding that the opposition had misled the voters for a two-and-a-half-year period from April 2000 to November 2002 and that the events surrounding Measure JJ illustrated that reforms are "urgently needed to improve the fairness of the initiative and referendum process."[38]

The Santa Monica Living Wage Struggle as "Social Movement"?

Based on the work and insight of numerous people, we describe a social movement as a sustained attempt by people on the margins of power, and/or those working on behalf of marginalized people, to effect change and thereby reallocate resources and/or power.[39] Social movements involve efforts to effect structural change, often through the creation of new rights or the enforcement of existing rights, as well as popular education about underlying social, economic, and political problems.[40]

The Santa Monica LWO leaders and activists had differing opinions regarding whether the living wage struggle was a "social movement." However, there is consensus that the fight for an LWO in Santa Monica was part of a nationwide effort to advance the rights of and secure more resources for low-wage workers, whether by passing LWOs, organizing unions, or effecting other types of changes that benefit the working poor[41] and bring the injustices they face into the national consciousness.

The Santa Monica LWO campaign[42] drew from related legal achievements such as the Los Angeles LWO (LA LWO), passed in 1997 and amended in 1998 and deemed by some to be a model of implementation and enforcement.[43] An LWO had also recently passed in nearby Pasadena.[44] These LWOs, all in Los Angeles County, were part of a nationwide trend of the enactment of LWOs.

Since 1994, when the city of Baltimore, Maryland, passed the first LWO, dozens of localities have enacted LWOs. There are currently approximately 123 LWOs "on the books" across the country.[45] Thus, it is fair to say that the Santa Monica LWO campaign was part of a broad movement for justice for low-wage workers via enactment of local ordinances.[46] The LWO movement involves localities taking into their own hands the responsibility to improve the conditions of low-wage workers given the inadequacy of the federal minimum wage.

The Santa Monica LWO campaign was separate from, but connected to, this larger living wage movement.[47] Paul Sonn, an attorney who heads the Brennan Center for Justice's (Brennan Center's) Economic Justice Project, suggests that LWO campaigns across the country are largely unconnected and decentralized, emerging as they do from local coalitions and political circumstances.[48] These local campaigns often draw on national resource providers such as the Brennan Center, the Economic Policy Institute, and the Association of Community Organizations for Reform Now (ACORN) Living Wage Resource Center for assistance with legal, organizing, and economic analysis issues. But their campaigns are not coordinated in any meaningful way. There are a few exceptions such as LWO campaigns organized across the country by ACORN. Also, HERE has actively supported a number of LWO campaigns in California in addition to the Santa Monica LWO.[49]

Although LWO campaigns are often unconnected to each other, they share the goal of shifting resources from profitable businesses to low-wage workers. The LWO initiatives in Los Angeles County may be considered a local movement for economic justice for low-wage workers.[50]

As might be expected, the living wage movement is often intimately connected with the labor movement—both of which seek to improve working conditions. The living wage movement is both broader and narrower in scope than the labor movement. The living wage movement is broader in scope than the labor movement because it encompasses many low-wage workers who are not members of labor unions. It is much newer and less institutionalized than the labor movement, but living wage coalitions are often broader than traditional labor movement coalitions, as exemplified by the range of constituency groups represented in SMART.[51] Ruben Garcia suggests that LWOs are part of a broader movement seeking economic justice for low-wage workers who work full-time but still live below the poverty line.[52]

The living wage movement is also narrower in scope than the labor movement. LWOs usually focus on only one or two terms of employment (typically wages and health benefits), as opposed to the labor movement's push for the right to collectively bargain over multiple and varied terms and conditions of employment. Also, although LWOs result in a government legitimated raise for low-wage workers, they do not confer ongoing, collective bargaining power to improve, monitor, and enforce the terms and conditions of employment. In fact, many LWOs are not even indexed to cost of living increases.

Although the centerpiece of the Santa Monica LWO campaign was an LWO, this was only one of many tools to achieve the broader goal of economic justice for the working poor. Other mechanisms included worker and community organizing, consciousness-raising, community education, and media. As Vivian Rothstein stated, the ordinance was part of a multifaceted strategy, a large part of which was changing public opinion.[53]

Cause Lawyering and the Santa Monica LWO

The Santa Monica LWO campaign illustrates an emerging theme in cause lawyering research: cause lawyers[54] often support, not dominate, the strategy and tools used in social movements.[55] Stuart Scheingold's refined view of cause lawyering, the "new politics of rights," is consistent with this trend.[56] Scheingold departs from his initial critique of activist, or cause, lawyering which claimed that the "myth of rights—according to which legal rights are *directly* empowering— is misleading. More often than not, rights articulated by courts go unrealized when they are embedded in contested matters of public policy."[57]

Scheingold's new politics of rights acknowledges that his initial "analysis of cause lawyers . . . resulted in two significant miscalculations that have been corrected by subsequent research . . . [including] that cause lawyers were socialized in ways that privileged litigation and marginalized the politicization that was essential to a politics of rights. . . ."[58]

The new politics of rights, as articulated by Michael McCann and Helena Silverstein, "[does] not deny that cause lawyers tend to privilege litigation, but point[s] out that, like other lawyers, cause lawyers view litigation as one arrow in a quiver that includes, for example, leveraging the threat of litigation, lobbying, and under the right circumstances, political mobilization. . . . [L]awyers working with and within organized social movements . . . are willing and able to deploy rights politically."[59] The Santa Monica LWO campaign provides an apt example of this revised view of cause lawyering.

In the Santa Monica LWO campaign, legislation, not litigation, was the primary legal tool. This model is consistent with other LWO campaigns that combine legislation with community education and political mobilization. Even if LWOs are challenged in court after their initial enactment, litigation is a reaction to and a defense of the ordinance as opposed to a proactive effort to create new rights or enforce existing rights.

Categorizing Cause Lawyers

To further understand the role of lawyers in the Santa Monica LWO campaign, it is helpful to differentiate among different types of cause lawyers. Cause lawyers, like social movements, do not fit neatly into specific categories. However, McCann and Silverstein's typology of cause lawyers provides a helpful reference point from which to examine the function and activities of lawyers in the Santa Monica LWO campaign. These categories are: "[First], *staff lawyers* who work (usually for a mix of salary and case fee) in established organizations such as unions or women's rights groups; [second] *independent cause lawyers* who work for fee as special counsel on particular movement cases; and [third] *nonpracticing lawyers* who have stepped out of professional roles to contribute in other ways to the cause...."[60]

McCann and Silverstein further classify *staff lawyers* into two subcategories: "*legal staff 'technicians'*... [who] tend to restrict themselves to executing the more narrowly technical legal aspects (consultation, negotiation, litigation) of campaigns initiated by others. [And] *[s]taff activists*... [who] formulat[e] group demands, develop[] group strategies, wag[e] broader political campaigns, and even challeng[e] their own organizations on behalf of constituent interests or principles."[61]

A new category of cause lawyers: pro bono, volunteer cause lawyers. The lawyers involved in the LWO campaign in Santa Monica do not fall neatly into the above-mentioned categories. However, they do resemble, with some overlap, *staff activists, independent cause lawyers,* and *nonpracticing lawyers.* Additionally, the Santa Monica LWO campaign illustrates another category of cause lawyers: *pro bono, volunteer cause lawyers.* They are "*pro bono*" because they do not charge fees for their services, and they are "*volunteers*" because they come to the movement in their spare time to act in whatever capacity—legal or nonlegal—they can be most useful.[62] As discussed below, these *pro bono, volunteer cause lawyers* play a support role to the movement. In this way, they are similar to McCann and Silverstein's "*legal staff technicians*," but they are not paid for their services and often take a more active role in the movement's political and community mobilization components. Additionally, *pro bono, volunteer cause lawyers* may also be employed as *independent cause lawyers* or *staff lawyers* for other, often similar, causes, or in the private sector, but they also donate their expertise and services to social movements outside their "day jobs."[63] Often these *pro bono, volunteer cause lawyers* play dual roles as attorneys and activists. The *pro bono, volunteer cause lawyers* often work at small or mid-sized, private, public interest firms (e.g., plaintiff-side employment or union-side labor law firms), not big, corporate law firms. *Pro bono, volunteer cause lawyers* may have the support of their law firms to do pro bono work as part of their jobs. Thus, there is overlap between *independent cause lawyers* and *pro bono, volunteer cause lawyers.*

Pro bono, volunteer cause lawyers do work that is significantly different from the type of *pro bono* work usually undertaken at large, corporate law firms. These firms generally avoid *pro bono* work that presents "positional conflicts" that are "directly adverse" to "commercial clients."[64] Cummings states that "the most noticeable effect [of positional conflicts] is to exclude pro bono cases that strike at the heart of corporate client interests, particularly employment, environmental, and consumer cases in which plaintiffs seek pro bono counsel to sue major companies." Ultimately, "[p]atronage shapes case selection."[65]

The fundamental goal of *pro bono, volunteer cause lawyers* in the Santa Monica LWO campaign was to change the economic power structure and challenge corporate, primarily luxury hotel, interests. Thus, the *pro bono, volunteer cause lawyers* active in the Santa Monica LWO campaign met a need that otherwise might not have been fulfilled by traditional *pro bono* resources.

Cause Lawyering Themes in the Santa Monica LWO Movement [66]

Two primary themes related to cause lawyering emerge from the Santa Monica LWO movement. First, while we focus on lawyers as individuals and in a group, it is clear that although lawyers played a strong support role in the Santa Monica LWO campaign, they were not often in the foreground.[67] Even when they were in the foreground, such as during the early shaping and later drafting of the LWO, they took direction from the community activists, who were primarily either nonlawyers or *nonpracticing lawyers* from SMART and LAANE.[68] Second, most of the lawyers involved in the Legal Team fit the *pro bono, volunteer cause lawyer* description more than any other category of cause lawyers, even when they were performing technical legal tasks.

The Role of Lawyers in LWOs Generally

Paul Sonn suggests that a role for lawyers in LWO campaigns emerges primarily if there are complicated legal issues regarding specific provisions of a proposed LWO.[69] These legal questions usually arise if the LWO is novel or contains unusual provisions, such as the Santa Monica LWO's Coastal Zone provision or the broader citywide LWOs that have been enacted in communities like San Francisco, Santa Fe, New Mexico, and Madison, Wisconsin. In cases with such complex legal issues, lawyers can be more important both in designing legislation that will withstand legal challenge and in persuading elected officials that proposals are legally defensible.[70]

Another factor that influences the need for lawyers in LWO campaigns is the position of the City Attorney.[71] If the City Attorney is sympathetic to the LWO, then the City Attorney him- or herself may help draft the LWO and argue for the legality of the LWO, decreasing the need for other lawyers to draft and defend the LWO.[72] The City Attorney's support for a LWO is particularly helpful because ultimately the City Attorney will defend and probably enforce the LWO. But even in such cases, having advice from lawyers who have expertise with LWOs and minimum wage laws can still be helpful because most city attorneys have not drafted such legislation before and are not familiar with the various issues that arise in designing them.[73]

LWO legal strategies are unique to each campaign, but many LWO campaigns (especially the more "traditional" LWOs) do not have access to lawyers and/or do not need lawyers because the legality of LWOs covering city contractors is generally not disputed.[74] Usually, campaigns for LWOs involve no attorneys. Where legal questions arise, many campaigns consult with the Brennan Center for long-distance legal support. Otherwise, lawyers often participate in LWO campaigns more as activists than as legal advisors.[75]

Notably, Sonn has not seen any other LWO campaign with a legal team as large as the SMART Legal Team.[76] Sonn thinks the SMART Legal Team was so large and well organized in part because Santa Monica has a long-standing, well-organized community.[77] Furthermore, lawyers may have played a larger role in the Santa Monica LWO campaign compared to other LWO campaigns because Santa Monica's proposed LWO was the first of its kind and supporters knew that opponents would challenge the ordinance in court.

SMART Legal Team Formation

Although many lawyers participated in SMART as laypeople, there was also a group of lawyers throughout the Santa Monica LWO campaign who supported the movement by contributing their professional expertise as members of the Legal Team. Leaders of HERE and LAANE were familiar with this model from a successful legal team in the movement to pass an LWO in Los Angeles.[78]

Stephanie Monroe, a LAANE staff person, began recruiting lawyers to the Legal Team in late 1997 or early 1998.[79] The Legal Team initially consisted of lawyers who had participated in the LA LWO, LAANE staff, and other community activist lawyers, including Ruben Garcia, Peter Marx, and Madeline Janis-Aparicio.[80]

At this early stage, lawyers played at most a marginal role in the Santa Monica living wage movement. According to Danny Feingold, Director of Communications for LAANE and a researcher and community organizer for SMART at the beginning of the anti-KK campaign, lawyers did not play a central role in strategizing, organizing, or framing the message against KK. SMART used media consultants and had a media message committee that included no lawyers.[81]

The SMART Legal Team's Role in Decision Making

Although the SMART Legal Team was one of the largest in the country, the Legal Team did not drive SMART's strategy, nor did it drive the specific strategy for passing a Santa Monica LWO. Instead, the Legal Team took its cues from SMART leadership, particularly the Task Force, and SMART's general membership.[82] Lawyers in the Santa Monica LWO played a support role for the movement rather than leading or directing the strategy.[83] As discussed above, the Legal Team, largely composed of *pro bono, volunteer cause lawyers* was an integral part of SMART, but it served largely in an advisory capacity for SMART leadership. Activists, workers, and community leaders, rather than lawyers, drove the Santa Monica LWO campaign strategy.

A number of the *pro bono, volunteer cause lawyer* members of the Legal Team, such as Davit Pettit and Rick Abel, were also SMART members. They participated in the SMART decision-making as long-standing residents and community activists, but not in their role as lawyers.[84]

The (voluntary) subordination of lawyers in the Santa Monica LWO campaign may have occurred because SMART's strategy did not consist of litigation or other labor-intensive, time-consuming technical legal tools. But the support role lawyers played most likely occurred because of SMART's commitment to an organic, community-based movement.[85] Community members, including workers, made key decisions. For example, the decision to propose an LWO covering the Coastal Zone was made by the Task Force, not the lawyers. The Legal Team responded to SMART strategies by researching and explaining how to craft an ordinance that was legally sound and accomplished SMART's goals.

Lawyers were on the front line of the Santa Monica LWO campaign only insofar as the campaign demanded their legal expertise in discrete tasks.[86] For example, Legal Team members and other legal scholars played a key role in lobbying City Council members and meeting with the City Attorney, the officials who would ultimately pass and defend a Santa Monica LWO.[87]

The City Attorney was cautious about the novel provisions of the Santa Monica LWO, namely the Coastal Zone. She wanted to minimize the risk that the city would be sued for enacting an LWO because such litigation would drain city resources.[88] Therefore, the Legal Team wrote many legal memoranda for the City Council and the City Attorney explaining the legality of the proposed Santa Monica LWO.[89] Members of the Legal Team also met on numerous occasions with City Council members, the City Attorney, and the City Manager to address their concerns about adopting a novel LWO and underscore the legality of the Santa Monica LWO.

The Role of SMART Legal Team Members

Pro bono, volunteer cause lawyers. In 1998, Ruben Garcia was a union-side labor lawyer working at the law firm Rothner, Segall, & Greenstone (Rothner, Segall) in Pasadena, California, who had much experience working on LWOs.[90]

He had worked on the LA LWO as a pro bono attorney while at Rothner, Segall. Garcia had also worked on the Pasadena LWO as a counsel for the American Federation of State, County, and Municipal Employees (AFSCME). Thus, Garcia was both an *independent cause lawyer* in his "day job," and a *pro bono, volunteer cause lawyer* for SMART.

Garcia helped draft the Santa Monica LWO in the early stages of the campaign, prior to Prop KK. As noted above, the fact that SMART's proposed LWO would apply to employees in a coastal zone, rather than to all employees covered by city contracts, set the Santa Monica LWO apart from all other existing LWOs. Garcia also researched and wrote legal memoranda about potential challenges to the groundbreaking provisions of SMART's LWO. Various iterations of these memoranda would be used to persuade the City Attorney that the proposed Santa Monica LWO stood on solid legal ground.[91]

Peter Marx was another community lawyer who volunteered his time in the beginning of the Santa Monica LWO campaign.[92] Marx, a National Lawyers Guild (NLG) member, practiced labor and employment law and was also a mediator. He became involved with SMART initially in support of the Miramar hotel workers.[93] As a member of the Legal Team, Marx researched and wrote a memorandum about antiretaliation and other potential provisions of a Santa Monica LWO.[94] Marx also participated in a nonlegal capacity: he helped plan one of SMART's major fund-raisers, a jazz concert.[95]

Additional *pro bono, volunteer cause lawyers* who were committed to social and economic justice joined the Legal Team at various stages throughout the Santa Monica LWO campaign. Steve Ury, a union-side labor lawyer at the Burbank, California firm Geffner & Bush, became a member of the Legal Team in late 1998. He initially heard about the Santa Monica LWO campaign by calling the NLG because he had recently moved to Los Angeles and wanted to become more involved in activism and the labor movement.[96] Ury was an active member of the Legal Team. Geffner & Bush supported Ury's pro bono work, but Ury also volunteered much of his spare time to the Santa Monica LWO.[97] Serving in his professional role as a lawyer, he not only conducted legal research and legislative drafting, but also lobbied the City Council and City Attorney by meeting with them, writing letters, and speaking at City Council meetings.[98]

Although Ury's primary involvement was as a member of the Legal Team, he also supported the Santa Monica LWO campaign in a nonlegal, activist capacity. He did extensive precinct walking, phone banking, and other get out the vote work for both the "No on KK" and "Yes on JJ" campaigns.[99] After the LWO was defeated in the November 2002 election, Ury also participated as an advocate in SMART's March 2003 Public Hearing to expose the LWO opposition's misleading and deceptive preelection campaign tactics.[100]

When legal issues surrounding the harassment of SMART volunteers during the signature revocation campaigns preceding Prop KK and Measure JJ arose, SMART asked Ury's advice on these discrete issues;[101] however, Ury and other lawyers were not the architects of this phase and, in participating in the ground campaign, they acted largely as other volunteers.

Rick Abel first became involved in the Santa Monica LWO campaign in the summer of 2000, shortly before the Prop KK campaign.[102] Abel not only lent his legal credentials as a law professor to the campaign, but also participated in community actions in support of Santa Monica low-wage workers and the LWO. For example, in May 2001 Abel sent a letter to the City Attorney, regarding the legality of SMART's proposed antiretaliation provision in the LWO.[103] He also phone banked, participated in demonstrations, and served as a SMART living wage spokesperson.[104] However, Abel views his participation in SMART primarily as a long-term Santa Monica resident, *not* a lawyer.[105]

David Pettit was another long-time Santa Monica resident and attorney who participate in the Legal Team as a *pro bono, volunteer cause lawyer.* Pettit had previously worked for the City of Santa Monica and had been active in the Santa Monica renters' rights movement.[106] Ultimately, Pettit's law firm, Caldwell Leslie, was ready to represent SMART as local counsel if the Santa Monica LWO had passed in 2002 at which point the opposition would have immediately challenged the ordinance in court.[107]

Nonpracticing lawyers. Cause lawyers involved in the Santa Monica LWO campaign also included *nonpracticing lawyers.* Madeline Janis-Aparicio had been intimately involved in the LA LWO campaign that LAANE spearheaded.[108] Although Janis-Aparicio was not acting formally in a legal capacity at LAANE, she had gone to law school and practiced law for four years before stopping legal practice and returning to full-time activism, armed with legal credentials and a familiarity with legal tools.[109] Janis-Aparicio participated in the Legal Team and provided leadership for the broader Santa Monica LWO campaign.

Independent cause lawyers. Although the Legal Team drew heavily on *pro bono, volunteer cause lawyers* throughout the Santa Monica LWO campaign, another important cause lawyer was labor attorney Rich McCracken and a number of associates from Davis, Cowell, & Bowe, a San Francisco union-side labor law firm that represents HERE Local 11 and other HERE clients.[110] In addition to providing counsel to HERE Local 11 in traditional union matters, McCracken assisted with the research and drafting of both the Los Angeles and the Santa Monica LWOs.[111] As such, he can be classified as an *independent cause lawyer* who was retained to represent a local union; although in the living wage campaign, his representation was not via litigation, but rather legislative research, drafting, and advocacy. McCracken provided tremendous experience and knowledge to the Legal Team and served in an advisory role throughout the campaign.[112]

Staff cause lawyers. The Legal Team also included *staff lawyers*. Erika Zucker began working as LAANE's General Counsel in March of 2000.[113] Zucker had previously advocated for the Los Angeles LWO as a *pro bono, volunteer cause lawyer* while she was working at a Los Angeles union-side labor law firm, Schwartz, Steinsapir, Dohrmann & Sommers. Soon after Zucker joined LAANE, the opposition's campaign to pass Prop KK began, and she became involved in SMART's efforts to defeat this proposition.[114]

At LAANE, Zucker functioned in part as a *legal staff "technician"* by conducting legal research, drafting legislation, and lobbying the City Council and City Attorney.[115] For example, Zucker conducted extensive research on possible enforcement options for the Santa Monica LWO as well as anticipated legal challenges to the Santa Monica LWO.[116] In addition, she did much legal work on the "Yes on JJ" campaign by coordinating challenges to the opposition's petition gathering for Measure JJ and working extensively with outside elections counsel.[117]

Zucker also functioned as a *staff activist* cause lawyer. She helped organize and mobilize community support for the Santa Monica LWO. For example, she did door-to-door canvassing and get-out-the-vote work.[118]

Participation of Lawyers Outside the SMART Legal Team

Although the primary contribution of lawyers in the Santa Monica LWO campaign came from members of the Legal Team, a number of other lawyers and lawyers-in-training contributed to the Santa Monica LWO campaign.

Paul Sonn was another *staff activist* attorney who supported the Santa Monica LWO campaign in a limited capacity. Sonn is the preeminent lawyer providing legal assistance to LWO coalitions across the country.[119] In approximately 2000, Sonn talked with Erika Zucker about organizing an amicus brief if and when there was litigation challenging a Santa Monica LWO.[120] Sonn secured a commitment from the firm Wilmer, Cutler & Pickering to act as *pro bono* counsel and help with the amicus brief if and when this challenge arose.[121]

Shortly before the November 2002 vote on Measure JJ, Sonn also helped mobilize legal scholars to publicly attest to the legality of the Santa Monica

LWO if necessary.[122] Because the Santa Monica LWO was ultimately defeated, the Brennan Center's involvement in the Santa Monica LWO campaign was limited to these efforts.[123]

Legal scholars played additional roles in the Santa Monica LWO campaign. Erwin Chemerinsky, one of the preeminent constitutional law scholars in the country and at that time a law professor at USC law school, also supported the Santa Monica LWO campaign.[124] For example, prior to the March 27, 2001 City Council meeting at which SMART's proposed ordinance was first officially considered, Chemerinsky wrote a letter to the City Council and Mayor stating that a Santa Monica LWO would not be preempted by state or federal laws and that the Coastal Zone provision would not violate equal protection or due process.[125]

Some of the key SMART members were lawyers who participated little in their role as lawyers, but largely as community activists. For example, Sonia Sultan, an active member of the Task Force, is a practicing lawyer, but did not participate in the Legal Team.[126]

Finally, many UCLA law students in Rick Abel's "Law and Social Change" and "Issues Affecting Low Wage Workers" seminars conducted legal research about the Santa Monica LWO. Students wrote papers addressing effective implementation and enforcement of the LWO, the national living wage movement, and strategies for implementing an LWO after the November 2002 electoral defeat, among other topics.[127]

Law students also participated in rallies, protests, precinct walking, media, and public education. For example, Kathleen Erskine, coauthor of this paper and currently a union-side labor lawyer at Geffner & Bush, was an active member of the Task Force and has participated in the Santa Monica LWO campaign since she was in law school. Erskine became involved in the Santa Monica LWO campaign while she researched and wrote a paper, with Abel as her advisor, about the history of the Santa Monica LWO campaign.[128]

Thus, although lawyers played diverse roles in the Santa Monica LWO campaign, in most cases, they provided a supporting, rather than directing, and a marginal, rather than central, role in the framing of the movement's goals and strategies.

The Santa Monica Living Wage Movement and the Framing of Social Movements

Various sociology of the law scholars have considered how disputes are translated into action. This section considers and sets the Santa Monica living wage movement within various theories regarding the framing of social movement goals and considers the role lawyers played in framing the movement's goals and strategies at various points during the Santa Monica LWO campaign.

William Felstiner, Richard Abel, and Austin Sarat describe the stages in the development of disputes as naming—identifying a particular experience or situation as injurious; blaming—attributing the injury to the fault of an individual or entity; and claiming—expressing the grievance and seeking a remedy.[129] Deborah Stone describes how the telling of "causal stories"[130] can help translate problems into political agendas and effectuate social change. In Stone's framework, various actors, struggle to control interpretations and images of difficulties in order ". . . to move situations intellectually from the realm of fate to the realm of human agency."[131]

In "naming" the problem and claiming the LWO as a solution, SMART has framed the problem of low-wage poverty in ways ultimately connected with the idea of fairness. For example, SMART emphasizes the financial support the city of Santa Monica has given to the businesses in the tourist industry in the past fifteen years, through improvements to tourist attractions such as the Third Street Promenade, Palisades Park, the Pier, and the beach, and antigrowth provisions that have limited competition for the hotels. SMART also portrays the adversaries as the moneyed corporate interests versus the people of Santa Monica and the workers in the tourist zone.[132] SMART has attempted to frame the issue in a normative way and attributed much of the problem to corporate greed on the part of hotels, thus employing Stone's intentional causal story, in which social problems are attributed willful bad actions that cause a foreseeable result.[133]

SMART's actions were also consistent with what Scheingold and others call a "constitutive conception" of rights, in which law influences ways of thinking rather than conduct.[134] In this conception of rights, "Law enters social practices and is, indeed, imbricated in them, by shaping consciousness, by making law's concepts and commands seem, if not invisible, then perfectly natural and benign."[135] In the context of the Santa Monica living wage movement, SMART's early attempts to mobilize the community focused on low-wage workers' right to a fair wage for their work by setting the wage level at the amount it would take to keep these workers out of poverty. The message SMART developed, created an idea of a right to "fairness," in many respects—fairness to workers as well as fairness to the community in not allowing hotels to take advantage of the benefits the community had already bestowed on them in the form of subsidies. In this way, SMART not only drafted and lobbied for passage of an ordinance that would create a right to a living wage, but also created a community consciousness that the proposed LWO's mandates were "natural" and "benign."

We found a notable absence of lawyers acting as lawyers in drawing people to the movement and in framing the movement initially. Although Erika Zucker and Madeline Janis-Aparicio at LAANE influenced the movement's direction in the early stages, they do not claim to have framed the strategy and the message around which SMART mobilized. As noted in "Cause Lawyering and the Santa Monica LWO," above, lawyers by and large assisted with technical matters at the direction of nonlawyer movement leaders and participated in community mobilization events organized by SMART.

The Santa Monica LWO movement also provides examples of counterframing and competing conceptions of rights.[136] Opponents of the ordinance employed two broad devices in framing their argument. One of these was an attack on the City Council for not conducting a more extended discussion of the city-commissioned study of the effects of an LWO and reviewing alternatives with all affected groups. FAIR publicly assailed the City Council for "irresponsible" regulation of community businesses and predicted disaster if the wage were to pass. Living wage opponents have employed a causal story in which the City Council could readily foresee the harmful economic consequences of passing a living wage and was, therefore, acting irresponsibly in doing so. The hotels did not argue that the City Council intended to drive them away or affirmatively hurt them financially; rather, they repeatedly suggested that the City Council was reckless with regard to the health of Coastal Zone businesses.

Living wage opponents also framed the issue as a voters' rights matter. Both in the campaign for Prop KK and in the referendum campaign to repeal the ordinance, the opposition used slogans like "let the people decide." Signature gatherers for the opponents also portrayed the living wage as a way to "force" businesses to unionize and warned that the living wage in the Coastal Zone would be simply a "foot in the door" to a city-wide living wage, which, they claimed, would have disastrous effects on the city economy. One signature gatherer told an elderly resident that the living wage would drive-up costs of food in restaurants and make buying a hamburger prohibitively expensive.[137] Mailers preceding the Measure JJ election displayed pictures of Santa Monica libraries and senior centers, with suggestions that a living wage would mean cuts to these programs. By predicting a catastrophic effect on the Santa Monica economy if the wage were passed, the opposition warned the public not to let the City Council meddle with the capitalist market.[138] In all of these ways, the hotels employed a countermessage of community rights that inspired fear and a sense of propriety among some residents.

Finally, the opposition responded to SMART's overall message of fairness by creating a competing right of businesses to nondiscrimination. One of the opposition's most effective arguments was that SMART's proposed living wage law would be discriminatory in applying only to hotels, and also only to hotels that were not unionized.

One of the most unfortunate aspects of the Santa Monica living wage movement was the opposition's deceitful distortion of SMART's message in the final week before the election on Measure JJ. What is not accounted for in the various theories of framing and cause lawyering is the reality that groups opposing social movements may employ such deceptive tactics to distort the "rights talk" that appeals to the public and aids the movement's proponents in mobilizing the populace. To the extent that cause lawyers and other movement activists can devise ways to anticipate and preempt such deception and message distortion, there may be greater hope that social movements will achieve their goals.

Conclusion

The attempt to pass a living wage in Santa Monica involved a large and diverse coalition including a team of lawyers that was larger than any other living wage campaign has seen. Nonetheless, as we have shown, lawyers played at most a supporting role in this localized movement. By and large, they did not develop a strategy, and lawyers acting in a traditional lawyer's role were not the leaders of the coalition. On the whole, lawyers were also not closely involved with the framing of the issue. In most cases, they took direction from the movement's leaders and provided specific assistance, or they acted simply as volunteers in the various mobilizing efforts of the coalition. The role lawyers did play in the Santa Monica living wage movement may suggest a new category of lawyers in the cause lawyer typology—that of the *pro bono, volunteer cause lawyer.* Additionally, viewing the ways the Santa Monica LWO was framed and the ways SMART's message was co-opted or distorted by the living wage opposition and its lawyers may provide a useful example of how conservative groups co-opt the rights talk of social movements to develop countermessages of rights and competing myths of rights to the detriment of those movements.

Notes

1. Portions of this chapter draw largely from Kathleen Erskine and Ellie Hickerson's unpublished paper about the history of the Santa Monica LWO campaign. "A History of the Living Wage Movement in Santa Monica, California," March 2002 (on file with the UCLA School of Law Office of Public Interest Programs).

2. See http://www.epinet.org/content.cfm/issueguides_livingwage_lwo-table (last visited Oct. 6, 2005); http://www.livingwagecampaign.org/ index.php?id2071 (last visited Oct. 6, 2005).

3. See http://www.epinet.org/content.cfm/issueguides_livingwage_livingwage faq (last visited Oct. 6, 2005).

4. See Stephanie Ann Luce, "The Role of Secondary Associations in Local Policy Implementation: An Assessment of Living Wage Ordinances," (unpublished Ph.D. dissertation, University of Wisconsin, Madison, 1999) (copy on file with author).

5. Leder-Pack, Beth, Interview with Stephanie Reynolds. Tape recording, Los Angeles, CA, Nov. 17, 2000 (hereinafter "Leder-Pack Interview").

6. On July 8, 2004 HERE merged with the Union of Needletrades, Industrial and Textile Employees to form a new union, UNITE HERE. See http://www.unitehere.org/about/ (last visited Feb. 7, 2005).

7. Rothstein, Vivian, Interview with authors. Los Angeles, CA, Jan. 6, 2005 (hereinafter "Rothstein Interview I"); Janis-Aparicio, Madeline, Interview with authors. Los Angeles, CA, Jan. 26, 2005 (hereinafter "Janis-Aparicio Interview").

8. Leder-Pack Interview.

9. Janis-Aparicio Interview.

10. Rothstein Interview I.

11. The proposal was different from the ordinance eventually passed in July of 2001 in several ways: the LWO passed by the City Council provided for a $10.50/hour, and only for those designated businesses with annual gross receipts of $5 million. See Santa Monica, CA. City Council. *Minutes of the Santa Monica City Council, July 24, 2001.* Available at http://pen.ci.santa-monica.ca.us/cityclerk/council/ agendas/2001/m20010724.htm (last visited June 12, 2005) (hereinafter "*City Council Minutes, July 24, 2001*").

12. See Robert Pollin and Mark Brenner, "Economic Analysis of Santa Monica Living Wage Proposal," Research Report No. rr2, Political Economy Research Institute, University of Massachusetts, Amherst, MA, Aug. 2000: 3. Available at http://pen.ci.santa-monica.ca.us/cityclerk/council/pdf/pollin.pdf (last visited June 12, 2005). See also Robert Pollin and Mark Brenner, "Supplemental Analysis of Santa Monica Living Wage Ordinance," Research Report No. 4, Political Economy Research Institute, University of Massachusetts, Amherst, MA, 2002: 5 (on file with authors).

13. Rothstein, Vivian, Interview with Kathleen Erskine. Santa Monica, CA. Nov. 12, 2001 (hereinafter "Rothstein Interview II").

14. Pollin and Brenner, 2000: 3.

15. Santa Monica, California. *City Staff Report to City Council, March 27, 2001* (hereinafter "*City Staff Report, March 27, 2001*"). Available at http://pen.ci.santa-monica.ca.us/cityclerk/council/agendas/2001/s2001032708-C.htm (last visited June 14, 2005). See Richard H. Sander, E. Douglass Williams, and Joseph Doherty, "An Economic Analysis of the Proposed Santa Monica Living Wage," Empirical Research Group, Los Angeles, CA, Sept. 2000.

16. Dr. Pollin concluded that the SMART proposal would benefit the intended population and would be affordable by the businesses covered. In contrast, Professor Sander argued that SMART's plan would be economically devastating: forcing lay-offs, driving down property values, and crippling Santa Monica's shopping district.

17. Gina Piccalo, "Anti-Living Wage Measure is Put on Santa Monica Ballot," *Los Angeles Times*, Aug. 3, 2000.

18. Kelly Candaele and Peter Dreier, "Living Wage: Big Money's Wolf in Sheep's Clothing in Santa Monica," *Los Angeles Times*, May 10, 2000; Jorge Casuso, "Living Hell: Santa Monica's Powerful Business Community Is Trying to Beat Workers on Fair Wage Issue," *Los Angeles Weekly*, March 31–April 6, 2000; Nancy Cleeland, "Santa Monica Living Wage Proposal Stirs Costly Fight," *Los Angeles Times*, Nov. 2, 2000.

19. Kelly Wilkinson, "Living Wage Proponents Rally Support," *Our Times*, April 20, 2000.

20. "Santa Monicans for a Living Wage, A Coalition of Santa Monica Hospitality Businesses, Local Merchants, and Neighborhood Activists," mailer, undated (on file with authors).

21. Rothstein Interview I.

22. Ibid.

23. SMART, "Voter Beware! Dirty Politics and the Sham Living Wage Ballot Initiative," *SMART TALK Newsletter*, March 2000 (on file with authors).

24. Santa Monica, CA. City Council. *Resolution of the City Council of the City Of Santa Monica Accepting the Los Angeles County Registrar Recorder/County Clerk's Official Canvass and Official Statement of Votes Cast for the Consoli-dated Municipal Election Held On November 7, 2000, and Declaring the Results Thereof*, Dec. 12, 2000. Resolution Number 9602 (City Council Series). Available at http://pen.ci.santa-monica.ca.us/cityclerk/election_archive/2000Election.pdf (last visited June 12, 2005).

25. For a detailed description of the SMART Legal Team, see "Cause Lawyering and the Santa Monica LWO," infra.

26. *City Staff Report, March 27, 2001.*

27. SMART Legal Team, Memorandum to City Council Regarding Legal Analysis of the Proposed Santa Monica Living Wage Ordinance, March 27, 2001: 4 (on file with authors).

28. Videorecording of Santa Monica City Council Meeting, KCET, March 21, 2001 (on file with authors).

29. Ibid.

30. *City Council Minutes, July 24, 2001.* These minutes state: "Councilmember Katz stated for the record that he voted in opposition because . . . [the Santa Monica LWO] is discriminatory within the City." See also Ari L. Noonan, "Living Wage Proposal Overcomes Opposition," *Santa Monica Bay Week*, May 29, 2001.

31. *City Council Minutes, July 24, 2001.*

32. SMART Task Force Meeting Minutes, June 19, 2001; "Living Wage Support-ers Rally in Its Defense," *Santa Monica Mirror*, July 18–24, 2001; Oscar Johnson, "Battle Continues over Wage Law," *Los Angeles Times*, Aug. 19, 2001.

33. "Living Wage Measure Qualifies, Will Be Placed Before Voters," *Santa Monica Mirror*, Sept. 12–18, 2001. "FAIR Submits Petition Calling for Repeal of Living Wage Law," *Santa Monica Mirror*, Aug. 22–28, 2001. Although the referendum campaign occurred in the Fall of 2001, the Santa Monica City Council decided to place Prop KK on the November 2002 ballot.

34. California Government Code § ∮ 81000, et seq.

35. Rothstein Interview I.

36. Feingold, Danny, Interview with Kathleen Erskine. Los Angeles, CA, Jan. 25, 2001 (hereinafter "Feingold Interview"); Janis-Aparicio Interview.

37. In March of 2005, the city of Santa Monica passed another living wage ordinance covering employees of businesses contracting with the City. The wage was set at $11.50 per hour, and the ordinance was to take effect on July 1, 2005. Text of the ordinance is available at: http://santa-monica.org/cityclerk/council/agendas/2005/20050308/S2005030807-A-1.htm. (last visited June 14, 2005).

38. Santa Monica Living Wage Commission of Inquiry, "Democracy Distorted: A Report on Electoral Deception and Manipulation by the Opponents of the Santa Monica Living Wage," Executive Summary, June 2003: 8. Available at http://www.democracydistorted.com/docs/DemocracyDistorted_ExecutiveSummary.pdf (last visited June 14, 2005).

39. Our working definition of a social movement draws from social movement theory founders Charles Tilly and Sidney Tarrow who have defined social movements as, respectively:

[A] sustained series of interactions between powerholders and persons successfully claiming to speak on behalf of a constituency lacking formal representation, in the course of which those persons make publicly visible demands for changes in the distribution or exercise of power, and back those demands with public demonstrations of support. Charles Tilly, "Social Movements and National Politics," in C. Gright and S. Harding (eds.), *Statemaking and Social Movements* (Ann Arbor, MI: University of Michigan Press, 1984), p. 306.

and

collective challenges by people with common purposes and solidarity in sustained interactions with elites, opponents, and authorities." Sidney Tarrow, *Power in Movement: Social Movements, Collective Action and Politics* (Cambridge: Cambridge University Press, 1994), pp. 3–4.

40. Rothstein Interview I; Janis-Aparicio Interview; Abel, Richard, Interview with authors. Los Angeles, CA, Dec. 15, 2004 (hereinafter "Abel Interview"); Ury, Steve, Interview with Judy Marblestone. Los Angeles, CA, Dec. 9, 2004 (hereinafter "Ury Interview"); Garcia, Ruben, Telephone conversation with Judy Marblestone. Dec. 29, 2004 (hereinafter "Garcial Interview").

41. Such initiatives, which are outside the scope of this chapter, include community benefit agreements. See, e.g., Scott Cummings, "Mobilization Lawyering:

Community Economic Development in the Figueroa Corridor," Chapter 13, in A. Sarat and S. Scheingold (eds.), *Cause Lawyers and Social Movement.* (Stanford, CA: Stanford University Press, 2006).

42. References to the Santa Monica LWO campaign throughout this chapter encompass the various iterations of the Santa Monica LWO that began in approximately 1998 with SMART's LWO proposal and ended with the November 2002 defeat by voters of the Santa Monica LWO that the City Council had passed.

43. Luce, 1999: 1.

44. On Sept. 14, 1998 the Pasadena City Council adopted a living wage ordinance. Available at http://www.cityofpasadena.net/councilagendas/agendas/sept_14_1998/AGENDARECAP.HTML (last visited May 15, 2005).

45. See http://www.livingwagecampaign.org/index.php?id=1958 (last visited Feb. 7, 2005).

46. The Santa Monica LWO campaign also relied heavily on civic participation and grassroots agitation not only to achieve the passage of the LWO, but also to mobilize the community around broader economic justice concerns. Janis-Aparicio Interview, Rothstein Interview I.

47. The living wage movement is similar to the pay equity movement that "was comprised of relatively decentralized campaigns that arose in dozens of states during the 1970s and 1980s...." Michael McCann and Helena Silverstein, "Rethinking Law's Allurements: A Relational Analysis of Social Movement Lawyers in the United States," in Austin Sarat and Stuart Scheingold (eds.), *Cause Lawyering: Political Commitments and Professional Responsibilities* (New York: Oxford University Press, 1998), pp. 261–92.

48. Sonn, Paul, Interview with Judy Marblestone. New York, NY Dec. 29, 2004 (hereinafter "Sonn Interview"). The Brennan Center is the primary legal resource center for LWO campaigns across the country.

49. HERE has also supported LWOs in Berkeley, Oakland, Los Angeles, and Hayward, CA. Sonn Interview.

50. Janis-Aparicio Interview; Zucker, Erika, Telephone conversation with Judy Marblestone. Los Angeles, CA, Jan. 30, 2005 (hereinafter "Zucker Interview").

51. Garcia Interview.

52. Ibid.

53. Rothstein Interview I. See also "A Brief History of the Santa Monica Living Wage Movement," supra.

54. Cause lawyers are defined as lawyers who "... deploy their legal skills to challenge prevailing distributions of political, social, economic, and/or legal values and resources. Cause lawyers choose clients and cases in order to pursue their own ideological and redistributive projects. And they do so, not as a matter of technical competence, but as a matter of personal engagement." Austin Sarat and Stuart Scheingold, *Cause Lawyering and the State in a Global Era* (New York: Oxford University Press, 2001), p. 13.

55. See also Anna-Marie Marshall, "Social Movement Strategies and the Participatory Potential of Litigation," Chapter 7, in A. Sarat and S. Scheingold (eds.),

Cause Lawyers and Social Movement. (Stanford, CA: Stanford University Press, 2006) ("[T]he organizations were dominated not by lawyers, but by the grassroots activists who were most directly affected by the environmental hazards being challenged."); Thomas Hilbink, "The Profession, the Grassroots, and the Elite: Cause Lawyering for Civil Rights and Freedom in the Direct Action Era," Chapter 2, in A. Sarat and S. Scheingold (eds.), *Cause Lawyers and Social Movement.* (Stanford, CA: Stanford University Press, 2006) ("Lawyers played a secondary, supporting role in the direct action phase of the [civil rights] movement."); but see Sandra Levitsky, "To Lead with Law: Reassessing the Influence of Legal Advocacy Organizations in Social Movements," Chapter 6, in A. Sarat and S. Scheingold (eds.), *Cause Lawyers and Social Movement.* (Stanford, CA: Stanford University Press, 2006). ("The analysis . . . suggests that legal advocacy organizations can and do occupy an influential role in the movement due largely to the sheer size, visibility and influence of these organizations relative to the rest of the GLBT community.")

56. Stuart Scheingold, "Preface to the Second Edition: The New Politics of Rights," *The Politics of Rights: Lawyers, Public Policy, and Political Change* (Ann Arbor, MI: University of Michigan Press, 2004), p. xvii.

57. Scheingold, 2004: xviii–xix. See also McCann and Silverstein, 1998: 261–92.

58. Scheingold, 2004: xxxvii, xix.

59. Scheingold, 2004: xxxviii, referring to McCann and Silverstein, 1998.

60. McCann and Silverstein, 1998: 265–66.

61. Ibid.

62. This category of *pro bono, volunteer cause lawyers* can be distinguished from the lawyers John Kilwein describes as "individual, *pro bono*" cause lawyers. The *pro bono* cause lawyers Kilwein describes typically represent individual plaintiffs, as opposed to representing an organization, or arguably, a movement, as did the *pro bono, volunteer cause lawyers* involved in the Santa Monica LWO. *See* Kilwein, "Still Trying: Cause Lawyering for the Poor and Disadvantaged in Pittsburgh, Pennsylvania," in Austin Sarat and Stuart Scheingold (eds.), *Cause Lawyering: Political Commitments and Professional Responsibilities* (New York: Oxford University Press, 1998), 1998: 187 ("For them, their job was to represent an individual client with a legal problem, guiding her or him through the legal system."). Kilwein does also discuss cause lawyers who "represent [local cause organizations] and their members in court," but it appears that he is referring to attorneys who do this work as part of their (paying) practice, more akin to *independent cause lawyers* as opposed to attorneys who volunteer during their own free time. John Kilwein, p. 196.

63. See Hilbink, Chapter 2, in A. Sarat and S. Scheingold (eds.), *Cause Lawyers and Social Movement.* (Stanford, CA: Stanford University Press, 2006). The Lawyer's Constitutional Defense Committee's "volunteer civil-rights lawyers" and the National Lawyers Guild volunteer lawyers who went to the south to do civil rights work also fit the *pro bono, volunteer cause lawyers* category.

64. Cummings, Scott L., *UCLA Law Review*, 1, no. 52, 2004: 116–19. See also Anna-Marie Marshall, Chapter 7, in A. Sarat and S. Scheingold (eds.), *Cause Lawyers and Social Movement.* (Stanford, CA: Stanford University Press, 2006).

65. Cummings, 2004: 130.

66. This section focuses on the role of lawyers in shaping strategy, drafting an ordinance, and waging campaigns to get the ordinance passed and defend against multiple anticipated challenges. By focusing on lawyers, our intent is not to overstate their importance among the various actors or to suggest their role as lawyers was neatly delineated; in fact, several attorneys who were very active in the Santa Monica LWO campaign rarely viewed themselves as "lawyers" in their participation. Many of them were drawn to the cause as interested citizens and volunteers and only acted as lawyers when specifically asked to do something requiring their particular legal knowledge and skills. For example, attorneys lent their professional expertise to help alleviate legislators' concerns about the legality of a Santa Monica LWO. And as activists they supported the movement's goals through nonlegal mechanisms such as direct actions, outreach, public education, and, in some cases, exercising their rights as residents.

67. Ury Interview; Garcia Interview; Marx Interview; Janis-Aparicio Interview.

68. Hilbink describes this type of cause lawyering as "grassroots lawyering," in which "lawyers *qua* lawyers do not play a leadership role in movement work... Lawyers work with grassroots social movements, often as supporting players. The movement is typically the lawyer's client..." Thomas M. Hilbink, "You Know the Type...: Categories of Cause Lawyering," *Law and Social Inquiry, Journal of the American Bar Foundation*, 29(3), Summer 2004: 681.

69. Sonn Interview.

70. Ibid.

71. Ibid.

72. Ibid.

73. Ibid.

74. Ibid.

75. Ibid.

76. Ibid.

77. Ibid.

78. Janis-Aparicio Interview.

79. Rothstein Interview I.

80. Janis-Aparicio Interview.

81. Feingold Interview.

82. Garcia Interview; Ury Interview; Abel Interview.

83. Garcia Interview; Zucker Interview; Ury Interview; Abel Interview.

84. Abel Interview, David Pettit, E-mail to Judy Marblestone. May 31, 2005 (hereinafter "Pettit E-mail").

85. Zucker Interview.

86. Ibid.

87. Zucker Interview; Ury Interview.

88. Ibid.

89. See, e.g., SMART Legal Team Memorandum to Members of the Santa Monica City Council Regarding Equal Protection Analysis of the Proposed Living Wage

Ordinance's Application to Employers in the Coastal Zone, Sept. 1, 2000 (on file with authors), explaining why an equal protection argument against SMART's proposed Coastal Zone would fail.

90. Garcia Interview.

91. Ibid.

92. Marx, Peter J, Telephone conversation with Judy Marblestone. Los Angeles, CA, June 13, 2005 (hereinafter "Marx Interview").

93. Ibid.

94. Marx Interview; Peter J. Marx, Memoranda to SMART Legal Team, May 17, 1999 and Aug. 5, 1999 (on file with authors).

95. Marx Interview.

96. Ury Interview.

97. Ibid.

98. Ibid.

99. Ury, Steve, E-mail to Judy Marblestone. Feb. 1, 2005.

100. See "A Brief History of the Santa Monica Living Wage Movement," infra.

101. Feingold Interview.

102. Abel Interview.

103. Richard Abel, Letter to Marsha Moutrie, Santa Monica City Attorney. May 1, 2001 (on file with authors).

104. Abel, Richard, E-mail to Judy Marblestone. Feb. 3, 2005.

105. Abel Interview.

106. Pettit E-mail.

107. Ibid.

108. Janis-Aparicio Interview.

109. Ibid.

110. Rothstein Interview I; Ury Interview.

111. Rothstein Interview I.

112. Rothstein Interview I; Janis-Aparicio Interview.

113. Zucker Interview.

114. Ibid.

115. Ibid.

116. Ibid.

117. Zucker, Erika, E-mail to Judy Marblestone. Feb. 1, 2005 (hereinafter "Zucker E-mail").

118. Ibid.

119. For example, Sonn has worked with ACORN and other living wage coalitions around the country by drafting numerous and varied LWOs, providing legal research and writing, writing amicus briefs, and assisting with litigation preparation when LWOs are challenged in court. Sonn, Paul, E-mail to Judy Marblestone. Feb. 5, 2005.

120. Sonn Interview.

121. Ibid. It is important to note that positional conflicts of interest, discussed in section "A new category of cause lawyers: pro bono, volunteer cause lawyers," supra, did not prevent a large law firm, Wilmer, Cutler & Pickering, from agreeing

to provide legal support in the form of an amicus brief. The absence of a positional conflict may have been because the Santa Monica LWO did not affect one employer, but rather it was an ordinance of general application. Sonn, Paul, E-mail to Judy Marblestone. June 10, 2005.

122. Ibid.

123. Ibid.

124. Zucker E-mail.

125. Erwin Chemerinsky, Letter to the Santa Monica City Council, Mayor, and City Attorney, March 27, 2001 (on file with authors).

126. Rothstein Interview I.

127. See, respectively, Tzvia Feiertag, "Implementation, Compliance and Enforcement of Living Wage Ordinances: Focusing on Los Angeles' Role as a Model and Challenges Facing Santa Monica in Its Attempt to Break New Ground,"; Andrew Elmore, "Counting a Movement: Why Do Groups Participate in Campaigns for a Living Wage?" Dec. 17, 2001; and Judy Marblestone, "Possible Strategies for Implementing A New Santa Monica Living Wage Ordinance After Measure JJ's Defeat," April 2, 2003 (on file with authors).

128. This chapter draws largely from Kathleen Erskine and Ellie Hickerson's paper about the history of the Santa Monica LWO campaign.

129. William S. F. Felstiner, Richard L. Abel, and Austin Sarat, "Transformation of Disputes: Naming, Blaming, Claiming . . . ," *Law and Society Review* 15, 1980–81: 632.

130. Deborah Stone, "Causal Stories and the Formation of Policy Agendas," *Political Science Quarterly*, 104, 1989: 281.

131. Ibid.: 283.

132. Video Recording of Santa Monica City Council Meeting, Santa Monica City Hall, May 22, 2001. Produced by KCET Broadcasting Service. (On file with authors.)

133. Stone, 1989: 285.

134. Scheingold, 2004: xxii.

135. Scheingold, 2004: xxii, citing Austin Sarat and Thomas R. Kearns, "Beyond the Great Divide: Forms of Legal Scholarship in Everyday Life," in Austin Sarat and Thomas R. Kearns (eds.), *Law in Everyday Life* (Ann Arbor, MI: University of Michigan Press, 1993), pp. 21–62.

136. Scheingold, 2005: xxxii–xxxiii.

137. Kathleen Erskine, Field notes of conversation with anonymous Santa Monica resident, Aug. 18, 2001.

138. This is an example of what Stone called an inadvertent causal story. Stone, 1989: 288.

A Movement in the Wake of a New Law

The United Farm Workers and the California Agricultural Labor Relations Act

JENNIFER GORDON

The passage of a law establishing new rights is a moment of great importance in a social movement's history. It is a triumph, a measure of the movement's power. It is also a pivotal time, when the movement must negotiate a shift in its relationship to the state as it moves from an outside force to at least something of an inside player. Ironically, the effect of new legislation on the movement that sought and won it is a matter that has received relatively little attention in the law and social movements literature, which has focused to a much greater extent on litigation (and, when it has turned to legislation, has tended to explore the impact of new rights on individuals rather than on collective action).

Most major legislative reforms that grant new rights are at least in part the product of social movements: the civil rights and voting rights acts, the Americans with Disabilities Act, and various pieces of environmental legislation, to name only a few passed between the 1960s and the 1990s. But the movements that produced those reforms are so varied—as are the reforms themselves—that any broad statement about their impact on collective action seems unlikely to hold water. Instead, I will concentrate my inquiry in one area, also under-examined in the law and social movements literature (although the subject of much debate outside it): labor law in the United States. By labor law I mean not only the National Labor Relations Act (NLRA), which has governed union organizing for the majority of workers in this country since the Wagner Act was passed in 1935, but also other legislation setting the rules for workplace organizing among employees excluded from NLRA coverage, including state and federal public employee labor relations law, and agricultural labor relations law that grew out of labor movements in states like California and Hawaii.

Labor law and its impact on the labor movement have received a wealth of attention from historians and legal scholars outside the law and social movements field (e.g., Forbath 1991; Pope 1997, 2002). Most who focus on the period immediately following the passage of the NLRA concur that the Act's initial effect on the movement was overwhelmingly positive, citing among other evidence the explosion of union membership from four million workers in the year after the Wagner Act's passage to fourteen million a decade later (Cox 1960; Ballam 1995). Not all agree (Montgomery 1979; Lynd 1981). But even many of the NLRA's sharpest critics—those who, like James Pope (1997, 2002), argue that the Act sowed the seeds of the labor movement's undoing when its drafters chose to base it on the Commerce Clause of the Constitution rather than on a Thirteenth Amendment right to be free of wage slavery; or who, like Karl Klare (1978), trace the path of what Klare has referred to as the law's "deradicalization" through a series of Supreme Court decisions constricting the acceptable range of worker protest in the name of preserving "industrial peace"—recognize that the NLRA initially provided an extraordinary source of support to worker organizing. Powerful a statement as it was, however, the Act could do nothing alone. The promises of the NLRA could only be realized on the ground through the work of a vital labor movement.

This remarkable melding of movement and law did not last. The propitious moment that began with the Wagner Act's passage and its upholding by the Supreme Court in 1937 faded when the Taft–Hartley amendments decisively curtailed the range of economic weapons legally available to workers and unions, and became an ever more distant memory in the following decades as courts and the National Labor Relations Board (NLRB) increasingly interpreted the Act against labor's interests (Klare 1978; Stone 1981). Union organizing levels for workers governed by the NLRA have famously plummeted from a high of nearly 35 percent in 1954 (Goldfield 1987) to the current 8 percent. Although structural factors bear the brunt of the blame for this decline, the law that had once facilitated labor organizing has also come to play a significant role in restraining it (Friedman et al. 1994).

The arc of the NLRA's relationship to the social movement that begat it— a sharp upward surge in movement in the wake of the new law, followed by a long, slow process of co-optation, restriction, and decline—contrasts with much law and social movement scholarship on what a movement should expect in the wake of the establishment of new rights. Such scholars have emphasized that the "implementation phase" immediately following the creation of new rights is particularly challenging for movements. Simultaneously, they have suggested that the legacy of new rights grows richer over time, as individual rights-bearers' identities and capacities change in extended interaction with the law. This chapter represents one part of an effort to bring law about labor rights into the fold of law and social movement scholarship, to see on closer comparison where and why those paths may intersect and where and why they diverge.

To this end, in this chapter I look closely at a less-studied time and place in the labor movement, exploring one union, the labor law that it won, and the effect of that law on its capacity to organize. In 1975, the United Farm Workers (UFW) capped more than a dozen years of farm worker organizing in the absence of a law governing labor relations (agricultural workers are excluded from the NLRA's coverage) by framing and successfully winning passage of the California Agricultural Labor Relations Act (ALRA) in 1975. This is a particularly apt case study for the purposes of this book, as the UFW was as much or more a social movement as it was a union. I focus on the evolution of the interaction between the UFW's organizing strategy and the law, as it began in a period in which farm labor organizing occurred outside an administrative framework, moved toward the passage of the ALRA, flourished in its immediate aftermath, and imploded when the union retreated from organizing several years later.

In many ways the UFW's story offers hope about the potential of good legislation. For several years, the UFW was more successful in organizing under the ALRA than at any other time in its history. The most important factor in the union's struggles a few years after the law's passage was a shift in its internal culture, not co-optation by the state. I offer explanations for why the law proved so helpful to the union during this period, both drawing on and contesting law and social movement scholarship that is more pessimistic about this implementation phase. At the same time, organizing under the ALRA brought the UFW new challenges, forcing it to grapple with the changes wrought by the state's comprehensive regulation of the unionization process. I conclude that the implementation phase is a richer one than we commonly recognize, with possibilities that depend greatly on the political environment, the type of law in question, and on the particular movement's history, experience with law as a part of its organizing strategy, and level of cohesion and engagement at the time of the law's passage. These possibilities coexist with the tensions that inevitably plague efforts to make new rights real.

The United Farm Workers Legal Strategy, 1962–80

The United Farm Workers combined a labor organization for the country's most disenfranchised workers with a mass movement attracting broad support across the continent and beyond.[1] When the UFW was founded in 1962 by Cesar Chavez and fellow Mexican–American community activists in Delano, California, wages on California's large ranches were pitifully low. Working conditions were inhumane. Agricultural workers were unprotected by national wage and labor laws such as the Fair Labor Standards Act and the NLRA. Farm workers were not completely without power, as decades of sporadically successful strikes had shown. But until the UFW, no farm worker organizing effort had been able to create an *organization* of farm workers with the creativity, persistence, and stability to fight for ongoing union representation and win, much less to negotiate multifaceted contracts and administer them over several seasons (Taylor 1975; Majka and Majka 1982; Ferriss and Sandoval 1997; Ganz 2000).

The UFW developed its unique organizing strategy in response to the particular circumstances of farm labor. In the face of vast ranches and the never-ending influx of new workers too mobile and too desperate to be effectively organized to stay out of work for long, traditional union organizing measures such as strikes and pickets were very hard to sustain. Chavez recognized that the union's capacity to build a stable worker organization would be critical to its success. He did this by creating not just a union, but a social movement, one that integrated Mexican Catholicism with Gandhian tactics such as the fast, strategies from the civil rights movement, and much-needed community services (Ganz 2000). The collective action of farm workers was, of course, central to the UFW's strategy. In some industries, particularly on vegetable ranches, where the workers tended to be more militant young single men rather than the families that migrated to pick grapes, the union carried out successful campaigns wholly based on worker organizing and strikes. Even where workers were unable to sustain direct pressure for long, the UFW continued to wrest all of the leverage it could from the perishable nature of the crops that its members harvested by cutting off the labor supply at key moments, beginning with its first strike in 1965.

Given the difficulty of winning contracts for mobile, replaceable farm workers through strikes, the UFW also sought to create a social climate in which the existing treatment of farm workers was seen as unjust, and to use that climate to generate moral, economic, and political pressure on growers to recognize the UFW as the legitimate representative of farm workers. To supplement and at times replace field organizing, the union called on middle-class consumers around the country to boycott nonunion fruits and vegetables, an effective year-round economic weapon that worked in complementary ways with the union's on-the-ground organizing, particularly between 1965 and 1970 (the first grape boycott) and at various times during the 1970s and 1980s (boycotts of other produce and wine as well as grapes). This combination of union and social movement strategies proved successful for the UFW in its early days. By early 1973, the UFW could boast an unprecedented 50,000 workers under contract with 150 California growers (Majka and Majka 1982; Ferriss and Sandoval 1997).

The creative use of law played an important role in the union's success. At its peak, the UFW legal department had seventeen lawyers and forty-four paralegals, high numbers indeed in the context of a leanly staffed and financially struggling movement. Although the general outline of the UFW's story is well known, the role of lawyers in that story has not received comprehensive treatment in published sources. Because of this, much of this chapter is drawn from interviews with former UFW attorneys and organizers as well as other original research.[2]

In the union's early years, it parceled out its legal work to volunteer lawyers and outside counsel, including lawyers at the newly founded California Rural Legal Assistance corporation (CRLA), one of the first federally funded legal service organizations in the country. It also experimented with hiring a staff lawyer whose principal responsibility was to provide members with services. But by 1967, it had become clear that the farm workers' union needed wholesale control of its own legal strategy. Chavez chose Jerry Cohen, a recent graduate of Boalt Hall, as the union's first general counsel. Over the next thirteen years, Cohen and his staff would break new frontiers in their exploration of how law could protect, open opportunities for, and advance the union's external organizing goals.

Cohen's role within the UFW was a broad one. After seeing "The Godfather," union staff jokingly came to refer to him as Chavez's "consigliere." Cohen strategized with Chavez not just about the legal aspects of the union's work but also about its overall direction. He and the attorneys he hired led the fight against restrictive farm labor legislation in several states. They negotiated contracts with growers. But most of all, in the UFW's early years, Cohen and his staff litigated. They went to court to defend the union, its volunteers,[3] and its members. They went to court to establish legal protections for farm worker organizing. And they went to court to spread the word about the UFW and to bring public pressure to bear on opponents in various ways. In each situation, the question was never only "what are our rights here?," but "how can we best turn this legal situation to the union's organizing advantage?"

Often, a lawsuit would serve several aims at once. As UFW lawyers defended the union in court, whether in cases that growers filed to impede organizing efforts or in those that were the result of the UFW's decisions to challenge the law by disobeying injunctions on a massive scale, they sought to wrest from the Constitution a web of rights—to use bullhorns, to picket, to reach workers in the fields—that could provide a basic framework for farm worker organizing in the absence of NLRA coverage. In these cases, victory in court was often important. But the union had other goals as well. During some court battles, the UFW sought to influence both public opinion and the legal outcome by using the courthouse as a stage on which to publicize the farm workers' plight. At several critical moments, the union mobilized members to sit vigils, sing, and pray in courthouse corridors as the judge decided a case involving the UFW. Another approach was to bring farm workers in to tell their stories in court or to use affidavits to bring farm workers' experiences in the fields and on the picket line into the courtroom. Unlike many of the big political trials of the 1960s and 1970s, the UFW was not trying to disrupt the actual court proceedings or to reveal the legal system as a fraud. The idea was to change the immediate cultural, political, and moral environment in which legal decisions were made. (Kinoy (1983) and Bellow (1996) offer examples of this approach in other contexts; see also Hilbink's description of the "grassroots" approach of Guild lawyers in the civil rights movement, this volume.)

Some of the UFW's most unfettered and creative legal work came when it practiced what Cohen calls "legal karate and the law of the jungle," using the law as an offensive weapon to advance the UFW's organizing goals and build power for the union. The union threatened and filed lawsuits designed to put collateral pressure on all fronts of its fight: to gain information about particular growers and the industry through discovery, to convince consumers and stores to respect the boycott, to increase the growers' legal bills and weaken their resolve, to pressure government officials to change their policies and practices, and to loosen the grip of the rival Teamsters Union. The fact that the union had its own legal staff was a critical factor in the success of these strategies. Although the UFW's opponents' legal expenses rose with each additional hour of court time, the union's costs were both fixed and low. A UFW staff attorney's annual salary cost roughly the same as two weeks of lawyer time at the rates that the Teamsters and sophisticated growers had to pay private law firms for representation.

In the context of the grape boycott, for example, highly publicized cases where union members were deprived of basic rights became as important for their effect on the sympathies of potential boycotters as for the outcome of the cases themselves (Taylor 1975). The union would use lawsuits seeking the names of pesticides used by the growers, or demanding toilets in the fields, to illustrate to consumers the dangers that they faced in choosing to eat grapes contaminated with unknown poisons and fecal matter. Simultaneously, such cases also pressured regulators to enforce laws on the books. Most importantly, they subjected growers to a triple whammy: the cost of defending the suit, the price of responding to heightened scrutiny from state regulators, and an economic squeeze from disgusted consumers. The combination pushed growers a step closer to seeing a settlement with the UFW on the union issue as a favorable alternative to continued resistance. Unlike the defensive cases or the constitutional protections that Cohen sought, the point in these particular suits was not to win the legal claim through the courts. Although these lawsuits originated in genuine grievances, the union had as least as much interest in the opportunities the litigation offered along the way as in its legal outcome.

All of the ways that the UFW used law made important contributions to the level of organization it had reached by 1973, the year that would prove to be the worst in the union's decade-long history. Although growers and their political allies were the UFW's chief opponents, they were not its only ones. At times, the UFW's most insidious adversary was another union, the International Brotherhood of Teamsters. Teamsters regularly turned out by the busload to intimidate UFW picketers, hurling racial epithets, bottles, and stones, and beating farm workers and their supporters. In 1973, the Teamsters raided UFW-organized ranches, working with growers to substitute "sweetheart" agreements that shortchanged farm workers and left the UFW reeling from the loss of 90 percent of its contracts. The union was left representing no more than 6,500 workers (Majka and Majka 1982; Ferriss and Sandoval 1997).

Fast running out of money and desperate to rebuild, the UFW debated whether to seek passage of a state law that would prevent such raids and create explicit rules for the organizing of agricultural workers. The UFW's staff and volunteers had wavered over the years about whether the union stood to lose or win in seeking to create a law that would govern its conduct. Chavez and others had observed how legislation had seemed to take the wind out of the sails of the civil rights movement in the South (Levy 1973). Certainly wholesale adoption of the NLRA seemed like the wrong solution, given the increasingly evident way that law was coming to shackle the labor unions that it governed (Taylor 1971). And the likelihood of wresting a good law from the California legislature seemed dim for many years. But the AFL-CIO was offering a strike fund of well over $1.5 million to the union on the condition that it make serious efforts to win an agricultural labor relations law (Cohen interview; Majka and Majka 1982). In 1974, victory in such an effort began to seem conceivable when Jerry Brown replaced Ronald Reagan as governor of California. The union decided that its best hope for rebirth was to create an administrative framework that would guarantee the UFW access to farm workers in the fields, bar sweetheart deals between Teamsters and growers, and set legal rules for elections and bargaining that would allow the UFW to recover the contracts it had lost. (On the UFW's efforts to win the ALRA, see Wells and Villarejo 2004.)

Cohen worked with the union's organizers and lawyers to develop a set of proposals that reflected what they had learned over the UFW's last hard-fought decade about the sort of protections that would facilitate farm labor organizing. Despite his campaign promises, the initial bill that Governor Brown introduced was far from the union's wish list, indeed so far that the UFW responded with protests around the state. Eventually, the UFW was successful in using a combination of pressure, back-room negotiations, and a divide-and-conquer approach that made allies (if somewhat ambivalent ones) out of some growers, the Teamsters, and local officials, to craft and pass a bill that hewed quite closely to their dreams.

The ALRA as passed offered the UFW a powerful new framework for organizing. It did not include all of the UFW's proposals. The law allowed the Teamsters to hold onto its contracts until elections were held, and it banned a form of secondary boycott pressure.[4] Nonetheless, the UFW's political clout and Cohen's negotiating acumen were clearly reflected in the bill signed by Brown, who would later claim it as "[t]he greatest accomplishment of my administration" (Wells and Villarejo 2004). The law began with an unabashed endorsement of the right of farm workers to organize, with a preamble that explicitly stated the Act's goal as "guaranteeing justice for all agricultural employees."[5] The law itself contained provisions that conventional unions could only dream of. It guaranteed farm worker unions a seven-day turnaround for secret ballot elections (compared to the month that is standard in the NLRA context), an essential time frame for such a highly mobile workforce. It gave workers much stronger remedies for employer violations than the NLRA, created more liberal rules for when strikers could vote in elections, and mandated ranch-wide or "industrial" groupings of workers for election purposes, a configuration that the UFW had favored.[6]

On top of these legislative provisions, the UFW was able to make the law more advantageous by using its political clout to guide the choice of members for the first Agricultural Labor Relations Board (ALRB), resulting in a pro-UFW supermajority of four to one. As it drafted regulations for the ALRA's implementation, that board made key additions to the law, including giving the union the right to a list of the names and addresses of the workers at each ranch they were organizing, putting symbols on the ballots so that farm workers who could not read and write would be able to put their mark next to the UFW's easily recognizable black eagle, and creating access rules that guaranteed at least two organizers the right to speak freely with workers in the fields at defined times during the workday.[7] The UFW had wanted these provisions from the beginning but felt it would be unable to get the law passed with them included. When the ink dried on the final rules, California could boast only the second pro-organizing farm labor law in the country (the first being the Hawaii Employment Relations Act, passed in 1945 before Hawaii was part of the United States).

The period that followed was intense and heady for the UFW. The UFW forged the ALRA, and an initially disorganized and foot-dragging ALRB, into powerful tools in its efforts to rebuild. The ALRB opened its doors on September 2, 1975. More than a hundred UFW members were waiting that morning to file election petitions from twenty-one different ranches, having spent the previous night in a vigil outside the ALRB office in Salinas.[8] And they were far from alone. The first five months after the ALRA's passage were a frenzy of activity for the UFW, for the Teamsters, and for California growers. By the UFW's contemporaneous tally, a staggering 45,915 farm workers voted in 382 elections during that time: an average of seventy-six elections per month.[9]

These early, exhausting, euphoric months ground to an unexpected halt when the ALRB closed its doors on February 6, 1976. Confronted with a tidal wave of elections, it had run through its annual budget in less than half a year. For the next eight months the ALRB remained closed, as growers (stunned by the over 90 percent level of union victory in the early elections) and Teamsters (who lost more often to the UFW than they had anticipated) pressured legislators to pass amendments to the legislation before it granted the agency further funding. Lawmakers refused to amend the ALRA, but neither could they muster the two-thirds majority required to pass an emergency appropriation. In the meantime, several pro-UFW members of the ALRB resigned (Majka and Majka 1982). During this time, the UFW mounted a large-scale effort to win Proposition 14, which would have guaranteed the ALRB a permanent funding and required voters statewide to ratify any proposed changes to the ALRA, thus securing the board a future independent of the state budget process. The UFW spent more than a million dollars on the initiative, but growers poured $2 million into a campaign to defeat it, and it lost in the Fall of 1976 by a considerable margin. In the process, however, the UFW succeeded in pressuring legislators to authorize the budget that the ALRA needed to resume functioning.

When the ALRB reopened on December 1, 1976, the volume of elections had fallen considerably, although it was still impressive. Over 150 elections took place in each of the following two years, with over 9,000 farm workers voting per year. The UFW won 55 percent of those elections; the Teamsters won 32 percent (Wells and Villarejo 2004). By January 1978, the UFW had brought 25,000 new workers under contract through ALRA procedures and represented perhaps three times that many on ranches where growers were resisting negotiating contracts (Majka and Majka 1984). The benefits for farm workers were immediate: wages rose by 30–50 percent, and many received health and pension benefits for the first time in their lives (Martin 2004). At its height in the early 1980s the UFW again had over 50,000 members under contract and as many as 50,000 more "affiliated" farm workers (King 1981; Majka and Majka 1982). The union's reputation stretched across the country and indeed the globe.

The ALRA offered the UFW a remarkable opportunity, and the UFW seized it and held on. And yet within a decade of the ALRA's passage, the UFW was all but dormant, as was the ALRB (Majka and Majka 1992, Wells and Villarejo 2004). Many factors contributed to this decline. On all fronts during the 1980s, organizing became more difficult. The political landscape changed and growers found much more support in Sacramento than they had previously enjoyed (Wells and Villarejo 2004). An influx of undocumented workers increased competition and made raising wages harder (Martin 2003). But the UFW had faced political opposition and intense labor competition before, and it triumphed. Internal changes in the UFW seem to have played the critical role in its inability to respond effectively to this round of challenges (Majka and Majka 1992; Wells and Villarejo 2004).

Beginning in the mid-1970s, Chavez began to show signs of concern that his control over the union was threatened. Others have explored this turbulent period in the UFW's history in greater depth (see, e.g., Majka and Majka 1992; Bardacke 1993; Wells and Villarejo 2004). For the purposes of this chapter, a few factors seem particularly relevant. In 1977, the Teamsters withdrew from farm worker organizing as part of the settlement of a long-running antitrust lawsuit brought by the UFW. The Teamsters' presence had been a thorn in the union's side but also a goad to continual organizing (Wells and Villarejo 2004). With the threat of competition in the fields gone, Chavez turned inward. He required union staff to participate in a psychological game run by the cult-like group Synanon to hash out internal problems, led the union into a retreat from the critical work of field organizing, and funneled increasing amounts of the UFW's money from the fields into direct mail and politics.

Among other concerns, Chavez focused on what he feared were two independent power bases developing within the union: the legal department (located in Salinas rather than at union headquarters in La Paz), which had become increasingly central to the UFW's organizing strategy after the passage of the ALRA; and Salinas-based vegetable workers organized through ALRA procedures by Ganz and Govea. Those workers' independence and strength rendered them more confident of their ability to strike for better pay and conditions and therefore less reliant on the social movement strategies that Chavez had to offer than the union's traditional mainstay, grape workers (Cohen interview; Ganz interview; Majka and Majka 1992; Wells and Villarejo 2004).

Matters came to a head when Cohen Ganz and Jessica and lead organizers Marshall Govea supported a call by organizers and paralegals that they be paid a regular salary, a move away from the "volunteer stipend" system that applied to most field and service staff. The lawyers also asked for an increase in their stipend. Disagreeing on both fronts, Chavez insisted that the UFW needed to go in the opposite direction, returning to its all-volunteer roots. He focused on the lawyers' request. In mid-1978, he proposed to the Executive Board that it begin this process by defunding the UFW's lawyers. The board split along generational lines, with younger members opposed to Chavez's proposal (such as Ganz, Govea, and Eliseo Medina) losing to a slim majority of older UFW leaders. Stripped of their income, most of the lawyers left in 1978 and 1979. During the same period, Chavez put down attempts by workers to run their own candidates for the union's executive board, and he froze out or fired almost all of his most experienced staff, including Ganz, Govea, Medina, and many other key organizers. Cohen stayed in a limited capacity until late 1980, when he too departed.[10] The impact of these changes on the UFW's organizing capacity was immediate. Before any of the transformation of immigration patterns or the political landscape that would mark the 1980s, the ALRB witnessed a steep drop in elections and union election victories starting in fiscal year 1978–79 (Wells and Villarejo 2004).

Chavez succeeded in retaining control of the UFW, but at a price. Over the course of the following decade, the union organized few new workers, and many of its contracts expired unattended. At the time of Chavez's death in 1993, the union was barely clinging to 10,000 members (Wells and Villarejo 2004). In the mid-1990s and early 2000s, the UFW began to regain some vigor under the leadership of Arturo Rodriguez, Chavez's son-in-law. The union received renewed attention and support from the AFL-CIO for its campaign to organize strawberry workers after John Sweeney's election in 1995, although that effort did not prove successful on a large scale (Martin 2004). Despite some noteworthy legislative victories, the venerable and embattled UFW has not yet managed to regain the public prominence or the level of worker representation it enjoyed in its heyday.

The Implementation Phase—A Closer Look

Law and social movement scholarship has focused much more on litigation than on legislation in relation to movements (Olson 1984; Milner 1986; Davis 1993; McCann 1994). This book continues that tradition, with only three chapters out of thirteen exploring legislative work in any detail (Erskine and Marblestone; Coutin; this chapter). The literature certainly contains explorations of legislative victories—a strong example is Engel and Munger's (Engel and Munger 2003) work on the Americans with Disabilities Act—but the focus of those studies tends to be on the impact of those rights on individuals rather than on a movement.

Using examples drawn from the litigation context, this body of scholarship has constructed an appreciative understanding of the complex "dialectic of rights," to use Elizabeth Schneider's phrase, in which law simultaneously contributes to and is in tension with movement efforts (Schneider 1986). The implementation phase that follows a major litigation victory—the period when the precise contours of the new right that the movement has won are delineated and the mechanisms for its enforcement are established and put into play—has emerged as a time where the challenges of integrating legal and organizing strategies have appeared particularly steep and the rewards for movements elusive. It seems worth wondering how this insight applies following a legislative, rather than court, victory.

The first person to offer a comprehensive account of the perils of the implementation phase from a movement perspective was Joel Handler (1978), who observes in his pivotal book *Social Movements and the Legal System* that "all too often the war is really lost in the stage after the rules are changed, where the group can no longer sustain its influence when enforcement problems take over." Handler studies law reform efforts associated with the environmental, consumer protection, civil rights, and welfare movements. Although his focus, too, is largely on litigation, the breadth of reform won in court by the case studies he highlights is comparable to legislative change in many ways. He concludes that the post–victory period is a critically vulnerable time for movements. Among other dangers, the rulemaking process that follows the announcement of the new right may fall captive to the influence of industry representatives. Personnel at the relevant agencies may resist the changes required to effectuate the new policy. And the site at which change is debated shifts from the public forum of the courtroom or legislature to the closed rooms of regulatory agencies, requiring "expert" intervention and making it harder for movement participants to influence outcomes. The problems are particularly acute when the new rights are not self-enforcing (because they require action by government officials, who may resist or stonewall), and when they impose costs on a relatively concentrated group, such as a set of businesses, but offer benefits that are more widely diffused (because it is easier for the concentrated group to mobilize in opposition than the diffuse one).

Others who have studied movements' staying power and success after legal reforms concur. In discussing the effort to bring about wage equity through litigation, for example, Michael McCann notes that ". . . both the overall remedial frame of comparable worth and specific legal leveraging tactics have proved less transformative at the implementation stage than at earlier phases of struggle."

The problems, he argues, are multifaceted. "...[E]mployers gain clear political advantages as disputes shift from the grand terms of general legal rights to more disaggregated, narrow, complex issues of wage system reconstruction." Furthermore, "[a]s implementation struggles shift to technical matters of job evaluation...they become less visible, dramatic, and public. And the more 'private' the disputes, the more that corporate employers and managers tend to have the advantage over workers" (McCann 1994).

Scholars have further emphasized the shift in legal skills that the implementation phase demands, a move from the blunt instrument of movement pressure to the technician's mastery of detail and the career-player's staying power. It is at this point, McCann has noted, that "...key political issues are often masked and 'depoliticized' by their redefinition as technical issues" (McCann 1994). This lawyerizes the implementation phase, favoring attorneys with a high level of specialization and the "insider" status that develops through repeated contacts with an agency. On this playing field, employers and other powerful opponents of new laws have advantages that grow from their greater access to technical knowledge, resources, and political clout (Handler 1978; McCann 1994; Foster 2002).

How do these insights translate to the situation where change is made legislatively, rather than through the courts? Some might argue that unlike a judicial holding, the fact that a new law is the product of a political consensus should curtail backlash in the implementation phase. Public choice theorists and other students of administrative agencies—as well as of the fates of specific pieces of legislation, such as in the environmental context—would surely beg to differ, citing a record of agency capture and bureaucratic foot-dragging in the wake of newly legislated rights (Stewart 1975). Although an in-depth exploration of this question is beyond the scope of this paper, I am inclined to believe that legislative proclamations of rights are at least as vulnerable to subversion as their judge-made cousins, given their highly public and—in comparison with litigation victories—often potentially more far-reaching character.

In light of this, it will come as no surprise that the ALRA posed challenges to the UFW's capacity to organize. These obstacles are important to note, both because they are common in the aftermath of new laws and because the fact that the UFW was briefly able to surmount them gives us occasion to imagine what might have happened differently had not the union in such short order withdrawn from the fields.

The first challenge for the UFW was to turn a paper law into a real one, a task that required the collaboration of a new agency, the ALRB. The ALRB looked to be an ideal partner for the UFW. After all, four of five initial board appointments had reason to favor farm worker interests over growers, and Brown's pro-UFW views were well known to the first general counsel he appointed, Walter Kintz. Matters on the ground, however, proved considerably less simple. The new agency was at once utterly disorganized and instantly bureaucratic. As former board attorney Ellen Greenstone recalls, "the first thing they taught us at orientation was how to fill out an expense report." Many of the ALRB staff were brought in from the NLRB, and were steeped in its rules and accustomed to its glacial pace. Few spoke Spanish, and according to observers at the time— including a fellow board attorney—many treated farm workers with suspicion or outright distaste. Meanwhile, many growers flaunted the law with impunity. Three weeks after the ALRB opened for business, Sandy Nathan, the UFW's lead attorney for ALRA matters, commented: "The growers are really lawless at this point. To them it's perfectly permissible to disregard the law and to do every-thing they can to subvert it. And the board is not recognizing that...They're just looking at it that everybody is a good faith participant." Most aggravating, Kintz proved indifferent to the UFW's complaints and its sense of urgency.[11]

The UFW responded in its customary style. When the board threatened that processing scores of elections would take months, the union carried out sit-ins, brought workers to the board and other government offices to protest, and called incessantly to prod the board to prioritize the cases where speed was of the essence and to deal with the rest expeditiously. Cohen called for Kintz's resignation at the first election hearing the ALRB held, and the UFW ratcheted up the pressure when he refused to step down. By November, 1975, Brown—at first a bystander to the chaos—responded to the union's demands by creating a task force of experienced outside attorneys who trained board staff and prosecuted growers themselves. The ALRB began working more effectively to enforce the new law.

The second challenge was delay. The ALRB was hampered by insufficient funding from the very beginning, and accumulated a large backlog of cases within its first year. By early 1977, workers faced prospective delays of up to two years after an election for the board to certify the union as their representative (Majka and Majka 1982). Under these circumstances, growers became increas-ingly savvy about the potential for postponing a final decision based on appeals under the ALRA. Delay worked entirely to the grower's advantage. In the gap it introduced between the moment of the union's demonstration of its power (in the ALRA model, the moment of the worker vote) and the time when bargain-ing happened, the group of workers who had voted to unionize almost always moved on to another ranch or another state. The union risked losing its leverage as months ticked by without an ALRB decision. So long as the UFW retained its vibrancy and its capacity to mobilize outside pressure, however, it could and did use pressure campaigns to convince growers to drop their appeals and begin negotiations with the union, just as it did when the ALRB itself initially obstructed the process of enforcing the law.

In addition to taking advantage of administrative delay, growers engaged in a range of other tactics to undermine the rights offered to workers by the ALRA. They recognized that as a law delineates whom it protects, it also lays out a roadmap for those who seek to avoid coverage. Growers reconfigured their businesses to make organizing under the ALRA more difficult, shifting out of certain crops and into others in order to evade coverage and changing owners and business structures once the UFW prevailed in the hopes of not being labeled a "successor enterprise" required to negotiate with the union. They also increased subcontracting, which made organizing harder despite the ALRA's recognition of the grower, not the subcontractor, as the legally responsible employer (Martin 2003; Wells and Villarejo 2004).

Most importantly, the lesson that the ALRA owed its passage and pro-worker implementation to the UFW's political support and power had not been lost on growers. Funding levels for the ALRB, political appointments to that board, and the future shape of the ALRA as a whole were all determined politically. Mobilized by defeat, growers turned to cultivating potential allies for the next round of battles. Their first success came with their victory over the UFW-backed proposition that would have guaranteed full funding for the ALRB. The UFW could—and did—fight back. For example, the union successfully advocated to defeat most grower-sponsored legislation to amend the ALRA, and Governor Brown vetoed every such bill that did pass (Majka and Majka 1982; Wells and Villarejo 2004).

It was not until the 1982 election of Republican Governor George Deukmejian that growers succeeded in changing the statewide political landscape (Majka and Majka 1984; Wells and Villarejo 2004). Under Deukmejian and then (to a somewhat lesser extent) his Republican successor Pete Wilson, ALRB members who had seen the law as a tool to encourage farm worker organizing were replaced with others who supported growers. By this time the UFW had largely withdrawn from the fields, and it is unclear that the UFW would have been in a position to take advantage of the ALRB's protections even had the agency been operating at full capacity (Wells and Villarejo 2004).

The UFW's Response to Implementation Challenges

In the case of the UFW, our ability to examine the interplay between law and movement is vastly complicated by Chavez's change in strategy in the mid- to late-1970s. In essence, there were only two to three years during which the

UFW was operating at full power after the passage to the ALRA, and during ten months of that period the ALRB was closed. During that time, however, the UFW built itself back up from almost total defeat, and then surpassed its earlier levels of representation and power. This success during the often-difficult implementation phase deserves further exploration. In particular, it illustrates that although a new law can pose new obstacles to a movement, those difficulties neither rob the movement of its agency nor necessarily determine the outcome of the battle. During a brief period following the passage of the ALRA, then, it is remarkable to review the organizing success the UFW enjoyed. The union continued to successfully exert its influence during rulemaking after the law was passed. It won most of what it sought at this stage. And in terms of sheer numbers of workers incorporated into the union and brought under contract, the period immediately following the passage of the ALRA was characterized by the most successful organizing that the UFW ever did. All of this was in spite of the considerable grower backlash and bureaucratic delay.

What accounts for the union's accomplishments during this period, accomplishments at odds with the more common assessment of the "implementation" phase as a particularly trying one for movements? I will argue that the sources of the divergence are twofold. First, the UFW had a different approach to the ALRB and the implementation of the new law, and was positioned differently in relation to its enforcement, than other movements that law and social movement scholars have studied. The fact that changes in context and strategy permit greater "bounce" from new rights should come as no surprise, but the law and social movements literature has thus far not documented many such examples, which in part accounts for its negative cant. Second, the ALRA was a different kind of law than most studied to date, in two interrelated regards. It was procedural rather than substantive, and it granted rights to groups rather than individuals. I will argue that both of these factors were important in facilitating movement success in the wake of the passage of a new law and in spite of organized opposition.

Again, the particular challenges that law and social movements scholars have identified with this phase include bureaucratic resistance to implementing new rules and procedures, the dominance of opponents in determining the regulations that will govern the new right, and the technicalization and lawyerization of the movement's fight.

With regard to bureaucratic resistance, as we have seen, the UFW responded to the obstacles that the ALRB initially posed by using its customary social movement pressure to demand greater responsiveness. Its influence was both reflected in and magnified by the supermajority of sympathetic board members.

Similarly, as for the problem of technicalization, technical negotiations about the regulations that would implement the ALRA's mandates did follow the law's passage. But unlike other movements documented by scholars, here UFW was successful in continuing to use movement pressure, or the threat of it, to continually politicize allegedly technical issues, while working on a technical level to use legal tactics to create a favorable regulatory environment. As former lead organizer Ganz recalls, "Sometimes it would be a sit in, and sometimes it would be a motion"; either way, the union sought to influence the development of board policy even as it vigorously fought to win each election. "Every step of every election procedure was contested, fought over—the order in which the regional offices accepted petitions, the scheduling of elections, election rules, worker education, pre-election conference proceedings, unfair labor practice processing, and throwing elections out. The whole process was political and subject to pressure" (Ganz quoted in Wells and Villarejo 2004).

Success in this arena was possible in part because of the union's unparalleled level of technical expertise with regard to the subject of the legislation. Unlike laws that require the definition of complex substantive standards (such as formulas for calculating wage equity) or command of a highly specialized field (such as the technology of pollution control), the ALRA established a relatively simple set of rules to govern organizing. And with regard to the content of those rules, no player knew more about what was needed to organize farm workers than the UFW in California in 1975. With the sympathetic ear of the majority of ALRB members, the union's high level of expertise, and the urgency born of the fact that it had tied its capacity to organize to the functioning of this new agency, the UFW had both the incentive and the ability to intervene in the rulemaking process in a way that was both persistent and very responsive to the needs of organizing on the ground.

The success of this collaborative approach involving lawyers and organizers was facilitated by the UFW's sheer level of legal firepower. Already well-staffed, the legal department quickly rose to its peak after the passage of the ALRA. The union's access to large quantities of low-cost in-house legal support, amplified by scores of law students and pro bono attorneys, gave it the upper hand over growers, who had to pay high rates for representation and whose attorneys (at least initially) were not nearly so well-versed in the new law as the UFW's. Equally if not more important was the union's long history of tight coordination between law and organizing strategy. When the ALRA went into effect, Cesar Chavez and Jerry Cohen had eight years of experience working together as a part of the same organization to use law as a leverage point to advance the union's capacity to organize. Both they and newer lawyers Cohen trained recognized that the new law was only as valuable as the opportunities it offered for organizing, and saw the legal staff's job as maximizing the opening for as long as possible.

These factors may account for much of the UFW's success after the passage of the NLRA. But they do not address another persistent concern about what happens in the wake of the creation of rights. Critical scholars have argued that once new entitlements appear, participants may turn away from the movement and toward the state as the source of individualized solutions to problems that they once viewed collectively (Freeman 1978; Gabel 1984; Tushnet 1984). Frustration about the difficulties of "getting one's rights" given the limits on those rights imposed by the new law and the flaws and obstacles in the procedures set up to deliver them further provokes dissatisfaction with and distancing from the movement.

Law and social movements scholars have quite effectively contested the idea that winning rights automatically pushes the new rights-bearers toward individualized dependence on the state. Through studies of the beneficiaries of civil rights, women's rights, and disability rights laws, among others, they have shown that rights have recursive effects, bolstering individuals' capacity to act even as they define and potentially limit the scope of that action (Schneider 1986; Polletta 2000; Engel and Munger 2003). But the literature has for the most part sidestepped the question of the effect that new rights have on *movements* as opposed to individuals (Handler 1992; McCann and March 1995; Polletta 2001).

After the ALRA, individual farm workers possessed new rights, to be sure. But those rights were experienced and expressed collectively. Both the ALRA's procedural character and its communal nature played roles in facilitating continued organizing. When a law is procedural, there is no confusing its passage with the achievement of the movement's substantive goals. The ALRA (like the NLRA) established the process by which workers could elect a union. That union would negotiate with a grower over the wages, benefits, and rules under which the workers would labor, but the ALRA nowhere specified a minimum or defined a level for those terms. This shifted the balance of power between farm workers and growers, and in that sense made more likely the achievement of substantive change, but the law itself and the ALRB on its own did not and could not create different workplace standards for farm workers. Something else—on-the-ground organizing—had to happen before the movement could deliver what it sought. This fact lessened the danger that the law would be seen as a victory in and of itself, and increased the likelihood that it will serve as a goad to continued action.

And yet other movements that have won laws with procedural qualities have not necessarily found that an emphasis on process leads to increased movement activity. Take, for example, environmental legislation that specifies the sort of information about pollution levels that companies must collect and make public, and creates triggers for the upgrading of plants and equipment, but does not set substantive targets for pollution reduction. As critics have pointed out, these laws have often set the stage for an implementation phase dominated by technician lawyers and industrial pollution experts, rather than encouraging broad-based participation (Dowie 1995; Foster 2002).

What is different about labor laws in general, including the ALRA, is that the procedure they establish for improving workplace rights is one that invites—indeed requires—collective use. Staughton Lynd (1984) has argued that labor-organizing statutes such as the NLRA establish "communal" rather than individual rights. A "communal right," as Lynd defines it, "articulate[s]... the values of community, compassion, and solidarity." In the labor context, this translates to "the right to act together, to engage in activity commonly and most effectively undertaken by groups." Although it is important to Lynd that individuals can exercise communal rights alone, the fact remains that at the threshold (when farm workers must decide by majority vote whether or not they will be represented by a union) and at the point when substantive rights are established (as the union negotiates with the employer over the contract), only the process of group decision making and the exercise of group power will result in the achievement of improved working conditions. In this setting, communal rights clearly required communal action to be realized. The scattering that happens to some extent after most substantive rights victories—"Now I'm going to sue to get my rights under law"—was simply not possible here. Winning change itself could never happen without active organizing by and among farm workers.

This is true to some degree for the realization of the promises inherent in laws guaranteeing substantive rights as well. That is, the enforcement of the victories won by a social movement always requires some (and sometimes a massive) amount of ongoing organizing. For a procedural and communal law like the ALRA, however, the law literally cannot deliver *any* improvement in the absence of a real organizing partner. This, of course, would quickly become the tragedy of the ALRA. With the UFW much less active in the fields starting in the 1980s, workers faced a nearly impossibly high bar to taking advantage of ALRA rights, where in the substantive rights case, the rights remain accessible to individuals even at points where there is little or no movement activity. But for a brief moment, in the two years after the law's passage when the UFW actively used it to organize tens of thousands of farm workers, the law's procedural and communal characteristics rendered it a most useful tool for movement-building.

Conclusion

The passage of a new law such as the ALRA creates new obstacles and opportunities for players already engaged in an ongoing game. By reconfiguring the rules it gives the advantage to one side or the other. The question then is, what do the players make of the new rules?

There is likely to be a window of opportunity in which the advantaged side can press its advantage if it is ready to do so. The opportunity is tempered by a variety of challenges that the law itself introduces. This is an inherently unstable situation. Administrative processes introduce administrative delay, and backlash is inevitable. In addition to the obvious route of repeal or amendment, neither of which occurred in the case of the ALRA, there are many other ways for powerful opponents to invalidate a law: identifying and exploiting loopholes in the legislation; gaining political control of appointments to the agency in charge of rulemaking, implementation, and enforcement; using the legislative process to reduce the agency's funding; supporting the selection of conservative judges who will interpret the law in ways that curtail its reach; reconfiguring business structures to avoid the law's confines; or, most simply, flouting the law outright and trusting that bureaucratic delay and minimal penalties will bring reward.

Yet these tactics do not rob a movement of its agency, its capacity to continue to work in innovative and strategic ways in the face of new challenges, or its ability to maintain an independent stance vis-à-vis the state.

The UFW knew that its advantages under the new law would not last forever. Chavez, Cohen, and others understood that the ALRA would offer them only a brief window of opportunity before growers gained the knowledge and political power they needed to roll back farm workers' new rights. Certainly the history of the NLRA confirmed their suspicion: the Wagner Act's pro-union provisions lasted a mere decade after they were upheld by the Supreme Court before they were devastated by Taft–Hartley, and much of that time both the law and the NLRB were embattled (Gross 1981). But during the first few years of that window, the UFW was able to use the ALRA to build its movement, continue its highly effective coordination of legal and organizing strategies, and leverage organizing of greater numbers of workers than ever before. This period of success was, of course, terribly brief. And the grower backlash to the ALRA plus the administrative delay introduced by the ALRB process doubtless played some role in frustrating the union's achievement of its goals. But by far the more powerful force was Chavez's dissolution of the legal department and his withdrawal of the union from the field of active organizing.

Had the UFW continued to hold up its half of the battle, it would still have had to fight growers on every front. The restructuring of the industry would have continued, to the union's disadvantage. Delays at the ALRB would likely have persisted. And there might have been nothing that the UFW could have done to forestall the election of a Republican governor. But the vibrant UFW of the early days had faced grower opposition and Republican administrations before, and had prevailed. Perhaps the union would have returned to its social movement organizing strategies, using boycotts to pressure employers to withdraw their appeals and begin bargaining. Perhaps it would have restructured the way it bargained for workers or created a different source of pressure than the boycott. It might have won another five or ten years of strong organizing before having to retrench and retool its strategy. We will never know for sure.

As the story of the UFW and the ALRA illustrates, even the best labor law does not do its work alone. It requires a union partner that is organizing actively, is configured in a way that makes sense in light of the structure of work in the industry, and is responsive to the particular needs of the workers who are or will be its members. Where such a union (or, better yet, such a labor movement as a whole) is present, the tools that good labor legislation offers can be powerful indeed. In the face of shifts that move the social equilibrium toward the relatively powerless, the powerful are creative, relentless, and eventually often successful in the quest to reestablish their dominance. But that is not the end of the story, nor is it a reason to avoid seeking new rights. It is just another point in the never-ending cycle of work for justice.

Acknowledgments

This chapter benefited greatly from the research assistance of Saru Jayaraman, Kristi Graunke, and Cynthia Isales.

Notes

1. The UFW changed names several times after its founding in 1962. It began as the Farm Workers Association (FWA) and in 1964 added "National" before its name (NFWA). In 1966, when the union merged with the AFL-CIO sponsored Agricultural Workers Organizing Committee, it became the United Farm Workers Organizing Committee (UFWOC). Finally, in 1972 when UFWOC formally affiliated with the AFL-CIO as a full member, it took the United Farm Workers of America (UFW) as its name. To avoid confusion, I use "UFW" throughout.

2. I interviewed CRLA founding attorneys James Lorenz and Gary Bellow; former UFW General Counsel Jerry Cohen; former UFW staff attorneys Bill Carder, Ira Gottlieb, Ellen Greenstone, Sandy Nathan, Peter Haberfeld, and Barbara Rhine; former UFW volunteer attorney Howard Richards; former UFW Executive Committee members and organizers Marshall Ganz, Jessica Govea, Eliseo Medina, and Gilbert

Padilla; and former UFW Service Center director LeRoy Chatfield. All quotes in this article are from these interviews unless otherwise attributed. The list of sources at the end of the chapter contains dates for all of these interviews.

3. The UFW operated on a "volunteer" basis, where most staff received a weekly stipend (initially $5 and later $10 per week) as well as room and board in lieu of a salary. Exceptions were made for lawyers, who received a monthly stipend that began at $600, and a few other professionals.

4. A primary boycott is when the union asks consumers not to buy a particular product grown or manufactured by an employer with which the union has a dispute. A secondary boycott broadens the focus beyond the immediate employer, as for example when the union asks consumers to avoid an entire store because it sells the boycotted product. With regard to the critical issue of secondary pressure, the ALRA preserved farm worker unions' right to call for secondary boycotts of stores that sold nonunion products, rather than limiting them as the NLRA did to only calling for a primary boycott of the product itself. Cal. Lab. Code §1154(d)(4). But a union that had not yet been elected as the bargaining representative of the farm workers in question was forbidden from setting up pickets in front of the store in support of the same boycott. Cal. Lab. Code §1154(d)(4). The union could still leaflet for the same purpose, however ("Secondary Boycotts . . . ," 1977).

5. Section 1 of Stats.1975, 3rd Ex. Sess., c. 1, p. 4013.

6. Cal. Lab. Code §§1140–66.

7. Cal. Admin. Code, tit. 8, div. 2.

8. Levy Collection, Interview with Sandy Nathan, 9/24/75.

9. Levy Collection, Box 29, Folder 563, File 31: "United Farm Workers of America, AFL-CIO: Elections Statistical Tally Up to and Including February 6, 1976: Statewide Results."

10. In his wake, the union turned for a while to a mix of in-house volunteers and outside pro bono attorneys. The need for paid representation eventually reasserted itself, however, and for a number of years now the UFW has been represented by its current General Counsel, Marcos Camacho, who serves the union through his private firm.

11. This description of the ALRA's early days is drawn from Jacques Levy's interviews with ALRB attorney Ellen Greenstone and UFW attorney Sandy Nathan, both on 9/24/75, less than a month after the ALRB opened (Levy Collection). The Nathan quote is from Levy's interview. This paragraph and the one that follows also draw on my interviews with Greenstone, Nathan, and Cohen. The Greenstone quote is from my interview.

References

Ballam, Deborah A. 1995. Commentary: The Law as a Constitutive Force for Change, Part II: The Impact of the National Labor Relations Act on the U.S. Labor Movement. *American Business Law Journal* 32: 447–79.

Bardacke, Frank. 1993. Cesar's Ghost: Decline and Fall of the UFW. *Nation* July 26: 130–35.

Bellow, Gary. 1996. Steady Work: A Practitioner's Reflections on Political Lawyering. *Harvard Civil Rights–Civil Liberties Law Review* 31: 297–309.

Cox, Archibald. 1960. *Law and the National Labor Policy.* Los Angeles, CA: University of California Press (Reprint, Westport, CT: Greenwood Press, 1983).

Davis, Martha F. 1993. *Brutal Need: Lawyers and the Welfare Rights Movement, 1960–1973.* New Haven, CT: Yale University Press.

Dowie, Mark. 1995. *Losing Ground: American Environmentalism at the Close of the Twentieth Century.* Cambridge, MA: MIT Press.

Engel, David and Frank Munger. 2003. *Rights of Inclusion: Law and Identity in the Life Stories of Americans with Disabilities.* Chicago: University of Chicago Press.

Ferriss, Susan and Ricardo Sandoval. 1997. *The Fight in the Fields: Cesar Chavez and the Farmworkers Movement.* New York: Harcourt.

Forbath, William. 1991. *Law and the Shaping of the American Labor Movement.* Cambridge, MA: Harvard University Press.

Foster, Sheila. 2002. Environmental Justice in an Era of Devolved Collaboration. *The Harvard Environmental Review* 31: 459–98.

Freeman, Alan. 1978. Legitimizing Racial Discrimination Through Anti-Discrimination Law: A Critical Review of Supreme Court Doctrine. *Minnesota Law Review* 62: 1049–119.

Friedman, Sheldon, Richard Hurd, Rudolph Oswald, and Ronald Seeber, eds. 1994. *Restoring the Promise of American Labor Law.* Ithaca, NY: ILR Press/Cornell University Press.

Gabel, Peter. 1984. The Phenomenology of Rights-Consciousness and the Pact of the Withdrawn Selves. *Texas Law Review* 62: 1563–98.

Ganz, Marshall. 2000. Resources and Resourcefulness: Strategic Capacity in the Unionization of California Agriculture, 1959–1966. *American Journal of Sociology* 105: 1003–62.

Goldfield, Michael. 1987. *The Decline of Organized Labor in the United States.* Chicago: University of Chicago Press.

Gross, James A. 1981. *The Reshaping of the National Labor Relations Board: National Labor Policy in Transition, 1937–1947.* Albany, NY: SUNY Press.

Handler, Joel. 1978. *Social Movements and the Legal System.* New York: Academic Press.

———. 1992. A Reply. *Law and Society Review* 26: 819–24.

King, Wayne. 1981. Chavez Faces Internal and External Struggles. *The New York Times* December 6: 1.

Kinoy, Arthur. 1983. *Rights on Trial: The Odyssey of a People's Lawyer.* Cambridge, MA: Harvard University Press.

Klare, Karl. 1978. Judicial Deradicalization of the Wagner Act and the Origins of Modern Legal Consciousness, 1937–1941. *Minnesota Law Review* 62: 265–339.

Levy, Jacques. 1973. *Autobiography of La Causa.* New York: W.W. Norton.

Lynd, Staughton. 1981. Government Without Rights: The Labor Law Vision of Archibald Cox. *Industrial Relations Law Journal* 4: 483–95.

———. 1984. Communal Rights. *Texas Law Review* 62: 1417–41.

Majka, Linda C. and Theo J. Majka. 1982. *Farm Workers, Agribusiness, and the State.* Philadelphia, PA: Temple University Press.

Majka, Theo J. and Linda C. Majka. 1984. Power, Insurgency and State Intervention. In *Research in Social Movements, Conflicts and Change,* Vol. 6, Richard Ratcliff, ed. Greenwich, CT: JAI Press, pp. 195–224.

————. 1992. Decline of the Farm Labor Movement in California: Organizational Crisis and Political Change. *Critical Sociology* 19: 3–36.

Martin, Philip. 2003. *Promise Unfulfilled: Unions, Immigration, and the Farm Workers.* Ithaca, NY: Cornell University Press.

————. 2004. Promise Unfulfilled: Why Didn't Collective Bargaining Transform California's Farm Labor Market? Center for Immigration Studies Backgrounder, Newsletter, January 2004.

McCann, Michael. 1994. *Rights at Work: Pay Equity Reform and the Politics of Legal Mobilization.* Chicago: University of Chicago Press.

McCann, Michael and Tracey March. 1995. Law and Everyday Forms of Resistance: A Socio-Political Assessment. *Studies in Law, Politics, and Society* 15: 207–36.

Milner, Neal. 1986. The Dilemmas of Legal Mobilization: Ideologies and Strategies of Mental Patient Liberation Groups. *Law and Policy* 8: 105–29.

Montgomery, David. 1979. *Workers' Control in America.* New York: Cambridge University Press.

Olson, Susan. 1984. *Clients and Lawyers: Securing the Rights of Disabled Persons.* Westport, CT: Greenwood Press.

Polletta, Francesca. 2000. The Structural Context of Novel Rights Claims: Southern Civil Rights Organizing, 1961–1966. *Law and Society Review* 34: 367–406.

————. 2001. The Laws of Passion (reviewing Susan Bandes, ed., *The Passion of Laws*). *Law and Society Review* 35: 467–93.

Pope, James Gray. 1997. Labor's Constitution of Freedom. *Yale Law Journal* 106: 941–1031.

————. 2002. The Thirteenth Amendment versus the Commerce Clause: Labor and the Shaping of American Constitutional Law, 1921–1957. *Columbia Law Review* 102: 1–122.

Schneider, Elizabeth M. 1986. The Dialectic of Rights and Politics: Perspectives from the Women's Movement. *New York University Law Review* 61: 589–652.

Secondary Boycotts and the Employer's Permissible Response under the California Agricultural Labor Relations Act. 1977. *Stanford Law Review* 29: 277–96.

Stewart, Richard B. 1975. The Reformation of American Administrative Law. *Harvard Law Review* 88: 1669–1813.

Stone, Katherine Van Wezel. 1981. The Post-War Paradigm in American Labor Law. *Yale Law Journal* 90: 1509–80.

Taylor, Ronald B. 1971. Why Chavez Spurns the Labor Act. *Nation* April 12: 454–6.

————. 1975. *Chavez and the Farm Workers.* Boston, MA: Beacon Press.

Tushnet, Mark. 1984. An Essay on Rights. *Texas Law Review* 62: 1363–403.

Wells, Miriam J. and Don Villarejo. 2004. State Structures and Social Movement Strategies: The Shaping of Farm Labor Protections in California. *Politics and Society* 32: 291–326.

Interviews with Jennifer Gordon

Gary Bellow, 9/10/99

Bill Carder, 4/25/05

Leroy Chatfield, 2/27/00

Jerry Cohen, 7/22/99 with multiple follow-up interviews

Marshall Ganz, 5/25/00

Ira "Buddy" Gottlieb, 3/23/05

Jessica Govea, 10/13/99

Ellen Greenstone, 4/21/05

Peter Haberfeld, 3/28/00

James Lorenz, 3/27/00

Eliseo Medina, 6/22/00

Sandy Nathan, 5/3/05

Gilbert Padilla, 2/28/00

Barbara Rhine, 3/27/00

Howard Richards , 6/28/04

Collection

Jacques E. Levy Research Collection on Cesar Chavez ("Levy Collection"). Collection of Western Americana. Yale University, Beinecke Library.

Mobilization Lawyering

Community Economic Development in the Figueroa Corridor

SCOTT L. CUMMINGS

Shifts in the American political system away from hard regulation and toward soft governance have provoked a reassessment of the role of cause lawyers in the United States. This reassessment reflects real changes on the ground, as trends of decentralization and privatization have reconfigured the terrain of cause lawyering (see Handler 1996; Freeman 1997; Minow 2002; Lobel 2004), producing new modes of legal advocacy and raising challenges to conventional rights-based practices (Trubek 2005). These field-level changes, in turn, have given rise to an emerging scholarly literature describing the arrival of a new style of cause lawyering that promotes stakeholder participation in designing flexible solutions to social problems and thus stands in contrast to the top-down impact litigation model of traditional public interest law (Simon 2004; Trubek 2005).

These developments draw attention to the importance of the state in structuring the relationship between cause lawyers and the mobilization of marginalized groups. The state sets the terms of legal intervention—supplying substantive rights, procedural rules, and legal resources—while also providing a primary target for reform. A central focus of cause lawyering scholarship has been on examining the effectiveness of lawyers in asserting the rights of marginalized groups as a means of moving state power on their behalf. This body of research largely calls into question the viability of legal rights strategies as a vehicle for social reform, emphasizing the demobilizing effect of law on political action (see McCann 1998: 76–77). The decentralization of political decision making and the expansion of public–private partnerships create new opportunities for cause lawyers to promote the type of community mobilization found lacking in the public interest law reform approach. Yet the decentered state also erects new challenges and reshapes traditional meanings (Handler 1996). A key issue concerns the kind of community mobilization that cause lawyers help to advance under localized, market-oriented governance structures. In particular, although new models of cause lawyering have the potential to promote participation and empowerment, they can also channel political action into processes of collaboration and negotiation that shape a more quiescent form of mobilization, resulting in the political disadvantage and co-optation of weaker groups.

The emergence of Community Economic Development (CED) as a distinct field of cause lawyering highlights the complexities of community mobilization in the postregulatory state. Defined by a set of social policies and grassroots practices that promote neighborhood revitalization, CED is associated with a *transactional* model of cause lawyering focused on negotiating deals between community-based nonprofit organizations, public funders, and private investors (Cummings 2001; Simon 2001). Whereas cause lawyers have traditionally sought to mobilize claims of *legal rights* to advance systemic reform, CED lawyers attempt to mobilize *community participation* to change local economic circumstances through the creation of innovative institutional structures.

However, CED does not neatly remove barriers to mobilization; rather it presents a different set of opportunities and constraints. For instance, CED is not connected with broad-based social movements. Instead, it is parochial, seeking to preserve community boundaries and increase community control of resources. Moreover, although CED establishes legal mechanisms for ongoing community participation in local governance, it does so through the design of partnerships with government and business elites that create disincentives for political confrontation seeking reforms in state practice or increased resources from private sector institutions. For this reason, the modus operandi of CED practice is not one of protest and disruption. Nor is CED designed to challenge the existing rules of the game; rather, it seeks to build partnerships and distribute resources within the framework of the law as constituted. As a technique of institutional design that extends contractual relationships between the community, the market, and the state, CED therefore fosters a version of mobilization that tends to de-emphasize adversarial organizing in favor of *collaboration* with business and governmental partners.

At the grassroots level, however, there are important recent examples of community mobilization within CED that depart from the collaborative model. In particular, the emergence of an "accountable development" movement in Los Angeles—where community–labor coalitions have pressured publicly subsidized developers into a series of agreements to provide benefits to low-income communities—has focused attention on more confrontational forms of collective action, flowing out of the traditions of community organizing and social movement activism (see Cummings and Eagly 2001). This chapter uses the advent of accountable development to reexamine the relationship between cause lawyering and community mobilization. It begins by describing the emergence of CED as a nonadversarial cause lawyering model, situating it within the context of the reaction against the social movements and legal rights strategies of the 1960s and 1970s. Drawing upon insights from social movement theory, it then analyzes the constraints that collaborative CED can impose on collective action by low-income communities. A case study of accountable development in Los Angeles follows, revealing an alternative approach to CED that mobilizes adversarial organizing to extract developer concessions and governmental reforms. It concludes with an analysis of cause lawyering in the accountable development context, suggesting continuities with conventional CED practice, while highlighting the ways in which the more confrontational approach of accountable development reshapes the lawyering role.

Community Economic Development as Cause Lawyering: A Genealogy

CED as a cause lawyering strategy that uses transactional skills to foster locally accountable development is a product of both the success and failures of the classic public interest law model of the 1960s and 1970s (Trubek 2005), which focused primarily on the use of impact litigation to achieve broad social reform through the courts (Handler, Hollingsworth, and Erlanger 1978). During this period, the configuration of governmental power created incentives for the rise of public interest law—with federal courts receptive to civil rights claims against the states, centralized administrative agencies susceptible to reform through impact lawsuits, and a system of welfare entitlements open to enforcement and expansion (Trubek 2005; McCann and Dudas 2006). Within this environment, public interest law was viewed as a means of advancing the interests of underrepresented groups in court, thus responding to the failures of majoritarian political processes (Weisbrod 1978: 22) and complementing social movement activism (Handler 1978).

The Politics of Community Economic Development

It was, in part, the very success of the public interest law model that fueled a conservative political reaction seeking to limit the federal governmental role in the areas of civil rights and civil liberties, economic regulation, and social welfare (Trubek 2005; see also McCann and Dudas 2006). As a conservative coalition gained political power in the 1980s and 1990s, the structure of the federal government was reshaped: An increasingly conservative federal judiciary became less hospitable to civil rights claims; federal agencies, criticized as inefficient and unaccountable, were decentralized and increasingly delegated decision-making power and service provision to private entities (Handler 1996; Freeman 2000); and core federal entitlements, most notably welfare, were curtailed (Handler and Hasenfeld 1997). These structural changes foreclosed legal advocacy opportunities for liberal public interest organizations at the federal level, while opening the door to claims by the growing number of conservative advocacy groups (Southworth 2005). In addition, the tools of public interest lawyers were restricted: Congress prevented federally funded legal services lawyers from bringing class actions, lobbying, collecting attorney's fees, and engaging in political advocacy; the Supreme Court limited attorney's fee awards in civil rights and environmental cases; and some states enacted caps on attorney's fees and damage awards, while restricting the ability of law school clinics to undertake controversial cases (Minow 2002; Luban, 2003).

At the same time, the changing political environment also generated new roles and opportunities for cause lawyers. In particular, the shift in social policy design from centralized federal regulation toward local, market-oriented governance brought a new emphasis on stakeholder participation in decision making, public–private partnerships, and negotiated rules (Lobel 2004). CED, focused on mobilizing community participation in economic revitalization efforts and creating public–private partnerships to promote affordable housing and job creation goals, emerged as an important component of this new social policy regime.

The theme of community participation in the design and implementation of urban poverty programs runs through CED policy, evolving in reaction to the failures of prior federal efforts to support local action (Simon 2001). The Urban Renewal program of the 1950s, which provided federal loans and grants to redevelop "blighted" neighborhoods, was criticized for subsidizing private development without sufficient input by affected low-income community members, leading to their displacement by high-end housing and commercial projects (Anderson 1964). The Community Action Program (CAP) of 1964 was faulted both for achieving too much and too little: Its mobilizing activities proved too confrontational for local municipal officials, who persuaded the federal government to assert greater control over militant community action agencies, while its goal of "maximum feasible participation" of community members was never fully realized (Halpern 1995: 114; Simon 2001: 14–15).

The urban policies and community organizations that grew out of these experiments shaped the terrain of modern CED, which created greater opportunities for community participation in the process of local development, while channeling that participation in ways that promoted collaboration with local governmental officials and private sector actors. The process of redevelopment is now undertaken primarily by local agencies, which finance private development through property tax increases and provide stronger requirements for community participation than Urban Renewal (Simon 2001: 10–11). The major federal urban policies since CAP—Model Cities, Community Development Block Grants, Empowerment Zones, HOME Investment Partnerships—have allocated funding for housing and economic development to local governments, while mandating specific requirements for community participation in the planning process.

CED is also defined by the centrality of private actors. Nonprofit community development corporations (CDCs) have been key vehicles for developing housing, creating jobs, and providing social services like child care, health care, and job training. Growing out of diverse strains of community activism, CDCs expanded in number and size in the beginning in the 1970s, spurred by federal funding as well as heavy investments by the Ford Foundation. Over the next two decades, CDCs became deeply involved in housing development, supported community businesses, and became highly professionalized, favoring collaborative partnerships with local institutions over adversarial organizing (Halpern 1995: 133–39).

In order to encourage private investment in low-income communities, CED policy has also created incentives to promote for-profit business involvement in local development activities. For example, the Low-Income Housing Tax Credit Program, which since its creation in 1986 has been the largest supply-side affordable housing program, subsidizes private development through the sale of federal tax credits to private investors. A similar program, called the New Markets Tax Credit, is now in place to subsidize business development in low-income neighborhoods. The HOPE VI program, which funds major public housing demolition and rehabilitation, is also designed to leverage private investment to develop mixed-income, low-density, affordable housing (Pindell 2003). In addition, there are federal subsidies available for community development financial institutions that leverage private resources to meet the banking needs of poor areas (Lento 1994).

The emergence of CED has thus called for a distinct type of lawyering in poor communities—one that, in contrast to litigation, is focused on helping community organizations develop accountable governance structures, access resources through CED programs, negotiate deals with private sector investors, and facilitate complex housing and commercial development projects.

From Rights to Empowerment

Although CED lawyering is a product of political changes driven in part by the right, it has also gained currency among activists and academics as a model of legal advocacy that responds to the critique of public interest law on the left. There were two main categories of criticism leveled by scholars at the legal rights strategies of the public interest law era. First, scholars articulated an *efficacy* critique, drawing on empirical research to demonstrate the inadequacy of law reform as a vehicle of social change. Handler's (1978) assessment of public interest law concluded that litigation alone could not reform field-level practice in the consumer, environmental, civil rights, and welfare rights arenas due to the exercise of vast administrative discretion by government bureaucracies— what he called the "bureaucratic contingency." Rosenberg's study (1991: 338) concluded that courts could "*almost never* be effective producers of significant social reform" because of their dependence on other political institutions and their lack of enforcement powers.

There was also a related *political* critique. Scheingold (1974) warned against the tendency of activists to mythologize rights, which he contended contributed to the breakdown of political organization and diverted attention from the political roots of social problems. Bell (1976) struck at the heart of the civil rights establishment, questioning whether the National Association for the Advancement of Colored People's commitment to desegregation—supported by its middle-class white and black constituents—ignored the needs of black communities by privileging litigation efforts designed to achieve integration over political strategies to promote educational quality. Other scholars suggested that litigation drained scarce movement resources, created confusion between "symbolic" and "substantive" victories (Rosenberg 1991), and co-opted potential movement leaders by paying them off with monetary awards (Gordon 1995: 438–39). Critical legal scholars went further, suggesting that the inherently individualistic nature of legal rights tended to "undermine collectivities rather than build them" (Abel 1985: 8–9), and that translating grievances into rights claims legitimated inequities inscribed in the legal status quo (Gabel and Harris 1982–83). Poverty law scholars warned of the potential of lawyers deploying legal expertise across dimensions of race and class to reinforce the marginalization of clients and argued for increased client participation in legal problem solving as a way of promoting client empowerment (White 1990; Alfieri 1991; López 1992).

CED lawyering responds to both categories of the critique of rights. With respect to the efficacy critique, CED, unlike rights strategies, does not rely on bureaucratic enforcement, but rather is a form of self-help that leverages existing community resources to gain access to outside investment, while mobilizing ongoing community participation to ensure project implementation. CED is also designed to promote collaboration with outside institutions in order to redress economic disparities that are resistant to law reform techniques. From a political perspective, CED values grassroots organization, accountability to community members, leadership development, and creative problem solving. CED has also been viewed as a model for promoting client empowerment: Because CED representation is focused on helping community-controlled groups design and implement local development projects, lawyer accountability to broad community interests is enhanced while the potential for lawyer domination recedes (Southworth 1996: 1154–55; Shah 1999: 232–33; Cummings 2001: 446; see also Southworth 1999).

Cause Lawyering Between Community, Market, and State

Scheingold and Sarat (2004: 101–02) suggest that cause lawyers can be arrayed along a spectrum according to their "dramatically different democratic dreams." Yet the picture is complicated within CED, which does not break down neatly along traditional political lines, but rather is characterized by its broad political appeal—claimed by proponents of free-market capitalism, radical egalitarianism, and civic republicanism. This is owing in part to the wide range of CED activities, but also to the ideological ambiguity of CED itself, which means that the same activity can have a different political valence depending on the advocate's views. Moreover, CED's legal complexity and potential for generating fees also means that it is undertaken by lawyers in different practice sites: corporate lawyers in large law firms, staff attorneys in nonprofit legal services groups, and solo and small-firm practitioners. The diversity of political viewpoints and professional roles within CED generates divergent conceptions of cause. For some, CED reflects a "grassroots" or "emancipatory" practice that promotes social justice, robust community participation, and nonhierarchical decision making (see Hilbink 2004: 683; Scheingold and Sarat 2004: 104). For others, CED's concern with providing under-resourced community groups with access to legal services also draws it toward a "proceduralist" vision of cause lawyering that seeks to achieve the best outcome possible for clients within the constraints of the existing political system (Hilbink 2004: 669).

With respect to professional role, the fact that the community organizations are the driving force of CED means that the lawyer–client relationship tends to be shaped by the norm of client-centeredness, with the client group making key decisions about goals and strategies. There remains considerable variation in the degree of lawyer–client collaboration, ranging from more passive facilitation of client projects (Marsico 1995) to greater lawyer participation in defining and executing community goals (Diamond 2000). The degree of lawyer participation in client decision making is a function of the governance style of the client organizations, the personal commitments of the lawyers (see Ellman 1992), and the influence of the lawyers' practice settings.

With respect to legal tactics, CED differs sharply from its litigation counterpart. In the litigation context, lawyers file claims of legal rights in an adversarial process to either change state practice vis-à-vis marginalized groups or invoke the power of the state to reform private conduct. The CED lawyer's role, in contrast, requires the type of nonadversarial transactional skills that are the stock-in-trade of the corporate bar: structuring business entities, arranging access to capital, counseling compliance with tax and corporate regulations, negotiating partnerships and other legal agreements, and navigating the process of real estate development (Southworth 1996; see also Glick and Rossman 1997; Shah 1999).

Scholars of cause lawyering have identified other models of collaborative practice, such as lobbying the state for passage of a new statute (Ziv 2001) or working closely with legal adversaries to advance the rule of law (Dotan 2001). However, in contrast to these examples, CED operates squarely within the context of the decentered state, where the focus of collaboration is not with central state authorities designated to enact legislation or defend state practices, but with the local governmental entities and private market actors empowered under the governance regime. Whereas other depictions of collaboration involve lawyers who are, at bottom, asking the state to redress a legal wrong, CED involves collaboration between community-based clients and state and market funders as a means to generate solutions to the problems of poverty and urban disinvestment.

CED's emphasis on collaboration as a form of legal action reflects its distinct orientation toward the fairness of the legal system (see Hilbink 2004: 666–81). In the cause lawyering literature, a contrast is typically drawn between procedural and substantive fairness, with substantive fairness associated with the domain of public law—the question being whether or not courts adequately use the power of the state to vindicate the rights of marginalized groups (Hilbink 2004). CED lawyering, however, is not directly concerned with the fairness of the legal system in this sense. Instead of looking to public law as a source of regulation or rights expansion, CED looks to private law as a resource for building collaborative institutional relationships in order to increase access to outside investment and expand community participation in development decisions. To be sure, CED relationships do not operate exclusively within private law: They purposefully cut across the traditional public–private divide, linking "private" sector activities, such as business operations and real estate development, with "public" sector financial and technical support. However, CED does not seek to reform public law rules through judicial decree or legislative change. Therefore, in contrast to traditional rights-oriented cause lawyering, which is designed to achieve universal public benefits, the goal of CED is, more modestly, the production of partial private benefits.

Community Economic Development: A Social Movement Perspective

The allure of CED lies in its potential to reconcile legal action and collective action. And because CED is itself a set of social policies and community practices designed to promote collaboration, there is a well-defined role for lawyers to play in advancing CED's mobilization goals. Although CED's emphasis on collaboration offers opportunities for innovative problem solving, it also imposes constraints on more adversarial forms of mobilization that seek structural reforms. This part uses the lens of social movement theory as a framework for examining the nature of mobilization within CED. The focus is on the *political context* within which CED operates and the *resources* CED actors are able to mobilize and deploy (McCann 1998: 80).

Social movement scholars emphasize the importance of the "political opportunity structure" in generating collective action (McAdam 1982; Kriesi 2004: 69). Formal political institutions constitute the key structural element, with the degree of political centralization shaping both the opportunity for intervention and the ability of the state to meet movement demands (Kriesi 2004: 70). Within CED, the benefit of decentralization is that community groups are closer to the decision makers they seek to influence and therefore may be able to more effectively hold them to account for community needs. On the other hand, decentralization localizes activism at the community level and routes it through market channels. There are opportunities for information-sharing and cooperation among CDCs, which may be generated by the need to respond collectively to policy initiatives or facilitated by intermediary groups. However, the local orientation of CED focuses mobilization on internal community-building strategies, rather than viewing economic inequality and racial segregation from a regional or even a national policy perspective (Foster-Bey 1997: 40; Barron 2003).

In order to take advantage of political opportunities, mobilization depends heavily on the capacity to gain access to resources and convert them into tools for advancing collective goals (Edwards and McCarthy 2004: 116). Resources are necessary to overcome the free rider problem faced by groups attempting to organize themselves to provide collective goods (Jenkins 1983: 537–38) and also to sustain organizational activity and mount campaigns to achieve strategic goals (Jenkins 1983: 533; Edwards and McCarthy 2004: 116). A critical insight of resource mobilization theory is that resources come with strings attached: They not only enable collective action, but also may steer it into channels favored by important resource suppliers (Edwards and McCarthy 2004: 135).

In the CED context, a key resource is organizational. CED values organizational formality, which can best be seen in the structure of CDCs, which typically incorporate community participation in governance, either through resident participation on the board or membership-based structures. Simon (2001: 60) argues in favor of organization, contending that "[a]t high levels of organization, the community has the capacity not only to prevent disruption that impairs the investment, but to facilitate support for investment and to bargain for a share of the returns." Within CED, organization is supported by a lattice of external institutional support designed to "induce" community participation (Simon 2001: 168). Legal rules play a critical role, promoting participation through an "*ex ante* structural approach," in which federal tax rules require charitable organizations to demonstrate a wide base of financial support and government funding programs require CED grantees to demonstrate community participation in governance (Simon 2001: 169–78). The government and private sectors also promote community accountability through an "*ex post* competitive approach" under which community organizations engaged in CED are graded on their performance in meeting community goals in the competitive process of applying for funding (Simon 2001: 178).

However, the same public and private actors whose funding induces mobilization in the CED context also impose significant constraints on its nature and scope (see Edwards and McCarthy 2004: 135). The National Congress for Community Economic Development's census of US CDCs reported that almost all received some type of government financing, almost one-half received money from banks, and nearly one-quarter were funded by corporations (The National Congress for Community Economic Development 1999: 6). Critics have charged that these relationships hamstring more adversarial tactics against government and business targets (Shah 1999), which can easily pull the plug on financial resources and partner instead with more cooperative community actors. The issue of constraints imposed by funding sources is not unique to CED organizations. The social movement organizations of the civil rights period relied not only on indigenous support from black churches and local organizations (Morris 1984), but also came to depend increasingly on a "conscience constituency" of Northern liberals and college students, and benefited significantly from the federal government (Jenkins 1983: 533–35; Barkan 1984: 553). However, unlike in the civil rights context where outside support was provided, at least in part, to promote confrontational organizing tactics, CED funders typically expect nonadversarial collaboration in order to achieve development aims.

The focus on cultivating and maintaining relationships with external state and market elites thus influences the *nature* of mobilization within CED, privileging collaboration over systemic disruption. In this sense, CED stands in contrast to social movements, which have historically been defined by direct challenges to "existing institutional authority—whether it is located in the political, corporate, religious, or educational realm" (Snow, Soule, and Kriesi 2004: 9). Moreover, unlike social movements that rely on "disruptive 'symbolic' tactics such as protests, marches, strikes, and the like that halt or upset ongoing social practices" (McCann 2004: 509), CED adheres closely to institutional channels of collective action. There are instances of disruptive activity within CED: Residents of Boston's Dudley Street Neighborhood Initiative, for instance, mounted a public demonstration to halt illegal trash dumping (Medoff and Sklar 1994: 81–86), and bank watchdog groups like the Greenlining Institute use the threat of disruption to compel compliance with the Community Reinvestment Act (CRA). However, disruptive activity is de-emphasized among CDCs (Dreier 1999: 180). The National Congress for Community Economic Development reported that while 82 percent of CDCs had engaged in housing development (National Congress for Community Economic Development 1999: 7), only 56 percent reported engaging in "advocacy and community organizing" (National Congress for Community Economic Development 1999: 15). Vidal's national study shows relatively more advocacy, reporting that 87 percent of CDCs engaged in housing development, while 75 percent conducted advocacy around housing issues (Vidal 1992: 64). However, Stoecker (1997: 11) has suggested that such advocacy may simply reflect CDCs "joining coalitions of other organizations and advocating around housing issues" not "bringing residents together to press for their needs collectively."

CED's collaborative approach to collective action reflects its political goals. Unlike many social movements, CED is not "state-oriented": It does not seek change in state practices, either through legislative enactment or rule enforcement (see Amenta and Caren 2004: 461). Instead, the goal of CED is neighborhood revitalization through the creation of public–private partnerships that leverage government programs. These partnerships may reconfigure the interests of the participants and therefore possibly reform their practices (Simon 2004: 182). Yet such reforms are "soft" and more difficult to measure than the "hard" regulatory reforms traditionally sought by movement actors. There is a redistributive element to CED, but it is built upon a preexisting legal framework. For example, the Low-Income Housing Tax Credit Program allocated approximately $50 billion in tax credits over its first fifteen years to build affordable housing units. However, the goal of CED is to implement such laws to create change at the neighborhood level, not to mobilize community groups to advance a radically different urban agenda.

The Accountable Development Movement

CED is therefore defined by a focus on *localism*, a commitment to bottom-up *neighborhood revitalization* over state-sponsored redistributive reform, and a version of mobilization that emphasizes *collaboration* over confrontation. Yet within CED, grassroots organizations have begun to experiment with different forms of practice that both extend and challenge these central CED principles, building upon community organizing, labor organizing, and social movement models to "redefine redevelopment" and promote "economic justice" (Cummings 2001: 478–83; Gibbons and Haas 2002). A prominent example has been the emergence of the "accountable development" movement in Los Angeles, which has sought to change city redevelopment practices through more confrontational grassroots campaigns aimed at increasing community participation in the planning process and forcing local developers and governmental officials to commit to redevelopment projects that are responsive to the needs of low-income residents. One important outcome of these campaigns has been the negotiation of "community benefits agreements" under which developers agree to provide specific levels of affordable housing, jobs, and other benefits in exchange for community support for project approvals and public subsidies. This part examines the first major community benefits agreement (CBA) campaign in Los Angeles and examines the role of cause lawyers within it.

Context

The campaign grew out of efforts to redevelop the Figueroa Corridor, a predominantly Latino working-class neighborhood that cuts southward from downtown Los Angeles along a 2.5 mile stretch of Figueroa Street toward the

University of Southern California (USC). Strategically located between the Los Angeles Convention Center downtown and the Los Angeles Memorial Coliseum just south of USC, the Figueroa Corridor has become a flashpoint for accountable development activism as city officials have sought to remake the Figueroa Corridor into Los Angeles's sports and entertainment hub. The key mechanism for implementing this plan is the state law of redevelopment, which empowers local redevelopment agencies to designate "blighted" neighborhoods as project areas, assemble private property through eminent domain, and subsidize private development by issuing debt backed by future property tax increases (known as "tax increment").

Situated at the intersection of five redevelopment project areas, the Figueroa Corridor has been shaped by the Los Angeles Community Redevelopment Agency (CRA). The southern part of the Figueroa Corridor lies within a redevelopment area established in the 1960s to allow USC to expand its campus borders and eliminate surrounding community blight as an inducement to remain at its South Los Angeles location. With the help of the CRA, USC has become the largest landowner in the Figueroa Corridor, with a real estate portfolio of over 100 properties, many of which are devoted to student housing. One of the most controversial sites is a property near the northeast border of campus, where the CRA helped USC to purchase property that it plans to use to build a $70 million sports arena to house its basketball and volleyball teams, having scrapped an earlier commitment to build a commercial center projected to create 2,700 jobs for local residents and generate $1.6 million per year in tax increment. The Memorial Coliseum, a 90,000 seat stadium located just south of the USC campus in Exposition Park, is another key site in the city's plan to promote the Figueroa Corridor as a sports and entertainment zone. The current home of USC football, the Coliseum is on the short list of stadium sites for a National Football League franchise, which the city has been working to attract by developing a subsidy package.

To the north, development pressures on the Figueroa Corridor have emanated from the redevelopment of downtown Los Angeles. The critical event was the 1997 announcement of a plan by Los Angeles real estate developer Ed Roski Jr. and Denver billionaire Phillip Anschutz of Qwest Communications (who together owned the Los Angeles Kings professional hockey team and part of the Los Angeles Lakers professional basketball franchise) to build the 20,000-seat Staples Center, which would become home of the Kings and Lakers and a venue for concerts and other entertainment events. The $375 million project, located immediately north of the Los Angeles Convention Center, was developed by the L.A. Arena Land Company (a Roski–Anschutz partnership) in a complex

public–private deal that involved billionaire Rupert Murdoch's Fox Group pur-
chasing a 40 percent interest in the arena. The deal was completed with a $70
million city subsidy, which included a $58 million loan from the city to the
developer (to be repaid through the dedication of revenues from parking fees
and a tax imposed on ticket sales) and a $12 million grant from the CRA, which
went to fund environmental approvals and assist in the acquisition of thirty
acres of property north and east of the arena to be used for interim parking. The
Staples Center project, which was completed in 1999, reconfigured the terrain of
downtown development, rising as a monument to the new vision of downtown
Los Angeles as a dynamic destination for affluent Angelenos and tourists. It
also disrupted the fabric of the existing low-income community, resulting in
the relocation of approximately 130 households and thirty-five businesses.

Coalition

Although the organizing that began after the Staples Center development
grew directly out of the resident response to the disruption, it was built upon
a foundation of community–labor cooperation that had evolved over several
years. On the labor side, part of the collaboration was the result of a deliberate
strategy by national labor leaders, who promoted grassroots coalitions through
programs like Union Cities and organizations like Good Jobs First, which was
created to build networks of local activists who would advance accountable development (Goodno 2004). But there were local factors as well. Los Angeles was
the site of innovative labor organizing among immigrant workers in the service sector, with the Service Employees International Union (SEIU) receiving
national attention for its Justice for Janitors and home health care workers campaigns (Stone 2004: 224–25; Gordon 2005: 62–63). The SEIU organizing model
forged ties between union organizers, workers, community activists, students,
and religious leaders in Los Angeles, and expanded union membership among
immigrant workers, many of whom lived in the Figueroa Corridor (Community Scholars Program 2004). In addition, the Los Angeles Alliance for a New
Economy (LAANE), a group created by the Hotel Employees and Restaurant
Employees (HERE) union in 1993, brought together grassroots organizations,
faith-based groups, environmental organizations, labor leaders, and worker representatives in its successful 1997 campaign to pass the Los Angeles Living Wage
Ordinance (Zabin and Martin 1999; Erskine and Marblestone 2006).

On the community organizing side, the key group in the Figueroa Corridor
was Strategic Actions for a Just Economy (SAJE), an economic justice and popular education center established in 1996 to build "economic power for working
class people in Los Angeles" (Strategic Actions for a Just Economy 2005). SAJE

was responsible for uniting the first community–labor network in the Figueroa Corridor, which grew out of a labor dispute at USC that began in 1995 when about 350 food and service workers, represented by HERE Local 11, demanded a guarantee from USC that it would not subcontract out their jobs. In 1998, SAJE organized USC employees, students, local clergy, community activists, and neighborhood residents as the Coalition for a Responsible USC (Haas 2002), initiating a series of protests, which included a rolling hunger strike, in support of the union's demands. After the Los Angeles City Council amended its worker retention ordinance in 1999 to prevent recipients of city economic development funds, like USC, from firing workers within ninety days of contracting out their work, the dispute was settled, with USC retaining the right to subcontract, but agreeing to a consultation process with the union in order to avoid doing so.

The USC campaign reinforced community–labor relationships, highlighting the common economic concerns of union and nonunion community residents and forging a sense of shared purpose among local block clubs, churches, and other community organizations that had not previously worked together. The campaign also led to changes in the coalition itself. As news stories began to circulate in 1999 about plans to further redevelop the area around the Staples Center, the coalition expanded its mission to focus on development pressures in the Figueroa Corridor, formally restructuring as the Figueroa Corridor Coalition for Economic Justice (FCCEJ) (Haas 2002).

The announcement in May 2000 by the owners of the Staples Center of plans to develop a Los Angeles Sports and Entertainment District adjacent to the arena set FCCEJ into motion on what would become its first major campaign. The plans for the proposed four million square foot, one billion dollar project—known as "L.A. Live"—included a forty-five story 1,200-room convention center hotel (with 100 condominium units) to be located directly north of the Staples Center, a second smaller 300-room high-end hotel, two apartment towers consisting of 800 units, a 7,400-seat live theater, restaurants, nightclubs, an office tower, a 40,000 square foot open-air plaza, and a 250,000 square foot Convention Center expansion. When the project was announced, FCCEJ initiated a community planning process and SAJE began organizing neighborhood tenants in buildings in the area of the proposed Sports and Entertainment District.

Then came the Democratic National Convention at the Staples Center in August 2000. The convention itself, though mostly peaceful, was marked by ugly moments, with armored police using rubber bullets and pepper spray in clashes with protesters in cordoned-off streets. After the convention ended, FCCEJ intensified its community organizing efforts, convening meetings at the First United Methodist Church for community members upset about the convention violence, as well as the ongoing nuisance of reckless drivers, unruly fans, vandalism, and increased parking tickets that were the byproducts of Staples Center events. By the time that FCCEJ held its first annual assembly meeting in late 2000, the focus of the coalition began to crystallize around one goal: forcing the Staples Center developers to address community needs in their plans for the Sports and Entertainment District. As this campaign began to take shape, FCCEJ expanded to its full size of twenty-nine organizations and approximately 300 residents. Reflecting the broad range of community concerns at stake, there were several categories of groups, which included *economic justice organizations* like SAJE and LAANE, the *environmental group* Environmental Defense, *community organizing groups* like the Association of Community Organizations for Reform Now (ACORN), Action for Grassroots Empowerment and Neighborhood Development Alternatives (AGENDA), and the community coalition; *community services groups; churches; housing and community development organizations* such as Esperanza Community Housing Corporation; *health advocacy groups; immigrant rights groups* like the Coalition for Humane Immigrant Rights of Los Angeles and the Central American Resource Center; *neighborhood groups;* the *student group* Student Coalition Against Labor Exploitation; and the *unions* HERE Local 11, and SEIU Local 1877.

Campaign

FCCEJ's relationship with the local unions proved to be one of its critical points of leverage with the developer, L.A. Arena Land Company. The FCCEJ campaign occurred against the backdrop of labor negotiations between the developer and five unions—HERE Local 11, SEIU Local 1877, Operating Engineers Local 501, Teamsters Local 911, and the International Alliance of Local Stage Employees Local 33—which were attempting to secure union contracts on the project. In contrast to the separate negotiations each union conducted during the original Staples Center development, the unions entered the negotiations on the Sports and Entertainment District project committed to a united front, agreeing under the leadership of the Los Angeles County Federation of Labor that "no one would sign an agreement until everyone had an agreement to sign" (Haas 2002: 93). Eager to demonstrate that labor and community groups could work together to achieve broad gains for working people, the five unions and the Federation, whose leaders had strong connections to LAANE and other coalition members, agreed to support FCCEJ in its own negotiations for community benefits. As a sign of union support, a labor representative was present at all of the meetings between L.A. Arena Land Company and FCCEJ. Meanwhile, as the unions worked to advance the goals of FCCEJ, LAANE was making efforts to help organize the unions.

The developer, which understood that organized labor's influence with local government officials could jeopardize city approval of the deal in the event of labor strife, was eager to reach an accord with the unions that would move the project forward. Not concerned with FCCEJ as such, the developer was nevertheless forced to recognize the coalition's concerns in order to garner the support of the unions that had come out behind FCCEJ's efforts. Although union leverage brought FCCEJ to the table with the developer, it also constrained its options in responding to the proposed project. Because the union partners were concerned with seeing through a project that would create jobs for their members, there were strong pressures on FCCEJ to negotiate a deal. In this process, FCCEJ could wield the threat of delay, but any expression of outright opposition to the project would have risked union support and weakened its bargaining position.

FCCEJ therefore focused its campaign on the negotiation of a CBA—a legally binding contract under which the developer provides specific community benefits in exchange for the coalition's promise to support the project (Gross, LeRoy, and Janis-Aparicio 2005). The CBA idea grew out of different strands of activism. Its formal legal structure mirrored the types of agreements entered into in the Community Reinvestment Act context, where community organizations commit to supporting bank applications for mergers or branch relocations in front of federal regulators in exchange for bank promises to increase loan activity and banking services in poor neighborhoods. SAJE's executive director Gilda Haas, who had been an organizer for the Center for Community Change, had extensive experience negotiating agreements such and brought expertise on this approach to the CBA process. The concept of the CBA—which used the leverage afforded by future developments to exact developer concessions—grew directly out of the strategy pioneered by the HERE and the SEIU, which used such an approach in their efforts to win card check neutrality and living wage jobs for immigrant workers.

A series of agreements between government entities and developers to target benefits to low-income communities also proved to be important precedents for CBAs (see Liegeois and Carson 2003: 174). In 1998, the public transit authority overseeing the Alameda Corridor transportation project—a twenty-mile railway linking the ports of Los Angeles and Long Beach with downtown Los Angeles—bowed to community organizing pressure in requiring the project's general contractor to provide $5 million for job training and to set aside construction jobs for low-income residents (Liegeois, Baxa, and Corkrey 1999:

290). That same year, LAANE worked to incorporate a community benefits package—which included provisions for living wage jobs, card check neutrality, local hiring, and job training—into the city's agreement with the developer of a large entertainment and retail project in Hollywood (Los Angeles Alliance for a New Economy 2005; Erskine and Marblestone 2006). Then, in 1999, AGENDA successfully pressured the Los Angeles City Council to require Dreamworks to fund a job training and placement program for low-income workers in exchange for public subsidies approved for the development of a new Dreamworks studio (Liegeois, Baxa, and Corkrey 1999: 286–89). However, the tactic of embedding community benefits within agreements between developers and the city did not include a mechanism for direct enforcement by community organizations, instead relying on government officials to hold developers to their obligations—which, after subsidies were awarded and projects were built, they often had little incentive to do. In response to this problem, LAANE came up with the idea of the CBA in connection with organizing it began in 2000 around a proposed mixed-use project next to the North Hollywood subway station, which was to receive public subsidies. That organizing eventually resulted in a CBA in late 2001, but not until after events had thrust the Sports and Entertainment District CBA to the fore.

As FCCEJ entered its crucial negotiation phase in 2001, its leverage against the developer was structured by law in key ways. First, there was the issue of term limits. In 1993, Los Angeles voters passed propositions restricting the mayor and City Council members to two four-year terms. That meant that Republican Mayor Richard Riordan, a staunch supporter of the project who had pushed the City Planning Commission for fast-track permitting approvals, was set to be termed out of office as of July 1, 2001, with a very tight run-off race underway between Democrats James Hahn and Antonio Villaraigosa, a strong pro-labor candidate (Padwa 2001). In addition, City Council—which also supported the Sports and Entertainment District—was about to be transformed, with six of its fifteen members—including Council member Rita Walters, whose district encompassed the project—termed out. As a result, the developer was pressing to secure all city entitlements before July 1, 2001, which meant ensuring that FCCEJ was on board and would not delay key approvals.

In addition to the leverage gained from timing, FCCEJ benefited from public participation rights embedded in the legal process for approving development. California state law sets the legal framework governing how cities structure the process of granting development entitlements such as land use and building ap-provals. In Los Angeles, developers typically must go through the City Planning Commission to obtain discretionary land use approvals, with a process for appeal to the City Council generally available. The structure of the entitlements process permits well-organized opposition groups with strong political connections to delay or even prevent key approvals. With labor unions as coalition members, FCCEJ could make a credible threat of disrupting the entitlements process for the Sports and Entertainment District deal, which would have increased costs and uncertainty for the developer. Moreover, the deal was from the beginning based on the assumption of public financing, which could only be approved by City Council after public hearings, providing another political opportunity for FCCEJ and its union supporters to disrupt the deal.

FCCEJ used the threat of disruption implicit in its participation rights to bring the developer to the negotiating table, where the goal was to hammer out a CBA. It was here that lawyers contributed key skills in moving negotiations forward and finalizing the agreement. Julian Gross was the coalition attorney primarily responsible for drafting the CBA. Gross had started out as a Skadden Fellow at the Employment Law Center in San Francisco, where he worked on developing the local hiring policy for the redevelopment agency in East Palo Alto and was involved in the Alameda Corridor Jobs Coalition project in Los Angeles. In 1999, Gross set up his own solo practice and began working with LAANE on the North Hollywood mixed-use development CBA campaign. When the Sports and Entertainment District deal was announced, Gross was retained by LAANE to represent the group and generally provided legal support to the negotiation team throughout the process.

The negotiation team itself was selected by FCCEJ members on the basis of expertise and negotiating skill. The key members were SAJE's Gilda Haas and Madeline Janis-Aparicio, the executive director of LAANE. Although not an attorney, Haas, who had a master's degree in Urban Planning from UCLA, had started the CED unit at the Los Angeles Legal Aid Foundation. Janis-Aparicio was a nonpracticing attorney who had previously done slum housing litigation and, after graduating from UCLA Law School, had worked as an associate at the Los Angeles firm of Latham & Watkins (which was representing the developer against FCCEJ in the CBA negotiations). The stringent criteria for selection to the negotiating team excluded Figueroa Corridor residents. To address this omission, FCCEJ put together a team of neighborhood leaders who attended all of the meetings with the developer, provided feedback on developer proposals, and conveyed information on the process back to the community (Leavitt 2006).

Another lawyer on the negotiating team who played an important role was Jerilyn López Mendoza, a graduate of UCLA Law School with law firm experience, who was an attorney in the Environmental Justice Project at Environmental Defense. In California, the process for gaining environmental clearance for development projects centers on the California Environmental Quality Act (CEQA), which requires that a public agency, such as the City Planning Commission, evaluate the environmental impact of projects before issuing discretionary development approvals or providing public subsidies. If the project is determined to have a significant environmental impact, an environmental impact report (EIR) must be prepared and circulated for public comment. The final approval of a project may be challenged in court on the grounds that it does not meet the substantive and procedural requirements of CEQA, forcing the agency to repeat the EIR process.

Knowing that a defective EIR could significantly delay the project, the FCCEJ environmental team, coordinated by López Mendoza, carefully reviewed the developer's draft EIR when it was issued in January 2001. FCCEJ's comprehensive forty-six-page response to the draft EIR was submitted to the City Planning Commission in late February highlighting a number of inadequacies, including the developer's failure to include an analysis of the energy impact of the project, which—coming on the heels of Southern California's 2000 energy crisis—was a significant omission. With the prospect of a CEQA lawsuit that could derail the project until well after the July 1 political transition suddenly a realistic possibility, the developer responded by intensifying the pace of negotiations with FCCEJ.

A final agreement was reached between FCCEJ and the developer on May 30, 2001. Under the agreement, FCCEJ agreed both to release its right to oppose the development project (which included bringing lawsuits, taking administrative actions, and expressing public opposition) and to provide affirmative support for the project (which included issuing a press release and testifying in support of administrative approvals). There was a split over the final terms of the agreement, with AGENDA and the Community Coalition refusing to sign on as Coalition members, citing the waiver of the right to oppose the project as incompatible with their organizational missions. This created a problem for the developer, which wanted to make sure that a few close FCCEJ allies could not opt out of the agreement and protest the project, while the developer bore the full contractual obligations. This was dealt with by designating FCCEJ members that did not sign the agreement as Interested Organizations, which—although technically not bound to the agreement—could nevertheless relieve the developer of its community benefits obligations by bringing a suit against the project. In exchange for FCCEJ's cooperation, the developer agreed to the following Community Benefits Program, which was also incorporated as part of the development agreement between the city and the developer:

- *Parks and Recreation*: The developer shall provide between $50,000 and $75,000 to fund "an assessment of the need for parks, open space, and recreational facilities" in the area and subsequently "fund or cause to be privately funded at least one million dollars ($1,000,000) for the creation or improvement of one or more park and recreation facilities."
- *Parking Permit Area*: The developer shall "support" FCCEJ's efforts to have the city establish a residential parking permit district, providing funding of $25,000 per year for five years to the city to develop and implement the program.
- *Living Wage Program*: The developer "shall make all reasonable efforts to maximize the number of living wage jobs" in the project and agree to a 70 percent Living Wage Goal for the anticipated 5,500 jobs.
- *Local Hiring and Job Training*: The developer shall provide $100,000 in seed funding to establish a First Source Referral System, a nonprofit organization that will recruit targeted job applicants—giving first priority to applicants displaced by the Staples Center or living within a one-half mile radius of the project—and refer them to project employers. The employers, in turn, will provide notice of job openings to the First Source Referral System and agree to hire only targeted job applicants for a designated period of time after notice of the jobs are provided. An employer who fills 50 percent of available jobs within a six-month period with targeted job applicants shall be deemed in compliance with the first source hiring policy.
- *Affordable Housing*: The developer "shall develop or cause to be developed affordable housing equal to 20% of the units constructed" within the project (100–160 affordable units in total). The units shall be targeted as follows: 30 percent to families earning 50 percent or less of Area Median Income (AMI); 35 percent to families earning from 51 to 60 percent of AMI; and 35 percent to families earning from 61 to 80 percent of AMI. Units may be built within the project area or off-site, provided that off-site housing is located "in redevelopment areas within a three-mile radius" of the Staples Center. Residents displaced by the Staples Center shall be given priority in housing selection. In addition, the developer must work cooperatively with community organizations to provide additional affordable housing by contributing up to $650,000 in three-year, interest-free loans to nonprofit housing developers that are building projects in the area.

Despite the timeliness of the CBA, the project itself did not receive the sought-after approval before the July 1 political transition because newly elected City Council members asked for a delay so that they could review the deal. The city made a number of attempts to move the project forward, which culminated with the 2005 approval of a $177 million subsidy for the hotel, consisting of up to $140 million in foregone revenue from hotel bed taxes, $22 million in city loans, $10 million in public improvements, and $5 million in building fees. Although construction is not set for completion until 2008, the developer has already made good on some of its CBA promises. In particular, the developer has gained commitments for nearly $1 million to fund Hope and Peace Park and a free family recreational facility in the neighborhood (Leavitt 2006). The developer also assisted in the establishment of Los Angeles's first Poor People's Preferential Parking District, which reserves evening parking for local residents, and paid for the first five years of resident permits (Leavitt 2006). The developer further provided $650,000 in low-interest loans to community-based affordable housing developers (Leavitt 2006), which have already opened some affordable units.

Implementation of the CBA, however, has not been without difficulty. The main issue has involved the application of affordable housing obligations to developers that have purchased discrete parcels within the project from L.A. Arena Land Company. In September 2005, one such developer, Williams and Dame, asked the city to be relieved of its affordable housing obligations in light of a preexisting agreement to contribute $8,000,000 toward the YWCA's development of an affordable housing project in the downtown area. After a flurry of negotiations, the parties agreed to a plan under which Williams and Dame was given credit for 200 units of affordable housing in exchange for a $400,000 contribution to the Figueroa Corridor Community Land Trust—an entity that FCCEJ had already established to build affordable housing in the neighborhood—as well as a commitment by Williams and Dame to potentially contribute another $700,000 in connection with future development. In addition, the parties agreed going forward that new purchasers of development rights in the Sports and Entertainment District may discharge their affordable housing obligations by providing a $40,000 payment for each required affordable unit to the Land Trust or other community-based developer in the Figueroa Corridor—an arrangement that could generate several million dollars in contributions.

FCCEJ's success in negotiating the Sports and Entertainment District CBA has lent momentum to related accountable development campaigns and policy initiatives. One direct outgrowth is the Share the Wealth Coalition, a joint organizing effort by FCCEJ and the LA Coalition to End Hunger and Homelessness, which has advocated for the rights of residential hotel tenants while promoting inclusionary zoning and policies to prevent the net loss of affordable housing in the central core of downtown Los Angeles. In addition, there have been a series of subsequent CBAs negotiated in Los Angeles and elsewhere, the most significant of which was the recent agreement between Los Angeles World Airports, the city department that owns and operates the Los Angeles International Airport (LAX), and a coalition of school districts, churches, environmental organizations, and labor groups that earmarked nearly $500 million for sound-proofing homes and businesses, setting up job training programs, and conducting environmental studies in connection with the modernization of LAX (LAX Coalition 2004). Finally, there has been an effort to convert the success of the CBA strategy into local policy reforms (Goodno, 2004). In Los Angeles, community groups pushed the CRA to adopt a Community Impact Report policy, which would have required developers within redevelopment project areas to take into account the impact of projects on affordable housing and jobs along the lines of the current environmental review system, but that proposal was tabled after strong developer opposition. The California Partnership for Working Families—an accountable development coalition that includes LAANE and similar community–labor organizations across the state—has been working to pass community benefits policies in San Diego, San Jose, and Emeryville.

Cause Lawyering and Community Mobilization

As the FCCEJ case study shows, accountable development advocacy attempts to confront government and market elites, create alliances and build networks, and change the rules of the game for redevelopment practice. In contrast to the "deal" orientation of conventional CED, accountable development focuses on local campaigns to mobilize low-income communities to achieve organizing "wins." It therefore presents distinct roles for cause lawyers who must navigate a complex set of organizational relationships and deploy a range of lawyering skills to advance mobilization goals. Drawing upon the lessons from the FCCEJ campaign, this part examines cause lawyering in the accountable development context, focusing on issues of professional role, legal tactics, and the impact of lawyering on community mobilization.

Professional Role

The picture of cause lawyering that emerges from the FCCEJ case resonates with Hilbink's (Hilbink 2004: 681) description of the grassroots cause lawyer focused on politically sophisticated advocacy that supports mobilization around community-defined goals (see Kilwein 1998). In the FCCEJ campaign, lawyers were viewed as one set of political actors who knew their role and used their skills to advance strategic ends, deploying rights when necessary, but also recognizing when to back off from rights tactics to build alliances, broker deals, and craft policy.

In this context, typical concerns about the disempowering impact of legal expertise on client mobilization were diminished for two reasons. One was the self-conception of the lawyers. FCCEJ lawyers Gross and López Mendoza adopted a complex view of social change, with legal and political advocacy seen as complementary strategies—the utility of each dependent on the particular context of struggle. Instead of top-down legal strategists, they viewed themselves as team members who attempted to cede as much control as possible to the organizers, providing technical expertise only to the limited extent necessary to advance the organizing goal. They were, in short, quite mindful of the critique of public interest lawyering and careful not to repeat mistakes of the past.

The other factor constraining lawyer domination was the presence of a powerful and politically savvy leadership structure for the coalition. Although the strength of the leadership structure created accountability issues as between the coalition leaders and their constituencies, it tended to insulate the leadership itself from undue influence by outside lawyers. Moreover, in the FCCEJ campaign, the existence of relatively powerful grassroots organizations counteracted the tendency that Levitsky (2006) identifies for legal organizations to exert more influence in strategic decision making due to their disproportionate size and visibility. Because the FCCEJ clients came to the campaign as empowered political actors, the lawyering was focused on achieving a political result defined by the coalition rather than promoting goals envisioned by the lawyers. From a lawyering perspective, the FCCEJ campaign can therefore be read as a story about the *potency* of legal advocacy operating within its appropriate sphere: FCCEJ's success in bringing the developer to the negotiating table, for example, was premised in large part on the threat that it could, in fact, successfully litigate the environmental claims.

Although it offered advantages from the perspective of community empowerment, the existence of a multigroup coalition as client also complicated the lawyer–client relationship (see Ellman 1992). This was apparent in the complex relationships that formed in the FCCEJ campaign. There was a loosely coordinated team of lawyers with different tasks—Gross focused on CBA drafting and López Mendoza on the environmental response—with a fluid specification of roles and no systematic effort to delineate the client. The lawyers themselves brought vastly different expertise to the project: Gross was trained as an employment attorney; Janis-Aparicio had experience in labor, immigration, and housing; and López Mendoza was an environmental lawyer. And there were times in which the lawyers were both outside and inside the coalition—providing legal advice to the group in their role as attorneys while hashing out policy issues and building group consensus in their role as coalition members.

Legal Tactics

The FCCEJ campaign also provides insights into the relationship between cause lawyering tactics and community mobilization. McCann defines *legal mobilization* as the translation of "a desire or want" into "an assertion of right or lawful claim" (McCann 2004: 508). In the litigation context, legal mobilization is achieved by bringing or threatening a lawsuit. Thus, legal mobilization can be an *end* in itself—lawyers filing an impact case to get "law on the books"—or a *means* for broader *community mobilization* (McCann 2004: 508). Legal mobilization in the public interest law reform mode has been critiqued as undermining collective action (the "myth of rights"), although scholars like McCann (1994) and Gordon (2005) have documented the strategic use of legal mobilization to promote collective action (the "politics of rights"). When CED lawyers mobilize law, in contrast, they generally do so by creating *legal frameworks for community organization*—taking advantage of the background legal rules that provide financial incentives for CED projects and promote community participation in CED organizations to design nonprofit corporations, partnerships, and other associational forms that promote CED goals.

The FCCEJ accountable development campaign reveals another model of legal mobilization that shares much in common with the CED approach, but differs in notable ways. The background rules that proved most critical to the FCCEJ campaign were *rights to participate in political decision making*, particularly those embedded in the land use and environmental review process. These rights were a function of the relationship between the city and the developer, with the city providing permits and subsidies that required public approval in exchange for future tax revenues and other economic benefits provided by the project. The participation rights provided an opportunity for legal intervention by FCCEJ, which exercised its right to comment upon the developer's EIR, with the potential threat of a lawsuit to prevent an inadequate EIR from being approved. In this way, FCCEJ lawyers were able to mobilize law through the *identification and navigation of routes of legal participation* for coalition members. Because the participation rights were backed by the threat of disruption, at the EIR stage of the campaign participation took on a confrontational tone, with the coalition positioned to derail a deal supported by the city and developer. In this sense, law was mobilized through what McCann (2004: 513–14) calls "legal leveraging"—the use of law "as a weapon to 'push' otherwise uncooperative foes into making concessions." Indeed, it was the "unfulfilled threat" that FCCEJ would stall the project on the basis of the faulty environmental report, imposing substantial costs and the risk of lost political support, that ultimately forced the developer to negotiate. The ability to deploy leveraging tactics was also a function of the client itself. Unlike in the typical CED deal where the organizational client is dependent on its public and private partners for ongoing financial support, the coalition was not financially dependent on the target of its organizing campaign, which gave it greater latitude to deploy more adversarial tactics.

The confrontational approach adopted by FCCEJ in the environmental review stage gave way to greater collaboration during the process of negotiating the CBA. Julian Gross's job as FCCEJ's lawyer was to help negotiate and draft a legal document that specified the rights and obligations of the coalition and developer—creating a legal framework for community participation in the development process. From a lawyering perspective, the skills deployed during this phase of the FCCEJ campaign closely resembled those of the conventional CED lawyer. However, the context and goals of the negotiation distinguished it from the typical CED process. Unlike a negotiation between a nonprofit housing developer and a private investor brought together by mutual financial incentives, the Sports and Entertainment District developer was pressured to the negotiating table through reinforcing political and legal threats. For this reason, the negotiation process in the FCCEJ context was at times more adversarial than the typical CED development deal, where the financial incentives promote a greater sense of cooperation and *espirit de corp.*

Community Mobilization

A key feature of accountable development is that the lawyering is undertaken to support community mobilization to change the redevelopment practices of private developers and city agencies. The immediate outcome of FCCEJ's community mobilization effort was the creation of a CBA. As a structural matter, a CBA operates like a development regulation in that it forces a private developer to action it would not otherwise undertake without the threat of community disruption. This outcome is redistributive because it extracts greater resources for the community through bargaining than it would otherwise be entitled to under law. It is true that the CBA represents a net gain for the developer to the extent that it calculates the costs of providing community benefits as less than the costs of delay, litigation, and the negative publicity associated with a contested approval process. But, in the absence of community challenge, the baseline position is that the developer can undertake the project without conferring benefits on the community. An agreement is struck only after organized community opposition to the project emerges. In this case, coordinated community participation constrains the developer's range of action, leveraging the background development rules in such a way that induces an agreement.

The CBA, however, is a complex tool—one that is highly dependent on the framework of governmental regulation of redevelopment while exposing its shortcomings. Although it operates within the domain of private law, the CBA strategy depends on state-created participation rights to confer negotiating power on community groups. The existing framework of legal rights thus operates to help induce negotiation, with the resulting CBA augmenting the current redevelopment regulatory scheme. The benefits of the CBA approach are that it constructs a public–private monitoring and enforcement mechanism. It allows both the community—through the CBA—and the city—through a development agreement that incorporates the CBA's terms—to watch over developer compliance and intervene to promote accountability. And even though many of the provisions do not provide for hard enforcement mechanisms, the goals and standards incorporated in the CBA provide political resources that can be used to pressure developer compliance by generating negative publicity when they are not met. From this perspective, the CBA highlights many of the advantages emphasized in the new literature on public–private collaboration (Lobel 2004; Simon 2004).

Yet the emphasis on multiple stakeholder accountability and the reliance on community persuasion to enforce benefits also raises questions about what is won and lost. For instance, the living wage provision in the FCCEJ CBA requires that the developer use best efforts, imposes flexible benchmarks, and creates mechanisms for dispute resolution. Ultimately, failure to comply with the 70 percent living wage goal does not breach the agreement. Instead, the CBA provides that even if the living wage goal is not met, developer compliance is presumed so long as it makes annual living wage reports (detailing the problems of meeting the living wage goal), notifies the coalition before selecting project tenants, meets with the coalition and prospective tenants to discuss living wage requirements, and "within commercially reasonable limits" takes into account "as a substantial factor" the impact of tenant selection on the living wage goal. Similarly, the CBA's first source hiring policy provides that businesses that do not meet the goal of hiring 50 percent of its workers from a pool of local applicants nevertheless are in compliance with the policy so long as they keep records, provide timely notice of job openings, and hold positions for targeted applicants open for designated periods.

In addition, although the FCCEJ CBA imposes strict support obligations on the coalition, the developer is allowed great flexibility in implementing benefits and in some cases is relieved of the direct obligation to fund aspects of the CBA. The provision for park and open space is an example. The developer was able to negotiate an agreement to "fund or cause to be privately funded" one million dollars for park space, which meant that it could use its foundation connections—which it did—to raise money for park construction without having to be out of pocket for the costs. Another example is the affordable housing provision, which requires the developer to "develop or cause to be developed" 20 percent of the total project units as affordable housing. Here again, the developer could use its access to philanthropic sources to reduce its out-of-pocket development costs. In addition, to the extent that nonprofit housing organizations build affordable units in the area with the assistance of interest-free loans provided by the developer, the developer's obligation to build units directly may be reduced, although not below 15 percent of the total units in the project. Thus, the strong bargaining power of the developer allowed it to negotiate a relatively soft set of obligations in exchange for a complete waiver of opposition rights by the coalition. From a regulatory perspective, then, the CBA could be read as a second-best solution reflecting the relative political weakness of accountable development actors to enact change through conventional political channels.

Moreover, the ultimate effect of the CBA approach on the mobilization of low-income communities is uncertain. Accountable development campaigns, although activating coalitions to move on targeted development projects, ultimately result in a waiver of the coalition's mobilization rights in exchange for the material benefits contained in the CBA. In the FCCEJ context, this caused AGENDA and the Community Coalition to split off, refusing to waive their power to disrupt in exchange for the benefits provided in the settlement agreement. Rights-stripping CBA's may be the necessary byproduct of a mobilization strategy premised on the threat of disruption, but the constraining effect runs counter to the ideological goals of many of the grassroots organizations involved. The FCCEJ CBA also raises questions about community accountability. Although community members actively participated in the formulation of FCCEJ's demands and attended negotiation meetings, it was inevitable in the heat of high-level negotiations under intense time pressure that community participation had to be compromised. There are also questions about the degree to which the CBA assigns financial rewards to groups involved in its negotiation, raising concerns about trading support for the promise of economic benefits (see Simon 2001: 182).

The longer term goals of accountable development advocacy seek to address some of the short-term trade-offs. FCCEJ and other accountable development coalitions around the state of California remain focused on the goal of passing community benefits policies, as well as other reforms such as no net loss housing policies guaranteeing that redevelopment does not result in the overall loss of affordable housing. More broadly, there are efforts to build upon the success of individual CBAs to deepen organizational connections, expand community resources, and develop higher level coordination in order to exert a sustained political influence over development decisions. LAANE has provided some coordination of CBA campaigns in the Los Angeles area, while the California Partnership for Working Families has emerged as a vehicle for statewide coordination. One consequence of these efforts has been that developers in Los Angeles now recognize that negotiating over community benefits is part of the overall redevelopment process. However, due in part to the local nature of redevelopment, accountable development continues to be a decentralized movement, comprising a fluid network of individuals and organizations that share information and strategies, but as of yet do not closely collaborate to promote accountable development as a national strategy.

It therefore remains to be seen whether accountable development can move beyond the particular circumstances of Los Angeles and take root in other urban centers and smaller scale jurisdictions. And it is an open question whether or not the CBA as a legal tactic—one that is embedded in the existing framework of legal rights—can help to fundamentally alter power relations between community groups and the development industry over the long term. Yet, particularly as accountable development strategies are diffused through organizing networks and CED practice groups, the role of lawyers in disseminating models, sharing resources, and experimenting with different tactical approaches will be crucial to efforts to build a movement that is national in scope.

References

Abel, Richard L. 1985. "Lawyers and the Power to Change." *Law and Policy* 7: 5.

Alfieri, Anthony V. 1991. "Reconstructive Poverty Law Practice: Learning the Lessons of Client Narrative." *Yale Law Journal* 101: 2107.

Amenta, Edwin and Caren, Neal. 2004. "The Legislative, Organizational, and Beneficiary Consequences of State-Oriented Challengers." In *The Blackwell Companion to Social Movements*, David A. Snow, Sarah A. Soule and Hanspeter Kriesi, eds. Malden, MA: Blackwell Publishing.

Anderson, Martin. 1964. *The Federal Bulldozer: A Critical Analysis of Urban Renewal 1949–1962*. Cambridge, MA: M.I.T. Press.

Barkan, Steven E. 1984. "Legal Control of the Southern Civil Rights Movement." *American Sociological Review* 49: 552.

Barron, David J. 2003. "The Community Economic Development Movement: A Metropolitan Perspective." *Stanford Law Review* 56: 701.

Bell, Derrick. 1976. "Serving Two Masters: Integration Ideals and Client Interests." *Yale Law Journal* 85: 470.

Community Scholars Program. 2004. *A "Just" Redevelopment: Lessons from the Figueroa Corridor Coalition for Economic Justice.* University of California, Los Angeles, School of Public Policy and Social Research, Department of Urban Planning.

Cummings, Scott L. 2001. "Community Economic Development as Progressive Politics: Toward a Grassroots Movement for Economic Justice." *Stanford Law Review* 54: 399.

Cummings, Scott L. and Eagly, Ingrid V. 2001. "A Critical Reflection on Law and Organizing." *UCLA Law Review* 48: 443.

Diamond, Michael. 2000. "Community Lawyering: Revisiting the Old Neighborhood." *Columbia Human Rights Law Review* 32: 67.

Dotan, Yoav. 2001. "The Global Language of Human Rights: Patterns of Cooperation between State and Civil Right Lawyers in Israel." In *Cause Lawyering and the State in a Global Era*, Austin Sarat and Stuart Scheingold, eds. New York: Oxford University Press.

Dreier, Peter. 1999. "Power, Money, and Politics in Community Development." In *Urban Problems and Community Development*, Ronald F. Ferguson and William T. Dickens, eds. Washington, DC: Brookings Institution Press.

Edwards, Bob and McCarthy, John D. 2004. "Resources and Social Movement Mobilization." In *The Blackwell Companion to Social Movements*, David A. Snow, Sarah A. Soule, and Hanspeter Kriesi, eds. Malden, MA: Blackwell Publishing.

Ellman, Stephen. 1992. "Client-Centeredness Multiplied: Individual Autonomy and Collective Mobilization in Public Interest Lawyers' Representation of Groups." *Virginia Law Review* 78: 1103.

Erskine, Kathleen and Marblestone, Judy. 2006. "The Role of Lawyers in Santa Monica's Struggle for a Living Wage." In *Cause Lawyers and Social Movements*, Austin Sarat and Stuart Scheingold, eds. Palo Alto, CA: Stanford University Press.

Foster-Bey, John. 1997. "Bridging Communities: Making the Link Between Regional Economies and Local Community Development." *Stanford Law and Policy Review* 8: 25.

Freeman, Jody. 1997. "Collaborative Governance in the Administrative State." *UCLA Law Review* 45: 1.

———. 2000. "The Private Role in Public Governance." *New York University Law Review* 75: 543.

Gabel, Peter and Harris, Paul. 1982–1983. "Building Power and Breaking Images: Critical Legal Theory and the Practice of Law." *New York University Review of Law and Social Change* 11: 369.

Gibbons, Andrea and Haas, Gilda. 2002. *Redefining Redevelopment: Participatory Research for Equity in the Los Angeles Figueroa Corridor.* Department of Urban Planning, School of Public Policy and Social Research, University of California, Los Angeles, available at http://www.saje.net/publications/redefineredevelopment.pdf (last accessed February 8, 2006).

Glick, Brian and Rossman, Matthew J. 1997. "Neighborhood Legal Services as House Counsel to Community-Based Efforts to Achieve Economic Justice: The East Brooklyn Experience." *New York University Review of Law and Social Change* 23: 105.

Goodno, James B. 2004. "Feet to the Fire: Accountable Development Keeps Developers and Community Groups Talking—and Walking." *Planning*, available at http://www.laane.org/pressroom/stories/ad/ad0403planning.html (last accessed March 13, 2006).

Gordon, Jennifer. 1995. "We Make the Road by Walking: Immigrant Workers, the Workplace Project, and the Struggle for Social Change." *Harvard Civil Rights-Civil Liberties Law Review* 30: 407.

———. 2005. *Suburban Sweatshops: The Fight for Immigrant Rights*. Cambridge, MA: Harvard University Press.

Gross, Julian with LeRoy, Greg and Janis-Aparicio, Madeline. 2005. *Community Benefits Agreements: Making Development Projects Accountable*, available at http://www.californiapartnership.org/downloads/CBA%20Handbook%202005%20 final.pdf (last accessed March 13, 2006).

Haas, Gilda. 2002. "Economic Justice in the Los Angeles Figueroa Corridor." In *Teaching for Change: Popular Education and the Labor Movement*, Linda Delp, Miranda Outman-Kramer, Susan J. Schurman, and Kent Wong, eds. Los Angeles: UCLA Center for Labor Research and Education.

Halpern, Robert. 1995. *Rebuilding the Inner City: A History of Neighborhood Initiatives to Address Poverty in the United States*. New York: Columbia University Press.

Handler, Joel F. 1978. *Social Movements and the Legal System: A Theory of Law Reform and Social Change*. New York: Academic Press.

———. 1996. *Down From Bureaucracy: The Ambiguity of Privatization and Empowerment*. Princeton, NJ: Princeton University Press.

Handler, Joel F. and Hasenfeld, Yeheskel. 1997. *We the Poor People: Work, Poverty, and Welfare*. New Haven, CT: Yale University Press.

Handler, Joel F., Hollingsworth, Ellen Jane, and Erlanger, Howard S. 1978. *Lawyers and the Pursuit of Legal Rights*. New York: Academic Press.

Hilbink, Thomas M. 2004. "You Know the Type . . . : Categories of Cause Lawyering." *Law and Social Inquiry* 29: 657.

Jenkins, J. Craig. 1983. "Resource Mobilization Theory and the Study of Social Movements." *Annual Review of Sociology* 9: 527.

Kilwein, John. 1998. "Still Trying: Cause Lawyering for the Poor and Disadvantaged in Pittsburgh, Pennsylvania." In *Cause Lawyering: Political Commitments and Professional Responsibilities*, Austin Sarat and Stuart Scheingold, eds. New York: Oxford University Press.

Kriesi, Hanspeter. 2004. "Political Context and Opportunity." In *The Blackwell Companion to Social Movements*, David A. Snow, Sarah A. Soule, and Hanspeter Kriesi, eds. Malden, MA: Blackwell Publishing.

LAX Coalition for Economic, Environmental, and Educational Justice. 2004. "Highlights of the LAX Community Benefits Agreement." *Environmental Defense*, available at http://www.environmentaldefense.org/documents/4174_LAX_CBA_Summary.pdf (last accessed February 8, 2006).

Leavitt, Jacqueline. 2006. "Linking Housing to Community Economic Development with Community Benefits Agreements: The Case of the Figueroa Corridor Coalition for Economic Justice." In *Jobs and Economic Development in Minority Communities*, Paul Ong and Anastasia Loukaitou-Sideris, eds. Philadelphia, PA: Temple University Press.

Lento, Rochelle E. 1994. "Community Development Banking Strategy for Revitalizing Our Communities." *University of Michigan Journal of Law Reform* 27: 773.

Levitsky, Sandra R. 2006. "To Lead with Law: Reassessing the Influence of Legal Advocacy Organizations in Social Movements." In *Cause Lawyers and Social Movements*, Austin Sarat and Stuart Scheingold, eds. Palo Alto, CA: Stanford University Press.

Liegeois, Nona and Carson, Malcolm. 2003. "Accountable Development: Maximizing Community Benefits from Publicly Supported Development." *Clearinghouse Review* 37: 174.

Liegeois, Nona, Baxa, Francisca, and Corkrey, Barbara. 1999. "Helping Low-Income People Get Decent Jobs: One Legal Services Program's Approach." *Clearinghouse Review* 33: 279.

Lobel, Orly. 2004. "The Renew Deal." *Minnesota Law Review* 89: 342.

López, Gerald P. 1992. *Rebellious Lawyering: One Chicano's Vision of Progressive Law Practice*. Boulder, CO: Westview Press.

Los Angeles Alliance for a New Economy. 2005. "Victories." Los Angeles Alliance for a New Economy, Accountable Development, available at http://www.laane.org/ad/victories.html (last accessed February 8, 2006).

Luban, David. 2003. "Taking Out the Adversary: The Assault on Progressive Public-Interest Lawyers." *California Law Review* 91: 209.

Marsico, Richard D. 1995. "Working for Social Change and Preserving Client Autonomy: Is There a Role for 'Facilitative' Lawyering." *Clinical Law Review* 1: 639.

McAdam, Doug. 1982. *Political Process and the Development of Black Insurgency, 1930–1970*. Chicago: University of Chicago Press.

McCann, Michael W. 1994. *Rights at Work: Pay Equity Reform and the Politics of Legal Mobilization*. Chicago: University of Chicago Press.

———. 1998. "How Does Law Matter for Social Movements?" In *How Does Law Matter?* Bryant G. Garth and Austin Sarat, eds. Evanston, IL: Northwestern University Press.

———. 2004. "Law and Social Movements." In *The Blackwell Companion to Law and Society*, Austin Sarat, ed. Malden, MA: Blackwell Publishing Ltd.

McCann, Michael and Dudas, Jeffrey. 2006. "Backlash: Mapping the Changing Context of Movement Lawyering." In *Cause Lawyers and Social Movements*, Austin Sarat and Stuart Scheingold, eds. Palo Alto, CA: Stanford University Press.

Medoff, Peter and Sklar, Holly. 1994. *Streets of Hope: The Decline and Rise of an Urban Neighborhood*. Boston, MA: South End Press.

Minow, Martha. 2002. *Partners, Not Rivals: Privatization and the Public Good*. Boston, MA: Beacon Press.

Morris, Aldon. 1984. *The Origins of the Civil Rights Movement: Black Communities Organizing for Change*. New York: The Free Press.

National Congress for Community Economic Development. 1999. *Coming of Age: Trends and Achievements of Community-Based Development Organizations*. Washington, DC.

Padwa, Howard. 2001. "Development for the People." *The Labor Research Association On-line*, available at http://www.laborresearch.org/story2.php/44 (last accessed February 8, 2006).

Pindell, Ngai. 2003. "Is There Hope for HOPE VI?: Community Development and Localism." *Connecticut Law Review* 35: 385.

Rosenberg, Gerald N. 1991. *The Hollow Hope: Can Courts Bring About Social Change?* Chicago: University of Chicago Press.

Scheingold, Stuart A. 1974. *The Politics of Rights: Lawyers, Public Policy, and Political Change.* New Haven, CT: Yale University Press.

Scheingold, Stuart A. and Sarat, Austin. 2004. *Something to Believe In: Politics, Professionalism, and Cause Lawyering.* Stanford, CA: Stanford University Press.

Simon, William H. 2001. *The Community Economic Development Movement: Law, Business, and the New Social Policy.* Durham, NC: Duke University Press.

———. 2004. "Solving Problems vs. Claiming Rights: The Pragmatist Challenge to Legal Liberalism." *William and Mary Law Review* 46: 127.

Shah, Daniel. 1999. "Lawyering for Empowerment: Community Development and Social Change." *Clinical Law Review* 6: 217.

Snow, David A., Soule, Sarah A., and Kriesi, Hanspeter. 2004. "Mapping the Terrain." In *The Blackwell Companion to Social Movements*, David A. Snow, Sarah A. Soule and Hanspeter Kriesi, eds. Malden, MA: Blackwell Publishing.

Southworth, Ann. 1996. "Business Planning for the Destitute? Lawyers as Facilitators in Civil Rights and Poverty Practice." *Wisconsin Law Review* 1996: 1121.

———. 1999. "Collective Representation for the Disadvantaged: Variations in Problems of Accountability." *Fordham Law Review* 67: 2449.

———. 2005. "Conservative Lawyers and the Contest over the Meaning of 'Public Interest Law.'" *UCLA Law Review* 52: 1223.

Stoecker, Randy. 1997. "The CDC Model of Urban Redevelopment: A Critique and an Alternative." *Journal of Urban Affairs* 19: 1.

Stone, Katherine V.W. 2004. *From Widgets to Digits: Employment Regulation for the Changing Workplace.* Cambridge, UK: Cambridge University Press.

Strategic Actions for a Just Economy. 2005. "Welcome to SAJE". Strategic Actions for a Just Economy, SAJE.net, available at http://www.saje.net/index.php (last accessed February 8, 2006).

Trubek, Louise G. 2005. "Crossing Boundaries: Legal Education and the Challenge of the 'New Public Interest Law.'" *Wisconsin Law Review* 2005: 455.

Vidal, Avis C. 1992. *Rebuilding Communities: A National Study of Urban Community Development Corporations.* New York: Community Development Research Center, Graduate School of Management and Urban Policy, New School for Social Research.

Weisbrod, Burton A. 1978. "Conceptual Perspective on the Public Interest: An Economic Analysis." In *Public Interest Law: An Economic and Institutional Analysis*, Burton A. Weisbrod with Joel F. Handler and Neil K. Komesar, eds. Berkeley, CA: University of California Press.

White, Lucie E. 1990. "Subordination, Rhetorical Survival Skills, and Sunday Shoes: Notes on the Hearing of Mrs. G." *Buffalo Law Review* 38: 1.

Zabin, Carol and Martin, Isaac. 1999. *Living Wage Campaigns in the Economic Policy Arena: Four Case Studies from California*, available at http://www.iir.berkeley.edu/livingwage/pdf/livwage.pdf (last accessed February 8, 2006).

Ziv, Neta. 2001. "Cause Lawyers, Clients, and the State: Congress as a Forum for Cause Lawyering during the Enactment of the Americans with Disabilities Act." In *Cause Lawyering and the State in a Global Era*, Austin Sarat and Stuart Scheingold, eds. New York: Oxford University Press.

Index